IRISH ARTS REVIEW YEARBOOK

Volume 11
1995

IRISH ARTS REVIEW
Yearbook 1995 : Volume 11

PUBLISHER : ANN REIHILL

EDITOR : HOMAN POTTERTON
ASSISTANT EDITOR : ELIZABETH MAYES
ADVERTISING MANAGER : VERA FINNEGAN

EDITORIAL ADVISORS
MAIREAD DUNLEVY is Director of the Hunt Museum, Limerick, on secondment from
the Art and Industrial Division of the National Museum of Ireland
BRIAN FERRAN is Chief Executive of the Arts Council of Northern Ireland and a practising artist
JOHN MEAGHER is an architect in private practice in de Blacam and Meagher and a director of the
Irish Museum of Modern Art
ALISTAIR SMITH is Director of the Whitworth Art Gallery, Manchester, and a former
Editor of Irish Arts Review
ROGER STALLEY is Professor of the History of Art at Trinity College, Dublin

COVER ILLUSTRATION
Eleazar Albin (d.1759), *The Red Crown Bird.*
(Marsh's Library, Dublin).

FRONTISPIECE
Kevin O'Dwyer, Architectural vessel. *Sterling silver and gold.* See page 222.

British Library Cataloguing in Publication Data
A catalogue record for this book is available from the British Library

ISBN 0 9523876 0 3 (hardback); 0 9523876 1 1 (paperback); ISSN 0791-3540

IRISH ARTS REVIEW YEARBOOK is published annually and is available by subscription
Price: Hardback - IR£30 (US $55) : Paperback - IR£20 (US $35)
(Postage and packing included)

Editorial and Advertising Address
Dunleary House
Dun Laoghaire
Co Dublin, Ireland

Tel: 01-280 8461
Fax: 01-280 4190

Address for Subscriptions
Irish Arts Review
P.O. Box 3500
Dublin 4, Ireland

Tel: 01-280 8461
Fax: 01-280 4190

IRISH ARTS REVIEW YEARBOOK receives grants from the Arts Council of Northern Ireland
the Irish Arts Council/An Chomhairle Ealaion   and assistance from the
Cultural Relations Committee of the Irish Department of Foreign Affairs

IRISH ARTS REVIEW YEARBOOK is published for Ann Reihill by Eton Enterprises Limited, Dunleary House, Dun Laoghaire, Co Dublin, Ireland
© *Eton Enterprises Limited, 1994*

Designed by John Power
Typeset by Pat Brennan
Printed in Singapore by C S Graphics Pte Limited

IRISH ARTS REVIEW YEARBOOK

CONTENTS
IRISH ARTS REVIEW YEARBOOK 1995 : VOL 11

CONTENTS
IRISH ARTS REVIEW YEARBOOK 1995 : VOL 11

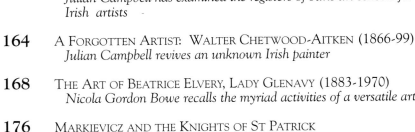

FOREWORD

BY
THE EXECUTIVE CHAIRMAN OF GLEN DIMPLEX
SPONSORS OF IRISH ARTS REVIEW YEARBOOK 1995

Glen Dimplex is delighted to support the 1995 edition of the Irish Arts Review. The Review is now well established having reached its 10th Birthday and each year provides a distinctive and eclectic view of the Arts spanning many centuries and disciplines. It celebrates the best of Irish and we are proud to be associated with it.

Martin Naughton
Executive Chairman Glen Dimplex

GLEN DIMPLEX

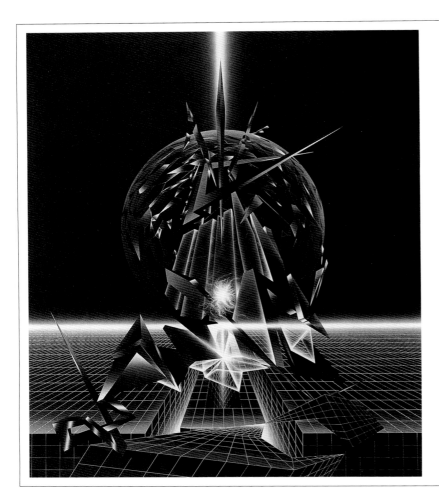

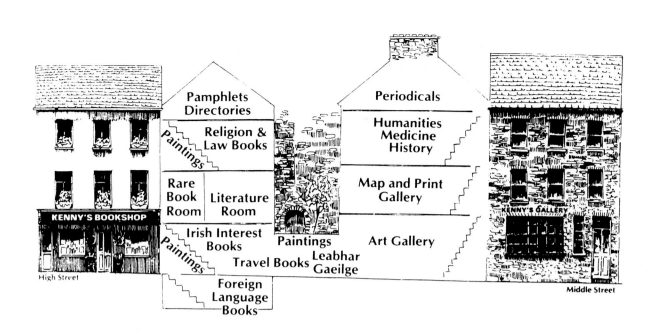

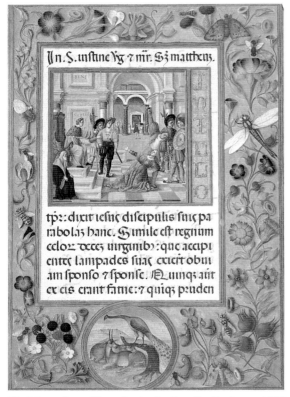

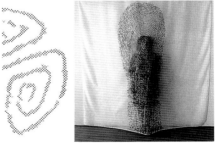

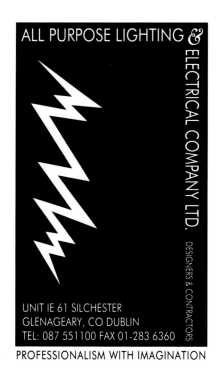

Bank of Ireland

College Green, Dublin 2

90-00-17

Date   *Valid for*
                    1995

Pay Bearer   *One Historic Day*

                    in

            The House of Lords

Signed _____

1783 - 1995   1808 - 1995

Guided tour dates for House of Lords 1995

Every Tuesday
during 1995
(except Bank Holidays)

Group Bookings

Tel: 6615933, ext. 2265

Tour Times:

10.30 am to 11.15 am
11.30 am to 12.15 pm
1.45 pm to 2.30 pm

Bank of Ireland

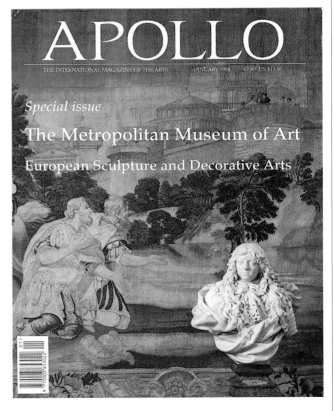

⇒Sullivan Antiques⇐

Victorian Brass eleven branch candleabra

Dealers in Fine Quality Georgian
and Victorian Furniture including Marble Chimney Pieces, Garden
Furniture and Objet d'Art.

Complete restoration service available.

43-44 Francis Street, Dublin 8, Ireland
Telephones: 01-454 1143/453 9659
Mobile: 088-543399 • Fax: 01-454 1156

Cork Public Museum

Fitzgerald Park, Mardyke, Cork. Tel: 021-270679

Admission Free

Open Monday-Friday 11.00-13.00 and 14.15-17.00 (18.00 June-August)
Sunday 15.00-17.00

BardasChorcai
Cork Corporation

NATIONAL MUSEUM OF IRELAND

KILDARE STREET, DUBLIN 2. TEL: 6618811.

Tuesday - Saturday 10 a.m. - 5 p.m. Sunday 2 p.m. - 5 p.m. Closed Monday.

Pyms Gallery, London

FINE PAINTINGS

Specialising in Eighteenth, Nineteenth and Twentieth century Irish paintings. Also British Post-Impressionist and French Nineteenth century works of Art.

Paul Henry R.H.A. 1876-1958
Woman Harvesting Wheat
Oil on canvas, signed Paul Henry
34.3 x 39.4 cm (13¹/2 x 15¹/2 ins)

Gallery Proprietors: Alan and Mary Hobart

9 Mount Street, Mayfair, London WIY 5AD
Tel: 071-629 2020 Fax: 071-629 2060
Hours: Monday to Friday 10am to 6pm. Other times by appointment

Cornice Detail

Decorative Ceiling

G R C Exterior

Restored Ceiling

Restoration Before

Restoration After

G R C Exterior

Centrepiece Detail

"WE DECIDED IT WAS TIME WE PAID THE CHANDELIER A COMPLIMENT."

Ireland's longest established decorative plaster moulding company isn't just about restoration work and specialist projects.

It's also about our wide range, now approaching three hundred different items. Everything from cornicing to centrepieces, wall plaques to fireplaces, corbels to panel mouldings. And much more.

Naturally, if you can't find it there we can happily make to order, undertaking to install our work to the highest standards.

And, using Glass Reinforced Concrete and Forton, all our work is today just as suitable for exteriors as interiors.

We've put most of our wide range of plaster mouldings into a most informative brochure.

It's yours for the asking.

The Old Mould Company,
8 York Road, Dun Laoghaire, Co. Dublin.
Telephone (01)284 2777. Fax (01)284 2814.

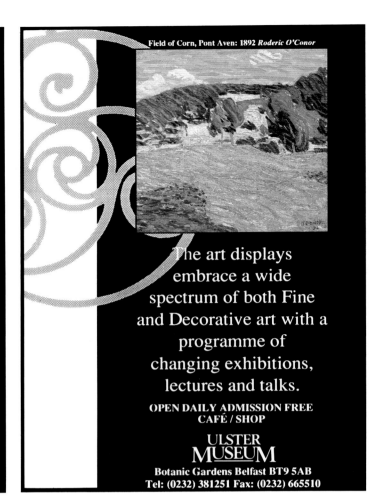

The Taking of Christ by Caravaggio (1571-1610)*

IRISH MASTERS ~ OLD MASTERS

THE NATIONAL GALLERY OF IRELAND

Merrion Square Dublin 2 ~ Telephone 01-661 5133 Fax 01-661 5372

Open *Mon.* to *Sat.* 10a.m.~5.30p.m. *Thurs*. 10a.m ~8.30p.m. *Sun.* 2p.m.~5p.m.

Restaurant and bookshop open during Gallery hours.

ADMISSION FREE

On indefinite loan from the Jesuit Community, Leeson Street, Dublin, who acknowledge the generosity of Dr. Marie Lea-Wilson

The Wild Geese

The term 'The Wild Geese' has been used romantically to describe Irish emigrants from the followers of Sarsfield after the Treaty of Limerick in 1691 to the present. These were the forerunners of the celebrated Wild Geese who swelled the ranks of continental armies and distinguished themselves for bravery in Landen, Fontenoy and many European battlefields in the seventeenth and eighteenth centuries. The great majority never returned to Ireland. Thousands died young. Small groups perpetuated Irish family traditions and their descendants can today trace their distinguished lineage back to the courageous men knighted by the Bourbons by virtue of their ancient Irish families. These were the men who left by reason of the confiscation of their ancestral lands in Penal Times, they were denied education or position. Others left to complete their commercial education abroad as merchant emigrès and integrated themselves by marriage; and still more left poverty behind to serve as mercenaries. The large scale migration to the United States of America of the nineteenth and early twentieth centuries is well known and the trend towards emigration is strong again in present times.

The Wild Geese have never been forgotten in Ireland as evidenced in story, song and poetry.

This foundry bronze portrayal of "Wild Geese rising on clamorous wing" depicts the Wild Geese mounted on a polished mahogany base and signed by the artist C. P. Breen. Each piece is numbered and authenticated in an edition of one hundred.

H. 12" x L. 8". £395.00.

Cuchulainn

Cuchulainn was known as Setanta until at the age of seven, he killed the Hound of Culan in self defence with a blow of his camán. Culan was so upset at the death of his favourite hound, that Setanta offered himself to guard Culan and his family and was henceforth known as Cuchulainn (the Hound of Culan).

He is the hero of Ireland's most famous tale of ancient times. The Táin Bó Cuailnge (the Cooley Cattle Raid). The oldest epic poem of Western Europe, tells of Queen Maedbh of Connacht's Cattle Raid on Ulster and how Cuchulainn single-handedly defended the land against the invaders. Mortally wounded in a subsequent combat, the young warrior tied himself to a tree, so that he might die on his feet as befitting a Red Branch Knight. So fearsome was his reputation for courage that the invaders only believed him dead on seeing the raven on his shoulder. Hence the association of Cuchulainn with the raven.

This foundry bronze portrayal of Cuchulainn shows him bent over in the shadow of the raven's wing, his shield upraised before the assault of the invaders.

Mounted on carbon dated bogwood over five thousand years old, the style of the finished bronze is dictated by the shape of the bogwood. Each piece is therefore one of a kind in a series of fifty and is signed and authenticated by the sculptor C. P. Breen.

12" x 18" (approx.). £395.00.

The Children of Lir

This foundry bronze sculpture represents the best loved of Ireland's legends. Fionnuala, the eldest and only daughter of King Lir supports on her wings her three brothers Aodh, Fiachra and Conn. Their images are reflected in the polished bronze base which depicts the surface of Lake Derravaragh over which the children as swans were condemned to fly for three hundred years; they spent a further three hundred years on the stormy Sea of Moyle, and the final three hundred years on the Isle of Inishgloire. With the coming of Christianity to Ireland, they regained human form on their baptism. They never lost there ability to speak or sing sweet music. This spell was cast on them by Aoife, sister of their dead mother Eva, who married their father King Lir and was jealous of the love he bore his beautiful children.

The Children of Lir, foundry bronze edition by C. P. Breen, mounted on a mahogany base, is limited to one hundred pieces, signed and authenticated.

H. 8" x L. 6½". £300.00.

Irish Times Collection Exclusives

National Library of Ireland

KILDARE STREET,
DUBLIN 2.

Photo: Peter Moloney
Courtesy of: Norton Associates

Jimmie Durham *A Map of the Sky* 1993 *36 1/4" x 36 1/4" x 2*
A recent acquisition to IMMA's collection

Irish Museum of Modern Art
Royal Hospital Kilmainham
Dublin 8
Tel: 01 671 8666
Fax: 01 671 8695

Museum and bookshop open
Tue - Sat 10 - 5.30   Sun 12 - 5.30
Coffee shop open
Tue - Sat 11 - 4   Sun 12 - 5

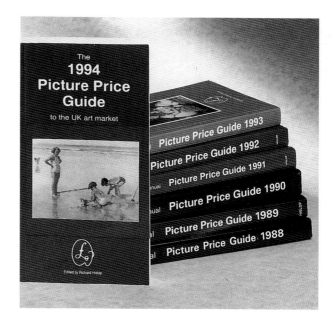

Upper Court Manor

A N T I Q U E S

Upper Court Manor, Freshford, Co. Kilkenny, Ireland
Tel: 056 32174. Fax: 056 32325

*See the largest collection of Irish, English, French, 18th, 19th
and 20th century antiques displayed in the ancient splendour of
Upper Court Manor.*

Open Mon to Sat 9am to 5pm
Sundays 2pm to 5.30pm

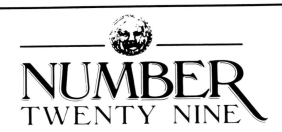

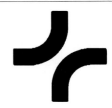

COLNAGHI

ESTABLISHED 1760

Master Paintings and Drawings
from the Fourteenth to the Nineteenth Centuries,
English Paintings and European Sculpture.

Valuations for Insurance and Probate

The Directors of Colnaghi are always interested in acquiring works of art from private sources and can
offer discreet financial services based on property consigned to the firm for sale.

RICHARD WILSON, R.A.
Penegoes c. 1713 – Mold 1782
A View of Tivoli with the Campagna in the Distance
Oil on canvas: 104 x 131cms (40 x 50ins)

14 OLD BOND STREET
LONDON WIX 4JL
TELEPHONE: 071-491 7408
FACSIMILE: 071-491 8851

108/112 RUE DU FAUBOURG ST HONORÉ
75008 PARIS
TELEPHONE: 1 42-66 14 51
FACSIMILE: 1 42 66 23 95

21 EAST 67TH STREET
NEW YORK, NY 10021
TELEPHONE: 212 772 2266
FACSIMILE: 212 737 8325

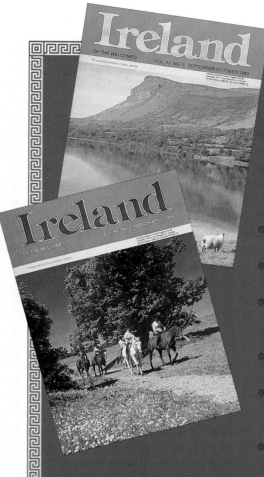

- ENJOY THE COLOUR AND BEAUTY OF IRELAND.

- MEET THE IRISH PEOPLE AND LISTEN TO THEIR STORIES.

- BE ENTRANCED BY THE CREAM OF IRISH LITERATURE AND POETRY.

- LEARN OF OUR CULTURE AND HISTORY.

- DELIGHT IN THE WORKMANSHIP OF TRADITIONAL ARTS AND CRAFTS.

- READ OF FAMILY HISTORIES AND GENEALOGY.

- SHARE IN THE MOUTH-WATERING RECIPES.

All this by simply subscribing to 'Ireland of the Welcomes'.

Ireland OF THE WELCOMES

Ireland of the Welcomes is a bi-monthly magazine published by Bord Fáilte Irish Tourist Board.

YES I wish to subscribe to Ireland of the Welcomes.
(Each year has six issues).

Rates:	1 Year	2 Years	3 Years
	(6 issues)	(12 issues)	(18 issues)
	IR £11.00	IR £19.00	IR £26.00

☐ *I enclose cheque for*

☐ *Please send me a bill / invoice*

☐ *Please charge my credit card*

☐ *ACCESS / MASTERCARD*   ☐ *VISA*

No.

Expiry date:

Name:

Address:

Send to: **IRELAND OF THE WELCOMES, PO BOX 84, LIMERICK.**

5-ADAB

Restoration of
Gilding and
Plasterwork,
Picture Frames,
Mirrors,
Furniture, etc.

Specialists in
conservation for
over 20 years

Susan Mulhall
Gilders Ltd.

Blackwood,
Robertstown,
Naas, Co. Kildare.
Tel: 045-60336

HULME-BEAMAN
PICTURE RESTORERS

**Conservation & Support treatment
cleaning and restoration
of oil paintings**

Consultancy work including
Care of collections - environmental monitoring,
inspection and condition reports,
and Crisis management.

30 Leeson Park Avenue
Ranelagh
Dublin 6

Tel: 01-660 4849/50
visits by
appointment only please.

Proprietor Roland Hulme-Beaman FABPR
Associate Teresa Viana

This studio is included on the Register maintained by
The Conservation Unit of the Museums & Galleries
Commission UK

Free
Expert
advice.

Gerard Dillon, R.H.A., *Mellifont Abbey*, signed, oil on board,
76 by 80cm (30 by 31½in). Included in the 22nd June 1994 sale of
Modern British & Irish Paintings. Estimate: £10,000-15,000.
In the early 1940's, the artist stayed with Nano Reid, on the outskirts of
Drogheda and together they painted the surrounding area,
including the Cistercian Abbey of Mellifont,
which became for him a symbol of Irish Antiquity.

Sotheby's Irish representatives, supported
by regular specialist visits, are able to advise
you on the saleroom value of pictures, silver,
jewellery, furniture and other works of art.
Their advice is free and without obligation.

Your enquiry will be treated in the strictest confidence.

For further information, or to make an appointment,
please contact:

In Dublin: Anne Dillon, 51b Dawson Street, Dublin 2.
Telephone: (01) 6711786/6711431
In Northern Ireland: William Montgomery,
The Estate Office, Greyabbey, Newtownards, Co. Down.
Telephone: (02477) 88668.

SOTHEBY'S
FOUNDED 1744

GRANT FINE ART

Tom Carr: *'Maghera Village, Newcastle, Co Down'* c 1940's

Specialising in fine paintings and sculpture nineteenth and twentieth century. Irish, British and European works of art.

Artists include:
Jack B. Yeats, Roderic O`Conor, Gerard Dillon, Dan O'Neill, Louis le Brocquy, Edward Delaney, Henry Moore, Josef Herman, Hector McDonnell, Tony O'Malley, Baselitz.

87c Bryansford Road, Newcastle, Co Down, Northern Ireland. Telephone/Fax: 03967-22349

A National Treasure

Dublin Castle - now restored to its former glory - is the home for a superb collection of paintings, fine art and historic artefacts. It's all part of a heritage of which we can be justly proud.

Together with our national parks and monuments, waterways and wildlife, this heritage is cared for and preserved by the Office of Public Works.

THE OFFICE OF PUBLIC WORKS
-caring for our heritage

EDITORIAL

The Editor, **Homan Potterton,** *writes on country-house legislation, the ruining of Merrion Square, and other matters.*

The *Irish Arts Review Yearbook* for 1995 is the first to be published without the sponsorship of GPA since 1986 when the *Review* was still a quarterly under the editorship of Brian de Breffny. It is appropriate to record here our gratitude for ten years of generous support without which the *Review* could never have continued and to say that, although on occasion GPA as sponsors were demanding, we miss them.

GPA, through the personal commitment to the arts of the Group's founder and chairman, Dr Tony Ryan, first emerged as significant sponsors of the arts in Ireland in 1980 when they came to the rescue of the international Rosc exhibition planned for that year. From that moment, with the fervour and panache that characterised the company's operations as a whole, they became the most generous, the most wide-ranging, and by far the most significant corporate patrons of the arts that Ireland had ever known. They led the way in this respect for other companies to follow and by their example they transformed, within the space of a decade, the whole attitude to corporate arts funding in Ireland.

Following Rosc, support of contemporary art took the form of biennial Awards to Emerging Artists. Music then attracted the Group's attention with a guarantee to the annual Festival of Music in Great Irish Houses. There followed, since its inception in 1988, substantial assistance to the triennial Dublin International Piano Competition and, also on a triennial basis, the establishment of the GPA Book Award. A large-scale restoration of the historic library of Archbishop Bolton at Cashel was financed by the Group in 1989 and reconstruction of the early-eighteenth

century Damer House, Roscrea as a cultural centre followed in 1990. A myriad other events and projects – such as the exhibition of Irish Women Artists at the National Gallery in 1987 – have also benefitted from the imaginative nature of GPA's generosity.

Irish Arts Review will continue to be published annually without the patronage of GPA but, as we enter our second decade, it is with a farewell and thanks to the benefactor who helped us through our first.

*　　*　　*

'The destruction of the likes of Coole Park and Bowenscourt and latent hostility or bureaucratic and commercial indifference is tending to give way more to a growing realisation and sense of pride that the many splendid monuments of the past such as Dublin Castle and the Royal Hospital, Kilmainham are jewels that now belong to an independent, democratic Irish nation and we need have no complexes about their origins.' Indeed; and note the word 'tending'. But, nevertheless, this was the Taoiseach, Albert Reynolds, speaking at a conference on 'The Future of the Country House in Ireland' in February 1993 – an occasion which would, like the sentiments the Taoiseach expressed, have seemed fairly improbable – if not entirely fantastic – ten (even five) years ago.

Then, as if to put his money where his mouth was, came the transfer (in January 1994) to the care of the Board of Works of the house that perhaps symbolised most the fight to preserve Ireland's post-Renaissance architectural heritage, Castletown, County Kildare (Fig. 1) – the Palladian mansion that, against

1. CASTLETOWN, CO KILDARE. The mansion, which was built for Speaker Conolly in the 1720s (to the designs of Alessandro Gallilei) was rescued from probable destruction when it was purchased by Desmond Guinness in 1967 as the headquarters of the Irish Georgian Society. From 1979 its restoration continued under the Castletown Foundation and then, in a remarkable turn of events, the house was taken over by the State in January 1994.

all odds and in face of the very latent hostility the Taoiseach referred to, Desmond Guinness had saved in 1967 from almost certain destruction. In an act of magnificent optimism and aided and abetted by others (most notably his father, Lord Moyne and late wife, Mariga) Desmond purchased the house and part of the estate and began the task of defending it from 'bureaucratic and commercial indifference'. Funds were raised, volunteers were co-opted, furnishings were obtained, and the house was opened to the public and used for concerts and other events mainly under the auspices of the Irish Georgian Society. In 1979 a charity was formed – the Castletown Foundation – which took over the ownership and management of the house and bravely saw it through another fifteen years of survival. At no time during all these years could it have been realistically envisaged that the State would one day take over the mansion and the fact that this has now happened is about as extraordinary and felicitous as the Taoiseach's remarks.

In the same speech the Taoiseach made the point that 'the most efficient way of protecting and preserving our great houses is to help the owners as far as possible to keep and maintain them.' If this is what the Taoiseach believes then, as anyone who has observed the gradual cloning of houses belonging to the English National Trust will

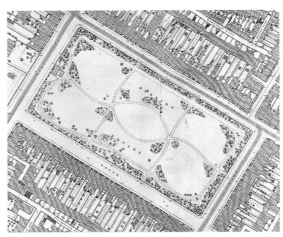

2. MERRION SQUARE, DUBLIN from a mid-19th century Ordnance Survey map of Dublin. The original layout of serpentine paths and the tree-planting plan is clearly shown. Although some evergreen trees were introduced at the end of the 19th century, the design of the gardens survived intact until very recently.

3. MERRION SQUARE gardens today. In an ongoing and inappropriate modernisation programme, the pleasant swards of green which were a feature of the late 18th century plan have been desecrated by the introduction of constellations of flower beds in blazing colours.

Council and Brussels being the main sources of funds. The Council has given grants (generally on a 50% of total cost basis) ranging from £100,000 (Bantry House) to £3,000 (Carriglas) with Tullynally, Glin, Markree, and Westport also sharing in the hand-outs. But there are problems – both practical and moral – with grants of this nature. In the first instance, even with all the will and endeavour in the world, some owners may not be able to raise any or all of the percentage of matching funds which are (justifiably) required before any allocation will be made and this means that an appropriate grant – although possibly available – cannot be obtained. Strokestown Park – the eighteenth century Roscommon mansion and former home of the Pakenham Mahon family which has been so sympathetically rescued from decline by a local businessman, Jim Callery, who bought it in 1979 – has been enviably fortunate in the largesse of the grants it has received; but then the estate is backed by Mr Callery's Westward Garages who are in a better position to pledge matching equity in their applications for grants than many a private owner is – and it shows. Decay to the house has been arrested, a garden that rivals that of the Hesperides has been laid out, and the stables have been restored and converted as a museum of the Famine. But Strokestown remains the property of Westward Garages (whose investment to date is said to be about £1.7 million) and as such it may be disposed of at any time. While its value has been enhanced by grants from Brussels and Dublin a new owner would not be required – and might not wish – to maintain the estate as a public amenity.

Therefore (as the Taoiseach said) while the most desirable means of preserving Ireland's country houses is to help owners maintain them, there may well be a case for insisting that a house or other property which has been grant-aided should provide – on a perennial basis – a public amenity. Then they really would be the 'jewels of a democratic nation' which the Taoiseach desires.

*　　　*　　　*

Sir Alfred Beit, Bt., whose magnificent and munificent gifts have so immeasurably enriched the cultural patrimony of his adopted country, died in May 1994 at the age of ninety-one. A stranger to Ireland, he and Lady Beit were tempted to come here when they saw photographs of Russborough in *Country Life* in

have observed, the Taoiseach has been well advised. And what steps have been taken to help country-house owners in Ireland? Well, income tax relief, whereby the costs of restoration and repair may be set off against tax, means, surprisingly, that (along with France and Denmark) Ireland has the best heritage income tax policy in Europe. The only problem with this provision is that many country-house owners simply do not have a level of income that is relevant. Country-houses are also exempt – if they are open to the public – from a punitive capital acquisition tax (at 40%) when the house passes from one generation to the next; but this provision does not apply to the adjoining lands which often, as a result, must be sold, thereby reducing income even further. In the case of capital gains tax – which arises if an object is sold, possibly to pay a major repair bill – there is no relief at all.

The situation with regard to grant-aid for repairs and other capital projects has improved significantly for country-house owners over the past few years with the National Heritage

1952. It was for sale and it appealed to them as possibly the ideal setting for the famous collection of Old Master paintings assembled by Sir Alfred's uncle and inherited by him from his father. They bought the house and moved in with their collection in 1953. Wintering in South Africa every year, the Beits would lend the cream of the Collection to the National Gallery of Ireland during their absence so that the pictures soon became both familiar and much-loved by the Irish gallery-going public. Then in 1976, in an act of great generosity, Sir Alfred established a charitable foundation to which he gave Russborough with the intention that the house should permanently be available to and enjoyed by the public. The Collection, although left in Russborough, remained his own property and it was not until 1987 in a further act of public-spiritedness that Sir Alfred gave it to the National Gallery. It was a stupendous gift – the envy of museums the world over – and it enhanced the Gallery's status in an immeasurable way. For it, and for Russborough, Ireland must be forever grateful and hold in reverence the name of Alfred Beit.

* * *

Is there really any hope left for Archbishop Ryan Park? What? Archbishop Ryan Park. Anyone making a dash across Merrion Square from the East will know that that is what the gardens in the centre of the Square are now called. A granite boulder at the gate tells us so. Now Merrion Square is a Conservation Area and even by the fairly reckless standards of planning which we have come to expect, it would be fairly inconceivable for anyone to even think of applying for permission to 'modernise' the facades of any of the houses around the Square much less being actually allowed to do so by Dublin Corporation.

Yet, for more than a decade now, the Corporation itself has been frenziedly modernising the gardens by indulging in a wild and riotous planting spree that is entirely inappropriate.

The gardens of Merrion Square are a very specific form of garden. By no means unique in style, they were planned as a city version of a 'country park' the design of which depended on an undulating ground form (the centre is sunken), serpentine paths, informally placed clumps of planting, single specimen trees, and the whole surrounded by a belt of trees. Very simple really and with no, absolutely no, provision for the energetic and regimented growing of tulips, wallflowers, daffodils, and other annuals which has, over the past decade, taken over the gardens and which shows no sign of abating.

There is no excuse for this as the layout of the gardens – the meandering transverse paths and the planting of the trees – is very well documented and is perfectly visible on almost all nine-

4. THE TYRONE GUTHRIE CENTRE, Annamakerrig, Co Monaghan. The witty restoration (by the Dundalk architects, Flynn Rogers & Rust) of derelict farm buildings as artists' residences further enhances the delights of this 'Workplace for Artists'.

teenth-century Ordnance Survey maps (Fig. 2). Furthermore the gardens retained their early-nineteenth century dignity until the time they became Archbishop Ryan Park in the late nineteen-seventies. True, in the latter decades of the nineteenth century the planting, principally of the enclosing belt, was modified in a very un-eighteenth-century way by the introduction of evergreens such as holly and laurel. This was part of an experiment conducted by an amateur plantsman and Dublin barrister, J G Adair, to disprove the theory, then widespread, that evergreen trees could not survive the polluted atmosphere of a city-centre garden. (Mr Adair published a pamphlet on the subject).

There is no such scientific reasoning behind the current epidemic of planting and not only should it be stopped but the gardens ought to be restored.

* * *

There are certain things which cheer the spirit. One of these is Annaghmakerrig, the former home of the theatre director, Tyrone Guthrie, in county Monaghan which, in accordance with his wishes, the Arts Councils of Ireland, North and South, administer jointly as 'A Workplace for Artists.' (See *Irish Arts Review*, Vol. 1, no.4). Artists – writers, musicians, painters – may stay here, working on their own projects, for anything from a week to three months. They pay only what they can afford. Annaghmakerrig, which has been in operation now for thirteen years, is a success and the credit for this must go to the Resident Director, Bernard Loughlin who, together with his wife Mary, have given the place its very special appeal and presence.

The house (although renovated) looks as though Guthrie might just have departed a day or so ago; gardens (for flowers and vegetables) are being laid out – but they seem merely to have sprung up; swans have returned to the lake in place of (noisy) local water-skiers; and a family atmosphere – with a warm kitchen as a focal point – has been generated that is unique. Most noteworthy of all, derelict farm buildings have been renovated as residences for artists who wish to stay in this idyllic place for as long as a year and a studio in the same area is shortly to be completed. This renovation is by the Dundalk architectural practice of Flynn Rogers & Rust and it is not just sensitive but extremely attractive and, above all, witty (Fig. 4). It strikes just the right note for Annaghmakerrig where any hint of bureaucracy seems (in spite of the involvement of the Arts Councils) to have been kept very firmly at bay. Annaghmakerrig, without ever complaining, always needs money to create further amenities and repair those already in existence. *Irish Arts Review* believes that it is about one of the worthiest projects around.

A Diary of the Art Year in Ireland

Elizabeth Mayes chronicles noteworthy art exhibitions and events from May 1993 to May 1994.

MAY 1993

■ Design Workshops, Rathfarnham, Co Dublin, Fine Arts Week (10-14). Distinguished lecturers included **Sybil Connolly** and **Roxane Moorhead.**

■ Kilkenny painter **Elizabeth Cope**, who has exhibited in Belfast, Dublin, London, Brussels, Boston and New York, has won the James Adam Salerooms Award, given to an artist with potential for future appreciation in value.

■ Irish Antique Dealers' Association Award at the Royal Hibernian Academy exhibition given to **Inez Nordell** for her painting of the Boyne Valley.

■ National Self-Portrait Collection, founded in 1977, at the University of Limerick, added 22 new works, including self-portraits by **Richard Gorman, Alice Maher, John Kindness**, as well as **Sarah Purser, James Sleator** and **Cecil Salkeld.**

■ Inspired by nature, recent mixed media works on paper by local artist **George Vaughan** at the Butler Gallery, Kilkenny.

■ Taylor Galleries, Dublin, showed recent paintings by **Jill Dennis** and bronzes by **John Coen.**

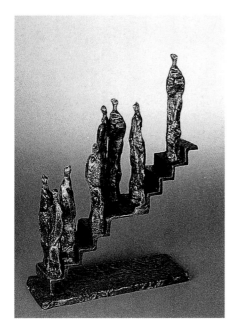

John Coen, Ascent/Descent, at the Taylor Gallery

Ger Sweeney, Firedance, at the Guinness Hop Store

■ Abstract expressionist canvases by Castlebar artist **Ger Sweeney** were exhibited in the Guinness Hop Store and toured to Castlebar, London, Edinburgh Festival, Brussels, Belfast and back to Galway.

■ **Alanna O'Kelly** video installation confronting painful memories of the Irish Famine 1846-48, No Colouring Can Deepen the Darkness of Truth, at the Walker Art Gallery, Liverpool

■ **Shirley MacWilliam**, Momart artist in residence at the Tate Gallery, Liverpool, made her video installation, A Bone to Pick, exploring the sense of territory associated with 'home', after a period of return to Northern Ireland - shown at the Bluecoat Gallery, Liverpool. Both in Video Positive 93, Liverpool's international festival of creative video and electronic media art.

■ **EuroThreshold** - Exhibition of important works of painting, print , sculpture and installation by major Irish artists at the Equestrian Centre, Millstreet, Co Cork, celebrated the Eurovision Song Contest

■ **Barrie Cooke's** recent paintings, some inspired by trips to New Zealand, were shown at the Kerlin Gallery, Dublin; **Aidan Dunne** found it 'as fine a show of painting as we are likely to see this or any year' .

■ **Sean Scully** - an exhibition to celebrate the publication of Heart of Darkness by Joseph Conrad with eight etchings by Sean Scully; signed limited edition of 300. Waddington Galleries, London

■ Belfast artist **Nuala Gregory**, born 1965, in new Works on Paper, explored themes associated with female subjectivity using a variety of techniques. A first major show for her, and for Edinburgh-based Co Armagh artist **Marcel O'Connor**, whose Boundaries, beautiful abstractions inspired by icon painting, were also on show at the Arts Council Gallery, Dublin Road, Belfast.

■ **Gavin Hogg** exhibited at the Green on Red Gallery, 58 Fitzwilliam Square, Dublin, 13-28 May

■ First showing in Dublin of work - complex orchestrations of canvases, dealing with concepts of rejection, humiliation, disaffection - by the American artist **Ida Appelbroog** in the Irish Museum of Modern Art. Her film, Belladonna, was also shown.

Sarah Purser's John B. Yeats RHA at the Gorry Gallery

■ **Sarah Purser** R H A (1848-1943) was the subject of an exhibition at the Gorry Gallery, Dublin, to mark the 50th anniversary of her death. Drawings and watercolours from eight sketchbooks were sold at prices from £120-£650. Facsimiles, and the original covers, were presented to the National Gallery of Ireland.

■ In Belfast, the Bell Gallery showed recent oils by **Cecil Maguire** RUA and recent watercolours by **James McIntyre** RUA, while new works by **Jasper McKinney** and **Gavin Weston** were exhibited at One Oxford Street.

■ Sligo Art Gallery showed recent works by **William Crozier**. The Vincent and Noeleen Ferguson Collection of contemporary Irish art (Blackshaw, Egan, Bourke, Cooke, Gingles, Magill, Mulcahy, O'Malley) opened at the Crawford Gallery, Cork.

■ An exhibition of 'Little Sculpture' at the Solomon Gallery, Dublin, featured the work of 16 artists in various media, mostly bronze and other metals, and included **Sean Mulcahy, Rowan Gillespie, Deborah Brown, Conor Fallon, Alexandra Wejchert** and **Linda Brunker.**

Dorothy Cross, Parthenon, 1991, at the Douglas Hyde Gallery

■ Work from the Power House, second exhibition at the Douglas Hyde Gallery, Trinity College, Dublin (27 May- 7 July) of work by sculptor **Dorothy Cross**, who represented Ireland at the 1993 Venice Benniale. Cross has been working in the disused power station near Dublin docks which, with an all-male work-force, supplied most of Dublin's electricity until 1975. These resonances fill her aggressive, iconoclastic pieces with explorations of feminine identity and power. A site-specific sculpture, Attendant, was simultaneously on view in the disused public lavatory in College Green.

JUNE 1993

Sharon O'Malley, Oracle, at European Modern Art

■ In Oracle, her exhibition of new oil paintings at European Modern Art in Clare Street, **Sharon O'Malley's** lyrical imagery was drawn from mythological subject matter.

■ The Director of the Irish Museum of Modern Art , **Declan McGonagle**, was appointed to the jury of the Tate Gallery's 1993 Turner Prize. The £20,000 prize, now in its ninth year, is awarded annually to a British artist under 50 for an outstanding exhibition or other presentation of their work in the preceding year.In 1987, McGonagle was himself nominated for the prize for making the Orchard Gallery, Derry, an'international centre for the artist'.

■ Ian Joyce's Paper Island, curated by **Jerome O Drisceoil**, was the inaugural exhibition at the new Green on Red Gallery, Fitzwilliam Square.

■ Mealys of Castlecomer handled the sale of the contents of **Paul Cooke's** well-known antique shop in Francis Street, Dublin on 3 June - a plethora of good lots.

■ On 8 June in Belfast , in a shopping arcade beside the Europa Hotel, a bronze Monument to the Unknown Woman Worker, by the young Irish artist **Louise Walsh** was unveiled. Controversy surrounded the commissioning of the £25,000 piece, which comments on woman's work, paid and unpaid, and the original commission from NI Dept of the Environment was taken over by the developers of the shopping centre, Glenbank Estates Ltd. The Arts Council of Northern Ireland contributed 25% of the cost.

■ On 15 June the IMMA/Glen Dimplex Award was announced. The prize of an exhibition, plus £15,000,will be awarded in February 1994 . Competitors may be Irish or non-Irish, but must have exhibited. The Award will be presented again in 1995 and 1996.

■ The President, Mrs Robinson, as Patron of The Friends of the National Collections of Ireland, received the members who presented her with the three-volume Catalogue Raisonné of the Oil Paintings of Jack B Yeats by **Hilary Pyle** (reviewed in this issue).

■ Bloomsday was 16 June . An additional celebration this year was a Joycean Art Exhibition at the James Joyce Cultural Centre, 35 North Great Georges' Street, which included what is believed to be the last portrait of James Joyce. It is by **Grace Henry** and was bought at auction 10 years ago in Dublin for £16,000; its Japanese owner, Mr Suzuki, had it sent from Tokyo and has offered it to the Centre for £20,000.

■ Bursaries of between £1,000 and £3,000 were awarded by the Arts Council/ An Chomhairle Ealaíon to the following visual artists: **Patricia Hurl, Alice Maher, Laura Venables, Nick Miller, Philip Napier, John Noel Smith** and **Louise Walsh.** Postgraduate awards went to **Liadin Cooke** and **Patrick Jolley**; two annual scholarships to the PSI International Studio Programme in New York went to **Mike Fitzpatrick** and **Thomas Bevan** and the Martin Toonder award was won by **Kathy Prendergast.**

■ The NI Arts Council announced that **Elizabeth Marie Caulfield** had won the Alice Berger Hammerschlag Trust Travel Award.

■ Pleasants Factory, 67 Pleasants Place, off Camden Street, Dublin 2. New creative arts venue with gallery workshops and library presented its inaugural exhibition of work by **Mark O'Kelly** and **Mark Duignan**. The National College of Art and Design degree exhibition took place at the RHA Gallagher Gallery.

■ Ulster artist **Shirley MacWilliam's** sound installation, This Meere, addressing the concept of the 'speaking voice' constantly distancing and seducing us, was featured at the Arnolfini Gallery, Bristol.

■ Work by two artists who received Arts Council grants for materials was displayed in the Arts Council reception area in Merrion Square - photomontage paintings by **Brian Palm** and photoscreen prints by **Kymberly Dunne**.

■ Paintings and drawings by Portadown artist **Nicola Russell** were exhibited in the Arts Council of NI Gallery in Belfast – 'the soft and hard sides of being a woman are all here.' **Padraic Reaney** Retrospective (1973-1993) at the Pantheon Gallery, Dawson Street, Dublin, (until 26 July). Trees and Woodlands, traditional watercolours from the bright and summery palette of **Joan Webb**, wife of Kenneth, were exhibited at The Kenny Gallery, Galway.

■ **Willie Doherty** from Derry and **Dorothy Cross** from Cork represented Ireland at the Central Pavilion of the Venice Biennale, June to October 1993

■ Project Arts Centre, Dublin, showed a series of impressive large scale wooden sculptures by Co Down artist

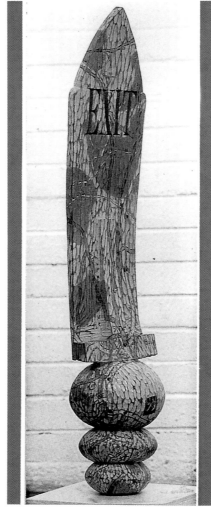

Graeme Hall, Exit 1, at the Project Arts Centre

Graeme Hall. Primeval Essence, his first solo show, although stemming from the artist's interest in monuments to the dead, was not morbid but was both tranquil and spirited.

■ The Kerlin Gallery, Dublin, hosted an exhibition of 17 lithographs by **William Scott** (1913-1989), arguably the finest post-war Irish artist; executed in 1972, they are built around a vers-libre poem by the artist called Poem for Alexander. Brian Fallon wrote 'The sensual and and the ascetic were close to each other in Scott, and his best work almost always comes from the tension between them.' This exhibition coincides with the opening of a room dedicated to Scott's work at the Tate Gallery London. ,

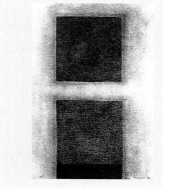

■ A two-person show at the Graphic Studio Dublin Gallery featured **James McCreary's** mezzotints of everyday objects, realised with great delicacy in rich colours, and woodcuts by **Jennifer Lane** on the theme of trees. Lane is one of five artists representing Ireland in the 1993 International Print Biennale in Ljubljana.

■ The Fenderesky Gallery at Queen's, Belfast, showed the work of Seven Women Artists- **Vivien Burnside, Marie Foley, Fran Hegarty, Patricia Hurl, Aileen MacKeogh, Moira McIvor and Alice Maher**- a catalogue accompanied the show.

■ West of Ireland exhibitions included new works by **John Andrew O'Regan** in Castlebar, and at the Sligo Arts Gallery an exhibition of watercolours by various major artists to commemorate the centenary of **W B Yeats'** poem The Lake Isle of Innisfree. Claremorris Art Gallery celebrated Mayo 5000 with The Mayo Landscape – an exhibition that included **Tony O'Malley, Louis Le Brocquy, Camille Souter** and **Barrie Cooke**.

JULY 1993

■ The 16th Galway Arts Festival (July 14-25) was opened by the President, Mrs Robinson and featured theatre, music, dance and film. Visual arts included Force Field, a massive elemental sculpture of grass, mud, mould and water in a disused warehouse, by **Daniel Harvey** and **Heather Ackroyd**; a multi-media exhibition 'On the Subject of Drink', at the Kenny Art Gallery; original photographic prints by **George Hurrell** at U C G Art Gallery and The Art of the Book at Galway Arts Centre.

■ A new chairman of the Arts Council/ An Chomhairle Ealaion was announced - **Ciaran Benson**, Professor of Psychology at University College, Dublin, who has written reports on the place of the arts in Irish education. 'With Michael D and his team, I think it is an exciting time to be developing cultural policy', said Professor Benson. He succeeded Mr Colm OhEocha, who had decided to step down.

A Diary of the Art Year in Ireland
July 1993

■ Boyle Arts Festival, Co Roscommon, now in its 3rd year, was opened by the Minister for the Arts, Culture and the Gaeltacht, Mr Michael D Higgins. Among the attractions was an exhibition of new work by *Gerard Bruen, William Crozier, Maud Cotter, Pauline Bewick* and more.

■ 'The Masters' Return' - an exhibition of the 42 master European paintings from the permanent collection returned from its acclaimed tour of New York, San Francisco, Boston and Chicago to the National Gallery of Ireland. In addition to the colour catalogue, this exhibition was complemented by an interactive computer system installed at the Gallery by IBM and the multi-media centre at Trinity College Dublin. An easy-to-use touch screen system which documents the paintings in the exhibition is available in the Shaw Room.

■ On 20 July, *Sean Scully* - Dublin-born, London-raised and New York-based artist - was shortlisted for the £20,000 Turner Prize.

■ Geneval's Tower, one of 14 towers in Dublin's 13th century Anglo-Norman city wall, is to be preserved, thanks to the intervention of the Minister for the Arts, Culture and the Gaeltacht, Mr Higgins, who promised Dublin Corporation £330,000. Pierse Contracting Ltd, the firm whose development near Christchurch uncovered the ruins, contributed £250,000 towards the excavation.

■ *Lord Dunsany* sold 12th century Trim Castle in Co Meath to the Office of Public Works 'for a six-figure sum' after more than twenty years of negotiation.

■ The Pantheon Gallery, Dublin, showed new paintings by *Margaret Tuffy*, followed by an exhibition of drawings by *Stephen Rinn* and *Rory Breslin*.

■ The Douglas Hyde Gallery brought to Ireland for the first time the work of a leading German artist, *Gunther Forg*, born in 1952, showing examples of his paintings, photographs, bronze reliefs and bronze steles.

■ Oil paintings by award-winning Portadown-born artist *John Long*

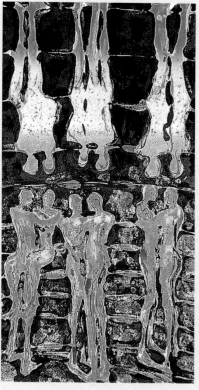

Frans Widerberg, Dancers (detail) at the Hugh Lane Gallery

■ The Hugh Lane Municipal Gallery showed a touring exhibition of 40 contemporary works by 16 *Norwegian Printmakers*, showing intaglio, woodcut, lithography and screen-printing. Printmaking was initiated in Norway by Edvard Munch, with techniques learned in Paris and Berlin.

were exhibited at European Modern Art, Clare Street, Dublin.

■ Cork City Artists were exhibiting in July in the Crawford Municipal Art Gallery, Cork. *John Hutchinson* made the selection.

■ Into the Wind was the title of an exhibition of paintings by *Ger Sweeney* at the Irish Club in Eaton Square, London. Equestrian paintings by artist *Susan Webb* were shown at the Kenny Gallery, Galway, in conjunction with Galway Races. The Carroll Gallery, Longford, showed work by Longford-born painter, *Charles Cullen. Una Sealy* and

Patrick Conyngham exhibited paintings at Pleasants Factory, Pleasants Place, Dublin 8

■ At the Graphic Studio Dublin Gallery, prints by *Terence Gravett*, 1992 printmaker in residence at the NI Arts Council, were on show; inspired by a visit to Graeco-Roman archaeological remanis in Ephesus in Asia Minor, Gravett's compositions were 'like looking into a deep river'.

■ In and Out of the Circle, work by 3 Belfast-based artists, was exhibited at the Kerlin Gallery in Dublin. Referring to the inner-city environment of Belfast, each artist explored themes of place and identity - *Padraig McCann* in abstracted charcoal drawings, *Michael Minnis* in large oil paintings on metal, transcribed from aerial photos of Belfast and *Philip Napier* in a huge kinetic sculpture consisting of rotating place names from 4 city bus routes

Malcolm Poynter, One Step Forward, at Kilmainham.

■ The first *Dublin Contemporary Art Fair* took place in the Royal Hospital, Kilmainham on 23-25 July. There were 24 stands representing galleries in Dublin and elsewhere in Ireland, England, Scotland and Hungary and a solo show of dramatic sculpture by British artist *Malcom Poynter*, and drawings by *John Lennon*.

■ The inaugural exhibition at the Jameson Heritage Centre, Midleton, Co Cork, was of paintings by *Elizabeth Cope*.

■ Selene, the moon goddess in Greek mythology, was the inspiration for a site-specific installation on the exterior and interior of the Project Arts Centre by

Rachel Joynt, the young sculptor whose 'footprints ' are on the traffic island between Westmoreland and D'Olier Streets, and whose 13 ft market lamp in Moore Street was commissioned by Dublin Corporation.

Edward Delaney, RHA, Horses Pass By, Joint Winner in Iontas,at Sligo Art Gallery

■ At Sligo Art Gallery, Iontas, the 4th annual exhibition of small works took place.

■ Open Air in the Square, organised by the Green on Red Gallery in Fitzwilliam Square, featured outdoor pieces by **Andrew Clancy, Liadin Cooke** and others, with oils by **Corban Walker**, a strong moulding in blue glass by **Kilian Schurmann**, and 'spider-lights' by **Brian McDonald** shown inside. Art critic Patrick Gallagher in his review, objecting to the frequently-used term 'site-specific', commented, 'were the fountains in the Piazza Navona "site-specific"? Are TDs in the Dail?'

■ At the Architecture Centre, Merrion Square, Dublin, an exhibition of 'organic architecture' by the renowned Hungarian architect **Imre Makovecz**. Also on display at the headquarters of the Royal Institute of Architects of Ireland were the 14 winners of the RIAI awards in 1993. Among other items, the catalogue noted the awards to **Arthur Gibney and Partners** for the renovation of Dr Steevens' Hospital as new headquarters for the Eastern Health Board, and for the Irish Pavilion at the World's Fair in Seville 1992(see IAR Yearbook 1994 pp.103-05) Sadly, the latter had to be demolished because nobody wanted to 'recycle' it. The

exhibition later travelled to Cork, Limerick, Kilkenny, London, Belfast, Derry, Galway and Waterford.

■ The work of the photographer **John Hinde**, whose popular colour postcards were produced at his factory in Cabinteely, Co Dublin, was exhibited at the Irish Museum of Modern Art from 6 July - 3 October (later shown at the Orchard Gallery, Derry, the Cornerhouse, Manchester and galleries

Hiroshige, Woodblock Print, at the Chester Beatty Library

■ Japanese woodblock prints by **Hiroshige,** born1797, from the collection in the Chester Beatty Library were displayed at the RHA Gallagher Gallery. Lacking the drama of Hokusai, the most popular Japanese artist in the West, Hiroshige's images have an almost melancholy stillness. Although Sir Alfred Chester Beatty never bought a complete cycle of the prints, the examples he acquired are, as always, of the finest quality and condition.

in the USA). Hinde was a pioneer colour photographer who believed 'pictures should always convey a positive, good feeling, something which makes people happy'. A colour book with an essay by David Lee accompanied the exhibition.

■ In the grounds of Kilkenny Castle, from July until the end of September, the Butler Gallery exhibited the American artist, **James Turrell**, who has been working for almost 30 years with light and space and the effects of light on space. The 'Air Mass' installation was a square room with continuous seating inside and a hidden light source affecting the changing colour of the sky. Dorothy Walker considered it 'magnificent', far surpassing the other two works in the series, in PSI, Long Island City and in the Hayward Gallery, London. Turrell has also been involved in The Irish Sky Garden, five permanent structures at the Liss Ard Foundation, outside Skibbereen, Co Cork.

AUGUST 1993

■ The Wyvern Gallery relocated across the street in No 2, Temple Lane, Dublin – the opening exhibition included **Eamon O'Doherty, Stuart White, Jack Donovan** and **Eileen Quinn**.

J H Craig, Sunday Morning, Cynthia O'Connor Gallery at the Antique Dealers Fair

■ The 27th Irish Antique Dealers' Fair was a showcase for the finest antiques available on the Irish market in the Mansion House, Dublin, from 2nd until 7th August.

■ A collection of 53 European Old Master paintings left the National Gallery of Ireland for a five-month tour of Japan. The exhibition, which includes the work of *Titian, Veronese, Rubens, Van Dyck, Poussin, El Greco, Murillo* and *Goya*, opened in Yokohama and was later shown in Chiba, Yamaguchi, Kobe and Tokyo. Exhibition costs were covered by the Tokyo Shimbun newspaper group, who also paid a fee of £300,000 to the Gallery towards their refurbishment programme.

■ A new Tate Gallery opened in Cornwall, at St Ives, for many years the centre of an artistic community which included *Tony O'Malley, Nancy Wynne-Jones, William Scott* and *F E McWilliam.*

■ At the RHA Gallagher Gallery, Dublin, the annual Oireachtas Art Exhibition took place. After last year's 'near-calamity'. Brian Fallon considered this one ' a partial recovery'. An entire section of *Michael Farrell's* work was 'an injection of brio' and other highlights were large works by *Michael Ashur, Michael Cullen*, and *Michael O'Dea*. Artists who are not called Michael also exhibited, and fine work was noted by *Sean McSweeney, Veronica Bolay, Anita Shelbourne, Charles Brady* and *Tony O'Malley.*

■ In the Pantheon Gallery there was an exhibition of recent work by *Paul Mooney* and *Helen Gibb*. At the Solomon Gallery there was a joint exhibition of the work of husband and wife artists, *Barry* and *Philip Castle*, now living in France and Italy. 'Dexterous professionals' with 'formidable technical skills', their paintings are sophisticated, colourful, faux-naif: his are meticulous cityscapes, hers are of lustrous girls and doves.

■ Kilkenny Arts Week took place at the end of August – exhibitions included work by *Alan Davie, Sonja Landweer, Bernadette Kiely, Henry Pim* and *Colin Rose.*

■ A significant collection of 18th and 19th century Irish landscape paintings

owned by a Cork businessman and noted collector, Mr Richard Wood, is to be hung in Plassey House at the University of Limerick, which is to be redecorated to house them. Included among the 30 oils and 40 watercolours are works by *William Ashford, George Petrie, James Arthur O'Connor, Francis Danby, Daniel Maclise, Thomas Roberts, Robert West, George Barret* and *Nathaniel Grogan.* The paintings were on display for 7 years until 1990 in Fota House near Cork, which had been restored by Mr Wood and opened to the public. Fota, which had won the European Museum of the Year award, has been allowed by University College Cork, who owns it, to deteriorate and has been closed for the past two years; controversy surrounds its future and that of the 700-acre Fota estate.

*Michael Ashur, Sentinel 1,
at the RHA Gallagher Gallery*

■ Number 85, St Stephen's Green, Dublin, part of Newman House, whose splendid interior restoration is described in Irish Arts Review Yearbook 1994, is to have its 1738 stone facade repaired. University College Dublin has raised £110,000 from the Getty Foundation and £75,000 from the National Heritage Council towards the cost of the project.

■ Paintings by Wexford based artist *Noleen Dempsey* were exhibited in the Arts Council in Merrion Square, Dublin.

■ *Paki Smith's* exhibition of paintings, The Garden of the Soul, was at the Project Arts Centre, Dublin, and the Arts Council Gallery, Belfast, showed work by two women artists: *Eileen Ferguson* - including collage, focused on 'the richness within decay' embodied in

the residences of former Irish landed classes - and Donegal-born *Mary McGowan's* colourful Giottoesque figures reflecting her interest in early Irish legend.

■ In the Irish Life Centre, Dublin, To the Baltic and Back was an exhibition of watercolours by 5 Irish and 5 Latvian artists ; although in a minor key, Brian Fallon found it had 'a freshness which lifted it beyond the ruck'.

■ The Angela Flowers Gallery in Rosscarbery showed *Anthony Daley's* flower paintings and, in contrast, monolithic sculptures by *Dave King*.

SEPTEMBER 1993

■ On Heritage Day, Sunday, 12 September, the Office of Public Works allowed free admission to many museums, galleries, concerts, walks and talks, in an annual event which is both imaginative and immensely popular.

■ Art Attacks was the title of RTE's 'aggressive' series of 11 television documentary programmes on the Arts in Ireland. The intention of producer Michael Garvey was to 'unnerve' viewers who thought that art was a sedate concert or a painting hanging in a quiet gallery'.

■ The Courthouse in Ballycastle, Co Mayo, the setting and inspiration for Jack B Yeats' well-known painting, Poteen-Makers in Court, was the location for an art exhibition organised by a husband and wife team from Philadelphia, *Peter Maxwell* and *Margo Dolan*. Drawing on more than 30 years' experience of the art world, they have established the Ballinglen Arts Foundation to revitalise the cultural and economic life of North Mayo, using diverse forms of the visual arts.

■ The City Arts Centre, in partnership with the National Rehabilitation Board, showed Celebrating Difference, an exhibition of work by disabled and non-disabled artists, which celebrated disability as difference rather than disadvantage.

Foundation Building, University of Limerick,
Designed by Pat Whelan

■ On 18 September, the new Foundation Building at the University of Limerick, designed by Cork architect **Pat Whelan**, was opened. The £15 million building, for which the University itself raised £10 million, contains a 1,000 seat concert hall, where an inaugural concert was given by the National Symphony Orchestra under **Colman Pearce**, with soloist **Barry Douglas**, and a specially commissioned work, Rivers of Paradise, by Limerick-born composer **John Buckley**. There are also 2 large lecture theatres, 3 art galleries, a museum (currently housing the Hunt Collection), a cafe, a bar and a dramatic atrium with a life-size model of Da Vinci's Flying Man, the gift of Dr Tony Ryan. The building has been described as 'a breathtaking creation', 'a treasure' and 'of unique importance to the arts in Ireland.'

Bronze bucket or situla, *Irish, late Bronze Age,
c. 700B.C, 46.5 x 36cm, at the Hunt Museum.*

■ The Hunt Museum was opened in the new building on 26 September. Its Director is **Mairead Dunlevy**, who was seconded from the National Museum of Ireland. This collection,which was donated by **John** and **Gertrude Hunt**, comprises 3,000 art objects, and includes neolithic and Irish Bronze Age work, medieval figure sculpture, the crucifix worn by Mary Queen of Scots on the day of her execution and drawings by Picasso. A newly-published handsome colour catalogue of the collection by Patrick Doran is reviewed in this issue.

■ In a week of celebrations, concerts and exhibitions in Limerick, the University also launched the permanent collection of The Water Colour Society of Ireland, pictures by 98 of the Society's current members.

■ A unique sculpture symposium for Co Laois was launched under the Department of the Environment's One Per Cent for Art in Public Places Scheme. Six top sculptors were commissioned to create original works of art to be sited permanently in Portlaoise, Mountrath, Mountmellick, Stradbally, Abbeyleix and Portarlington. Based in Stradbally, the sculptors are **Cliodhna Cussen, Dick Joynt, Dave Lambert, Eileen MacDonagh, Mary McGinty** and **Kieran Melody**, and **McKeon Stone** are providing materials and machinery.

■ Two new art galleries opened in Dublin: The Peter Hogan Gallery, owned and run by the eponymous round- the -world yachtsman and artist, specialising in Dublin and marine paintings, on the top floor of 57 Dame Street, Temple Bar, and The Guinness Gallery in the centre of Foxrock village, owned by glass expert Elizabeth Guinness, exhibiting an exciting range of modern art works, and featuring young Cork artists.

■ See Through Art, an exhibition of 22 innovative sculptures and installations, opened at the Hugh Lane Municipal Gallery of Modern Art, in association with the Sculptors' Society. The 'See Through'media were glass, perspex, water, mirrors, cathodes and fibre-optics; artists included **Maud Cotter, Eilis O'Connell, Brian Connolly,**

Michael Minnis, Rhona Henderson, and the exhibition was set to tour to Limerick, Tralee, Belfast and Sligo. Aidan Dunne found it 'smart, slick, cerebral, very now...a medium-sized leap forward for the Society'. It was also fun.There were 4 short 'soundworks' and a series of children's workshops.

Johannes Vermeer, The Letter, (detail)
Beit Collection, NGI

■ Four of the most important paintings stolen from the collection of Sir Alfred and Lady Beit in 1986 were recovered outside Brussels on 1 September, when four men were arrested. **Vermeer's** The Letter, **Vestier's** The Princesse de Lamballe, **Metsu's** Man Writing a Letter and **Goya's** Dona Antonia Zarate were safe and intact. Of the 11 paintings stolen, only a painting by Rubens and 2 by Guardi remain missing.

■ Two interesting exhibitions took place at the Green on Red Gallery, Dublin. Interface was the first solo show by Dublin artist **John MacMenamin**, works on canvas, paper and in bronze, exploring themes of thesis and antithesis. Later we saw **Ciaran Lennon's** Scotoma III/C 1993 (last in the series of his Scotoma Group of 3 large paintings which he completed after his 1992 retrospective in the Douglas Hyde Gallery). In an attempt to lend a further dimension to his abstract art, Lennon published a small 'box book', The Scotoma Group, in which all the pages fold over, just as in his paintings he 'folds' the paint. Lennon's work is in the Hugh Lane Gallery and appears in their new Images and Insights catalogue.

■ At the Irish Museum of Modern Art, an exhibition of work belonging to members of the Contemporary Irish Arts Society displayed interesting, and often surprising, trends in private art collecting in Ireland in the past 30 years. *Gordon Lambert*, who is himself a major collector of contemporary Irish art, succeeded Sir Basil Goulding as Chairman in 1977 and became Honorary Patron in 1992 of CIAS.

■ The Crafts Council of Ireland Gallery in the Powerscourt Townhouse Centre had an interiors exhibition with a difference. Five people, who had to be 'fun to work with', were asked by freelance curator *Anya von Gosseln* to create their own rooms using Irish crafts. Pricelist in hand, one browsed through architect *Alfred Cochrane's* luxurious Hotel Lobby, filled with Alfrank tables and candlesticks. Architect *Sean O'Laoire* presented a neat hi-tech Home Office. *Shay Healy*, the musician, had done a dull Bedroom; *Robert O'Byrne* an enchanting coppery Bathroom, in which one seemed to be asked to shower inside a rough brick chimney; but everyone fell for architect *Rachael Chidlow's* Bedsitter, where the centrepiece was an irresistible white 'Venus flytrap' sofa by *Niamh Barry*. There was a cooking trolley with chopping-boards, wonderful colours and

Robert O'Byrne, The Bathroom, Interiors, at the Crafts Council of Ireland Gallery

a high bed nest, under which was a dining or reading area inside a muslin curtain - perfect for narrow, high-ceilinged bedsits everywhere.

Paul Kelly, Tomato Picking, Rush, at the Gorry Gallery

■ The Gorry Gallery had a delightful exhibition of oils by the young Dublin artist *Paul Kelly*, while the Pantheon Gallery showed paintings and lithography by *John Breakey* and late in September, work by *Maurice Quillanan* and *Paddy Lennon*. The Arts Council showed work done by *Doris Affeldt* in Mayo since 1983 and the Bobby Dawson Gallery in Dun Laoghaire exhibited paintings by 3 young artists - *Marie McDonald, Peter Pearson* and *Ries Hoek.*

■ The Douglas Hyde Gallery showed a new installation by *Willie Doherty*, who lives and works in Derry. Inspired by Bloody Sunday (30th January 1972), it comprised 2 large projected images and crowd sound effects. It was in collaboration with Matt's Gallery, London and Grey Gallery, New York. Aidan Dunne found it 'remote...shyly oblique' and 'understated'.

■ *Ronnie Hughes*, 'a painter of formidable gifts' showed a fine set of paintings of Belfast office blocks in City Reformed at the Rubicon Gallery, Dublin and New Arts Studios celebrated their tenth anniversary with a bumper group exhibition at the RHA Gallagher Gallery.

■ In Cork, the Crawford Gallery showed abstract oils, 'indecipherable, but lovely' by *Richard Gorman* and the Triskel , new works by *Suzanna Chan*; in Galway, the Kenny Gallery showed Vagabondage, Women in Music, drypoint etchings and lithographs by German *Gertrude Degenhardt*, which are both 'wild, witty and sexy' and 'quintessentially West of Ireland'; in Derry, the Orchard Gallery showed Home Rule, work by American *Elaine Reichek*; in Belfast, the Ulster Museum showed dramatic wind- and rain- swept landscapes by *Len Taubner*, the Emer Gallery works by *Gladys MacCabe*, and the NI Arts Council showed Akshun Artifax, dramatic, even shocking, paintings and installations by Belfast artist *Andre Stitt*, done since the 1970s.

Stephen McKenna, Red Sea (detail) at IMMA

■ At IMMA an exhibition of *Stephen McKenna's* paintings made between 1985 and 1993 was shown; Brian Fallon sees him as 'currently at the height of his powers'. McKenna deals with seascapes, still life, landscapes and interiors; a disquieting tension between past and present is characteristic of his art. His alluring painting of sunlight on stone may come from his sojourns in Tuscany, while the coastline of Donegal, where he also has a studio, was the inspiration for the oil paintings on concurrent exhibition at the Kerlin Gallery, Dawson Street.

*Patricia Jorgensen, In Full Bloom,
at the Solomon Gallery*

■ At the Solomon Gallery, lovely floral watercolours and brilliant tapestry work by the multi-talented **Patricia Jorgensen** showed her patient observation and increasing expertise. **Sarah Walker's** exhibition, Real Life, attracted a lot of interest at the Hallward Gallery, Dublin. A graduate of NCAD, Sarah Walker lives and works in West Cork.

OCTOBER 1993

■ **George Morrison,** one of Northern Ireland's best known watercolour artists, died in Belfast at the age of 78.

■ **The Office of Public Works** won the Incorporated Association of Architects and Surveyors' James Culleton Award, which is presented every 6 years, for its restoration work on the Islandbridge Irish National Memorial Park, which was originally designed by Sir Edwin Lutyens.

■ The Royal Institute of Architects of Ireland presented medals for conservation to the practice of **de Blacam and Meagher** for the Dining Hall and Atrium, Trinity College, Dublin and to **Costello Murray Beaumont** for the Royal Hospital, Kilmainham. The winner of the restoration medal, the first ever

presented, was **Mr Austin Dunphy** for 'scholarly restoration' of the Casino at Marino, Dublin.

■ At the Boston College Museum of Art, Irish Watercolours and Drawings from the National Gallery of Ireland went on exhibition. A full-colour catalogue is available from the NGI.

*Beatrice Glenavy, Sea Shanty ,
at Pyms Gallery*

■ At Pyms Gallery, London, An Ireland Imagined was a prestigious exhibition of Irish art, including works by **O'Conor, Lavery, MacGonigal, Orpen, and Beatrice Glenavy** (see article by Nicola Gordon Bowe in this issue); it was

accompanied, as usual, by a very high quality catalogue.

■ The collection of the late antique dealer, **Ronald McDonnell** of 16 Kildare Street, Dublin, especially rich in 18th century art and furniture, was auctioned by Mealy's of Castlecomer in the Royal Hospital, Kilmainham.

*Philippa Bayliss, The Rosarie, Lodge Park (detail),
at the Kennedy Gallery*

■ **Philippa Bayliss'** exhibition of recent work - more than thirty canvases - at the Kennedy Gallery, Dublin, focussed on trees and was inspired by scenes in Louth and Kildare.

.■ A new TV series on antiques and collectibles, Treasure Ireland, presented by James O'Halloran (of James Adam and Sons) and Helen Comiskey began on Sunday evenings on RTE. Better than Antiques Roadshow because of its local interest, it showed us inside some beautiful houses, with lots of polish, in both senses of the word.

■ Irish artists of the late 19th and early 20th century who painted in France, such as **Osborne, Leech, O'Conor, Hone** and **Swanzy,** were the subject of Onlookers in France, an exhibition, reviewed in this issue, at the Crawford Municipal Art Gallery in Cork.

W J Hennessy, Fete Day in France, Onlookers in France Exhibition, at the Crawford Gallery

■ *Rita Duffy* was Artist in Residence at the Ulster Museum.

■ Antiques fairs took place in Cork and Kilmainham. *Louis O'Sullivan*, of the Irish Antique Dealers' Fair, organised one in Templeogue to raise funds for the St Vincent de Paul Society. Among the items on sale was a rare set of George III silver buttons made by the Dublin silversmith *Jane Stone* about 1785.

Brian Ferran, Drumceat, at Jorgensen Fine Art

■ *Brian Ferran's* exhibition of recent work, his first in Dublin for 10 years, was opened at the Jorgensen Fine Art Gallery by James White. In these large works, assured and positive, the brilliant colours spoke of a new direction in Ferran's painting; a well-deserved success.

■ The NI Department of the Environment's collection of contemporary Irish art was on show at the Arts Council Gallery, Dublin Road, Belfast, and later toured in the province. The 600 works, which are usually located in public service offices, represent a concise history of painting in Northern Ireland in the past 25 years, and include work by *T P Flanagan, Tom Carr, Basil Blackshaw* as well as younger artists.

Brian Maguire, Black, Blue, and White at the Kerlin Gallery

■ *Brian Maguire*, more recently shortlisted in the IMMA Glen Dimplex Award, showed American Paintings at the Kerlin Gallery; further showings at D'arte Galleria in Helsinki and the Orchard Gallery in Derry are scheduled. Brian Fallon found the big, aggressive canvases had impact, luminosity and lightness which 'reaffirmed (Maguire's) place among living Irish painters of any generation.'

■ In connection with the Wexford Festival Opera, Signature, an exhibition of Irish painting and sculpture, was opened by the Earl of Rosse at the Westgate Heritage Centre in Wexford. Grant-aided by the Arts Council and sponsored by Guinness, the artists included *Felim Egan, Veronica Bolay, Richard Gorman, Tony O'Malley* and *Vivienne Roche*.

■ *Gerald Davis* of the Davis Gallery, Capel Street, Dublin, affirmed his 55th birthday with an exhibition of 55 paintings. Canadian artist *Jeff Wall* employed the advanced technology of mainstream cinema in his new works on show at IMMA, Dead Troops Talk. Also at IMMA, Four Artists from France - paintings, collages, sculptures and prints by new generation French artists, all born in the 1950s, *Jean-Charles Blais, Helene Delprat, Philippe Favrier* and *Gerard Gaouste*.

■ *Stephen Rothschild* exhibited, at European Modern Art, Dublin, paintings and drawings related to Fossett's Circus and Smithfield Horse Market.

Carmel Benson, Haystack Print, Graphic Studio

■ New prints by *Carmel Benson*, exuberant in colour and rich in significance, went on show at the Graphic Studio Dublin Gallery.

■ At the Douglas Hyde Gallery, German artist *Nikolaus Lang* used his background in woodcarving to explore an anthropological interest in Australian aborigines. The title, Nunga and Goonya, means 'black fellow and white person'.

Carey Clarke, Still Life, *at the RHA*

■ At the 4th Annual Banquet Exhibition of the Royal Hibernian Academy, a wider aspect was presented as each Member of the Academy had selected an artist they admired to hang their work alongside their own. The President of the Academy, *Carey Clarke*, PRHA, Hon RA, Hon RSA, welcomed the President, Mrs Robinson.

NOVEMBER 1993

■ At the beginning of November, the Water Colour Society of Ireland held its 139th Annual Exhibition at the Royal Hibernian Academy Gallagher Gallery in Dublin, where the 288 paintings hung to advantage. For all those who complain that contemporary Irish art is neither affordable nor accessible, this is an annual exhibition not to be missed.

■ The National Gallery of Ireland unveiled The Taking of Christ, now known to be by the 17th century Italian master *Caravaggio*, in an exhibition entitled The Master Revealed. The exhibition, catalogue and RTE video told the fascinating story of the rediscovery of the painting by NGI restorer Sergio Benedetti, and paid tribute to the generosity of the Jesuit Community, who have placed the picture on loan in the Gallery. The painting, which has both beauty and intrigue, has attracted thousands; it hangs currently with the Italian collection. International scholars contributed to a symposium at the Gallery and The Burlington Magazine published an article by Sergio Benedetti in the November 1993 issue. Guinness Mahon sponsored the events.

Christina Steenson, Silver, Red Gold Brooch, *The Crafts Council Gallery*

■ The Crafts Council Gallery in Dublin showed the work of 10 contemporary Irish jewellers.

■ In a major exhibition,the Hugh Lane Municipal Gallery of Modern Art in Parnell Square showed a selection from its Irish and international collection of paintings and sculpture from mid-19th

Daniel Mc Donald, Discovery of the Potato Blight, in the *UCD Folklore Dept.*

■ At Newman House, the Department of Irish Folklore at University College Dublin held an exhibition of paintings entitled Amharc Oidhreacht Eireann - Folk Tradition in Irish Art. The documentary value of these works is high in that they give a unique insight into aspects of folk life. Many were gifts, such as The Discovery of the Potato Blight in Ireland by *Daniel McDonald* (1821- 1853), which was purchased by Mrs Cecil Woodham-Smith at Christie's of London in 1966 and presented to the Irish Folklore Commission in gratitude for the help she received in research for her book The Great Hunger. The exhibition which included work by Brocas, Lover, Williams and Mulvany, and the interesting colour catalogue were sponsored by First National Building Society.

century to the present day. Entitled Images and Insights, it was accompanied by a colour catalogue, the Gallery's first ever and sponsored by ABN Amro Bank in association with Dublin Corporation. The exhibition and catalogue are reviewed in this issue.

■ The disposition of the 39 paintings in the Bequest of Sir Hugh Lane, who was drowned in the Lusitania in 1915, was the subject of a new agreement between the National Gallery, London, and the Hugh Lane Gallery. As is appropriate, the substantial part of Lane's original collection will remain on view in Dublin. While keeping picture movement to a

minimum, the new arrangement will allow the public in London and Dublin to enjoy the fullest possible access to these celebrated paintings.

■ Historic St Brigid's Cathedral in Kildare, whose main fabric is Norman, is the centre of a major and splendid FAS restoration scheme on which 23 people are working and which has attracted apprentices from Portugal and Greece. The stonework is supervised by *Pat McAfee*, who worked on Drimnagh Castle; he has immortalised Bishop Walton Empey and Archbishop Desmond Connell in two of the stone corbels.

■ More than 130 artists, Irish and international, young and long-established, entered for the first IMMA/Glen Dimplex Artists' Award. The 4 on the shortlist were *Terry Atkinson, Brian Maguire, Patricia McKenna and Alanna O'Kelly*.

■ Seven Irish museums received awards, made for the first time, from the Calouste Gulbenkian Foundation. The Tower Museum in Derry won the £2,000 award for institutions with annual income of more than £500,000. The £2,000 Norwich Union Award (for those with annual income of less than £500,000) was shared by the Chester Beatty Library and Fermanagh County Museum- two very different collections. A £1,000 award for the Most Improved Museum/Gallery with Limited Resources went to the Crawford Gallery, Cork. The £1,000 Best Visitor Care Award was shared between the Linen Hall Library, Belfast, and Number Twenty-Nine Fitzwilliam Street, a Dublin townhouse restored by the Electricity Supply Board, now open to the public.

■ The Arts Council/An Chomhairle Ealaion published their Annual Report in which the outgoing Chairman, Colm O hEocha accounted for the expenditure of more than £10 million in 1992 and referred to an increase of almost 70% in Arts Council's State funding from 1988 to 1993. The Council welcomed the Taoiseach's commitment to bring funding to £12.5 million by the end of 1994, bringing it nearer to the 'plateau' of £13 million.(See IAR Yearbook 1991-92, pp.99-106).

Felim Egan, Sculpture, *Awarded by Cothu for Arts Sponsor of the year*

■ Awards for Arts Sponsor of the Year were made by Cothu/The Business Council for the Arts in conjunction with The Sunday Business Post. The Best Established Arts Sponsor was Toyota for the National Youth Orchestra; the Best Single Arts Sponsor was IBM Ireland for The Masters' Return, an exhibition marking the return from the USA of the Master European Paintings from the National Gallery of Ireland touring exhibition for which IBM were shortlisted in 1992; the Best First Time Arts Sponsor was Kilkenny Limestone for involvement with Irish sculptors and a Special Recognition Award went to the Tokyo Shimbun newspaper group for its sponsorship of the NGI exhibition of Master European Paintings touring 5 Japanese cities in 1993/94.

■ The Arts Council of Northern Ireland sold 31 pieces from its collection of over 1000 paintings at Sotheby's in London and raised just over £100,000. Two works, by **Gerard Dillon** and

Patrick Hennessy, were withdrawn, believed bought by the Ulster Museum, and the highest prices (£11,000) were fetched by a **Dillon** and a **William Conor.** Some controversy surrounded the sale, which the Council defended on the grounds that it 'needed funds to help a new generation of young artists'.

■ Jewellery expert **John FitzPatrick** was appointed Master Warden of the Company of Goldsmiths of Dublin, which was established by Charles I in 1637 and controls the Assay Office.

■ *Desmond Shortt* showed new paintings at the Pantheon Gallery and at the Guinness Gallery, Foxrock, there were paintings by **Suzanna Chan** and ceramic sculpture by **Michael O'Brien.**

■ **Michael Kane** exhibited at the Rubicon Gallery, Dublin - Aidan Dunne found his style still in essence confrontational, but labelled this a good show. 'Liberation for the eye' was Dunne's view of the exuberant, lyrical paintings of **Robert Armstrong** at the Hallward Gallery, Dublin. At European Modern Art, *Evelyn Montague's* exquisite quilted wall hangings were seen to have broken the divide between craft and contemporary art.

■ The Ulster Museum showed 14 watercolour studies by **Louis Le Brocquy** - Images Towards Seamus Heaney - on loan from the Taylor Galleries, Dublin, as well as Exploring Materials: The Work of **Peter Rice**. Dublin-born Rice, educated at Queen's University, Belfast, who died in 1992, was an internationally acclaimed and highly innovative structural engineer. Ceramic sculpture made recently in the Netherlands by *Deirdre McLoughlin* was also exhibited.

■ In Munich, at Galerie Bernd Kluser, *Sean Scully's* paintings and drawings illustrating **James Joyce's** Pomes Penyeach were on exhibition, accompanied by a colour catalogue.

■ A copy of Ulysses illustrated with 6 etchings by **Matisse** and published in New York in 1935 was auctioned at Christie's London salerooms for £5,000 (est. £3,000). It was one of 250 signed by Joyce and Matisse.

■ The Arts Council displayed paintings and monoprints by Monaghan artist and feminist activist **Carissa Farrell**. The Arts Council of Northern Ireland showed brightly coloured constructions in metal and wood by **Brian Ord** and a window installation/performance by **Dougal McKenzie**. Prints by **Geraldine O'Reilly** inspired by the Monaghan landscape were on show at Monaghan County Museum.

■ At the Kenny Gallery, Galway, was Portfolio, an exhibition of paintings, fine bone china figurines and bronzes by **Rick Lewis**, while the Butler Gallery in Kilkenny was host to the exhibition of works from the collections of the members of the Contemporary Irish Art Society which had earlier been in IMMA, and the Triskel in Cork exhibited an installation by **Bernadette Cotter**.

■ Some 40 bronzes by the German painter, printmaker and sculptor **Max Ernst** (1891-1976) were on show at IMMA. Sculpture 1934-1974, drawn from collection in Europe and America, dated from his early work with Arp and Giacometti.

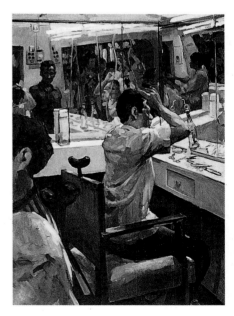

Hector McDonnell, Hairdresser in Bubaneshwar, *Solomon Gallery.*

■ Antrim artist **Hector McDonnell** had an exhibition at the Solomon Gallery.

■ At the Kerlin Gallery, Dublin, The Last Kiss was an exhibition of paintings by **David Godbold** based on the newspaper reproduction of the 'Odessa copy' of the Caravaggio painting in the National Gallery of Ireland.

*Mary Rose Binchy, Antenna,
at the Green on Red Gallery*

■ November exhibitions at the Green on Red Gallery, Dublin, were A View by **Pauline Flynn**, New York by **Mary Rose Binchy** and humorous Monotypes by **Peter Jones**.

DECEMBER 1993

■ An auction of 126 works by Irish artists took place in the RHA Gallagher Gallery in aid of the RHA Building Fund. In the same venue later in December, 25 dealers presented an Aladdin's cave of quality antiques 'for middlebrows' in the first Dublin Antique & Fine Arts Fair, organised by **Louis O'Sullivan**.

■ The collection of ceramics and Irish works of art assembled by the late **Angus MacDonald**, one of the best-known figures in the antiques world in Northern Ireland, was auctioned by Christie's for more than £200,000. The ceramics made more than £45,000, with top prices for the Staffordshire ware which was his particular favourite.

■ The President, Mrs Robinson, officially reopened the grand stairwell and salon at Newman House, which had been restored at a cost of £400,000 by Gallaher(Dublin) Ltd under the supervision of architect, **David Sheehan**, and is now open to the public.

*Augustus Burke, The Little Laundress (detail),
at Milmo-Penny Fine Art*

■ At Milmo-Penny Fine Art there were paintings by Lavery, Leech, Burke, Somerville and Williams.

■ An exhibition of drawings by **Alexander Williams** opened in the Lombard and Ulster Building, Waterford.

■ Designyard, the Applied Arts Centre at Temple Bar, opened with an exhibition of enamelling and jewellery by

Patrick Swift, Boy with Pears, IMMA

■ A major exhibition of the work of the Irish artist **Patrick Swift** (1927-83) opened at IMMA. The exhibition and its accompanying catalogue are reviewed in this issue, as is the biography of Swift published by Gandon.

Joan MacKarell, Alexandra Raphael and **Tamar Winter**.

■ A Tribute to **Sidney Nolan** was held by IMMA in the Baroque Chapel at the Royal Hospital, Kilmainham.

■ At the RHA, Minister Michael D Higgins launched the Irish Contemporary Art Gallery Association. In December, the Minister also initiated a radical restructuring of the framework within which the national institutions under his authority operate, beginning with contemporary arts.

■ A revolving fund for the restoration of historic buildings in Dublin was launched by the Minister for the Environment, Mr Smith, with £75,000 from his Department. He spoke at the inauguration of the restoration of two early Georgian houses in South Frederick Street by the newly-formed Dublin Civic Trust.

■ To mark the 75th anniversary of **Countess Markievicz's** election to the House of Commons, Group 84, the club for female members of the Oireachtas, negotiated a loan from the National Gallery of Ireland of the full-length portrait by her husband of the Countess in evening dress (see the article on **Count Markievicz** in this issue), to hang in Leinster House, on the stairs leading up to the Seanad.

■ Artist books from the Kaldewey Press in New York were featured in IMMA, coinciding with the launch of Sandymount Strand, a book with texts by **James Joyce** and **Seamus Heaney**, illustrated with 12 etchings by **Felim Egan**.

■ The Royal Institute of the Architects of Ireland gold medal, awarded every 3 years, was presented by the President, Mrs Robinson, to the Dublin practice **Gilroy McMahon** for their extension to Bolton Street College of Technology.

■ The President, Mrs Robinson, presented a gold torc, the symbol of Aosdana, to the artist, **Tony O'Malley**, who was elected to the honour of Saoi. There can be no more than five Saoithe in Aosdana at any one time; there are now 4, including **Patrick Collins**, **Mary Lavin** and **Louis Le Brocquy**.

■ Northern Ireland's museums are to be served by a new Museums Council, funded by the NI Department of Education, which met for the first time in December under the Chairmanship of **Lord O'Neill**.

■ Gorry Gallery's Christmas exhibition was of delightful landscapes by **Andrea Jameson**, the Norwegian- Irish artist from Waterford.

■ The Burren College of Art, a unique conference venue, purpose-built for the study of Fine Art, opened near Ballyvaughan, Co Clare.

■ Dancing around my Ghost was the title of an exhibition in the Douglas Hyde Gallery of delicate and soothing geometric drawings, based on Sufi meditation, by a young Iranian woman artist, **Shirazeh Houshiary**.

■ **Hughie O'Donoghue's** richly textured abstracts were strikingly successful at the Kilkenny Arts Week a couple of years ago. At the Atlantis Upper Gallery, Brick Lane, London, work on his huge new project, The Passion, was exhibited.

■ The Ulster Museum showed work by the influential Ulster painter **John Luke** (1906-75) drawn from their own collection.

■ The Arts Council exhibited paintings by Angela Fewer, while the Arts Council of Northern Ireland showed work by 2 young Ulster women artists, **Deborah Mulvenna Murphy** and **Sharon Kelly**, which dealt with the human consequences of terrorism and loss.

■ The Kerlin Gallery showed new paintings by **Brian Ballard**, inspired by his Donegal island home.

JANUARY 1994

■ Europa Nostra awards 'for distinguished contribution to the conservation of Europe's heritage' were given for the restoration of Dr Steevens' Hospital as the Eastern Health Board headquarters and for the 'creative adaptation' of an old distillery as the Jameson Heritage Centre, Midleton, Co Cork.

Scott Tallon Walker, UCD Biotechnology Building, *Shortlisted for the Sunday Times/RIAI Award*

■ There were 68 entries for the new Sunday Times/RIAI competition Irish Building of the Year. The shortlist included the Ashtown, Waterways and Ceide Fields visitor centres by **OPW**; Glenveagh School, Belfast, by **Kennedy Fitzgerald**; the Irish Film Centre(**O'Donnell and Tuomey**); UCD Biotechnology Centre(**Scott Tallon Walker**); Clyde Mews(**Grafton**); the Beckett Theatre(**de Blacam and Meagher**) and Dr Steevens' Hospital.

■ The Arts Council was requested by the Department of the Arts , Culture and the Gaeltacht to submit a Three Year Plan for the arts in Ireland by June 1994. A working party was established under **Ciaran Benson**, Chairman.

■ **Joan O'Connor** was elected President of the Royal Institute of the Architects of Ireland. The RIAI presented awards to Dublin Corporation's housing architects for flats at Cambridge Court, Ringsend and Woodstock Gardens, Ranelagh.

■ The restoration of a Georgian house at no 35 North Great Georges Street as the James Joyce Cultural Centre was funded by Guinness Ireland Ltd. The original 1784 plasterwork by **Michael Stapleton** was completely restored from photographs under Dublin architect **Jim O'Connor**.

■ The death occurred of **Miss Aideen Gore-Booth** of Lissadell House, Co Sligo.

She was a niece of Countess Constance Markievicz and of Eva Gore-Booth.

■ Among a number of new developments for 1994, the Irish Museum of Modern Art announced plans for 18 new projects for the Artists' Work Programme in the studio blocks in the restored coach-houses and for the rebuilding of the studio of **Edward Maguire**, who died in 1986, in a ground floor room in the Museum.

■ In association with the Anthony d'Offay Gallery, London, IMMA showed Works on Paper by **Barnett Newman, Joseph Beuys, Cy Twombly, Yves Klein** and **Jasper Johns**.

■ The Minister for Enterprise and Employment, Ruari Quinn, appointed **Cyril Forbes**, Chairman and Managing Director of the corporate insurance brokers Kennedy Forbes, as Chairman of the Crafts Council of Ireland in succession to Dr John Maguire, Chief Executive of Rehab Lotteries.

Nancy Crow, Colour Blocks #27, at the RHA Gallagher Gallery

■ The Crafts Council of Ireland showed 41 Contemporary American Quilts at the RHA Gallagher Gallery.

■ *Elizabeth Magill* showed a bewildering diversity of styles in her Kerlin Gallery exhibition; in January she also began the Momart Fellowship at the Tate Gallery, Liverpool.

Vivienne Roche, Silent Pool, at the Green on Red Gallery

■ The Arts Council showed mixed media work by *Jacqueline Duignan*, whose sculpture Mother and Child was erected in Lough Key Forest Park last year; she also acted as facilitator for the Finglas community project, A Woman's Place, shown in the City Arts Centre.

■ Tulira Castle, Co Galway, former home of *Edward Martyn* (see IAR 1994, pp.167-73) was offered by Sotheby's for sale at $3million.

■ The Pepiniere Programme, spanning 16 European cities, enables young artists to live and work abroad. The 4 artists who worked for 3 months at the National Sculpture Factory in Cork showed their work at the Crawford Gallery - *Peter Sinclair* and *Caroline Duchatelet* from France and *Simcha Roodenburg* and *Danielle Kray* from the Netherlands. Irish artists *Julie Merriman* and *Maurice O'Connell* were selected for residencies in Norwich and Niort.

■ City Arts Centre showed Machinations, kinetic figures based on the story of Adam and Eve by *John White*, whose permanent installation, Party Piece, is in IMMA. Also on exhibition were the results of workshops facilitated by *Corban Walker* for Cerebral Palsy Ireland and the Polio Foundation.

■ The Head Gallery, Ormond Quay, Dublin, showed North, new sculpture by *Aisling O'Brien, Lorraine Burrell* and *Michael Donaghy* from Belfast, using material from steel to soap.

■ The Green on Red Gallery exhibited works on canvas and paper by a young artist from Cork, *Catherine Kenny*, whose 'subtly drawn shapes tantalize the senses', and later in January, new sculpture by *Vivienne Roche* was shown.

■ At One Oxford Street, Belfast, there was a *Basil Blackshaw* retrospective, 1980-93; at the Boole Library, UCC, paintings and sculptures by *Eilis Ni Fhaolain*; the Gordon Lambert Collection from IMMA toured to the Galway Arts Centre and See Through Art from the Hugh Lane was in the Sligo Arts Centre.

FEBRUARY 1994

■ A new post of Arts Officer to promote co-operation between North and South, at a salary of £20,000, to be funded jointly by both Arts Councils, was announced. The Director of the Arts Council of Northern Ireland,

Brian Ferran, also announced details of allocations from ACNI's £6.448 million budget for 1994, which had been increased by 4 per cent.

■ The Arts Council/An Chomhairle Ealaoin received an additional £1million from the Government this year, bringing their grant to almost £13.2million. There were other beneficiaries from January's Budget; the current funding for heritage arts institutions in 1994 is as follows : National Gallery - £1,426,000; National Museum - £600,000; National Library - £400,000; Chester Beatty Library - £380,000. In addition, the National Library received £214,000 to develop the Photographic Archive in Temple Bar. The Irish Museum of Modern Art's grant increased by £100,000 to £1,150,00

Dorothy Cross, Spurs, at the Kerlin Gallery

■ Sculpture by *Dorothy Cross*, using cow hides with found and fabricated objects to confront viewers with the complexity of their own sexual identity, was shown at the Kerlin Gallery, Dublin.

■ The Wonderful Barn, part of the Castletown Demesne, Co Kildare, built in 1743 and one of the finest follies in Ireland, was the subject of a public meeting in Leixlip to protest against rezoning of agricultural land which would leave it sandwiched between a housing estate and a motorway. *Desmond Guinness*, who saved Castletown from destruction in 1967, has agreed to sell 120 acres to the Office of Public Works, to whom the house has formally been handed over, thereby ending his long association with the demesne.

The Sand Mandala, at the Douglas Hyde Gallery

■ The Kalachakra sand mandala, and the 4 Tibetan Buddhist monks who spent 3 weeks creating it in the Douglas Hyde Gallery, enthralled thousands of visitors. The symbolic design was created in coloured sand before our eyes, and, when complete, was ceremonially swept up into a chalice and carried in procession to the Liffey, where it was cast upon the waters 'to purify the environment'.

■ The new President of the Water Colour Society of Ireland, founded in 1870, is the well-known Irish artist **Kay Doyle**. She succeeds James Nolan RHA, who is stepping down after 12 years.

■ New religious works by two leading RHAs went on exhibition at the RHA Gallagher Gallery. **Patrick Pye's** Stations of the Cross, painted for a church in Kilcroney, has ' a kind of Expressionist edge and urgency' and **Imogen Stuart's** cedarwood Madonna, for the Church of the Resurrection, Ballycasheen,Killarney, is 'tall, simplified..with a genuine emotional presence'.

■ An exhibition by 12 young Irish printmakers, Dispatches, was on view at the Crawford Municipal Art Gallery, Cork, as well as prints and sculptures by **Sue Melling**.

■ In The Colonnades, Trinity College, Dublin, an exhibition entitled Le grand siecle: the genius of France in the 17th century,was opened of superbly illustrated books from the College Library's extensive collection; focusing on the growth of the image of the magnificence of the state and showing the expertise of Parisian engravers and printers, the exhibition remains on view until December 1994.

■ **Cathal O'Flaherty** exhibited romantic paintings in the Head Gallery, Ormond Quay, Dublin; **Rory Donaldson** showed new photoworks at the Orchard Gallery, Derry; **June Fitzgerald's** paintings were exhibited at the Triskel Arts Centre, Cork.

■ The Solomon Gallery held an exhibition of contemporary glass, designed by 4 young artists and produced by Waterford Crystal. Designyard Jewellery Gallery in East Essex Street, Dublin had an exhibition of contemporary rings.

■ At the Rubicon Gallery, Dublin, **Pam Harris's** paintings on a silver-grey background explored analogies between music and colour. At the Taylor Gallery, **Michael Farrell's** paintings chronicled a meeting between James Joyce and Pablo Picasso at the Cafe de Flore. The centrepiece, reportedly a statue and some sketches of a couple, one of whom was wearing a mitre, was not exhibited, on legal advice.

*Mark Joyce,Rostyly,
at the Green on Red Gallery*

■ The Green on Red Gallery, Dublin showed new paintings and computer images by **Mark Joyce**.

■ A major retrospective of the work of the German artist **Joseph Albers** (1888-1976), who became one of the most influential teachers in America, was shown at IMMA. He is perhaps best known for his series'Homage to the Square', one of which is in the Hugh Lane Gallery and featured in their new catalogue.

■ Also at IMMA, an exhibition of paintings, drawings and notebooks by **Rob Smith**, who taught at the National College of Art and Design from 1974 until his death in 1990.This was linked with a residency by Coracle, a small publishing house specialising in producing artists' books.

■ Portraits by **Cathy Callan** were on show at the Arts Council, while at the Arts Council in Belfast, light-filled paintings were shown by **Sophie Aghajanian**, who was born in Haifa of Armenian extraction, but now works in Northern Ireland. Recent paintings by **Mary Fitzgerald** went on exhibition at the Hallward Gallery, Dublin and at the Pantheon Gallery, new work by **Pat McAllister**. At Dublin Airport, there was Gateway to Art , the 7th annual exhibition comprising works by more than 60 artists.

■ In Belfast, at One Oxford Street, there was **Terry Gravett's** Ephesus series, and at the Fenderesky Gallery at Queen's, monoprints by **John Ford**, an installation by **Brian Connolly**, followed by an exhibition of paintings and prints by **Richard Gorman.** In Londonderry, Gordon Galleries showed new paintings by **Melita Denaro**

MARCH 1994

■ The inaugural exhibition at the Jo Rain Gallery, 23 Anglesea Street, Dublin, was of paintings and sculpture by various artists including **Mike Duhan** and **Rachel Ballagh.** Paintings and watercolours by **Michael Cullen** were on exhibition at the Fenderesky Gallery at Queen's, Belfast.

■ The annual Exhibition of Visual & Art (EV+A) took place in Limerick from 21 March until 30 April. The adjudicator for 1994 was **Jan Hoet**, Director of the Museum of Contemporary Art, Ghent, Belgium and Artistic Director of Documenta IX, Kassel, 1992. Mebh Ruane considered this EV+A 'one of the finest shows in Ireland for years', containing an open section,Young EV+A, and a new invited section. Encompassing multiple venues with its indoor and outdoor/public works, 'EV+A settles on the city like a cloud of magic dust'.

■ The distinguished Irish artist **Patrick Collins** died on 2 March at his home in Dublin. Born in Sligo in 1911, he was described as' an exceptional painter' and 'a shining figure for a number of generations

■ The well-known antique dealer **Alain Chawner** opened a shop called Shed Antiques at 120, The Coombe, Dublin, where he plans to sell country furniture.

■ Mayo poet **Paul Durcan** has produced another book of poems inspired by paintings, this time in the National Gallery in London. Give Me Your Hand was published by Macmillan in association with National Gallery Publications, price £9.99 stg. (paperback), and an exhibition of the poems and paintings took place at the Gallery. Those who liked his Crazy About Women poems in the National Gallery of Ireland will be glad to find more of the same kind here,'so artful in its vernacular ease'.

Alanna O'Kelly, The Country Blooms.......A Garden and a Grave, IMMA/Glen Dimplex Winner

■ The winner of the first IMMA Glen Dimplex Artists Award was multi-media artist **Alanna O'Kelly**, who was born in Co Wexford in 1955. The £15,000 prize was presented by the President, Mrs Robinson, for her 1992 IMMA exhibition The Country Blooms...A Garden and a Grave. Using video,installation and photoworks, it created a series of compelling images to explore themes from the Great Famine evoking feelings not only of pain, fear and hurt but also the possibility of a journey of discovery and healing. The other shortlisted artists were Terry Atkinson, Brian Maguire and Patricia McKenna.

■ A Victorian bookcase by the Dublin furniture maker **Strahan** was sold by Town & Country in Loughlinstown, Co Dublin for £1,950.

■ A white-lacquered 5-panelled screen, 6 ft. in height, by the Irish furniture designer **Eileen Gray** of 1929 was on sale at Christie's, New York(est. $100-$150,000).

Murillo,The Meeting of Jacob and Rachel, at the NGI

■ A painting by the Spanish artist **Bartolome Esteban Murillo**(1617-82) was unveiled at the National Gallery of Ireland by the Minister for Arts, Culture and the Gaeltacht, Mr Higgins. The Meeting of Jacob and Rachel, which is one of a set of 5 compositions on the Biblical story, was given to the Gallery in 1987 by Mrs Alice Murnaghan, from the collection of her late husband, the Supreme Court judge, Mr Justice Murnaghan, who had been Chairman of the Gallery Board from 1939 to 1963 and a member until his death in 1973.

■ Two Irish artists exhibited at the Arnolfini Gallery, Bristol. Derry artist **Willie Doherty's** unique video installation, The Only Good One is a Dead One, simulated the fear of both aggressor and victim in Northern Ireland. Preparatory designs by **Eilis O'Connell** for St Augustine's Footbridge in collaboration with **Ove Arup & Partners** were shown to illustrate this major public art commission for Bristol City Council.

■ Jorgensen Fine Art spring exhibition featured mostly 19th and 20th century works of art, many of them Irish, including Osborne, Lavery, Rose Barton, Mary Swanzy, Dan O'Neill, Norah McGuinness and Tony O'Malley.

■ The Kenny Gallery exhibited new work by Co Down artist **Sue McNeill** featuring paintings of heavily textured bog oak as well as waterlilies and cottage interiors.

■ A new arts and crafts retail and gallery outlet opened in Belfast - Vivid Earth Trading, 93 Dublin Road, Belfast. Also in Belfast, Catalyst Arts has established at 5 Exchange Place an exhibition space and 4 studio spaces; run by and for artists, its emphasis is on art, culture, creativity and diversity. The Rubicon Gallery exhibited **Jack Crabtree's** visual record of Patterson's Spade Mill in Templepatrick, Co Antrim - 'harsh and nostalgic'.

Walter Verling, The Curragh, Ardmore, at the Gorry Gallery

■ The Gorry Gallery held an exhibition of delightful 'plein air' landscapes from France and Ireland by **Walter Verling**, who lives and paints in Limerick and had recently been elected to Honorary membership of the Royal Hibernian Academy.

■ At the Old Museum Centre, Belfast, the widely acclaimed touring exhibition **Unspoken Truths** was opened on International Women's Day, 8 March, with a series of talks and workshops. The works are by 32 Dublin women, from Inchicore and from Sean McDermott Street, many of whom had little previous involvement with the visual arts.

■ The Ulster Museum was the March venue for a touring exhibition of watercolours by HRH **The Prince of Wales** to mark the 25th anniversary of his investiture.

■ The Arts Council exhibited paintings by the Cork artist **June Fitzgerald**, and the Arts Council of Northern Ireland showed a window installation by **Amanda Dunsmore** inspired by the 1993 Dublin Road bombing.

■ Parallel Windows, an abstract site-specific installation/series of paintings by the Korean-born artist **Chung Eun-Mo**, and later in March, South African Works 1991-92 by **Nick Miller** were shown at IMMA, and the Douglas Hyde Gallery showed work by **Jimmie Durham**, a Native American Cherokee sculptor, painter and political activist.

■ Armagh artist **Hugh McCormick**, who is Head of the Art Department in Galway RTC, spent 6 months in New Zealand as an artist in residence in 1993. He exhibited 50 works inspired by the landscape there at the Kenny Gallery, Galway.

Hugh McCormick, The Land of the Long White Cloud, Kenny Gallery

■ The Kerlin Gallery showed a new series of densely surfaced, richly textured abstract paintings made in Dublin by the German artist **Sibylle Ungers**, together with a set of monoprints from her studio in Cologne. **Ger Sweeney** exhibited at the Art Center Jean Rigaux, Brussels and at Espace Leopold, at the European Parliament Building. More than 30 artists from the Graphic Studio Dublin Gallery exhibited framed and unframed prints in the Armory in New York.

■ At the Triskel Arts Centre in Cork, abstract paintings and drawings by local artist **Billy Foley** were on show.

Billy Foley, Formation 10 (detail), at the *Triskel Arts Centre*

■ The landmark house built by architect **Michael Scott** in 1938 beside the Joyce Tower in Sandycove, Co Dublin, was sold for £274,000. The new owner is a Dublin banker interested in Irish literature who intends to use the house as a family home.

APRIL 1994

■ St Helen's House, Stillorgan, Co Dublin was registered by the Office of Public Works under Section 5 of the 1987 Historic Monuments Act. Built in 1754 by **Thomas Cooley**, the house has been deteriorating since it was sold by the Christian Brothers in 1988 and conservationists have urged the Taoiseach to take it into State care.

■ A neolithic court tomb, 5,500 years old and 30 metres long, was discovered near Clifden, Co Galway, by local archaeologists, and a new exhibition of prehistoric artefacts was opened at the National Museum of Ireland by the Minister for the Arts, Culture and the Gaeltacht.

■ The founder-proprietor of the Oriel Gallery, Clare Street, Dublin, **Oliver Nulty**, celebrated its 25th anniversary with the publication of a book, 100 Years of Irish Art, while the City Centre Arts Centre, held an Open Day which included an Open Forum to air views on the Arts Council Three Year Development Plan.

■ An exhibition organised by the Island Trust, founded in 1987 to foster the development of Ireland's off-shore islands, was opened in the Irish Life Centre, Dublin. Featuring works by **Tony O'Malley, Derek Hill, Veronica Bolay** and other island artists and artists who have worked on the islands, the exhibition toured to Inis Mor, Co Galway, the Glebe Gallery, Co Donegal and the Yawl Gallery, Achill Island.

■ In Dublin the Jo Rain Gallery in Temple Bar exhibited work by Dutch and Belgian artists; the Hallward Gallery showed work by **Helen Richmond** and **Liadin Cooke** was showing at the Green on Red Gallery.

Martin Mooney,Ramelton, Co. Donegal, at the Solomon Gallery

■ **Martin Mooney**, born in Belfast in 1960, but now working in Donegal, has won a reputation for himself in the unfashionable 'academic' style. An exhibition of his recent work, accomplished, warm-toned, but 'cool', according to Brian Fallon, was in the Solomon Gallery, and two of his paintings were also included in the 164th Annual Exhibition of the Royal Hibernian Academy of Arts at the RHA Gallagher Gallery.

■ The Gardens at Heywood House, Ballinakill, Co Laois, designed by *Lutyens* in 1909, were officially opened. (See Irish Arts Review 1991-92, pp.95-98).

■ A solo exhibition by **Ciaran O Cearnaigh** began in the Arts Council in Dublin, while the Arts Council Gallery in Belfast displayed charcoal drawings by Omagh artist **John Mathers**. There was also a window installation in this gallery by Belfast-born artist **Nora Gaston**, artist-in-residence at Musgrave Park Hospital since 1992, who has carried out a number of stained glass commissions in Canada.

■ Margo Dolan, co-founder of the Ballinglen Arts Foundation, opened an exhibition of works by **Brian Maguire** at the Model Arts Centre, Sligo. In association with Living Art Projects (formerly the Irish Exhibition of Living Art founded in 1943) the Centre also exhibited an installation, Domestic Shrubbery, by Longford-born artist **Daphne Wright**, now working in Manchester. This was third in a series of projects by artists of the Irish Diaspora, examining the effects of dislocation.

■ Other Dublin exhibitions in April included **Corban Walker's** mixed media pieces in the City Arts Centre; landscapes and still-life in oils, as well as some pastels, for which she is better known, by **Veronica Bolay** at the Rubicon Gallery; pictures on Irish and Tibetan themes by **Dymphna Hayden** at the Hallward Gallery; a large sculpture-installation by **Remco de Fouw** at the Project Arts Centre and new paintings by **Nicola Bunbury** at the Head, the gallery now relocated at Ormond Quay which shows the work of recent NCAD graduates.

■ In the North, Gordon Galleries, Derry, showed Peace of Ireland paintings by **Trevor Geoghegan**; Tom Caldwell Gallery, Belfast, showed paintings by **Brian Ballard**; Grant Fine Art in Newcastle showed paintings by **Mary Lohan**; Fenderesky at Queen's, Belfast showed work by **Diarmuid Delargy**, by John Keys and a retrospective (1954-94) of **Barrie Cooke's** works on paper, while in Flowerfield, Portstewart, a NI Arts Council touring exhibition of Still-life Painting had been selected by artist **Neil Shawcross**.

■ The Crawford Gallery in Cork exhibited ceramic figurines by Cork-based artist **Stephanie Dinkelbach**; the UTV Art Collection, which is mainly contemporary 20th century art, and colourful naive canvases by **Desmond Shortt.**

■ The Gorry Gallery, Dublin, held a retrospective exhibition of delightful paintings by **Henry C O'Donnell** (1900-92) including landscape, still-life, portraits and equestrian subjects, as well as his brushes, palette, catalogues, cuttings and photographs.

Imogen Stuart, Brid Dara, at the 164th RHA Exhibition

■ The **164th Annual Exhibition of the Royal Hibernian** Academy took place in the RHA Gallagher Gallery. This year a number of non-Academy Members were exhibiting, including the winner of the new Elizabeth FitzPatrick Bursary, **Catherine Harper**. Work by 6 Members of the Royal Academy in London was also shown as well as a panel of his work in memory of the late **Patrick Collins**, Honorary RHA, which included his first oil painting, Howth Castle, done in 1946. Although there are circles within which this exhibition is regularly deplored, it was clear from the large number of red stickers that the 1994 works were more popular than ever with collectors.

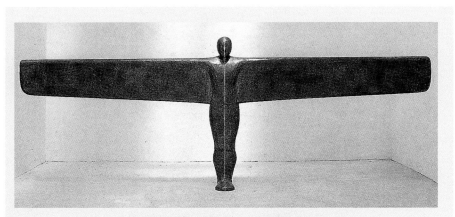

Antony Gormley, A Case for an Angel III, IMMA

■ Recent work by **Antony Gormley** (b.1950), one of Britain's foremost sculptors, was on exhibition in IMMA; showing the development of his pioneering work based on the human body, the sculptures were on a challenging scale, notably Case for an Angel III, whose wingspan filled the room, and the startling Field for the British Isles, 40,000 hand-sized terracotta figures which filled the floor of a 130 ft. corridor.

Kate Robinson writes of the RHA Annual Exhibition:

'The land of Ireland – the love of most artists – was the inspiration for the many subtle delights that the landscape painters gave us: **Richard Kingston's** brilliant colours; **Andrew Folan's** etching, A Living Landscape. **Peter Collis** winds into deeper colour and stronger shadow, but **Barbara Warren** stays with her seascapes and boats and gives us lovely drawing and gentle shapes. I had to return to **Eithne Carr's** lusciousness and overblown flowers. Nature's Grandeur at Mirabello, a strong contrast to **Mark Duffy's** swathes of light and colour in Reflections.

The sculpture section was exceptional.

Richard Kingston, RHA Poppy Fringe (Wicklow) *at the 164th RHA Exhibition*

Thomas Ryan PPRHA, The Artist's Studio, *at the 164th RHA Exhibition*

Conor Fallon's steel Horse and **John Behan's** Ikarus Falling dominated the lower floor. Two pieces in particular were very badly placed, I thought. **Imogen Stuart's** ... In The Shadow of His Hand...(Isaiah 49/1) was raised to such a level that it was impossible to see it as an object, while the lovely, flowing rhythms of **Rowan Gillespie's** Reclining Bodyscape, were entirely lost in the conflicting window-light.

Small sculptures which are not presented in cases are difficult to place in large spaces; they tend to lose their identity when simply placed against walls or pillars. Such was the case with **Imogen Stuart's** Brid Dara and **Marjorie Fitzgibbon's** Girl's Head. The penetrating observation that created Butterfly by **Annette McCormack** in delicately polished elm wood suffered the same fate.

John Behan's Cock a Doodle Dandy was arrogantly appropriate as Homage to O'Casey but then all his sculptures tend to be eminently appreciable at first glance. **John Coll**, on the other hand, deliberately emphasises eccentricity in his studies of Vincent Van Gogh.

Problems arose among the portraits. The fine robes that clothed Professor Patrick Masterson, the President of UCD in his portrait by **Carey Clarke** PRHA were not sufficient to give life to the mask-like features of his face. Perhaps Clarke, skilful painter that he is, who gives us such delights as his elegant still lifes, did not achieve the state of mutual relaxation with this subject that was obvious in his portrait of Mrs Susan Doyle, a lovely calm study.

Similar problems beset **John Coyle's** Portrait of Professor Stephen Doyle M D, President of the Royal College of Physicians and Surgeons, Dublin, while his Sailing Boats, Dun Laoghaire, is a rich study of shapes and colour. It is interesting that **John F Kelly's** Study for Portrait of the Late Harry Brogan was so much more successful and natural than the later portrait.

The President, Mrs Mary Robinson, was shown in photographic likeness by **Carol Graham**, but the attempt by the **Hon Edward Plunkett** to capture either the physical appearance or the complex character of ex-Taoiseach Charles Haughey in my view quite failed. It was a strong exhibition which kept the lines of academic art intact.'

Brett McEntagart RHA, Paysage Lot et Garonne, *at the 164th RHA Exhibition*

THE RENAISSANCE GARDEN IN IRELAND

1. UNKNOWN ARTIST: Bird's-eye view of Trinity College, Dublin. *(Coll. The Marquis of Salisbury, Hatfield House)*. The drawing was made in 1591 for Lord Burghley who as Secretary of State was responsible to Queen Elizabeth I for the foundation of the College in 1592.

In recent years, many books and articles have been published on Irish gardens and their history. Only one, *Lost Demesnes* by Edward Malins and the Knight of Glin,[1] attempts to trace their history as far back as the seventeenth century. However, even it does not describe Irish gardens of an earlier period, of the late sixteenth and early seventeenth century – the period of the Renaissance garden in Ireland. It is the aim of this article to rectify this omission for the first time.

The idea of the Renaissance garden – of a formal, symmetri-

The earliest Irish formal gardens date from the time of Queen Elizabeth I. **Patrick Bowe** *pieces together the evidence.*

cal garden integral in design with the house to which it is attached – grew up in Italy in the fifteenth century[2]: the idea was taken up in France in the early sixteenth century and subsequently in other countries in Europe. In England, it was pioneered by the Tudor king, Henry VIII (1509-1547)[3] but its introduction to Ireland does not appear to have taken place until later, in the reign of his daughter, Elizabeth I (1559-1603). The first visual evidence of this new type of gardening in Ireland is in the bird's-eye view of Trinity College, Dublin

THE RENAISSANCE GARDEN IN IRELAND

which was submitted to William Cecil, Lord Burghley in 1591.[4] Burghley, who as the Queen's Secretary of State was responsible for the foundation of Trinity College in 1592, had an intense personal interest in gardening. His own gardens in London and at Theobalds in Hertfordshire[5] were justly famous and were superintended by the great herbalist, John Gerard, who dedicated his celebrated *Herball* to him. It is not surprising, therefore, that the view of Trinity College presented to him should contain provision for an elaborate formal garden (Fig. 1).[6] By the great formal entrance court to the college is shown a large enclosed rectangle of ground divided symmetrically into four large plots, each of the plots having a distinctly different design. In the Elizabethan period, such plots were conceived not only in decorative patterns but also as 'emblems' of the Queen and of her power and graces. When the Queen was received by Lord Burghley at Theobalds in 1591, she was entertained by a masque in which the principal actor played the part of a gardener who extolled to her the garden at that time being made by her host's son which was deliberately designed to be such an emblem of herself.[7]

In one part of this garden a maze had been planted, not with the usual hedges of hyssop or thyme, but with flowers which would be representative of her virtues and the glories of her reign – the Twelve Virtues were represented by twelve types of roses, the Three Graces by pansies and the Nine Muses by divers other flowers. The entire garden was overlooked by an arbour on which the eglantine rose grew. *Rosa rubiginosa*, an English native rose, known as the sweet briar or eglantine rose had already become, both in the English literature and painting of the time, a symbol of her grace and beauty. This kind of horticultural symbolism is closely followed in the Trinity College design. For example, in the north-eastern plot, that nearest the college buildings, the violet, emblematic of the Three Graces, is shown in the centre of the formal pattern, perhaps of box hedging. In the south-eastern plot, an eglantine rose represents the Queen. The remaining two plots are decorative rather than emblematic in design. The south-western plot is designed as an open 'knot', the term used at the time to define an intricate pattern of dwarf hedging such as box, the spaces in between being filled with flowers. This particular design – a combination of diamonds and rectangles decreasing in dimensions towards the centre of the design – derives perhaps from the engravings of contemporary French gardens which were published by Jacques Androuet du Cerceau,[8] whose books *Les Plus Excellents Bastiments de France*

2. LISMORE CASTLE, CO WATERFORD. The garden was laid out by the Great Earl of Cork. Its walls, dating from 1626, turrets, and great terrace form part of the present-day walled kitchen-garden and are the earliest extant remains of any garden in Ireland.

were published in 1576 and 1579 respectively and were widely circulated in Europe. The north-western plot is only sketchily portrayed. However, an intricately interwoven 'knot' garden can be discerned. No flowers are depicted, suggesting that, in this

3. PORTUMNA CASTLE, CO GALWAY. Built c.1618, Portumna is the first great Renaissance style house in Ireland and although no record of its garden survives, the axial plan of the house with the garden was one of the keystones of Renaissance garden design.

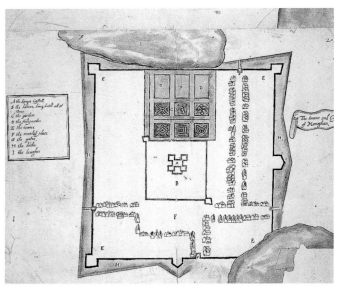

4. UNKNOWN: The town and castle of Monaghan. (*National Library of Ireland*). This undated plan shows the castle which was built c.1606 for Sir Arthur Chichester. The symmetrically planned garden on an axis with the castle is the first in Ireland to be designed in a fully Renaissance style.

case, the spaces between the dwarf hedging were filled with coloured sands rather than with flowers. Of the subsequent history of this scheme, little so far has been uncovered save for a

tantalisingly brief reference to it fourteen years later when one Henry Hollander was given a contract for the maintenance of the garden and great orchard (shown in the background of the Burghley drawing). He was obliged by this 'to dig, dung, prune, set and plant the garden' in return for which he was allowed to take 'half of all the herbs that grow, lavender, roses, fruit'.[9]

It is disappointing that there is not more detailed evidence of the flowers which were grown in gardens such as that of Trinity College. One has to rely on indirect or circumstantial evidence to build up a detailed picture in one's mind of the colourful creations these gardens undoubtedly were. The poems of Edmund Spenser, for example, are very helpful in so doing. His *The Faerie Queene* was written at Kilcolman Castle, Co Cork, the estate he was granted as part of the Plantation of Munster in 1585.[10] Spenser was foremost in promoting the 'horticultural' vision of the queen and the poem is a rich source for Elizabethan garden flowers. Here, for example, he compares the fragrances of his beloved's body with the fragrances of a variety of garden flowers:

Her lips did smell lyke unto Gillyflowers
Her ruddy cheekkes lyke unto Roses red
Her snowy browes, lyke budded Bellamours,
Her lovely eyes, lyke Pincks but newly spread
Her goodly bosome, lyke strawberry bed
Her necke, lyke to a bounch of Cullambynes
Her brest, lyke lillyes, ere theyr leaves be shed
Her nipples, lyke young blossomed Jessemynes.
Such fragrant flowers doe give most odourous smell
But her sweet odour did them all excell.

'Gillyflowers' (wallflowers), roses, 'pincks' (pinks), strawberries, 'cullambynes' (columbines), 'lillyes' (lilies) and 'jessamynes' (jasmine) were all common flowers of the Elizabethan flower garden. In his other poems, there are references to the damask rose, 'daffodowndillies' (daffodils), primroses, violets, cow-slips, kingcups and bay trees[11]. By examination of Spenser's poems alone, a detailed picture of the planting of a garden like that at Trinity College can be arrived at.

By the end of the Elizabethan reign, the garden aesthetic of the period with its knots, emblems and mazes was already outmoded in European terms. Developments in garden design in France would soon ensure a transition in England and in Ireland from the Elizabethan emblematic garden to the Jacobean mannerist one.

Of the gardens created in Ireland during the reign of James I, called the Jacobean period (1603-1625), that made by the Great Earl of Cork at Lismore Castle, Co Waterford is not only the best documented but also the best preserved (Fig. 2). Whereas the problem in studying the Elizabethan Trinity College garden has been a lack of evidence with regard to its detail design and planting, the problem in studying the Lismore Castle garden is exactly the reverse – while there is a wealth of detailed information contained in the meticulously-kept diaries and account-books of the Great Earl,[12] there is only the slightest visual evidence of its overall design.

The story of the Great Earl's gardening activities in Ireland begins, like those at Trinity College, with Lord Burghley. Burghley, the Queen's Secretary of State, was unhappy with the way in which certain parts of the 1585 Plantation of Munster had gone. In particular, he was unhappy with the administration of the large estate which had been granted in counties Waterford and Cork to Sir Walter Raleigh[13]. As this had fallen into disrepair due to Raleigh's prolonged adventures abroad, Burghley prevailed on him in 1602 to sell it to a young man from Kent called Richard Boyle who had come to the queen's notice.[14] During the remainder of his life in Ireland, Boyle prospered to such an extent that he became the country's richest man, earning himself, after his eventual ennoblement, the title 'The Great Earl of Cork.'[15] He was a genuinely Renaissance-style patron of the arts – a collector of pictures, furniture, jewellery, plate, tapestries and fine costume[16], a connoisseur of music[17] and an inveterate builder and gardener. In his lifetime he made three important gardens – at his house in Youghal, Co Cork, at Lismore Castle, Co Waterford and at Stalbridge Park, Dorset – each one more elaborate than the last as might be expected of a man whose power and prestige were constantly increasing.

On his arrival in Ireland, Boyle first lived in Raleigh's house, today called Myrtle Grove,[18] in the walled town of Youghal. He subsequently bought the adjoining house known as The College and joined the two estates. Over the next forty years, his diaries and account books record,[19] among many other projects, the creation and maintenance of his garden there. Perhaps the most important entry as far as the history of the Renaissance garden in Ireland is concerned is in a letter in 1613 from his agent in Youghal saying: 'your Terras in the garden be a covern'. This is the earliest recorded instance in Ireland of the creation of a garden terrace,[20] a key feature in Renaissance garden design. A later entry in his diary records his plan to harness the water from a natural spring on the hill behind the house to form 'delightful throws of water' in the garden below. This is the first reference to the construction of a garden fountain – another key feature of the Renaissance garden – in an Irish garden. Although there are many other references to

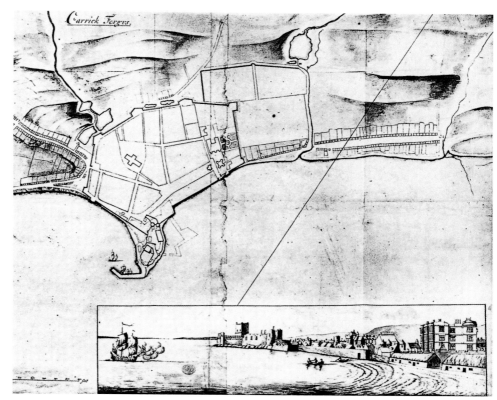

5. UNKNOWN: Drawing from Sir Thomas Philipp's Survey of Carrickfergus, 1635. *(Lambeth Palace Library, London)*. The garden and house (inset) is Joymount which was built c.1618 by Sir Arthur Chichester, Lord High Treasurer of Ireland.

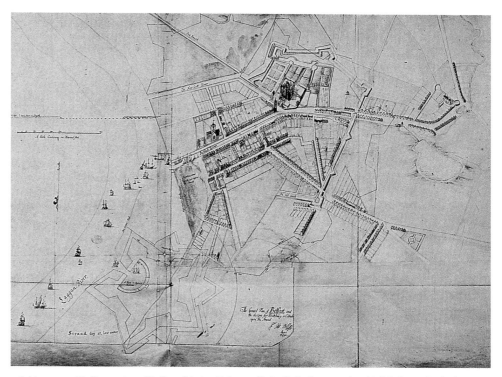

6. UNKNOWN: Bird's-eye view of Belfast. *(National Library of Ireland)*. In this view, dated 1685, the garden laid out at Belfast Castle by Sir Arthur Chichester is visible.

his Youghal garden and estate over the years – for example, his 1616 importation of apple trees from England for the orchard, his 1617 importation of forty-six deer from Devon for his deer park and his 1628 payment for poles and wattles to make an arbour – the references to his construction of a terrace and fountain are of the greatest significance for the introduction of the Renaissance garden in Ireland.[21]

The Great Earl created a more elaborate garden at Lismore Castle. As it was not within the safety of a walled town, the garden itself was walled, the walls being built in the year 1626, already one year into the reign of Charles I. The Great Earl records his indebtedness to his mother for seeing their construction through: 'I owe to make up to my mother for compassing my orchard and garden at Lismoor with a wall of two foot and a half thick and twelve foot high and lyme and stone and turrets at each corner'.[22] This was obviously not only a garden wall but one built for defence also (for which purpose it was indeed used later during the rebellion of 1641). Such defensible garden walls were common also in English gardens of the period, notably at the great house of the prominent Suffolk family at Audley End, Essex.[23] The walls, the turrets, and the great terrace at the upper end of the garden, which was built later, are still in existence at Lismore today and form part of the present walled kitchen garden. They are, therefore, the earliest extant substantial remains of any garden in Ireland and so are of the utmost importance in the study of Irish garden history. Sadly, no evidence remains of the garden's detail design and planting. One might assume from the existence of its great terrace that its design was elaborate since such terraces were usually only built when it was desirable to be able to look down over a garden pattern. Terraces were especially desirable when the garden was in such a position that its design could not be seen from the chambers of the house itself as was the case at Lismore.

One of the developments which characterised the Jacobean garden was the tendency to extend the enclosed garden of the Elizabethan age outwards by the creation of formal orchards around it.[24] These orchards were formally planted and traversed by straight walks and vistas and were, in a way, an anticipation of the extensive formal groves which characterised the later baroque garden. Although there is no visual evidence of such orchards at Lismore, there is abundant documentary evidence that they existed. There are payment records for walling, hedging and ditching a number of different orchards, for the purchase of many hundreds of fruit trees, mostly apples, pears, plums and cherries, for the purchase of nails and wattles to train or espalier fruit trees against the walls, for mowing the walks and, in one case, for repairing a hedge after it had been broken down by foxhunters'.[25]

The Great Earl also provided at Lismore facilities for the many outdoor activities which were an essential part of Jacobean aristocratic life. An extensive terrace, paved and walled in stone, was constructed in 1635 overlooking the river Blackwater and which was only accessible from his Little

Smaller yet equally formal gardens were made in the new towns of the plantation of Ulster from 1608.

Dining Chamber. It seems to have been built for the formal exercise of walking, so important at that time that all great houses provided indoor or outdoor galleries or rooftop 'leads', as well as terraces like that at Lismore to facilitate it.

In 1627, there were many payments recorded in his account books for the laying-out of a bowling green. Bowls was an important game at that period and the groundsmanship required to make and maintain a smooth grass surface on which the bowls might run true resulted in the creation of the first 'lawns' as we know them today. At Lismore, the bowling green was protected by a high palisade fence and was only accessible through a door which was normally kept locked. Later, the green was augmented by a pair of timber summerhouses with seats.

Finally, there are frequent references in the accounts to the deer park. Although, strictly speaking, the creation of a deer park does not come under the heading of garden design, it can, nonetheless, be included under the broader heading of landscape design. The entire deer park at Lismore, like the bowling green, was surrounded by a timber palisade fence – a major undertaking. Inside the palisade, fish ponds, a brick dovecote and a hunting lodge were later erected. It would seem there were about ten ponds with their attendant sluices and watergates. The banks of the ponds were constantly under repair after they had been broken by flooding. This also meant that the ponds had to be restocked frequently and there are many payments for sending his men to obtain fresh quantities of carp, tench and pike for this purpose. The dovecote was an extensive building, eighteen feet high, forty long and twenty wide. We do not have any detailed description but the fact that it was built in an expensive material like brick indicates that it was conceived as an ornamental as well as a practical structure. Likewise, there is no detailed description of the hunting lodge. However, we do know that Jacobean hunting lodges, in general, were conceived as ornamental buildings, almost pleasure pavilions, to which the owner, his family and guests could escape on occasion and that their architecture often reflected this somewhat frivolous function. They were frequently built in the form of a tower, the upper floor and flat roof of which could be used as a stand for watching the progress of the hunt.[26]

Although many individual features of the Renaissance garden were prominent in the garden at Lismore, it did not have an overall, cohesive plan. Its plan remained that of a series of isolated enclosures dotted apparently at random and fenced around. It does not have the breadth of composition, the close integration of house and garden or the use of optical principles of planning which characterised the Jacobean garden elsewhere. Perhaps this is because the garden was laid out around an irregular building of medieval origins. In fact, the two gardens already discussed – Trinity College and Lismore Castle – were both attached to rambling courtyard structures which had seemed sensible during the Middle Ages and afterwards from the point of view of security.[27] Increasingly, however, there was a tendency for even very large houses to do without courtyards and cohere into a single dominating symmetrical mass. Houses which had been compressed into one soaring stately whole were an irresistible advertisement of the dignity and glory of their owners. Such a house was Portumna Castle, Co Galway (Fig. 3).[28]

Portumna was built around 1618 for the 4th Earl of Clanrickarde, scion of an old Norman-Irish family, who had been brought up at the English court.[29] He had contracted a most prestigious marriage to the daughter of Sir Francis Walsingham, the Secretary of State.[30] She had already been twice widowed. Her first husband had been that epitome of the Elizabethan age, the poet and soldier, Sir Philip Sidney. Her second husband had been the Earl of Essex, at one time the Queen's favourite but who was later disgraced and beheaded. The Clanrickardes had built, around 1610, the impressive mansion of Somerhill Park, near Tonbridge in Kent. When they came to build their Irish house, they chose to build a scaled-down version of Somerhill. In its architectural planning and detail, Portumna is the first great Renaissance-style house in Ireland. Although no record of any garden survives, its inclusion in this survey of Irish Renaissance gardens is justified on the basis of the axial plan on which the house and its forecourts — both inner and outer — are assembled.[31] Such axial planning was, of course, one of the keystones of Renaissance landscape design.

Axial planning and the integration of house and garden design is also a feature of the undated plan in the National Library of Ireland showing 'The Town and Castell of Monaghan' (Fig. 4).[32] The castle was built for Sir Arthur Chichester, Lord Deputy of Ireland, around 1606 and it is thought the plan dates from soon afterwards. If this is the case, the castle's garden, being both fully symmetrical and axial with the castle and within itself, is the first garden in Ireland to be designed in a fully-realised, mature Renaissance style. It is laid out like a carpet on the ground and is designed to be seen from the windows of the castle above. Its six compartments have complex geometrical patterns, probably carried out in dwarf box or other similar hedging. The patterns, similar but different in their detail, are based on those of French Renaissance gardens which were depicted in the engravings by du Cerceau which were already mentioned above in connection with the patterns of the Trinity College garden. However, there is one original feature in the Monaghan Castle design, that is the way in which the three fishponds are incorporated as part of the parterre design. Fountains were an integral part of the Renaissance parterre but not still pools of water. Such pools of water were usually placed to one

side of the parterre or in another part of the garden. Still water was thought by many to be unhealthy so close to the house. Francis Bacon, in his essay 'Of Gardens' published in 1625, wrote, for example, that such pools 'mar all and make the garden unwholesome and full of flies and frogs'. In spite of this, one cannot but admire the way in which the Monaghan Castle pools are integrated so seamlessly in the garden's overall design.

In 1616, Sir Arthur Chichester, for whom the Monaghan Castle scheme was prepared, became Lord High Treasurer of Ireland. Two years later, he embarked on the building of a new house and garden which he called Joymount at Carrickfergus, Co Antrim (Fig. 5). Its very name 'Joymount' was indicative of the

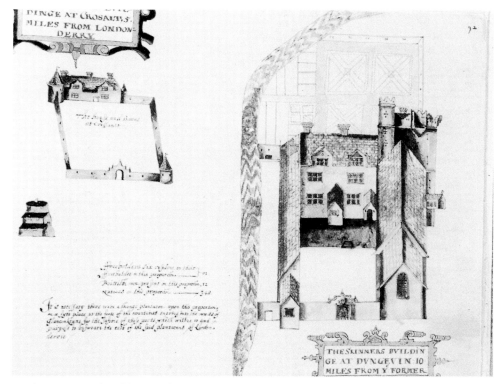

7. Thomas RAVEN: Plan of the town of Dungiven, Co Derry from Sir Thomas Philipp's Survey of 1622. *(Lambeth Palace Library, London).* The drawing is of the garden attached to the house of Captain Edward Doddington which was laid out shortly after 1608.

fact that it was built not as a fortified defensible castle but as a house of relaxation and enjoyment. Of three stories, with an elegant balustrade rather than a battlemented parapet, with large mullioned windows (including three tiers of bay windows to the seaward side) rather than narrow openings, the mansion was the most progressive in its design in the Ireland of its day.[33] Demolished in the eighteenth century, it is now only known to us through Sir Thomas Philipp's survey of Carrickfergus in 1685.[34] Its garden, shown on the same map, was in the form of a conventional four-part parterre, although the central crossing of the paths has been developed in the form of a circle containing, perhaps, a pool or fountain. Although such a central feature became common later, this is its first use in Ireland, so far as can be ascertained. A contemporary continental plan of Carrickfergus shows the garden extended outward from the parterre in the form

THE RENAISSANCE GARDEN IN IRELAND

of a grove crossed and recrossed by vistas.[35] This grove may well have been a grove of orchard trees as was typical in a Jacobean garden and as we know to have existed at the time at Lismore Castle. On the seaward wide of the mansion was an onion-domed banqueting house. A banqueting house in the Jacobean period had a very specific use.[36] It was a place to which the owner, his family and guests would often retire in order to eat desserts and sweetmeats after a formal banquet in the house. Its architecture, as in the case of the onion-domed Carrickfergus example, often reflected its conception as a place of relaxation. Only one contemporary account of the garden survives which describes it thus: 'a stately house, a stately gate house, and a graceful terrace; and a

destroyed by fire in 1708.[38] There are, however, a number of entries in the 1666 Great Roll of Belfast,[39] quoted in Benn's History of Belfast which are particularly interesting for what they tell us about the details of construction, planting and maintenance of the garden. Benn tells us that the Great Roll 'abounds with allusions to the gardens, to the bowling green, to the cherry garden and the apple garden, and to the arbours and walks which were the cool shades, the favoured retired retreats of the castle inmates and guests of rank who were frequent visitors ... There were also payments of wages for rolling, cleaning, weeding, wheeling in ashes and cinders for the improvement of the walks referred to.' While strawberries, currants and gooseberries are mentioned, no notice is taken of flowers, except this: 'Paid for making boarders at the Rampier, and for women gathering violatts in ye fields to sett in the Gardens.' Uniquely interesting are the facts that the walks were surfaced with ashes and cinders rather than with gravel and that wild violets were used in the flower borders.

8. Thomas RAVEN: Plan of the town of Limavady, Co Derry from Sir Thomas Philipp's Survey of 1622. *(Lambeth Palace Library, London)*. The fortified castle and garden of c.1610 belonged to Sir Thomas Philipp himself.

We have been considering the gardens laid out by the great magnates of Elizabethan and Jacobean Ireland. Smaller yet equally formal gardens were made in the new towns of the Plantation of Ulster from 1608. Thomas Raven's pictorial plans of these towns which were part of Sir Thomas Philipp's Survey of 1622 show the gardens attached to the castles which were erected in these new towns.[40] The plan of the town of Dungiven, Co Londonderry, for example, shows a formal garden attached to the gabled house[41] erected by Capt Edward Doddington who undertook the plantation of the area for the Skinners' Company of London (Fig. 7). Its classic design of a four-quartered parterre around a central feature, perhaps a well-head, is augmented by diagonal paths leading to the four corners. Sir Thomas Philipp's own garden at Limavady, Co Londonderry is also depicted in the same series of plans (Fig. 8). Although the garden is depicted in a very simplified form, three topiary-lined plots with a central arbour are nevertheless clearly evident.

The progress of the Renaissance garden in Ireland was brought to an abrupt halt by the Rising in Ireland of 1641 and by the outbreak of the Civil War in England. Gardening was not to move forward again until the Restoration of Charles II as king in 1660. By that time the Renaissance garden style had given way to the Baroque, a style introduced to Ireland by men like the Duke of Ormonde who had been in exile at the court of Versailles and had become familiar with the new Baroque gardens of France.[42]

walk before the house as is at Denton, my Lord Fairfax's house. A fine garden and mighty spacious orchards and they say they have a goodly store of fruit. I observed on either side of this garden and twixt the garden and the orchard, a dove house placed one opposite the other, a most convenient place for apricockes'. The comparison of the walk before the house with that at Denton[37] is certainly a flattering one as Lord Fairfax's garden, celebrated by Andrew Marvell in his poem *Upon Appleton House, to my Lord Fairfax*, was one of the most famous in England.

Sir Arthur Chichester had two further gardens, one at Chichester House in Dublin (on the site of the present Bank of Ireland in Dame Street) which had a garden extending to a banqueting house and terrace overlooking the river Liffey, and another at Belfast Castle which is only known to us through a bird's-eye view of the city dated 1685 (Fig. 6) since it was

PATRICK BOWE is a landscape designer and garden historian.

1. Edward Malins and The Knight of Glin, *Lost Demesnes, Irish Landscape Gardening, 1660-1845*, London, 1976.

2. The most important recent works on the subject of the Italian Renaissance garden are: David Coffin, *The Villa in the Life of Renaissance Rome*, Princeton, 1979 and Claudia Lazzaro, *The Italian Renaissance Garden*, Yale, 1990.

3. Roy Strong, *The Renaissance Garden in England*, London 1979.

4. The view is still in the possession of Lord Burghley's descendant, the Marquess of Salisbury, at Hatfield House, Hertfordshire.

5. Burghley's London house was located off the Strand (on the site of the present Shell-Mex building). Theobalds was inherited by Burghley's second son, Robert (future Earl of Salisbury) who swopped it with James I for Hatfield House.

6. The fullest account of Lord Burghley's garden at Theobalds is in Martin Andrews, 'Theobalds Palace: the Gardens and Park,' *Garden History*, Vol. 21, no. 2, Winter 1993.

7. Roy Strong, *The Renaissance Garden in England*, London, 1979, p.45 et seq.

8. For an extended treatment of the French Renaissance garden and, in particular, Jacques Androuet du Cerceau see Kenneth Woodbridge, *Princely Gardens*, London, 1986, p.87 et seq.

9. Trinity College Ms. 1209/67.

10. Spenser returned to England after Kilcolman Castle was burned in 1595 during an attack by its previous owner.

11. These flowers are referred to in The *Shepheard's Calendar* (1579)

12. All of the detailed information which follows in relation to the Earl of Cork's gardening activities is derived from Grossart (ed.) *The Lismore Papers*, London 1886-88, 10 vols.

13. Sir Walter Raleigh also took part in the Plantation of Virginia as a result of which he is credited with the introduction to Ireland of two useful American plants, the potato and the tobacco plant. He is also said to have introduced to Ireland a sweet-smelling wall-flower from the Azores and the common myrtle, *Myrtus communis*, from Southern Europe. He later called his house at Youghal, Myrtle Grove, after this plant. He was the first to lay out cherry orchards in Ireland. It was from a tree in one of these orchards at Affane, Co Waterford that Katherine, wife of the 16th Earl of Desmond and known as 'The Old Countess of Desmond', fell to her death. It is never satisfactorily explained what an old lady, reputed to be over a hundred years of age, was doing climbing in a cherry tree!

14. Boyle, who had begun life as a man of little means, had already contracted an advantageous marriage to an heiress, Joan Apsley of Limerick. She had died in 1599.

15. In 1600, Boyle married the daughter of Sir Geoffrey Fenton, Principal Secretary of State of Ireland. In 1616, he was created Baron Boyle of Youghal and in 1620, Earl of Cork.

16. Anne Crookshank and The Knight of Glin, *The Painters of Ireland* c. 1660-1920, London, 1978, p.19.

17. Barra Boydell, *Music in Seventeenth Century Ireland*. Thesis in preparation, Trinity College, Dublin.

18. Myrtle Grove is almost the only completely unfortified c. 16th century house in Ireland to have survived intact and in anything like its original state. The adjoining house, known as The College, was part of the 13th century St Mary's Abbey which had by then been secularised. The Collegiate Church remains to this day in use as a church.

19. The Earl of Cork's diaries are in the muniments room of Chatsworth, Derbyshire and are the property of his descendant and the present owner of Lismore Castle, the Duke of Devonshire. The Earl of Cork's account books are in the National Library of Ireland.

20. This terrace was later dismantled when the lead, with which it was dressed, was melted down to make shot during the Rebellion of 1641.

21. Sadly, no visual depiction of these features is available to help us in our understanding of their design and placement. A map of the town of Youghal, thought by some to date from 1585, by others to be later in date, does, however, contain a simplistic depiction of a 'knot' garden.

22. There are frequent references in the Great Earl's diaries and account books of later date to the maintenance and rebuilding of this wall.

23. Strong, *op. cit.*, notes.

24. The reference in the Cork papers to orchards are too numerous to mention. The size of the orchards can be gauged from one January 11, 1639 reference to the fact that only a hundred trees were required at that time for the completion of one of the orchards. This would imply that the orchard being laid out comprised many hundreds of trees.

25. Another idea of the size of the orchard and farm development taking place at Lismore during those years can be gauged from the fact that between 1637 and 1639, over forty-nine thousand white-thorn plants were paid for, to form hedging on the estate.

26. Mark Girouard, *Life in the English Country House*, New Haven and London, 1978, pp.76-77.

27. In 1636, the Great Earl purchased his last and most prestigious estate, Stalbridge Park, Dorset. It was situated close to Wilton House, Wiltshire, the seat of the Earl of Pembroke, who was employing the great Isaac de Caus as the designer of his new gardens. Cork was able to take advantage of de Caus's proximity while he was carrying out these works to have him come and design his garden at Stalbridge. The house and garden of Stalbridge have, however, long vanished.

28. An interesting example of the mutual assistance rendered by the creators of the great Jacobean mansions of Ireland is the entry in the Earl of Cork's diary of 31 January, 1625: 'Capt. St. barbe came to me from my lo. the earl of clanrickarde to gett some young deer to begin to store his new parcke at portum-nagh: by whom I sent 12 deer'.

29. Another old Irish family which had come to terms with the new regime in Ireland, the O'Briens were also able to boast a substantial house and garden at this time. In 1639, their castle at Lemeneagh, Co Clare had 'walled gardens, fish ponds, a pair of summer houses and a brick tower'.

30. Sir Francis Walsingham had been the recipient in 1586 of some young arbutus trees. They were sent from Killarney with the accompanying note from an unnamed official: 'You shall receive herewith a bundle of trees called the wollaghan tree whereof my Lord of Leicester and Mr Secretary Walsingham are both very desirous to have some, as well for the fruit as for the rareness of the manner of bearing which is after the kind of the orange to have blossom and fruit, either green or ripe, all the year long, and the same of a very pleasant taste, and growing nowhere else but in one part of Munster, from whence I have caused them to be transported immediately to you, praying you to see them safely delivered and divided between my said lord and Mr Secretary, directing that they may be planted near some ponds, or with a great deal of black moory earth, which kind of soil I take will best suit them for that they grow best in Munster around loughs and prove to the bigness of cherry trees and continue long'.

31. The present layout and planting of these forecourts as gardens by the late Sidney Maskell, landscape architect to the Office of Public Works, while making the site more attractive for the visiting public, do not seem to have any basis in historical fact.

32. National Library of Ireland. Ms. 1209(32).

33. For its position in the development of domestic architecture in Ireland, see Brian de Breffny and Rosemary ffolliott, *The Houses of Ireland*, London, 1975 and Maurice Craig, *The Architecture of Ireland*, London, 1982.

34. This drawing is in the Lambeth Palace Library, London.

35. This undated plan is titled *Plan de la Ville de Karikfarus*, is signed by one Goubet and was presented to the Duke of Wittenberg. It is in the National Library of Ireland. While the town in general and the garden of Joymount seem to be accurately depicted, the house of Joymount is drawn in a simplistic almost primitive way.

36. Girouard, *op. cit.*, p.105.

37. Lord Fairfax's house at Denton was called Appleton or Nunappleton House. Located in Yorkshire, its garden is described in Strong, *op. cit.*, p.123.

38. Philipp's Maps: Ms. 3137 Pt/2 91(2) Map 41(2), National Library of Ireland.

39. George Benn, *A History of the Town of Belfast.*, Belfast, 1823, p.242.

40. These maps are in the Lambeth Palace Library, London.

41. The house was attached to an earlier 16th century tower house.

42. For the Duke of Ormonde's Restoration garden at Kilkenny Castle, see Edward Malins and The Knight of Glin, *op. cit.*, p.6.

THE MENAGERIE OF THE DERRYNAFLAN PATEN

The Derrynaflan Hoard has been much discussed since its sensational discovery in 1980. In this article **Michael Ryan** *assesses the fabulous filigree decoration that is a feature of the silver paten.*

The Derrynaflan Paten (Fig. 2) was found in a hoard of altar plate in the monastic site of that name in Co Tipperary, Ireland in 1980. The find was published in preliminary form in 1980 and more extensively in 1983.[1] The objects found included a chalice, a sieve and a basin together with an ornamental hoop which has been interpreted as a foot-ring for the paten. In its restored form the paten measures 35.6 – 36.8 cm in diameter and stands 3.35 cm in height excluding the foot-ring. It is an extremely complex structure consisting of many separately manufactured components which have been elaborately assembled in a manner which would have enabled the piece to be dismantled for repair or cleaning.[2] There is evidence that the object was disassembled and reconstructed in antiquity at least twice. An assembly code of letters and symbols engraved on the components had evidently been modified in ancient times. It is not intended to discuss the constructional history of the piece here – the code has been studied in detail by Raghnall Ó Floinn and the letters and a faint inscription by Michelle Brown[3] – but it is important to note that decorative components have been moved from their original positions, or been found not to fit the positions already chosen for them and this must have a bearing on the question of whether a symbolic sequence had been originally intended by the craftsman and designer. As we shall see, if such a scheme had originally existed it is not now evident, nor does it seem to be mathematically recoverable although given the sophistication of the piece and the general tradition of paten-design throughout the early church, the creators of the Derrynaflan communion plate are likely to have had something of the sort in mind.

It is enough to note that the paten is essentially a large silver plate with around its rim a series of filigree ornaments displayed in pairs in contiguous cast copper alloy frames. They are further embellished with polychrome glass studs, some in the familiar insular pseudo-cloisonné manner, others with cast false-relief decoration and inset metal trays of filigree. The elaboration of the filigree, the stamped ornaments of the side of the paten, the glass settings, the knitted mesh of its rim and the organisation of the ornament place the paten clearly within the same aesthetic as the Ardagh Chalice.[4] It belongs to the mainstream of Irish style metalwork of the eighth century and is to date the most elaborate and accomplished piece to come to light from that tradition. I see no reason to modify the view which I expressed in 1987 that the two pieces stem from the same workshop tradition, a phrase carefully chosen so as not to imply that they were made by the same person nor indeed on the same premises. Although that fine distinction has often been missed in recent

discussion, it finds new support in the comments of Brown about the significance of the lettered assembly code.[5] I also maintain that it flies in the face of commonsense to deny that the two are 'effectively contemporary' in so far as one may use the highly-charged term 'contemporary' in discussing phenomena which are essentially without dating indications independent of art-historical speculation.[6]

There are twenty-four filigree ornaments placed in double frames around the rim. Of these, three are abstract and the remaining twenty-one are either anthropomorphic or zoomorphic. They may be listed as follows:

Zoomorphic/Anthropomorphic
Two kneeling men 4; Kneeling quadruped 5; Two squatting addorsed beasts 3; Raptorial bird with snakes 1; Stag with snake 1; Interlaced snakes 2; Stag with interlace 1; Narrow-bodied quadrupeds 3; Interlace with bird-heads 1.

Abstract
Plain interlace 1; Interlocked peltae 1; S-scroll with trumpet devices 1.

Rynne has argued that the latter described by me as abstract is to be read as zoomorphic. The ornament of the panel consists of an S-scroll composed of interlocking spirals linked to the arms of miniature trisceles. The spiral endings contain pendant half-loops of wire with short lengths dividing them. These, he argues, are long-snouted beasts of general Salin Style II derivation, similar to those on the well-known belt-buckle from Lagore Crannog and widespread in the curvilinear art of the Tara – Lindisfarne style.[7] This is not entirely to be ruled out although it is worth pointing out that the wire loop which forms the eye of the beast is precisely the same as that used to render the bell-mouths of the trumpet scrolls on the panel where the motif is undoubtedly an entirely abstract one composed of peltae.[8]

The motifs are executed with a variety of beaded wires and ribbons of gold, together with granules. These wires are built up in combinations to form more complex structures, designed to highlight detail, fill out bodies and create depth of field. The filigrees are all executed on foil on which, in some places, the motif has been previously traced by repoussé or stamping. In these cases, the background foil has been cut away and the motif displayed in its frame against a further foil sheet. The technique, known as hollow-platform, is well attested on insular pieces. It is not the purpose of this paper to discuss the filigree in great detail; suffice it to say that it is highly accomplished and extends the range already known from the major pieces of the period considerably.

Paired arrangements – more or less symmetrical – are the most common on the paten, six zoomorphic, one ornithopomorphic and four anthropomorphic are disciplined in that way. Only two motifs represent solitary beasts – the stag with interlace and the kneeling beast, of which there are five examples. The remaining

1. THE DERRYNAFLAN PATEN. Irish, mid-late 8th Century. Detail of the rim showing a filigree ornament with a pair of kneeling men. (*National Museum of Ireland*). The rim of the paten consists of the twenty-four framed filigree panels, which are the subject of this article, interspersed with polychrome glass studs. Three of the panels are abstract but the remaining twenty-one consist of animals, birds, and men.

panels depict either creatures of unlike type on the same panel – two examples – or interlaced serpents. It would seem reasonable to conclude that pattern was especially important in the design of the symmetrical motifs and that those with beasts of two different types represent – either overtly or by derivation – scenes or symbols which had been less subordinated to ornament.

The paired men panels (Fig. 1) have already been the subject of a detailed discussion by the writer in which it was argued that they derive in the main from the human figures frequently represented with beast motifs on the rim friezes of Late Antique silver plates from which it may be argued Christian patens derived.[9] This impression is reinforced by the use on vessels in several Gaulish finds of silver of back-to-back human heads and human heads used almost as scene dividers[10] Early Christian patens tended to carry complex iconographical symbols or figured scenes – the Riha and Stuma patens, for example, are well-known as is the later fifth century Plate of Paternus now in the Hermitage in St Petersburg. The latter bears a rim ornament of doves, chalices and vines to which secondary settings for applied ornaments are soldered, the dished interior bears a large Chi Rho monogram.[11] Later medieval patens in western Europe often carry elaborate engraved scenes. The majority of surviving early medieval western patens are small examples made en suite with grave or travelling chalices and preserved because they were placed in tombs. The sample which survives is unrepresentative. References in inventories and documents such as the *Liber Pontificalis* make it clear that very large patens were once fairly common in the great churches of western Christendom and the Derrynaflan Paten is of special interest because it is the only example of its type to survive from early medieval western Europe.

The Paten is an extremely complex structure consisting of many separately manufactured components.

The raptorial bird shares its panel with two snake-heads on a common body which forms the interlace within which it is displayed but with which it is not involved. The form of the bird is clearly dependent on manuscript representations where the general type, usually and for obvious reasons, is the eagle, a symbol both of the evangelist John and of Christ Himself. While bird and beast combinations are common, I know of no other insular metalwork scene which specifically relates the eagle with the serpent. One may be an evangelist's symbol, the other (because it sloughs off its skin) in the *Physiologus* tradition may represent repentance.The eagle and snake in combat is a very ancient and widespread motif in both literature and the visual arts. In the Roman world it appeared on tombstones and in medieval Christian art appears in manuscript illumination (in the Valerian Gospels, Staatsbibliothek, Munich; the Douce MS 176 in the Bodleian Library, Oxford) and on Byzantine and Romanesque sculptures. Its use as a Christian symbol can be traced continuously into modern symbolic systems. Its general Christian import seems to have been the triumph of Christ over the forces of evil.[12] The Derrynaflan scene does not portray a struggle: instead the serpents (two heads on a common body)

provide an interlaced setting within which the eagle is placed. It seems reasonable to see it as nevertheless dependent on eagle and serpent combat scenes of widespread distribution. It has therefore a christological symbolism. It is not unknown elsewhere in insular art – a very fine example dominates the head of the Keills Cross.[13]

The same may be said for the stag and snake scene (Fig. 3) – the animal is not involved in the coils of the snake. The serpent does, however, rear up in front of the stag and a dependence on stag and snake combat scenes elsewhere is very likely. It is represented on another Irish object of the same general period, a slab from Gallen Priory,[14] but it is one that we can recognise from a number of early Christian sources depicting the combat of the stag and snake from the *Physiologus* tradition.[15] The mosaic of the baptistery at Messaouda in Tunisia depicts on its central panel a pair of stags flanking a tree, each with a serpent grasped in the jaws. Parallels are not common; Puech[16] however, lists a detail on the apse mosaic of San Clemente, in a Romanesque baptistery at Freudenstadt, Württemberg, a wall painting at Bawit, Egypt, and on a mosaic from the Imperial Palace in Byzantium. A mosaic fragment from Carthage, now in the British Museum, also depicts a stag with a snake but Puech does not list it. The stag and snake enmity was known to the Latin fathers and St Ambrose refers to it twice in his *Breviarium in Psalmos* in his commentary on Psalm 41 ('As the hart panteth for fountains of waters') and in a sermon addressed to neophytes in which the stag is associated with baptismal imagery and the slaying of the serpent is given symbolic value. St Augustine, commenting on the same psalm, also makes the same references to the stag and serpents, the latter he specifically identifies as the sins; the serpents of iniquity must be consumed by those who desired the Waters of Life. In a number of liturgies Psalm 41 was recited at the vigil on Easter Saturday night when the catechumens achieved their initiation. The Mass of the Catechumens Good Friday in the Roman rite still uses Psalm 139, 2-10, 14 as the tract: 'Deliver me O Lord from the evil man: rescue me from the unjust man … They have sharpened their tongues like a serpent: the venom of asps is under their lips.' Psalm 41 is the tract for the blessing of the font during the Easter Vigil. It was chanted by Pope, clergy and catechumens in the early Roman Ordines. The symbolism of the stag and serpent is appropriate also to monastic life according to Puech, because the stag ejects the snake from caves and clefts in the rock just as the anchorites and contemplatives destroy their enemy the allegorical serpent. Doubtless some of the Desert Fathers had to evict the real thing too. In Ireland St Patrick had taken care of the problem.

The panel depicting a stag in a field of interlace (Fig. 4) is worthy of comment. It is quite clearly an antlered beast, not a horned one. Alone of all the animal panels found *in situ* in its frame, it was placed so as to be read looking from the inside of

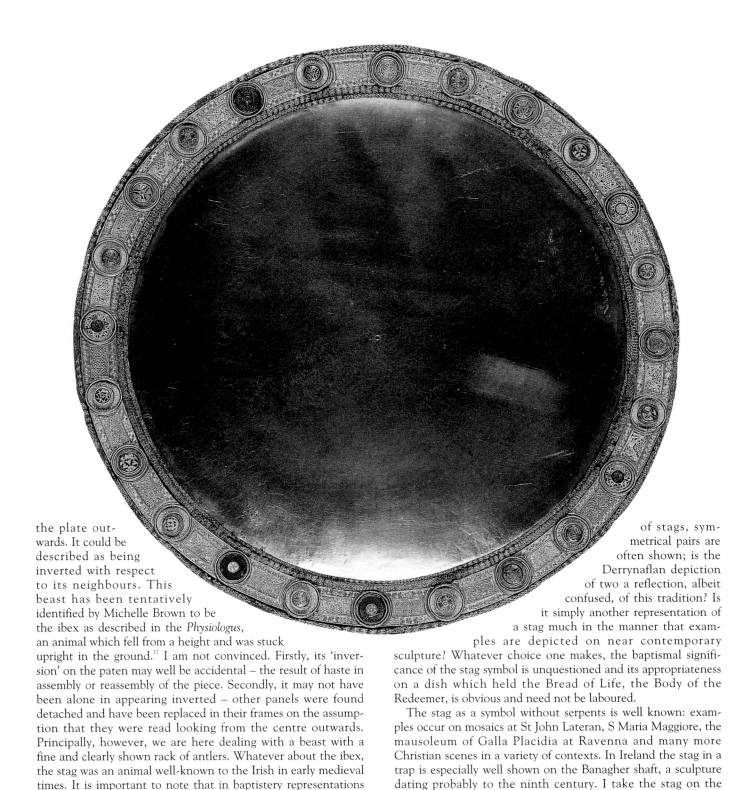

the plate outwards. It could be described as being inverted with respect to its neighbours. This beast has been tentatively identified by Michelle Brown to be the ibex as described in the *Physiologus,* an animal which fell from a height and was stuck upright in the ground.[17] I am not convinced. Firstly, its 'inversion' on the paten may well be accidental – the result of haste in assembly or reassembly of the piece. Secondly, it may not have been alone in appearing inverted – other panels were found detached and have been replaced in their frames on the assumption that they were read looking from the centre outwards. Principally, however, we are here dealing with a beast with a fine and clearly shown rack of antlers. Whatever about the ibex, the stag was an animal well-known to the Irish in early medieval times. It is important to note that in baptistery representations of stags, symmetrical pairs are often shown; is the Derrynaflan depiction of two a reflection, albeit confused, of this tradition? Is it simply another representation of a stag much in the manner that examples are depicted on near contemporary sculpture? Whatever choice one makes, the baptismal significance of the stag symbol is unquestioned and its appropriateness on a dish which held the Bread of Life, the Body of the Redeemer, is obvious and need not be laboured.

The stag as a symbol without serpents is well known: examples occur on mosaics at St John Lateran, S Maria Maggiore, the mausoleum of Galla Placidia at Ravenna and many more Christian scenes in a variety of contexts. In Ireland the stag in a trap is especially well shown on the Banagher shaft, a sculpture dating probably to the ninth century. I take the stag on the

2. THE DERRYNAFLAN PATEN. Irish, mid-late 8th Century. *Silver with cast copper alloy and polychrome glass, 35.6-36.8 cm diameter. (National Museum of Ireland).* The ornament of the paten places it within the same aesthetic as the Ardagh Chalice and it is the most accomplished example of Irish style metalwork of the 8th century that has so far come to light.

THE MENAGERIE OF THE DERRYNAFLAN PATEN

3. THE DERRYNAFLAN PATEN. Irish, mid-late 8th Century. Detail of the rim showing two filigree ornaments. *(National Museum of Ireland)*. The panel on the left is one of three that shows two squatting addorsed beasts; the panel on the right is of a serpent rearing up in front of a stag.

paten to be an explicit reference to baptism and redemption.

The interlaced snakes need not detain us long. In Christian terms the serpent is an ambivalent figure. Snake forms are endemic to insular metalwork and whether we should see anything more than conventional ornament in their use is arguable. I believe that we must accept the sophistication of the artists and their mentors, but the overt use of the serpent in a symbolic way is an open question. What is not questionable is their disposition to form an interlaced cross and this is reflected also in the panel of plain interlace where there is a cross evident in the void created by the interlacements.[18] Some of the glass studs of the rim also repeat the cross theme.

The paired motifs do not lend themselves to quite such detailed interpretation. I have suggested for some time that they are closely related to paired beast patterns, inhabited plant-scroll derivatives which seem to emerge in a secondary phase in the Anglo-Saxon province of insular art. This has some chronological value: it might be taken to suggest that the paten belongs to the later rather than the earlier eighth century when equivalent motifs make their appearance in Anglo-Saxon art. Here I must continue to declare that the taste represented by the narrow strip of panelled ornament, alternating animal, curvilinear and interlace patterns is that identified by Professor Cramp in the Durham manuscript of Cassiodorus commentary

on the psalms and in the Breedon sculptures in general terms. It is not the aesthetic of the Tara Brooch and the Lindisfarne Gospels of the later seventh and earlier eighth centuries AD. This suggests to me that the paten and the Ardagh chalice belong to a later phase of the Irish tradition. Having said that, I should add that I simply do not accept that there is any precision in this. Far too many certainties have been claimed in the field of Early Irish art history.

The plant-scroll phenomenon is, of course, explicitly iconographical in import. I doubt, however, if we can see the entire corpus of Derrynaflan animal panels as an integrated scene, a procession of the *tria genera animantium* of Genesis. What I have suggested elsewhere is that the composition in a general way reflects the rim ornament of beasts found on late antique silver dishes, but this is no more than a re-emphasis of a truism about the origins of early altar plate as a whole. Individual scenes within the circle of the rim embody specific Christian themes but it is difficult to see them married to form on the paten a coherent integrated symbolic cycle.

DR MICHAEL RYAN is an archaeologist who has published extensively on early Irish art. He is currently seconded from the National Museum to the Directorship of the Chester Beatty Library. He was awarded the Frend Medal of the Society of Antiquaries of London in 1989 for his contribution to the archaeology of the Christian Church.

4. THE DERRYNAFLAN PATEN. Irish, mid-late 8th Century. Detail of the rim showing two filigree ornaments. *(National Museum of Ireland)*. On the left, two narrow-bodied quadrupeds; on the right a stag in a field of interlace.

1. Michael Ryan, 'An Early Christian Hoard from Derrynaflan, Co. Tipperary,' *North Munster Antiq. Journal,* 22 (1980), pp.9-26; (ed.) *The Derrynaflan Hoard: A Preliminary Account,* Dublin 1983 (hereafter Ryan 1983) and with R Ó Floinn in S Youngs (ed.) *The Work of Angels,* London 1989, pp.130-33.

2. Ryan and R Ó Floinn in Ryan 1983, pp.17-30.

3. Ó Floinn forthcoming; M Brown 'Paten and purpose': the Derrynaflan paten inscriptions in R M Spearman and J Higgitt (eds.) *The Age of Migrating Ideas,* Edinburgh, National Museum, 1993, pp.162-67 (hereafter cited as Spearman and Higgitt).

4. M Ryan, 'Some aspects of sequence and style in the metalwork of eighth-and ninth-century Ireland' in M Ryan (ed.) *Ireland and Insular Art AD 500-1200,* Royal Irish Academy, Dublin 1987, pp.66-74 at p.68.

5. Brown in Spearman and Higgitt 1993, pp.163-64.

6. Ryan 1987 *loc. cit.*

7. E Rynne, 'The date of the Ardagh Chalice,' *Ireland and Insular art,* pp.85-89, at p.89. His general conclusions as to the relationship of the paten and Ardagh and Derrynaflan

chalices should be treated with reserve. Similar whorls are to be found in the ornament of, *inter alia,* the Lindisfarne Gospels and one of two discs from the Donore Hoard. The presence of stylised zoomorphic elements does not affect the general arguments for dating the paten.

8. Compare Ryan 1983, pp.19-20, pls 42 and 43.

9. Ryan, 'A suggested origin for the figure representations on the Derrynaflan Paten' in E. Rynne (ed.) *Figures from the past: Studies on figurative art in Christian Ireland,* Dublin 1987, pp.69-72.

10. Examples in F Baratte and K Painter (eds.) *Tresors D'Orfeverie Gallo-Romains,* Paris 1989, Nos. 24,75, 88, 103, 104, 107, 125, 174, 184, 197, 201, 202 ranging in date from the first to the third centuries AD.

11. E C Dodd, *Byzantine Silver Stamps,* Dumbarton Oaks Studies 8, Washington 1961,Nos. 20 (Riha), 27 (Stuma), 95, 108: and *ibid,* No. 2, 54 (Plate of Paternus).

12. The motif has been surveyed in detail by R Wittkower in an article 'Eagle and serpent' reprinted in *Allegory and the migration of symbols,* London, 1987, pp.16-44.

13. Douglas MacLean, 'The Keills Cross in Knapdale,the Iona School and the Book of Kells' in J. Higgitt (ed.) *Early Medieval Sculpture in Britain and Ireland,* British Archaeological Reports, British Series 152, Oxford 1986, pp.175-97.

14. F Henry, *Irish Art in the Early Christian Period to 800 AD,* London 1965, p.123 and pl.64, Ryan, *loc. cit.* p.72. The interlaced cross, panelled ornament including a fretted frame for the stag and snake scene and the symmetrically-placed beasts above it, perhaps also associated with snakes, make this sculpture an interesting parallel for the ornament of the Derrynaflan Paten in other ways also.

15. G L Feuille, 'Une mosaïque chrétienne de l'henchir Messaouda (Tunisie, région d'Agareb)', *Cahiers Archéologiques* IV, 1949, pp.9-5 and H-C Puech, 'Le cerf et le serpent; note sur le symbolisme de la mosaïque découverte au baptistère de l'henchir Messaouda,' *ibid.,* pp.17-60.

16. Puech, *op.cit.,* p.26.

17. Brown, *op. cit.,* p.164.

18. R B K Stevenson, 'Aspects of ambiguity in crosses and interlace', *Ulster Journ. Archaeol.* 44-5 (1981-82), pp.1-27.

1. Eleazar ALBIN: (d.1759), The Hoopoe. *Gouache on vellum, 30 x 23 cm. (Marsh's Library, Dublin).* The paintings are contained in two volumes bound in contemporary calf and were originally part of the famous collection of the Duchess of Portland which was sold as the Portland Museum in 1786.

ELEAZAR ALBIN'S WATERCOLOURS OF BIRDS

Among the rare treasures of Marsh's Library in Dublin are the original watercolour drawings for a celebrated Natural History of Birds which was published in the 1730s. **Muriel McCarthy** *examines them.*

On 15 June 1803 the assistant librarian of Marsh's Library accepted a bequest of two volumes of Eleazar Albin's 'Original water-colour drawings of birds'. Albin's drawings were bequeathed by Alexander Mangin (d. 1802).[1] They had been sent to Mangin on 6 February 1787 by the Hon General John Fitzwilliam as a 'Memorial of his friendship'.[2] They had originally belonged to Margaret Cavendish, Lord Harley's daughter, afterwards the Duchess of Portland (1715-85) to whom as a child Matthew Prior (1664-1721) the English poet addressed the lines beginning 'My noble lovely little Peggy'.[3] Albin's drawings were sold at the Portland Museum sale in 1786, lot 2809.[4] These charming watercolours on vellum were the original drawings for Albin's *Natural history of birds* which was published in London in three volumes in 1731, '34 and '38.[5]

The early details of Eleazar Albin's life (c.1713-59) are obscure[6] but it is known that he was a professional watercolour painter and that he taught drawing and painting in London. Albin also wrote *A natural history of English insects* (1720) and painted natural history objects for Sir Hans Sloane, and for Mary Somerset, Dowager Duchess of Beaufort. Albin's daughter Elizabeth assisted him with the hand colouring of the illustrations.

Many writers on natural history have criticised Albin's work and said that he was both 'lacking in imagination' and 'a very indifferent artist'. He has also been criticised for his lack of scientific knowledge of birds' habits and his writings have been compared unfavourably with those of the great English ornithologists, John Ray and Francis Willoughby. One suspects that these comments have been made by writers who have not seen the original drawings but have criticised the hand-coloured etchings in the printed versions which may not have been coloured by Albin. The first volume of the original watercolours contained ninety-nine drawings and there were one hundred and two drawings in the second volume. There is a manuscript list of the birds in the front endpapers of both volumes and the names of the birds have been written in English at the bottom of every drawing. In some instances the names may have been cropped by a bookbinder. (This probably occurred when the volumes were being rebacked). There is no text and the drawings are unsigned. Unfortunately some of the drawings are missing. In volume l, no. 56 the 'House Sparrow', and nos. 92 and 93 the 'Paroquets' and the 'Crown Paroquet' are missing. At some later stage a hideous attempt was made to 'replace' nos. 92 and 93.

Albin's birds were not painted from the imagination but were

The colours used by Albin are delicate and in some instances vivid and intense and the different species of birds are very recognisable.

copied from live specimens or dead skins. Considering the difficulties and limitations of getting live birds over two hundred years ago, these beautiful drawings are regarded as fairly accurate representations and the species are very recognisable.

The birds are a curious mixture and are in a strange order. They include Arctic, American and European birds. Albin has also included some birds from Bengal. Although they are described in the manuscript catalogue in Marsh's as 'Watercolour paintings on vellum', they were in fact executed in gouache heightened with white. The background and remainder of the paintings are in watercolours. The birds are placed on a tree stump, on the branch of a tree, on the ground, or in the sea. They are very much of the 'bird and branch style' which is a bit dull and monotonous. The branches of the trees are rather bare with very little foliage or berries.

Although it is difficult to be precise in avian structure, Albin has been very successful in the majority of cases. This is particularly noticeable with the arrangement of the feathers and the right number of bars in the wings of the 'Chaffinch'. The colour patterns on the 'Blue Tit' and the head and back stripe are also accurate. The 'Bull Finch' is very impressive. All the birds are recognisable although a few are fanciful and some have incorrect names. It is possible that these incorrect names may have been commonly used at the time. Albin's 'Bohemian Jay Hen' is in fact the Hawfinch and the 'Great Speckled Diver' is really a Red Throated Diver in winter plumage. The claws on most of the birds are curious and do not overlap on the branches of the trees.

Inevitably some licence has been taken. In order to get the 'Crested Grebe' (now the Great Crested Grebe) to balance, Albin (or his daughter) painted the bird bolt upright. The Great Crested Grebe cannot stand upright or walk as its legs are at the back and are used only for swimming. When it is on the ground it shuffles along on its belly. It is interesting to note that Albin was able to include the Guillimot (sic). This bird is really Brünnich's Guillemot and rarely occurs south of Iceland. Very few have been seen in Ireland. The only drawing in these volumes which consists of a detail is of a bird not named in the list of birds in the book. According to the index in the printed version this detail is the 'Head and Bill of the Man of War Bird which is also called the Albitross'. No. 95 in the list in Marsh's is called 'Bergonde', in the printed version this bird is called 'The Sheldrake of Bergander'.

A comparison between the two original volumes of drawings by Albin and the printed volumes of his *Natural history of birds* is

The Kingfisher from Bengall

2. Eleazar ALBIN (d.1759): The Kingfisher from Bengall, *Gouache on vellum, 30 x 23 cm. (Marsh's Library, Dublin)*. Albin's three-volume printed work was the earliest British bird book to contain coloured plates.

3. Eleazar ALBIN (d.1759): The Brazil Pie. *Gouache on vellum, 30 x 23 cm. (Marsh's Library, Dublin)*. Bequeathed to Marsh's in 1803, the paintings are one of the finest gifts ever made to the Library and they are here reproduced extensively for the first time.

problematic due to the fact that one volume appears to be missing from the set in Marsh's. There is a further complication. A second three-volume set of original watercolour drawings by Albin which belonged to the well-known American book collector, J H Bradley Martin[7] were sold by Sotheby's in New York in 1989. The priority of these drawings and the drawings in Marsh's, and their precise relationship to Albin's *Natural history of Birds* as it was published, have not yet been established. The problem of identification is further complicated by another one volume collection of sixty-six original watercolour drawings by Albin which belonged to the Dutch book collector W J de Bas.[8] De Bas's collection was sold in the Anderson Galleries in New York in November 1924. The Bradley Martin and the de Bas collections have not been seen by the author.

In order to make a comparison between the originals and the printed books, the edition in the Claudius Gilbert Collection in Trinity College Dublin was consulted. Albin's printed edition contains three hundred and six copperplate etchings. They were the first British bird books to have coloured plates, but there is no evidence as to who etched them.

The first volume contains a hundred and four unsigned plates. Volumes 2 and 3 contain a hundred and one twelve plates in each volume. The plates in volume 2 are signed by 'E. Albin', 'Eleazar Albin' and 'Eliz Albin'. There are at least twelve or possibly fourteen unsigned plates in this volume although it is difficult to be exact due to the fading of the ink in the corner of the plate. There are two additional names on the plates in volumes 2 and 3. In volume 2 there is a delightful etching of the 'Quail'. This plate is signed by 'Eliz Albin' and it also bears the name of 'G Thornton Sculp.' According to Christine E Jackson 'Nothing is known of this craftsman'.

The plates in volume 3, with one exception, are signed by 'Eleazar Albin', 'E. Albin' and 'E. A.' The exception is plate no. 72 the 'Red Linnet Cock', which is signed by 'F. Albin' who was Eleazar Albin's son, Fortin. It is interesting to note that another plate, no. 73 the 'Red Linnet Hen', which is signed by 'E. Albin' also bears the name 'H. Fletcher Scpt.'. Jackson records that Henry Fletcher was an excellent etcher of flowers, fruit and birds and that he worked in London from about 1710 to 1750.

The names of the birds on the plates in the printed volumes are given in various ways. Sometimes they are in English or English and Latin, or in English, Latin and French. Albin occasionally added interesting details such as in volume 1 plate 54, the 'Pied Chaffinch was taken the 20 April 1732 at Havering Bower in Essex where Edward the Confessor was born'. In volume 3 plate 127 Albin wrote 'The Bird was brought from Bengal in the year 1734 and is called the Dial Bird'.

There are however striking differences between Albin's original beautiful watercolour drawings in Marsh's and the three printed volumes. In the printed version the colouring of the

Albin's printed edition contains three hundred and six copperplate etchings, but there is no evidence as to who etched them.

birds has been carried out in an uneven and very amateur fashion. A limited range of colours has been used and the birds look dull and 'grainy'. Although the originals in Marsh's are not perfect they are much more sophisticated. The colours used by Albin are delicate and in some instances vivid and intense. But these are not the only differences. The background in the paintings of the birds in the printed version is a little more detailed. The branches of the trees have more foliage, blossoms or berries, and in a few cases Albin has also included insects.

There are also bibliographical differences between the printed edition examined by the author and the edition mentioned by Christine E. Jackson. Ms Jackson said that the plates in volume 1 were signed and the plates in volume 2 were unsigned. This is reversed in the volumes in Trinity College. The plates in volume 3 in both sets appear to be identical. The copy in Trinity College, Dublin may have been misbound.

The two volumes in Marsh's were bound in a contemporary brown calf binding. Unfortunately the upper and lower covers in both sets appear to have been 'decorated' with a liquid mixture made of iron filings in vinegar or iron gall. As this substance is very acidic, it has completely degraded the grain leather. The original binding was later rebacked in a red calf and decorated in gold.

The drawings are on single vellum leaves. They were gathered along with their paper interleaving to form gatherings to a total of eight individual leaves. These were then overcast to form a single section which was then sewn all along through a paper guard in the centre of the section. The paper used in the bindings bears the watermark of the paper maker 'C. Taylor' and the initials 'G. R.'. These probably refer to Clement Taylor who had a paper mill in Kent in England in the eighteenth century.[9]

As already stated, it does not seem possible to come to a conclusion as to the priority of these drawings, and their precise relationship to Albin's *Natural history* as it was published, without being able to consult the various 'original' paintings[10] together with the plates in the printed editions.[11]

While there may be identification and bibliographical problems associated with Albin's paintings and printed books, these magnificent watercolours on vellum are of great interest to ornithologists, scholars and visitors. They are one of the finest bequests made to Marsh's Library.

MURIEL MCCARTHY *is the Keeper of Archbishop Marsh's Library, St Patrick's Close, Dublin.*

ACKNOWLEDGMENTS
I am grateful to Mr Charles Benson and the librarians in the Early Printed Books and Special Collections Department of Trinity College, and to Ms Patricia Butler in the National Library, and the staff in the National Archives for all their help and assistance. I am particularly grateful to Mr Hugh Brazier in the Royal College of Surgeons for his advice on the identification of the birds in the Albin watercolours.

4. Eleazar ALBIN (d.1759): The Brown Owl. *Gouache on vellum, 30 x 23 cm. (Marsh's Library, Dublin).* The illustration is one of a collection of almost two hundred original paintings by Albin in Marsh's that were made for his famous *Natural History of Birds* published in London in the 1730s.

5. Eleazar ALBIN (d.1759): The Carason Hen. *Gouache on vellum, 30 x 23 cm. (Marsh's Library, Dublin).* Both Albin's daughter and his son assisted him with the hand-colouring of the printed plates.

THE SUMPTUOUS SILVER OF THOMAS BOLTON (1658-1736)

Irish example of an ostrich egg cup (Fig. 5), are to be seen in the National Museum of Ireland. One of the most notable was a silver-gilt Monteith or punch bowl (Fig. 2). Dated with a hallmark for 1704, it stands 22cm high. The bowl is semi-spherical with ring handles, while the body has vertical fluting and a chased coat of arms within a cartouche. The foot is gadrooned. The bowl is engraved with the inscription 'The gift of the Honble City of Dublin to Capt. Geo. Sanders Commandr of her Maties Ship the Seaforth for his Signal Services in taking two French Privateers being the first that were brought into this Harbour this warr Anno. Dom. 1704'.[5] This very fine Monteith has a fixed scalloped collar which was said to hold glasses suspended in the punch. Another interesting Bolton piece in the National Museum of Ireland is a fine gold Freedom Box, dated 1707, which was presented to Richard Freeman on his appointment as Lord Chancellor of Ireland (Fig. 8). This is a rare piece, as not only is it the earliest Irish-made freedom box extant, but it is also the earliest hallmarked Irish gold piece. Dublin Assembly Roll of 1707 records that Richard Freeman Esq., Lord High Chancellor of Ireland, 'be presented his freedom in a gold box not exceeding twenty five pounds sterling'.[6]

2. Thomas BOLTON, (1658-1736): Punch Bowl or Monteith. *Silver-gilt, diameter 22 cm., height 22 cm. Dublin hallmarks for 1703-04. (National Museum of Ireland).*

There was demand not only for Bolton's ceremonial ware, but also for church plate. The parish churches of Killaloe, Ettagh, Ballingary, Dunkerrin and Kilmore in the Church of Ireland diocese of Killaloe all boast of work by him. Lismore Cathedral has flagons of 1704-05, Youghal a flagon of 1710-12 and Galbally a paten dated 1702.[7]

Two fine items of domestic silver made by Bolton were in the executor sale of George W Panther of Foxrock in July 1929.[8] One of these was a remarkable chocolate pot (Fig. 4). Of plain hexagonal tapered body, it has a swan-shaped spout and wooden handle at right angles. Because of the quality of chocolate at that time regular stirring was necessary and therefore the finial on the lid was hinged to admit the stirring rod. This chocolate pot has its original burner, made as a separate stand and retaining its original wooden handle. The second item was a magnificent two-handled cup and cover nearly twelve inches high, which George Panther had bought from the collection of Mary, Lady Carbery of Castle Freke, Co Cork.[9]

Thomas Bolton was elected Warden of the Company of Goldsmiths in 1690, became Master in 1692 and the following year was elected Assay Master by twenty-two votes to three. He

3. Thomas BOLTON: (1658-1736): The Sir Joseph Williamson Standing Cup & Cover. *Silver, overall height 79 cms. Dublin hallmarks for 1696.* (left) and The Sir William Fownes Standing Cup and Cover. *Silver, overall height 69 cm. Dublin hallmarks for 1770 (Dublin Corporation).*

4. Thomas BOLTON: (1658-1736): Chocolate Pot, Stand, and Burner. *Silver, height 37 cm. Dublin hallmarks for 1708-09. (National Museum of Ireland).* The hexagonal-shaped pot with swan-necked spout has a hinged lid and hinged finial which allows for the insertion of a stirring-rod.

5. Thomas BOLTON: (1658-1736): Ostrich Egg Cup and Lid. *Ostrich egg and silver, height 24.5 cm., diameter of rim 8.75 cm. Dublin hallmarks of 1693-95. (National Museum of Ireland).* The ovoid bowl is an ostrich egg.

6. Thomas BOLTON, (1658-1736): The Mace of Trinity College, Dublin. (Detail) *Silver, overall length 153 cm. Dublin hallmarks of 1708-09 on head and shaft. (Trinity College, Dublin).* The shaft is decorated with roses and thistles. The head, which is linked to the shaft by four caryatids, bears the College arms on four escutcheons with the Royal arms on the upper surface beneath the crown.

7. Thomas BOLTON, (1658-1736): The Sir William Fownes Standing Cup & Cover. (Detail) *Silver, overall height 69 cm. Dublin hallmarks for 1700. (Dublin Corporation).* The cover of the cup is surmounted by the crest of the donor which was a falcon.

remained in that office until 1697. He became Alderman in Dublin Corporation in 1706 and Lord Mayor of Dublin in 1710-11.[10]

As Lord Mayor, Thomas Bolton wore the impressive gold chain of office created in 1697. It was made after the then Lord Mayor, Sir Michael Creagh, fled, carrying the original chain, with James II after his defeat at the Battle of the Boyne. Creagh's successor, Bartholomew Van Homrigh, a Dutchman, procured from King William a new gold collar with a portrait medallion appended.[11]

In 1697 the Minute Books of the Company of Goldsmiths recorded that 'Thomas Bolton has served this Corporation for some years past as assay master, but there having been lately some differences between this Corporation and Thomas Bolton, Mr. Bolton is now willing to quit this office and and rights and titles thereto provided the Corporation will reimburse to him the sum of £10 for what rent he has heretofor paid for the Hall'. This being agreed, Bolton's discharge was passed by sixteen votes to three. Tantalisingly, the books do not specify the reasons for the differences and one can only speculate on these.

One other point of interest recorded in the Minutes in 1694 was 'Thomas Bolton, Assay Master, to charge ld per oz. and to be charged 1/2d per oz. for assaying his own plate'. This is of interest because in the year of Bolton's death, 1736, a resolution was passed saying 'that the assay master, if a shopkeeper, shall not buy or sell any manner of plate during his continuance in said office, nor shall after a limited time, which will be granted him by the Corporation, keep open shop, nor work up, nor cause to be wrought up, any manner of gold or silver plate'. The introduction of that resolution was found to be so valuable that it pertains until today.

Thomas Bolton still remained an important force as in 1703 he

8. Thomas BOLTON (1658-1736): Freedom Box. *Gold, diameter 8 cm. Dublin hallmarks for 1706-07. (National Museum of Ireland).* The box is engraved on the lid with the arms of Freeman and on the underside with those of the City of Dublin. It was presented to John Freeman who was Lord Chancellor of Ireland from 1707-17.

9. The maker's mark of Thomas BOLTON (1658-1736): The letters 'T' and 'B' are conjoined in a shaped shield.

was an official when Dublin Corporation entertained the Lord Lieutenant, the Duke of Ormonde. As late as 1708, it is recorded that Bolton made a loan of two hundred pounds to the Company of Goldsmiths. This was for their building programme to build new premises in Werburgh Street, opposite Hoey's Court. The Minute Books show that the loan was at seven per cent interest and they also record the various payments of interest and of the principle.

The Company of Goldsmiths' records for 1730 mention that Alderman Thomas Bolton petitioned the Company for a pension. Ten pounds a year was granted to 'our reduced brother' and this sum was given each year until his death in 1736. The records show that after Thomas' death his daughter, Mary Bolton, petitioned and was granted five pounds a year but this was reduced to three pounds a year in 1737. In August 1740, by a majority vote of Council, her pension ceased. She again petitioned them on 1 May 1741 without success. She then applied to the City where it is recorded that 'Mary Bolton settling forth that she is the daughter of Alderman Thomas Bolton, deceased and being reduced to very low circumstances prayed the City's Charity: where upon it was ordered that the receiver general of the city revenues do, in the Lord Mayor's warrant, pay the petitioner £10 sterling, the same to be allowed the treasurer on his accounts'.

JOHN MCCORMACK *is a retired medical practitioner who has made a special study of the work of the silversmith Thomas Bolton.*

ACKNOWLEDGEMENTS
My thanks are due to Douglas Bennett for much help and advice; to Captain Ronald Le Bas for allowing me to study the Assay and Minute Books of the Company of Goldsmiths in Dublin; to Mairead Dunlevy, Director of the Hunt Museum in Limerick for her help and advice and to Mary Clark, Archivist in Dublin Corporation

1. Douglas Bennett, *Collecting Irish Silver, 1637-1900*, Dublin 1984, p.139.
2. Sir Charles Jackson, *English Goldsmiths and their Marks*, 1921.
3. Douglas Bennett, *The Silver Collection, Trinity College Dublin*, Dublin 1988, p.30
4. Both of these cups and the City Mace were exhibited in The Armoury, The Bank of Ireland, Easter-September 1991 in Dublin City Treasures.
5. John Teahan, Company of Goldsmiths

exhibition catalogue, pp.13 and 33.
6. Ida Delamer, 'Irish Freedom Boxes' *Dublin Historical Record*, Vol. XXXII, no. 1, December 1978.
7. Robert Wyse Jackson, *Irish Silver*, Dublin 1972, p.57
8. Henry Naylor, 'Eighteenth Century Irish Silver', *Dublin Historical Record*, Vol. XII, no. 1. George Panther lived at The Bawn, Foxrock, Co Dublin. The sale was at Sotheby's London saleroom where the

chocolate pot was sold for £1,280.
9. Sold at Sotheby's, London, for £2,570
10. The strength of the Goldsmiths was such that in 1716 not only did Bolton become Mayor but another leading Goldsmith, David King, became Sheriff. To mark the occasion, the Company presented the Lord Mayor with a piece of plate valued at £35 and the Sheriff with plate valued at £15.
11. Maurice Craig, *Dublin 1660-1860*, Dublin 1980 (pb), p.72

A WAX BAS-RELIEF BY PATRICK CUNNINGHAM

A rare and unusual eighteenth-century portrait group is identified by **Christine Casey.**

During the course of conservation work at Newman House (Number 86, St Stephen's Green, Dublin) a remarkable eighteenth-century wax portrait has come to light which depicts the family of Richard Chappell Whaley, the builder of the house (Fig 1).

Nine figures are represented in the wax. At the centre is Richard Chappell Whaley standing alongside the seated figure of his young wife, Anne Ward, who cradles the couple's seventh and last child, William Whaley. On Mrs Whaley's right is the kneeling figure of her eldest daughter, Susanna. Touching the sleeve of his father's coat is the eldest child, also Richard Chappell Whaley. To the right of the central group are the couple's four remaining children: a profile portrait of Anne Whaley in a contemporary dance posture; Sophia Whaley kneeling with fruit in her lap; and three-quarter portraits of the two younger Whaley boys, Thomas (later to achieve notoriety as 'Buck' Whaley) playing innocently with a rattle and his younger brother John kneeling next to Sophia.

The Whaleys were married in 1759. He, a widower and childless, was by then considerably advanced in years while his wife was just eighteen years old. Within nine years the couple had seven children and then less than a year after the birth of his youngest son, Richard Chappell Whaley died in January of 1769. After the death of her husband Anne Whaley lived at Number 86 St. Stephen's Green while Number 85 was bequeathed by Whaley to his father-in-law, the Rev Mr Bernard Ward. In 1772 Anne married John Richardson MP and continued to live at St Stephen's Green.

The Whaley's eldest son, Richard, died before coming of age and their second son, Thomas 'Buck' Whaley, inherited the very considerable family estates. During the late 1780s and 1790s Whaley squandered his inheritance on foreign travel and gambling pursuits. He eventually retired to the Isle of Man and died in 1800 at the age of thirty-three. John, the third son of Richard and Anne Chappell Whaley, inherited Number 86 St. Stephen's Green where he lived until his death in 1847. A decade later his widow, Mary Anne Whaley, sold the property to Charles Bianconi who acquired it on behalf of the Catholic University of Ireland. William Whaley, who is depicted as a baby in the wax portrait, became a lieutenant-colonel in the army and died in 1843. Susanna Whaley married Sir James Stewart of Fort Stewart, Anne married the Rt Hon John Fitzgibbon, afterwards Earl of Clare and Lord Chancellor of Ireland, and Sophia Whaley later married the Hon Robert Ward, son of Lord Bangor.

The group is set in a rather puzzling architectural framework with a floor of black and white stone flags and a curious dual backdrop which suggests that the family occupies two distinct interiors. On the left is a pedimented Ionic doorcase flanked by classical female figures which are not dissimilar to the stucco ornamentation of Number 85 St Stephen's Green. On the extreme right, a large panel depicting an urn in a verdant landscape may represent a painting or tapestry or indeed a view to a garden. The figure of Richard Chappell Whaley stands at the junction of these ill-matched backdrops. While the oddities of the portrait's scenic framework elude certain explanation, the architectural history of Newman House offers some food for thought in its elucidation. Five years prior to his marriage with Anne Ward, Richard Chappell Whaley acquired Number 85 St. Stephen's Green and the adjoining land which would later become the site of Number 86. Number 85 had been built in 1738 by Captain Hugh Montgomery and contained a wealth of late baroque stucco ornament by the Lafranchini brothers. In 1765, prompted perhaps by his rapidly expanding family, Whaley embarked on the construction of Number 86. His will, made on 5 July 1768, made provision for the completion of the house after his death.[1] It is possible that the curious duality of the portrait's background reflects the building history of the Whaley family home.

A document recently discovered among the Faulkner papers by Mr Conor O'Brien has thrown new light on the history of this remarkable family group.[2] A memorandum dated 27 August 1767 records an agreement between Richard Chapell Whaley and Patrick Cunningham, sculptor.

> *Memorandum that Richard Chap Whaley Esq has agreed this day with Mr Patrick Cuningham statuary to make and finish for him the different figures of himself and wife and seven children in bass relieffe in a groupe together on a piece of marble of the very best kind of statuary marble the piece of marble to be of the dimensions of the cleere of the chimneypiece in the grate room in his new house at Stephens Green for which the said Whaley is to pay Sd Cuningham for said piece together with a tablet agreeable to a moddle now delivered by Sd Cuningham the sum of eighty pounds sterling, said Cuningham has agreed to finish the tablate with the greatest speed and the groupe of figures on or before the first day of March next and Sd Cuningham doth herby acknowledge to have recd. from Sd Whaley by Saml. Faulkner the sum of two pounds five shillings and sixpence. Dublin the 27th August 1767. Present S Faulkner, Pat. Cuningham.*[3]

Patrick Cunningham was a Dublin sculptor who trained at the Dublin Society Schools and in the studio of John Van Nost.[4] Best remembered for his busts of William Maple and of Jonathan Swift, he was recognised among his contemporaries primarily as a wax modeller.[5] John O'Keefe's memoirs of the Dublin Society Schools claimed for Cunningham the invention of 'small basso-relievo portraits, in wax of the natural colours; they had oval frames and convex crystal glasses and were in great fashion'.[6] While Cunningham's exhibits at the Society of Artists in Dublin included a number of busts in terracotta and marble the majority were portraits 'modelled in coloured wax'. Remarkably no surviving example of Cunningham's work in wax was hitherto known.

Samuel Faulkner was Richard Chappell Whaley's agent; a cultivated man who produced many designs for buildings on Whaley's extensive estates.[7] Faulkner's memorandum of the Whaley-Cunningham agreement is somewhat difficult to decipher. Is Whaley commissioning two separate items; a figurative bas-relief and a chimneypiece tablet? Is the 'moddle' referred to a model for the Whaley family group or another item entirely?[8] Confusion stems initially from the specified dimensions of the marble piece namely 'the cleere' or breadth of the chimneypiece. A figurative bas-relief approximately four to five feet wide incorporated in a chimneypiece would produce a frieze-like composi-

A Wax-Bas Relief by Patrick Cunningham

1. Patrick CUNNINGHAM (d. 1774): Wax portrait of the Whaley family. *38 x 51 cm*. Cunningham was best known as a marble sculptor.

tion quite unlike traditional family groupings in contemporary painting and sculpture. A marble tablet set in its usual location at the centre of such a frieze would further complicate matters. It seems more likely that an awkwardly phrased memorandum records the commission for a marble chimneypiece lintel with a central figurative tablet. While the high relief of the figures in the wax portrait certainly stretches current definitions of bas-relief, the dimensions of the Whaley wax are concurrent with those of a chimneypiece tablet and it is tempting to assume that the portrait and the 'moddle' brought to St Stephen's Green in August 1767 are one and the same object.

Whether or not the wax portrait was the model for a marble bas-relief or an entirely separate work, it now seems certain that Patrick Cunningham was responsible for its execution. In April

of 1768 Cunningham exhibited at the Society of Artists 'a family piece in coloured wax', the only documented wax group portrait in his oeuvre. Large wax tableaux were more usual in the later eighteenth century and Cunningham's family group must have been considered as something of a virtuoso exercise.[9]

Richard Chappell Whaley died in January of 1769, almost a year after the agreed delivery date of the marble bas-relief. Whether that work was ever completed remains in doubt. The chimneypiece in the Saloon or great room of Number 86 St Stephen's Green has long since been removed and to date no record of its appearance is known and no other instance of a marble family group on an eighteenth-century chimneypiece is known.[10]

DR CHRISTINE CASEY *was Curator of Newman House, 85 and 86 St Stephen's Green and is now a Newman Scholar at the School of Architecture, UCD.*

1. 'Whereas I am now building a house and offices next adjoining my present dwelling house situated at the south side of St. Stephen's Green, Dublin. My will is that in case the same should happen not to be finished at the time of my death that my executors ... should compleat and finish the same according to the plan thereof and under the direction of my servant, Samuel Faulkner.' NLI MS D.6597.

2 I am grateful to Mr Conor O'Brien for bringing this item to my attention and to Mrs Amy Monaghan for kindly granting

permission to publish material from the Faulkner Papers.

3 Samuel Faulkner papers, Castletown, County Carlow.

4. Walter Strickland, *A Dictionary of Irish Artists* (Dublin, 1913) Vol. 1, pp247-49.

5 Homan Potterton, *Irish Church Monuments* (Ulster Architectural Heritage Society, 1975), p. 83.

6. *Recollections of John O'Keefe, written by himself*, 2 vols. (London, 1826) Vol. i, p.16.

7. Information from Mrs A Monaghan.

8. A fine marble tablet depicting Orpheus

among the animals adorns a chimneypiece in the room adjoining Whaley's Saloon or 'grate room'. The artist is unknown.

9. Dublin-born Samuel Percy (1750-1820) specialised in elaborate wax tableaux during the 1790s and early 1800s. See C Bernard Hughes, 'Wax portraits by Samuel Percy', *Country Life*, 12 May 1955 pp.1255-57. I am grateful to Jim Murrell of the Victoria and Albert Museum for his observations on the Whaley portrait.

10. I am grateful to Desmond FitzGerald and Homan Potterton for their observations.

A Life devoted to Landscape Painting William Ashford (c.1746-1824)

Anne Crookshank *catalogues an important Irish artist.*

1. William ASHFORD (c.1746-1824): Flowers in a Vase. *Oil on canvas, 63.5 x 86.4 cm. Signed and dated, 1766. (National Gallery of Ireland). (Cat.no. 1.)* This very early painting by the artist is a rare example of his work as a flower-painter as he is known almost exclusively as a landscape artist.

William Ashford was born an Englishman in Birmingham, where he was christened on 20 May 1746 in St. Martin's Parish Church, the son of Richard Ashford. Unfortunately his mother's name is not mentioned in the register,[1] neither, but less surprisingly, is his father's occupation given. He may have been the youngest of three brothers, for a Richard Ashford had a son, Thomas, christened on 8 April 1740, and Joseph on 17 August 1744, as well as William. We know absolutely nothing more about our man until he was eighteen. He must have gone to school, for he could read and write; he must have learnt to ride a horse as his work from eighteen onwards demanded it; and he must also have belonged to a family of some standing who were accustomed to travel out of Birmingham as in 1764, under the patronage of Ralph Ward, he came to Ireland. Ralph Ward was an Englishman and from what we know (and that is not much) he came from London. He had been Second Architect to the Tower of London and in 1763, under the patronage of the Marquess of Kildare, later first Duke of Leinster, he was brought to Dublin as Surveyor General of the Ordnance[4] of which the Marquess had become Master in 1761. What Ashford's links were with Ward we do not know but in the *Life of Gandon* which was written and edited by two men who would have known Ashford, Thomas Mulvany and James Gandon the Younger, it is said that Ashford 'was a favoured protégé of Mr. Ward, then at the head of the Ordnance Department in Dublin'.[5] From 1764 Ashford made his home in Ireland though he did not loose his English links and from time to time made visits to London and often exhibited there.

Pasquin[6] says that 'he [Ashford] was appointed to a lucrative situation in the ordnance office.' This was an exaggeration as he was paid £40 a year, as Clerk to the Comptroller of the Laboratory section of the Ordnance. It cannot have been a full-time post, as a fellow employee, Thomas Ivory, who earned £60 as Clerk to the Surveyor General was at the same time in charge of the Architectural School at the Dublin Society and a practising architect. The £40, as opposed to £60 for Ivory, might have been an age distinction as Ashford was certainly not trained for his job

A Life devoted to Landscape Painting: William Ashford

though the salary was never increased. His task, rather surprisingly, was going round Ireland checking on the armaments stored at the various forts and barracks. A few records exist in the House of Commons Journals of expenses he clocked up of which the largest was in early 1765 when he was paid £38 'for his travelling Expenses, and to Viewers to assist him to examine the Arms of the Army at the different Parts of this Kingdom'.[7] In June of the same year he got a mere £3 'for his Disbursements for a Horse, hired for a labourer to assist when sent to survey Arms'[8] and in Sept. 1765 £2.12s.6d. 'for twentyone Days travelling Expenses going to the Laboratory at Chapel-Izod'.[9] No other expenses are recorded and how long he carried out this boring job is not known, but he did not leave the Ordnance until 1788.

It is impossible to say when exactly he stopped doing any serious work for the Ordnance, but by 1767 he was already exhibiting in the Society of Artists in Ireland and if by 1775 he was able to get £57. 9s. 3d for three pictures (nos. 6-8), he must

2. William ASHFORD (c.1746-1824): Moore Abbey, the Garden Front. 1775. *(Cat.no. 8)*.

have outgrown his £40 salary and was probably employing, or about to employ, someone else to do the work. The addresses given in the records of Society of Artists in Ireland show that he must have been in lodgings when he first came: in 1767 in Aston's Quay, in 1770 at the Indian Queen, Dame Street and from 1771 to 1777 he gave the Ordnance Office, Castle-Yard as his address. In 1780 he moved to a more permanent home, 27 College Green, and maybe this represents his break with more than nominal work for the Ordnance. In about 1792 he got his friend Gandon to design a house for him in Sandymount[10] which remained his home for the rest of his life.

Of more interest is how Ashford learned to paint. He may well have been apprenticed before he came over to Ireland in 1764, but he was by no means a fully trained artist. He clearly had connections with the Dublin Society Schools; he would have known the masters and when in Dublin he could easily have slipped in to the odd lesson, after all the Duke of Leinster was one of the Schools' patrons, and there is no doubt that in many ways his work links with that of his Irish contemporaries. He is not mentioned in any Dublin Society School records except that he won in 1772 a second premium for one of the landscapes he exhibited in that year. The first premium was won by Thomas Roberts who must have been a rival, and whose early

tragic death opened up Ashford's career for him. After 1777 when Roberts left Ireland to die in 1778, there was no serious competition and as a landscape painter Ashford reigned supreme for thirty to forty years.

Ashford's earliest exhibited works from 1767-1771 were all still-life and flower-pieces. None of the still-life paintings has yet been identified but two more flower-pieces can reasonably be added to the two always known, which belonged to the descendants of that great Irishman, Samuel Madden. It was probably on account of his constant travelling that Ashford turned to landscape painting: six roughly done drawings, inscribed 'Askeyton', 'Timoleague (abbey ruins)', two of 'a mill near Bantry' and two pen and ink sketches of Limerick (Fig. 22), all of which were signed 'W Ashford' on a covering sheet of paper, indicate that he did in fact sketch on his trips. Another more finished sketch of Drogheda can be added to these early efforts; these are, except for the twenty-four Mount Merrion drawings which will be discussed later, the only drawings we know by Ashford. None of them are studies for oils.

He exhibited his first landscapes in 1772, and though none before 1774 is certainly identifiable, by then he was already very good. His talent was recognised almost at once for when he exhibited a landscape at the Royal Academy in London in 1775 (from the Ordnance) an unidentified critic wrote 'We don't remember this artist's name before in any exhibition; notwithstanding this, he is so far from being a novice in his profession, that if he is young and attentive, he may well expect to reach the first form in this department of painting'.[11] This is precisely what he did.

The fashion of commissioning sets of views of one's house and park was in full flood in Ireland during Ashford's lifetime. He worked for General Cunningham, later the first Lord Rossmore, the Earl of Drogheda, the Duke of Leinster, the Earl of Charleville, the Viscount Fitzwilliam, the Earl of Bessborough, the Earl of Kilmorey, Lord Rockley, and the Hon William Wellsley Pole and probably a number of others. Of these his masterpieces are certainly those done of Charleville Forest in 1801 (Figs 10 & 11) where his remarkable capacity for painting trees, in sunlight or in shade, and in painting water reach a high point of excellence.

It is sometimes difficult to see much stylistic change in Ashford's work but if one compares the views of Moore Abbey, 1775 (Figs. 2 & 3), with those of Charleville (Figs. 10 & 11) one sees at once how much more developed the latter are. Ashford was never at his best with architecture – one has only to remember his stage set views of Maynooth which are as late as 1780 – and in the Charleville pictures he hardly has to contend with buildings at all as the castle was not completed. An unknown diarist was rightly thrilled by them: 'There is here abundant scope for an exertion of the artist's genius in the delineation of foliage ... the colouring so beautifully rich, and various, that I could with pleasure have spent hours in viewing them'.[12]

In London, Ashford exhibited not only at the Royal Academy but also at the Society of Artists, an organisation on the downward trend because of the Academy. He first showed there in 1777 when he used a Dublin address as well as a London one, 'At the Castle Dublin, or 69, Margaret St Cavendish Square:' He was elected a Fellow of the Society of Artists in 1778 but this does not seem to have impressed him as he didn't show with them again till 1783 and then in 1790 he sent eleven works from a London address: 'Gt Russel St Covent Garden'. These pictures included several views in North Wales where he may have stayed on the journey over from Ireland, as well as a house view in Henley-on Thames. He last showed with the society in 1791. To the Royal Academy he sent a single landscape in 1775 and again in 1776, giving the Ordnance office as his address. The move to 27 College Green had taken place before he exhibited again – in 1785, his two views of Bessborough – and he sent again in 1786 and 1787. In 1789 he exhibited eight pictures and was living at 34 Leicester Fields. He must have been in lodgings as his London addresses change so often. Having returned to the Society of Artists in 1790 and 1791 he exhibited again at the Royal Academy in 1795, two subject pictures and one landscape. He sent three pictures in 1804 from 2 Berners Street, three more in 1805 from 20 Lower Brooke Street, and one English view of Hammersmith in 1811 from 22 Hanover Street, Long Acre.

After its establishment in 1806 he sent a lot of works in the following three years to the British Institution. A number of these were old stock, works which had clearly not sold in the past, notably his efforts at subject pictures, like *Jacques and the Wounded Deer* (Fig. 13) which was first exhibited at the Society of Artists in 1790 and *Celia and Orlando*, first shown in the RA in 1795 and then at the British Institution in 1806. He painted at least four scenes from *As You Like It* as, apart from the two already mentioned, two others were exhibited at the Royal Hibernian Academy after his death. He may have been spurred on to paint them because of the Shakespeare mania of the time. It was not only London that had a Shakespeare Gallery but for a brief three months, May to July 1793, there was one in Dublin.[13] The importance of subject pictures can be gauged by the fact that after his death the RHA showed works by him in six exhibitions, but six out of the eight paintings were subject pictures.

There was one other event of note in Ashford's London visit of 1789/90. His friend, J T Serres, was planning to go abroad and on 22 and 23 April 1790 he held a sale of his work in London which included works by his friends. From the titles of his pictures it is clear that Serres made a number of trips to Ireland, visiting down the coast from Dublin to Waterford. As well as the paintings by Ashford, works were included by three other Irish artists, George Barret, Thomas Roberts and Robert Carver. The five Ashfords were of general scenery, Killarney and Wicklow, not country houses which would have been commissioned works; there was also one rather surprising Stubbsian effort, not now known, entitled *Lions and Leopards in a Landscape*. This unusual sale must have been in Ashford's mind years later in 1819, when as an old and distinguished man he decided to hold a one-man show. This was held in February/March 1819 in the Board room of the Dublin Society's House in Hawkins Street.[14] If there was a catalogue it has not survived but it would be fascinating to know what he wanted to show. Possibly the large number of views of Dublin and Dublin Bay which living in Sandymount had clearly inspired him to paint. I feel it likely that he had a theme in mind as the most obvious example of an exhibition was Thomas Sautell Roberts's show of 1802 of watercolours of the new Military Road over the Dublin mountains.

The large commission from the seventh Viscount Fitzwilliam to record his estate and house at Mount Merrion was the last commission for a set of views that he seems to have had. W B Sarsfield Taylor said that from 1801 'until his decease, (1824) ... he had received but one order, and that was from a Mr. Hodges, for two pictures'.[15] This remark was based on similar comments made in Ashford's uninformative obituary in Faulkner's *Dublin Journal* for 23 April 1824 and makes one wonder if this had been written by Taylor. The Fitzwilliam commission must have been given about 1804 as one of the six views is dated then but the volume of twenty-four drawings has a title page dated 1806 and it seems likely that these are the boundary dates for the entire set. The oils are impossible to evaluate as they appear never to have been cleaned and are shadows of what they must have been. In size there are three 64.8 x 76.2cm, two 64.1 x 111.1cm and one 95.9 x 131.5 cm so that they must have been designed for a specific room as indeed would all the sets have been.

The drawings on the other hand, because they are in a volume, are in perfect condition and extremely beautiful. They are the

3. William ASHFORD (c.1746-1824): Moore Abbey: the Entrance Front. 1775. (*Cat.no. 7*).

only finished drawings known. Ashford's love of depicting the various types of trees is beautifully shown in *The Woodhouse*, where the charming summer house is inhabited by people and a child and her dog are playing on the grass outside (Fig. 19). At this time Mount Merrion was inhabited by Mrs Barbara Fagan,[16] the Fitzwilliam's agent, and her husband Mr Richard Verschoyle. Mrs Fagan's mother had been agent before her to the sixth Viscount and this very unusual role for a woman at this date seems, from the drawings, to have been wholly justified. The park, at any rate, was superbly maintained and apparently full of deer; they wander freely near the Gothic building at the end of the North terrace as well as in the less cultivated and more distant parts of the park. One drawing entitled *View from the rear of the Ash Grove* (Fig. 21) shows deer roaming amid the hay field where Ashford's favourite prop, a hay cart, is being filled. The workers include women as well as men and the background is again a much concealed silhouette of the Dublin mountains from the Sugar Loaf to the sea. The album is completed with two views of Lord Fitzwilliam's house at Richmond which, with its neat, brick wall, herbaceous border, urns and wrought iron work, has a trim precision not to be found in Ireland.

Ashford is a painter of summer. If he paints an open landscape it is full of haymaking or people driving in open carriages

4. William AsHFORD (c.1746-1824): The Park at Carton. 1779. *(Cat.no. 13)*

5. William AsHFORD (c.1746-1824): The Duchess of Leinster in a horse-drawn carriage crossing the bridge at Carton. 1779. *(Cat.no. 14)*.

6. William ASHFORD (c.1746-1824): Figures with cattle and sheep by a stream in a wooded landscape. c.1780. *(Cat.no. 18).*

7. William ASHFORD (c.1746-1824): Shane's Castle, Co Antrim. 1786. *(Cat.no. 31).*

or, as in the utterly charming *Cloghoughter Castle*, of fashionable trippers boating out to see a famous ruined castle. Only one picture has autumnal colouring, *Jacques and the Wounded Deer* (Fig. 13) Ashford's trees are nearly always heavy with foliage, everyone is happy, well-fed, well-dressed and you would think that he hadn't lived through the terrible year of 1798 with its rebellions, its merciless guerilla warfare and the attendant dreadful retribution. After the Act of Union of 1801, Dublin must have been a very different place, empty of the glamorous high society which had filled it since his arrival nearly forty years before. The one winter landscape, which is an illustration of a poem, is, by some odd fate, now in his birthplace, Birmingham, and dates quite early, 1780. He does seem in his later years to have painted a number of stormy seascapes, no doubt seen from his house; the critic of the 1800 exhibition complains of a picture of Dublin Bay that it is 'rendered unpleasant by a predominant, grey tone'.[17] The critic waxes eloquent on more summery views, as one of Tollymore Park, 'The colours are natural; the verdure is warm and mellow ... the shadows on the water are broad and deep ... the skies cool and pleasant ... The union of the picture is so perfect... we leave it each time with regret, and return to it with fresh pleasure, as a master-piece fit to rank with Ruysdael and Waterloo in the cabinet of a Prince, and for which no price can prove too high a compensation'.[18]

Despite Pasquin's remarks that Ashford's figures are inaccurate, they do add to the charm of his landscapes and it is not surprising that he took an interest in the fashion for genre painting which gripped Dublin painters in the early part of the nineteenth century. His last dated works, 1821, (Figs. 8 & 9) though landscapes, are studies of peasant conditions.

8. William ASHFORD (c.1746-1824): A village with many ruined buildings by a lake. 1821. *(Cat.no. 56).*

Ashford certainly made money; he married but we don't know who, and had children. One grandson was clearly known to Strickland which makes his account particularly important.[19] One hint of his interests is found in a resolution taken on 23 February 1792 in *The Proceedings of the Dublin Society* that a committee of members should 'be appointed to examine the Statues and Models now to be disposed of by Mr William Ashford, Landscape Painter ... and that they might report ... their opinion, whether it might not be proper for them to Purchase the said statues.' The Dublin Society, on the advice of this committee, agreed to purchase them on 15 March 1792 for eighty guineas, and ordered 'That the sum of £91 sterling, be paid to Mr Wm Ashford for the collection of Statues and Casts offered for Sale by him to the Society'. Eighty guineas was a sizeable sum; the collection must have been quite large and of quality. It was bought for the Schools but no other mention of them seems to occur in later lists of the Society's works of art. They prove that Ashford was a collector and the fact that it took four days by auction to sell his 'Paintings, Drawings, Field Studies and Sketches' after his death may indicate that it was more than the remains of his studio that were on offer. No catalogue is now known but the sale was advertised in *Faulkner's Dublin Journal* for several days before the auction, held between 18 and 21 May 1824 at M Gernon's Rooms at 38 Dawson Street, Dublin.

In 1813 Ashford was elected President of the Irish Society of Artists and was involved in the complicated negotiations which resulted in the foundation of the Royal Hibernian Academy. Of this he was voted first President in 1823 at the age of seventy-seven, which must have been an honour and a pleasure for a man who had devoted his life to landscape painting. He didn't live to see the first exhibition.

1. International Genealogical Index: Parish register for St Martin's Church, Birmingham, County Record Office, Warwickshire.
2. *Victoria History of the County of Warwick*, Vol. 7 (London, 1964), p.258.
3. *ibid.*,Vol. 2,(London, 1908) p.211.
4. *Freeman's Journal*, 2-4 Sept. 1788 Information kindly given by Dr Edward McParland.
5. James Gandon and Thomas J. Mulvany, *The Life of James Gandon*, first ed (Dublin, 1846); second edition ed. Maurice Craig, (London, 1969) p.141.
6. Anthony Pasquin, *Memoirs of the Royal Academicians and an Authentic History of the Arts in Ireland* ... London 1796, reprinted with an introduction by R W Lightbown, London 1970. p.40.
7. *Journals of the House of Commons of the Kingdom of Ireland*, Vol. VIII, Dublin 1796, Appendix p.li. 'Sums expended ... for March Quarter 1765.'
8. *ibid.*, June. Quarter 1765
9. *ibid.*, Appendix plii, Sept. Quarter 1765
10. Registry of Deeds, Vol. 458, p.59; no. 294171: Deed dated 13 June 1792 concerned with the acquisition of the land for his house by Ashford from Lord Fitzwilliam. Information kindly given by Dr Edward McParland.
11. Unidentified newspaper cuttings, Courtauld Institute of Art.
12 Diarist, usually called the Unknown Diarist, 2 vols covering 1 Feb 1801-9 May 1803 survive in the Royal Irish Academy, 24k 14-15. Vol. 2, p.258
13. Robin Hamlyn, 'An Irish Shakespeare Gallery', *The Burlington Magazine*, Vol. cxx, no. 905, Aug. 1978, pp.515-29
14. *Proceedings of the Dublin Society*, Vol. LV, 1819, pp.55 and 63. Letters concerning this exhibition.
15. W B Sarsfield Taylor, *The Origin, Progress and Present Condition of the Fine Arts in Great Britain and Ireland*, 2 vols. London, 1841. Vol. 2, p.282
16. F E Ball, 'Mount Merrion and its History', *Journal of the Royal Society of Antiquaries of Ireland*, Vol. 28, pp.329-44.
17. Author unknown. *Critical Review of the First Annual Exhibtion of Paintings, Drawings and Sculptures, The Work of the Irish Artists, at No 32 Dame Street, Dublin*. June 1800. p.10
18. *ibid.*, p.14.
19. W G Strickland, *Dictionary of Irish Artists*, 2 vols, Dublin and London 1913, Vol. 1, pp.7-11.

FLOWER PAINTINGS

1 **Flowers in a vase.** (Fig. 1)
Oil on canvas, 63.5 x 86.4 cm. S &
D: W M Ashford 1766. Exh.: 1767,
Society of Artists in Ireland, No. 1 or
2. Prov: Christie's, 19 July 1985, lot 52.
National Gallery of Ireland,

2 **Flowers in a vase**
Oil on canvas, 63.5 x 76.2 cm. Exh.
1767, Society of Artists in Ireland,
No. 1 or 2
Private collection.

3 **A Vase of Roses**
Oil on canvas, 54.2 x 76.8 cm,
Pair to no. 4.
Christie's 18 Nov. 1988, lot 83.

4 **Two vases of flowers**
Oil on canvas, 54.2 x 76.8 cm. Pair
to no. 3. Nos. 3 and 4 are unsigned
and are only attributed to Ashford
but appear to be early works.
Christies' 18 Nov. 1988, lot 83.

VIEWS OF KNOWN PLACES

5 **Gibraltar**
Oil on canvas, dimensions unknown. Exh: 1821,
Cork Society for Promoting the Fine Arts, no.
43. Lent by T. Gibson Esq. Painted for Sir John
Irwin who was Governor of Gibraltar 1766-68
and Colonel-in Chief in Ireland 1775-82. A label
on the back is said to have stated that it was
painted by Ashford in 1773. The date sounds
unlikely. Ashford must have painted this picture
from a watercolour or drawing provided by Irwin
though Col.Vallencey of the surveying branch of
the Board of Ordnance has been said to be the
author of the drawing. Its primitive style is not
similar to Ashford's later landscape work.
Private collection.

6 **Moore Abbey, showing the Deer in the Park**
Oil on canvas, 91.5 x 152.4 cm. The river and
house are to the left.
Private collection.

7 **Moore Abbey, the Entrance Front** (Fig. 3)
Oil on canvas, 91.5 x 152.4 cm
The river occupies the left hand side of the pic-
ture, a sailing boat being poled mid-stream.
Private collection.

8 **Moore Abbey, the Garden Front** (Fig. 2)
Oil on canvas, 91.5 x 152.4 cm. The river winds
in the background. Nos. 6, 7, and 8 were exhibited as 'Views of Moore Abbey' in the Society of
Artists in Ireland, 1775 and one again was lent to
the First Winter Exhibition of Old Masters,
Dublin in 1902, No 75, when the size is mentioned and an account book from Moore Abbey
is quoted 'Paid Mr. Ashford 17th July 1775, paid
£57. 9s. 3d. for three pictures of Moore Abbey' It
is an assumption on the author's part that the
three pictures are the same size and it is impossible to tell which work was exhibited or if the
measurements included frames.
Private collection.

9 **Killarney Mountains with Lough Lene and the
round tower of Aghadoe in the foreground**
Oil on canvas,60 x 100.5 cm. S & D: 1778..
*Christie's 23 March 1979, lot 72, and 26 June
1981, lot 77*

10 **Muckross Abbey, Killarney**
Dimensions unknown.S & D: 1779. Exh. 1780,
Society of Artists in Ireland, No. 10; Spring 1953,
Arts Council, *English Landscapes from Col. Grant's
Collection,* No 3. Lit. Col. Grant, *Old English
Landscape Painters from the XVIth century to the
XIXth century,* London, 1959. Vol IV p 266.
Private collection.

11 **Killarney, from Aghadoe**
Oil on canvas, 61 x 99 cm. Exh.1780, Society of
Artists in Ireland, No. 7.
*The Richard Wood Collection, on loan to the
University. of Limerick*

9. William ASHFORD (c.1746-1824): Howth Harbour and Ireland's Eye,
beyond. 1821. (Cat.no. 55).

12 **Killarney**
Dimensions unknown. S & D: 1779
Possibly the picture exhibited in the Society of
Artists in Ireland, 1780,no. 9 as a 'View in the
passage to the Upper Lake'.
Tryon Palace, New Bern, N. Carolina

13 **The Park at Carton, Co Kildare, the seat of the
Dukes of Leinster.** (Fig. 4)
Oil on canvas, 111 x 153 cm. S & D: 1779. Exh.
1780, Society of Artists in Ireland, no. 1 or 2.
Lit. *Notes of the Pictures, Plate, Antiquities ... at
Carton ...* Dublin 1885 p.52; Edward Malins
and the Knight of Glin, *Lost Demesnes,*
(London, 1976, p.58, illus.) Prov: the Dukes of
Leinster. An angler and a sportsman with his
dogs are standing near the weir.
Sotheby's 14 July 1993, lot 77.

14 **The Duchess of Leinster in a horse drawn carriage crossing the bridge at Carton.** (Fig. 5)
Oil on canvas 110 x 150 cm S & D: 1779.Exh.
and Lit. as for no 13. Prov: the Dukes of
Leinster. This pair of landscapes, commissioned by the second Duke of Leinster, formed
part of a set of six views of Carton, four of
which were by Thomas Roberts who died in
1778 and therefore presumably left the commission unfinished and Ashford was asked to
complete the set. The Duchess is Olivia, wife
of the second Duke.
Sotheby's 14 July 1993, lot 76.

15 **The ruins of Maynooth Castle, with other
buildings**
Oil on canvas, 57.2 x 80.7 cm. S & D: 1780 Exh.
1780, Society of Artists in Ireland, no. 3
Though this picture is not part of the set of six
mentioned in no. 14 it must have been commissioned at much the same time and shows the
earlier home of the Earls of Kildare.
Private collection.

16 **The ruins of Maynooth Castle, with other
buildings**
Oil on canvas, probably 57.2 x 80.7 cm. as
no.15. This is certainly a pair with no. 15 and
both are framed identically. This view has a broken bridge and a stream or pond in the
foreground where women are washing and a
horse is being watered
Private collection.

17 **Kilkea Castle**
Oil on canvas, dimensions unknown.
According to Strickland, the Duke of Leinster
owned four Ashfords, apart from two of
Carton. Nos 15 and 16, above, were of this set
and probably also this painting of Kilkea
Castle, though it is in bad order. The fourth,
described as a landscape, was perhaps no. 18.
Private collection.

18 **Figures with Cattle and Sheep by a
stream in a wooded landscape** (Fig. 6)
Oil on canvas, 93.5 x 122.5 cm.
Signed but undated. Said to be a view
near Carton, Co. Kildare, in which
case it was probably painted about
1780 at the same time as nos. 15-17.
There are sheds and a cottage on
the far bank and what looks like a
canal bridge in the distance.
Sotheby's 19 July 1978, lot 96

19 **The Scalp, Co. Wicklow**
Oil on canvas, 35.5 x 24 cm. Exh.
1780,Society of Artists in Ireland,
no. 6. Engraved, T Milton's *Views of
Seats,* 1783, second set, Pl. viii.
Christie's 3 July 1964,lot 131

20 **A Storm Scene also called The
Thunderstorm**
Oil on canvas, 56.2 x 66.8 cm. S &
D: 1780. Exh. 1780, Society of
Artists in Ireland, no .13, where it is
described as being from Whyte's
Shamrock; 1975, Milan, *Pittura
Inglese 1600 -1840.* Engraved in reverse by Esdall
in a circle over the following poem taken from
Samuel Whyte's *Shamrock,* Stanza 10, p. 113:
*Bless'd be the Hand, which then, with timely
Power
Humanely Strong, and generously brave,
Approch'd the Traveller in his needy Hour,
And snatch'd the Poet from a watery Grave.'*
Birmingham City Museum and Art Gallery.

21 **An Open Carriage passing Frescati [Frascati],
Blackrock, Co Dublin** (Fig. 12)
Oil on canvas, 100.4 x 124.5 cm. S & D: 1781
Ulster Museum, Belfast.

22 **and 23 Lismore**
Oil on canvas, both 46.9 x 63. 5 cm. and
S & D: 1783. Exh. 1804, Society of Artists in
Ireland, nos.59 and 65.
A pair in which the bridge is seen from the right
in one and from the left in the other.
Christie's 19 Nov. 1976, lot 23, as a pair.

24 **Barmeath Castle**
Dimensions unknown. S & D: W Ashford 1783
Private collection.

25 **Belan House, Co. Kildare**
Oil on canvas, 78.4 x 106.7 cm
A carriage waits at the door of the house and the
stables can be seen to the right while a large dove-
cote is prominent to the left of the house. In the
foreground there are swans and a group of fashion-
able people in a boat being poled across a pond.
*The University of Michigan Museum of Art, gift of
Booth Newspapers, Inc. in memory of George
Gough Booth and Ralph Harman Booth.*

26 **Belan House from the Park**
Oil on canvas, 78.4 x 106.7 cm. *Signed (falsely)*
Wilson.This picture may well be a pair with
no.25, above.Engraved in T. Milton, *Views of
Seats in Ireland,* second set, 1783, no. vi.
A Chinoiserie bridge is seen at the end of a long
avenue beside a stream. This is peopled by fig-
ures and deer. On the far side of the stream a
carriage and four drive towards the house.
Private collection.

27 **Dawson's Grove, Co. Cavan.**
Oil on canvas, 40.7 x 34.3 cm. S & D: 1785 An
artist sketching is seated near a classical urn in
the grounds of the Doric Mausoleum. Another
work entitled *View of Dawson's Grove* was
exhibited in the Society of Artists of Ireland
exhibition in 1774.
Christie's 3 July 1964, lot 128.

28 **Castleward from the Doric Temple**
Oil on canvas,109.2 x 142.3 cm. S & D: 1785 Exh.
1961, Belfast Museum and Art Gallery, *Pictures
from Ulster Houses,* no. 105. Figures, including
children and dogs, are seen in the foreground.
The National Trust, Castleward House, Co Down.

10. William ASHFORD (c.1746-1824): The Gothic Dairy at Charleville. 1801. *(Cat.no. 35).*

11. William ASHFORD (c.1746-1824): The River on the Charleville Estate. 1801. *(Cat.no. 36)*

12. William ASHFORD (c.1746-1824): An open carriage passing Frescati, Blackrock. 1781. *(Cat.no. 21)*.

13. William ASHFORD (c.1746-1824): Jacques and the wounded deer. 1786. *(Cat.no. 72)*.

14. William ASHFORD (c.1746-1824): A horseman on a country lane with children playing by a gate. *(Cat.no. 87)*

15. William ASHFORD (c.1746-1824): Mountainous river landscape with ruins. 1778. *(Cat.no. 71)*.

16. William ASHFORD (c.1746-1824): A water-mill near Lucan. 1791. *(Cat.no. 62)*.

17. William ASHFORD (c.1746-1824): Dublin Bay from the Charter School, Clontarf. 1794. *(Cat.no.47)*.

29 **Mount Kennedy House, Co. Wicklow**
Oil on canvas, 42 x 61 cm. *S & D*: 1785.
Engraved in T Milton's Views of Seats, fifth set,
1787, no. xviii. A lady and gentleman are riding towards the house pointing out its new
glories. This picture is almost certainly a pair
with no. 30. Neither of them seem to be the
work exhibited at the Society of Artists in
Ireland in 1772, no. 2 as 'A View of Mount-
Kennedy, and part of Col. Cunningham's
improvements.'
Private collection.

30 **Mount Kennedy House, Co. Wicklow**
Oil on canvas, 41 x 61 cm. Almost certainly a
pair with no. 29 and therefore of the same date.
It shows a different view of the house, looking
towards the Wicklow mountains. In the park, a
shepherd with his dog watches a large flock of
sheep and other figures discuss the view.
Private collection.

31 **Shane's Castle, Co Antrim** (Fig. 7)
Oil on canvas, 72 x 102.5 cm. *S & D*: 1786.
Engraved in T Milton', Views of Seats, sixth set,
1793 no. xxiv. The village of Edenduffcarrick
has been left out. It stood close to the shore
near the castle and appears in a naive view of
the castle which probably dates from much the
same time as the Ashford. The Castle was
burnt in 1816. According to the Sotheby's catalogue 'Mrs. Siddons visited Shane's shortly
before the picture was painted and noted how
the guests would pluck their dessert from the
conservatory whilst the waves splashed outside,
and likened the luxury of the house to "an
Arabian Nights entertainment". During the
storms, however, the noise of the wind and
waves was considerable and spray is said to
have reached the attics of the castle'. Another
very similar picture of Shane's Castle exists
though much more open in aspect. It has
always been given to Ashford but it seems more
likely that it is by Jonathon Fisher whose
known work in the north of Ireland has considerable similarities.
Sotheby's 18 Nov. 1992, lot 68

32 **Tourin Castle**
Oil on canvas, 76.2 x 104.2 cm. *S & D*: 1786.
Exh. 1963, *Irish Houses and Landscapes*, Ulster
Museum, Belfast and the Municipal Gallery of
Modern Art, Dublin, no. 3. A pair with no.32.
Private collection.

33 **Scene on the Blackwater at Tourin,
Co. Waterford**
Oil on canvas, 76.2 x 104.2 cm. *S & D*: 1786
Exh. 1963, *Irish Houses and Landscapes*, Ulster
Museum, Belfast and Municipal Gallery of
Modern Art, Dublin, no. 4. A pair with no. 33.
Tourin Castle was the seat of Sir Richard
Musgrave
Private collection.

34 **The Powerscourt Demesne looking towards the
Sugar Loaf. Deer in the foreground**
Dimensions unknown. Possibly the picture
exhibited at the Royal Academy in 1789.
Private collection.

35 **The Gothic Dairy at Charleville,** (Fig. 10)
Oil on canvas, 106 x 127 cm. *S & D*: 1801.
In the foreground, a man is hauling to the side a
punt containing three figures.
Prov. The Earls of Charleville; Allen and
Townsend Dublin, 1. Nov. 1948; Leger Gallery,
May 1973.
Christie's 12 July 1991, lot 67.

36 **The River on the Charleville Estate at
Tullamore** (Fig. 11)
Oil on canvas, 106 x 129 cm. *S & D*: 1801. *Prov.*
The Earls of Charleville; Allen and Townsend,
Dublin 1 Nov. 1948; Leger Galleries, May 1973.
There are three figures and a dog on a path to
the left and a man, by a rock in the foreground.
Christie's 12 July 1991, lot 68.

18. William ASHFORD (c.1746-1824): The stables,
from the Mount Merrion Album. 1806.
(Cat.no. C5).

19. William ASHFORD (c.1746-1824): The wood-
house, from the Mount Merrion Album. 1806.
(Cat.no. C9).

37 **A Landscape with Fisherman in the Park at
Charleville**
Oil on canvas, 102 x 126 cm. *S & D*: 1801. *Prov.*
The Earls of Charleville ; Leger Gallery, 1950;
M. Bernard, 1972;
The National Gallery of Ireland

38 **The River with trees and a Rustic Bridge on the
Charleville Estate at Tullamore.**
Oil on canvas, 101.6 x 127 cm. *S & D*: 1801. *Exh.*
1801, Society of Artists, Dublin, one of five views
by Ashford, nos, 5, 51, 58, 71 and 78. A gardener
sweeps the path and three men, two virtually in
the river, may be fishing, though they hold no
rods. Another man stands on the bridge. One
picture is now not known and of the other four it
is impossible to tell which is which, as no titles
were given but nos. 35-38, above, are four of the
set of five. The pictures are discussed in Edward
Malins and the Knight of Glin, *Lost Demesnes,*
London, 1976, p. 88 and illus. 97, 98, 99.
Private collection.
THE FOLLOWING SIX PICTURES, NOS.39-44, WERE
ALL COMMISSIONED BY LORD FITZWILLIAM AND
THOUGH ONLY ONE IS DATED (1804) IT SEEMS
LIKELY THAT THEY WERE ALL PAINTED BETWEEN
ABOUT 1804 AND 1806, THE DATE ON THE TITLE-
PAGE OF THE BOOK OF DRAWINGS OF TWENTY
-FOUR OTHER VIEWS OF THE PARK, DISCUSSED IN
THE ARTICLE, ABOVE.

39 **Mount Merrion Park looking towards the sea.**
Oil on canvas, 64.1 x 111.1 cm. A small part of
Howth can be seen; most of the left hand back-
ground is hidden by trees. Deer are prominent
in the foreground.
Fitzwilliam Museum, Cambridge.

40 **Mount Merrion Park looking towards the Hill
of Howth.**
Oil on canvas, 61.9 x 111.1 cm. *Signed.* Two
men are on the terraced walk and are said to be
Lord Fitzwilliam giving orders to his steward.
Fitzwilliam Museum, Cambridge.

41 **Mount Merrion Park**
Oil on canvas, 95.9 x 131.5 cm. *S & D*: 1804. A
large classical portico to the left and a number
of figures, including children and dogs.
Fitzwilliam Museum, Cambridge.

42 **Mount Merrion Park** showing the Lodge.
Oil on canvas, 64.8 x 76.2 cm. Viscount
Fitzwilliam's house with two other buildings to
the right and left, and a carriage and four
approaching the main house.
Fitzwilliam Museum, Cambridge.

43 **Mount Merrion Park** showing part of the Lodge
and Stables and two columns on the right.
Oil on canvas, 62.2 x 76.2 cm. Signed.
Fitzwilliam Museum, Cambridge.

44 **Mount Merrion Park** showing a pool among
rocks with deer. Oil on canvas, 64.8 x 76.6 cm.
The view is near Mountainville Gate.
Fitzwilliam Museum, Cambridge.

45 **The classical portico of the Temple in the park
at Mount Merrion.**
Oil on canvas, 91.5 x 128.2 cm. *Signed.* Exh.
1805, Royal Academy, no 32.
Lit. E. Malins and the Knight of Glin, *Lost
Demesnes,* 1976 p.10 and illus. p.116. This picture is a version of no. 41, above, Fitzwilliam
Museum no. 462, with considerable differences
in the figures, details of trees etc. Presumably it
was painted at much the same time as the
Fitzwilliam Museum series. It is a view of a now
demolished summer house.
*Christies' 17 April 1964, lot 46; 15 July 1983,
lot 25.*

46 **The North Terrace Walk at Mount Merrion**
Oil on canvas, 91.5 x 128.2 cm. This was sold as
pair to no. 45 and is a version of no. 447 in the
Fitzwilliam Museum. (no. 40 above)
Christie's 17 April 1964, lot 45

VIEWS OF DUBLIN OR THE COUNTRYSIDE IN THE
IMMEDIATE VICINITY

47 **Dublin Bay from the Charter School, Clontarf.**
(Fig. 17)
Oil on canvas, 69 x 126 cm. *S & D*: 1794. *Lit.*
Michael Wynne, 'William Ashford and the
Royal Charter School', *Irish Georgian Society,*
Oct.-Dec.1967 pp.20-24.
National Gallery of Ireland.

48 **Monkstown Castle with Dublin Bay**
Oil on canvas, 91.5 x 127 cm. *S & D*: 1794. *Exh.*
1963, *Irish Houses and Landscapes,* Ulster
Museum, Belfast and the Municipal Gallery of
Modern Art, Dublin, no. 1, ill. no. 14
Arthur Guinness and Son

49 **Dublin from the Phoenix Park**
Oil on canvas, 129 x 191 cm. *S & D*: 1797.
This panoramic view is taken from a point of
view closer to the city than that in the
National Gallery of Ireland painting, no. 52,
below. The Magazine Fort, which is prominent
in the latter, is omitted but a number of
mounted figures, probably soldiers, approach
along the road. A pair with no. 50, both were
donated to the Brighton Museum by the Earl
of Chichester in 1891. Presumably, therefore,
they were commissioned or bought by the second Earl who was Lord Lieutenant in 1788 and
again in 1795. They cannot be the pictures
exhibited at the British Institution in 1809,
nos. 293 and 304, which were smaller measuring with frames 114.3 x 152.4 cm.
Brighton Museum and Art Gallery

50 **Dublin from Clontarf, Haymakers in the
foreground**
Oil on canvas, 129 x 191 cm. *S & D*: 1797. For
details of provenance, see no. 49 above, with
which this is a pair.
Brighton Museum and Art Gallery

51 Dublin from Clontarf
Oil on canvas, 114 x 183 cm. A pair with no. 52. These two pictures came from the Camden collection and were therefore presumably commissioned by the second Earl, later first Marquess Camden, when he was Lord Lieutenant, 1796-98.
National Gallery of Ireland.

52 Dublin from Chapelizod
Oil on canvas, 114 x 183 cm. For details of provenance, etc. see no. 51 with which this is a pair.
National Gallery of Ireland.

53 Dublin Bay towards the Dublin mountains
Oil on canvas, 59.5 x 84 cm. S & D: 1798
Sotheby's 20 Nov. 1985, lot 83

54 Ireland's Eye with Lambay in the distance, from Howth
Oil on canvas, 92.5 x 126 cm. S & D: 1808.
Probably Exh. 1809, British Institution, no. 289, 3.9 x 4.9 ft. (114.3 x 144.8cm including frame)
Sotheby's 20 March 1974, lot 27.

55 Howth harbour and Ireland's Eye beyond.
(Fig. 9)
Oil on canvas, 50.8 x 71.1 cm.
A pair with no. 56.
Private collection.

56 A village with many ruined buildings by a lake, mountains in the background. (Fig. 8)
Oil on canvas, 50.8 x 71.1 cm. A pair with no. 55. One of these is S & D: 1821. There are peasants talking in the foreground with a dog and cattle. The landscape is not identifiable, but might be by Carlingford Lough with the Mourne Mountains in the background.
Private collection.

57 Ireland's Eye from Howth.
Oil on canvas, 94 x 124.5 cm. Figures in the foreground with a horse and cart. This view became popular in the nineteenth century and is probably a late work by Ashford.
The Richard Wood Collection, on loan to the University of Limerick.

58 Dublin Bay from Clontarf.
Oil on canvas, 92.7 x 129.5 cm. Exh. 1963, *Irish Houses and Landscapes*, Ulster Museum, Belfast and the Municipal Gallery of Modern Art., no 2; 1972, *Irish Art in the 19th century*, Rosc, Crawford Art Gallery, Cork, no. 2. *Lit.* Michael Wynne,' William Ashford and the Royal Charter School Clontarf, County Dublin' *Irish Georgian Society Bulletin* Oct-Dec 1967 p.24. This picture appears to have been painted from the grounds of Lord Charlemont's estate at Marino. It probably dates from the first decade of the nineteenth century when Ashford painted several views of Dublin Bay.
Arthur Guinness and Son

59 A Wooded River Landscape looking towards the Sugar Loaf from the Scalp, Co Wicklow.
Oil on canvas, 110.5 x 144.7 cm.
Christie's 24 June 1977, lot 67

60 Romantic Landscape, the River Dargle, Co Wicklow.
Oil on canvas, dimensions unknown.
Exh. 1800, Society of Artists of Ireland, no. 27 possibly as *The Dargle in the County Wicklow*; 1988, Royal Hibernian Academy of Arts 158th Exhibition. A party of fashionable picnickers are commenting on the scenery on the right hand side of the picture. This gorge in the Dargle was a very popular subject in the eighteenth century.
Royal Hibernian Academy, Dublin.

61 Capriccio view of Bray Head and the Hill of Howth
Oil on canvas, 100.3 x 137cm. *Exh.*1908, Winter Exhibition of Old Masters, Dublin, no. 122, lent by Lord Massey
Christie's 18 Nov. 1983, lot 84

20. William ASHFORD (c.1746-1824): A view near the great willow, from the Mount Merrion Album. 1806. (Cat.no. C12).

21. William ASHFORD (c.1746-1824): View from the rear of the ash-grove, from the Mount Merrion Album. 1806. (Cat.no. C23).

VIEWS OF IDENTIFIED PLACES OUTSIDE DUBLIN

62 A Watermill near Lucan (Fig. 16)
Oil on canvas, 68.5 x 101.5 cm. *Signed.*
*Exh.*1975, Cynthia O'Connor and Co., Dublin, 'Irish Paintings and Drawings', no.1. This catalogue informs us that to-day, 'a similar view can be observed from the bridge over the Griffin stream, with the town [Lucan] in the distance on the left and Moat Hill on the right. While only part of the mill remains, the race still runs under what is now the paved road. The figures on the hill in the picture walk, we presume, in the grounds of Canon Brook House, where James Gandon, Ashford's close friend, lived for fifteen years.' The only mill scene Ashford exhibited was *A Mill at Beggarsbush*, Society of Artists, London, 1791. As, however, the topography still suits the Lucan mill, the identification is probably correct. *Lit.* Col Grant, *Old English Landscape Painters from the XVI century to the XIX century*, (London, 1959), Vol IV, p.266, illus. p.266, no 275.
Sotheby's 26 March 1975, lot 13 and 13 March 1985, lot 81.

63 Figures on a Beach below a Castle, said to be Conway Castle.
Oil on canvas, 34 x 49.55 cm. The figures appear to be fisher folk. Two boats are drawn up on the beach. From the description given by the Critic of the 1800 exhibition, this is not the Conway Castle exhibited in that exhibition.
Sotheby's 14 Sept. 1977, lot 11

64 Llyn Gwynant, Caernavonshire
Oil on canvas, 46.5 x 6.8 cm.
Sotheby's 9/16 July 1986, lot 283

65 Cloghoughter Castle, Co. Cavan
Oil on canvas, 62 x 85 cm
A group of tourists dressed in costumes of the 1790s are examining the ruins. Their two boats are drawn up on the shore of the island. According to Strickland, this picture belonged to Lord Farnham who sold it in June 1827 when it was bought by an English dealer, Peacock. *The Richard Wood Collection*, on loan to the University of Limerick.

66 The park at Emo, Co. Laois, looking towards the temple and Spire Hill .
Dimensions unknown. Cows graze in the foreground.
Private collection.

67 View perhaps of the lake at Killarney
Oil on canvas, 86 x 105 cm. Two men on the bank look towards two approaching in a boat.
Private collection.

UNIDENTIFIED VIEWS AND SUBJECT PICTURES, DATED

68 Landscape with Sheep and Goats
S & D: 1777. *Lit.* Crookshank and Glin, *The Painters of Ireland*, p. 136, fig 22.
Private collection.

69 A Morning Landscape with a Triumphal Arch
Oil on canvas, 109 x 149.2 cm. S & D: 1777. A pair with no. 70. This has also been called 'Evening: A River scene with town, and ruined arch among trees' (ill. as such *Apollo*, July 1963, Frank Sabin Gallery and 'A wooded river landscape with shepherd and his dog resting a ruined classical arch and distant town'.
Christie's 16 July 1965, lot 112

70 An Evening Landscape with Mercury and Argus
Oil on canvas, 109 x 149.2 cm. S & D: 1777. A pair with no. 69. This has also been called 'Morning : A Coast scene with the story of Mercury and Argus' and 'A rocky coastal landscape with Mercury and Argus and ruins on a cliff.' Despite the different titles and minor differences in the photographs (perhaps due to cleaning). I think there is only one version of this pair of landscapes.
Christie's 16 July 1961, lot 111

71 Mountainous river landscape with ruins and a town in the background. (Fig. 15)
Oil on canvas, 111 x 151 cm. S & D: 1778. There is a bridge over the river and in the foreground a peasant girl riding, talking to a man who may be in charge of the goats. It is an imaginary view.
National Gallery of Ireland.

72 Jacques and the Wounded Deer (Fig. 13)
Oil on canvas, 79 x 104 cm. S & D: 1786. A figure reclining within the wood looking at a stag by the banks of the river. This picture is almost certainly *Jacques and the Wounded Deer* from *As You Like It* (Act 2, scene 1) which Ashford exhibited in the Society of Artists in London in 1795, no. 193 as 'Jacques Description' and again in the British Institution, 1808, no. 210. Here the measurements are given as 3 x 4 ft, (91.4 x 121.9 cm inclusive of frame), which would be possible if the frame was fairly slight. It is the only example the author knows of autumnal colouring in Ashford's work.
Private collection.

73 An extensive river landscape
Oil on canvas, 74 x 100 cm. S & D: 1796. A pair with no. 74. *Prov.* Aldric Young (Antiques) Edinburgh, 1965;
Sotheby's 4 April 1973, lot 42.

74 A Wooded River Landscape with a bridge and a mill in the foreground.
Oil on canvas, 74 x 100 cm. S & D: 1796. A pair with no.73. *Prov.* Aldric Young (Antiques Edinburgh, 1965);
Sotheby's 4 April 1973, lot 43

22. William ASHFORD (c.1746-1824): Limerick. (Cat.no. A5).

75 *Lake Scene with a man fishing* with his wife and dog and an urn on a pedestal behind them
Oil on canvas, 76.2 x 101.6 cm. S & D: 1797.
Leger Galleries l950.

76 *Wooded Rocky River Scene with two sportsmen*
Oil on canvas, 66 x 99 cm. S & D: 1799
Christie's 28 July l961.

77 *Wooded landscape* with peasants driving cattle, sheep and goats along a path.
Oil on canvas, 50.8 x 71.1 cm. S & D: 1809.
Extensive ruins and a mountain are seen in the background.
Christie's 20 Nov. l981, lot 75.

UNIDENTIFIED AND UNDATED LANDSCAPES

78 *River Landscape with castle and figures*
Oil on canvas, 95.2 x 134.5 cm
Christie's 20 April l990, lot 64.

79 *A Wooded River Landscape* with labourers resting and cattle watering
Oil on canvas, 73 x 94 cm.
Christie's 27 March l981, lot 87.

80 *Sportsman in a Wooded River*
Oil on canvas,89 x 124 cm. Landscape with a house on a hill in the background.
Sotheby's 9 July l980, lot 97.

81 *Landscape with Haymakers and a Distant View of a Georgian House*
Oil on canvas, 76 x 106.5 cm. *Exh.*1982, Yale Center of British Art, Louis Hawes, *Presences of Nature, British Landscape l780-l830*
Private collection.

82 *Landscape and a distant view of the sea.*
Dimensions unknown.
Private collection.

83 *Paesaggio con figure e Animale* (Landscape with figures and Animals)
'Lord W'm Fowler' sale, Milan, 12/15 Dec. l955, lot 173

84 *A Ravine*
Oil on canvas, 68.6 x 90.2 cm. This could be a view of the River Dargle.
Christie's 12 April l920, lot 102

85 *A Rocky River Landscape* with fishermen and other figures in the foreground and a castle beyond. Oil on canvas, 75.5 x 99 cm.
Sotheby's 6 July l977, lot 123

86 *A wooded landscape with Lake and Herdsman.* A ruined chapel on the hillside
Oil on canvas, 39.1 x 50.5 cm.
Christie's 15 April l988, lot 53

87 *Horseman on a country lane with children playing by a gate* (Fig. 14)
Oil on canvas, 70 x 90 cm.
Sotheby's, 14 March l984, lot 68

88 *An extensive landscape* with travellers on a woodland track and others resting beside a river
Oil on canvas, 95.2 x 135.8 cm.
Christie's 20 April l990, lot 64.

89 *Cephalus and Procris*
Oil on canvas,71.2 x 91.4 cm.
Oscar and Peter Johnson Ltd.

90 *Landscape with castle and bridge with figures, cows and sheep*
Oil on canvas,58.4 x 73.7 cm.
Royal Dublin Society

91 *A river landscape with weir and a rocky bluff to the left.*
Oil on canvas, 96.5 x 119.4 cm.
Royal Dublin Society

92 *Wooded landscape with river and cows watering,* mountains in the background
Private collection.

DRAWINGS

A. This is a list of six drawings recently on the Dublin market which were signed on an additional piece of paper. They are in different media, and their titles are inscribed roughly, usually in the sky. They were all numbered but as there are two '3s', the present set cannot be the original sequence. They were approximately 17.8 x 11.4 cm

1 Inscribed 'A mill near Bantry' with the number 3 in the right hand corner.Pen, ink and wash.

2 Inscribed 'A mill near Bantry' but taken from another angle to the above. The number 2 is inscribed in the corner. Pen, ink and wash.

3 Inscribed 'Askeyton' with a number 6 in the right hand corner. Pencil.

4 The ruins of Timoleague Abbey. Inscribed 'Timoleague' with the number 4 in the right hand corner. Pencil.

5 Inscribed 'Limerick S: W' with a number 3 in the right hand corner. Pen and ink (Fig. 22)

6 Inscribed 'Limerick N W'. Pen and ink.

B. A single drawing of Drogheda, in pen, ink and watercolour, more highly finished than the set of six is almost certainly by Ashford. It is not inscribed.

C. This is a list of the drawings in the Mount Merrion Album in the Fitzwilliam Museum, Cambridge. Each drawing is in grey monochrome wash on paper, 32 x 43 cm. Most of the drawings are on paper with a watermark, 1801, but that of Lord Fitzwilliam's house at Richmond has a watermark dated l805.

1 Frontispiece, inscribed 'Mount Merrion/ 1806' in an oval medallion in the centre
2 The Lodge seen from the lawn
3 The Lodge seen from the east advance
4 The Lodge seen from the island
5 The stables (Fig. 18)
6 The kitchen garden
7 The lawn seen from the lodge
8 The lawn seen from the fir grove
9 The wood-house on the north terrace (Fig. 19)
10 View from the rear of the fir grove
11 View of the fir grove from the west side of the north avenue
12 View near the great willow (Fig. 20)
13 View from the gate in Owenstown avenue
14 View of the bay from the upper end of the north avenue
15 View near the spring in the warren
16 View of the north terrace from the upper end of the north avenue
17 View near the north terrace of the bay and hill of Howth
18 View near the gothic building of the bay and hill of Howth
19 View near Mount Anoillegate [Anville?]
20 The Gothic building at the end of the north terrace
21 View from the south side of the fir grove
22 View from the rear of the kitchen garden
23 View from the rear of the ash grove (Fig 21)
24 View near the farm
25 The farm

26 Lord Fitzwilliam's house at Richmond, fronting the garden
27 The rear of Lord Fitzwilliam's house on Richmond green.

WORKS EXHIBITED IN ASHFORD'S LIFETIME, NOW UNTRACED

(Works with titles such as 'Composition' or 'Landscape' are not listed).
Exhibited at the Society of Artists in Ireland
1770 *Dead Game*
Fruit and Dead Game
1771 *A Dog, Dead Game, etc.*
Dead game.
Ditto
A Trout from Nature
1772 *A View of Mount Kennedy, and part of Col. Cunningham's improvements*
A view of Tinney park
l773 *A View of Dunran wood and Kiltman castle,* illus Milton, sixth set, l793, Pl XXIV
View of St. Woolstans
Part of the domain of St. Woolstans
Cashell, from a gentleman's sketch
Portraits of dogs
A herring from nature
1777 *View of Chapelizod*
1780 *View of Part of the Sugar loaf hill*
View of Innisfallen Island
Exhibited at the Society of Artists of Great Britain
1790 *A View of Bangor*
A View of Carwyn
A View of Lanroost Bridge
View from Lanroost Bridge
View of Gen. Conway's Park, near Henley-on-Thames
The Aged Oak in As You like It
Exhibited at the Royal Academy, London
1785 *Lord Bessborough's Park, Ireland* one of these is Milton, third set 1785, plate IX
A second view of the same
1786 *Sullivan's Cascade*
1789 *View of Conway Castle, Wales*
View of an Irish Cabin
View of Donnybrook Road
1795 *View in Avon Dale Ireland*
1804 *Opening of the Docks at Ringsend*
Tollymore Park, Co. Down, Milton
1805 *Dublin and the Harbour from Mount Merrion*
1811 *Part of Hammersmith.*
Exhibited at the British Institution.
Measurements include frames.
1806 *Cecilia discovering Orlando under an oak*
1808 *A view in Avondale taken from Mount Merrion* 4 x 4.10 ft.
A View in Tollymore Park 4.0 x 4.10 ft.
1809 *View of Dublin from the Phoenix Park,* 3.9 x 5.0 ft.
View of Dublin Harbour from the back of Clontarf, 3.9 x 5.0 ft.
View of Loughlinstown, near Dublin, 3.9 x 4.9 ft.
Milton's Views of Seats adds, fifth set, l787, plate XIX, *Ballyfin,*

ACKNOWLEDGEMENTS
The author would like to thank Dr Edward McParland and Desmond FitzGerald, the Knight of Glin and Christie's for help in this article also Sotheby's who have been extremely generous in lending colour transparencies.

ANNE CROOKSHANK *was Professor of History of Art in Trinity College Dublin. She is co-author with the Knight of Glin of* The Paintings of Ireland *(c.1660-1920) (London, 1978) and* The Watercolours of Ireland: works on paper in pencil, pastel and paint, *c. 1600-1914 (Barrie & Jenkins, London 1994).*

SIR JOSHUA REYNOLDS AND RICHARD ROBINSON, ARCHBISHOP OF ARMAGH

Joshua Reynolds (1723-92) was the most successful British portrait painter of the latter half of the eighteenth century. Although he does not appear to have ever visited Ireland, he painted a large number of the most important members of the Anglo-Irish Ascendancy – landowners, peers and office holders. His Irish sitters included the first and second Dukes of Leinster, Emily, wife of the first Duke and her sister, Lady Louisa Conolly of Castletown.[1]

Richard Robinson (1709-94) as Archbishop of Armagh (1765-94) held the most important position in the Church of Ireland for the greater part of the latter half of the eighteenth century; he was also a notable patron of architecture in Ireland. Richard Robinson was on familiar terms with Reynolds and there is a copy of his *Seven Discourses delivered at the Royal Academy by the President*, first published in 1778, in Armagh Library with the inscription 'To His Grace The Lord Primate of All Ireland from the Author'.[2] Reynolds painted Richard Robinson's portrait on three separate occasions. These portraits are examined in this article in the context of Robinson's career and the way he self-consciously used portrait images to express and even reinforce his public image. Other portrait images of Archbishop Robinson are also considered.

Reynolds painted a small number of portraits of Irish bishops and clerics, including two archbishops, two bishops and two other Irish churchmen.[3] As with all of Reynolds's Irish sitters, the bishops and other clergy who sat for him for their portraits had close personal associations with England.

The Church of Ireland episcopacy occupied a significant position in the fabric of eighteenth-century Irish society. The majority of those appointed as bishops throughout the century were Englishmen.[4] Of English bishops, during the same period, John Ingamells had remarked that

They were, however, the Church's absolute aristocracy, as far removed from the Parish Priests as a Duke from his tenants. The Bishop was a nominated official of Royalty or government, but a life peer in an age of hereditary titles ... preferment finally rested on a combination of piety and learning, political loyalty and wealth.[5]

The see of Armagh was particularly important in the Irish

The eighteenth-century Irish Primate, who was an active patron of Irish architecture, was depicted in three separate portraits by Reynolds.
John Coleman *interprets the different images.*

1. Joshua REYNOLDS (1723-92): Portrait of Richard Robinson, Bishop of Killala. 1758. *Oil on canvas, 68 x 55 cm. (Private Collection, England).* Robinson (1709-94), the son of Yorkshire landed gentry, first came to Ireland in 1751 as Chaplain to the Lord Lieutenant, the Duke of Dorset. He was almost immediately appointed Bishop of Killala.

church, with its lineal descent from St Patrick. Its incumbent was the head of the church in Ireland and was usually named as one of the three Lords Justice who governed the country in the frequently long absences of the Lord Lieutenant.

Richard Robinson, like his predecessors as Archbishop of Armagh, was an Englishman. Born into a landed family, he was a younger son of William Robinson (1675-1720) of Rokeby, Yorkshire and Merton Abbey, Surrey.[6] He had been educated at Westminster School (1720-26) and Christ Church College, Oxford (1727-48).[7] He came to Ireland in 1750 as chaplain to the Lord Lieutenant, the Duke of Dorset and in the same year was appointed Bishop of the remote western diocese of Killala (1751-59).[8] He was advanced to Ferns (1759-61), then to Kildare (1761-65) and finally to Armagh.[9]

In 1758, while Bishop of Killala, Robinson sat to Reynolds for a bust-length portrait, referred to in the eighteenth-century as a 'head' (Private collection, England) (Fig. 1).[10] In 1763, while Bishop of Kildare, two years before his elevation to Armagh, he again sat to Reynolds, on this occasion for a splendid half-length. He presented this portrait to his Oxford college and it still hangs in the Dining Hall of Christ Church College (Fig. 2).[11] There is also a fine full-size copy of the picture in a private collection in Ireland which came from the house Robinson built for himself, Rokeby Hall, Co Louth.[12] There is a further signed version of this portrait in Church House in Armagh.[13] Finally, in 1775 he had himself painted in a three-quarter length, now in the Musée des Beaux Arts in Bordeaux (Fig. 3).[14] He also paid for a second version of the 1775 portrait painted by Reynolds in 1779, now in the Barber Institute, Birmingham (Fig. 4).[15] Contemporary engravings were made of both the 1763 and 1775 portraits, a popular method of promoting public recognition and repute.

As well as the Reynolds portraits there are other representations of Richard Robinson. In 1776 his Oxford college commissioned a bust in marble, by John Bacon the Elder RA (1740-99), (Christ Church College, Oxford) (Fig. 7).[16] There is another bust by Joseph Nollekens (1737-1823) on his memorial on the south aisle of Armagh Cathedral.[17] He had a medal engraved with his portrait on one side.[18] The medal, in bronze,

Sir Joshua Reynolds and Richard Robinson, Archbishop of Armagh

by William Mossop (1751-1805), the Dublin medallist, which was struck in 1789 to commemorate the construction of the Observatory in Armagh, bears the inscription 'The Heavens declare the Glory of God.' (Fig. 6).

As important public figures, bishops in eighteenth-century Ireland, as with their English counterparts, frequently had their

2. Joshua REYNOLDS (1723-92): Portrait of Richard Robinson, Bishop of Kildare. 1763. *Oil on canvas, 125 x 99 cm. (Christ Church College, Oxford).* Painted when the Bishop was fifty-four, this is his second portrait by Reynolds. As one of Robinson's first acts as Archbishop was to establish a library at Armagh, it is entirely appropriate that he should be shown holding a book.

portraits painted.[19] Perhaps the most often portrayed Irish bishop of the eighteenth century was George Berkeley (1685-1752), Bishop of Cloyne (1733-52).[20] The only contemporary Irish bishop portrayed as often as Richard Robinson was Frederick Augustus Hervey, Bishop of Derry and 4th Earl of Bristol, who

was painted by Pompeo Batoni, Angelica Kauffman, Vigeé Le Brun (twice) and Hugh Douglas Hamilton (twice).[21]

Reynolds's first portrait of Richard Robinson, painted in 1758, depicts the forty-nine-year-old bishop in a modest head size (Fig. 1). In it the bishop is shown full face wearing a white collar with two short, very broad, white bands and a short 'physical' wig. Wigs were generally worn by bishops throughout the eighteenth century; a reflection of the general pattern of wig wearing by males of the period as an essential reflection of masculine power and authority.[22]

Reynolds's second portrait of Richard Robinson, at Christ Church College, Oxford was completed in 1763 when he was aged fifty-four and Bishop of Kildare (Fig. 2).[23] The portrait has an inscription on the top right corner 'Richard Robinson DD Primate of all Ireland 1765', added after his elevation. The walls of the Hall of Christ Church College are lined with portraits of graduates, many of them bishops in the English and Irish churches. Robinson later paid for the construction, to the designs of James Wyatt, of the south side of Canterbury Quadrangle at the College, 1775-78, and the frieze bears a bold inscription recording his generosity. By 1783 he had donated £6,000 to the scheme.[24]

The half-length portrait shows Robinson wearing his official 'convocation dress' of white rochet and black chimere.[25] He is portrayed against a background of shaded pilasters, seated in an ample purple damask-covered armchair. Robinson's substantial form is shrouded in extensive draperies and the billowing lawn right sleeve of his rochet overflows from the chair and fills the centre of the canvas. The sitter's head is shown almost in profile as he turns in a contrapposto position to return the viewer's glance out of the corner of his right eye. We feel like intruders who have interrupted the prelate in the privacy of his studies. Yet, the portrait conveys a sense of calm, grand, benevolent authority and assurance.

Books are frequently deployed as emblems in portraits, particularly those of bishops, reflecting the requirement of scholarship for episcopal appointment.[26] It is particularly appropriate that Richard Robinson is shown seated before an open book. He had spent a large part of his life at Oxford and one of his first acts

SIR JOSHUA REYNOLDS AND RICHARD ROBINSON, ARCHBISHOP OF ARMAGH

when appointed to Armagh was to set about the establishment of a public library there. His personal collection of books, which formed the core of the Armagh Public Library, included a wide range of subjects reflecting his Enlightenment interests – Latin, Greek, philosophy, theology, medicine, law, history, travel, local history and agricultural innovation.[27]

Houston's mezzotint engraving, first produced in 1764, is a fine representation of Reynolds's work, particularly in the depiction of the background props and drapery.[28] Sitters frequently initiated publication of prints, including private plates for circulation among family members only. Robinson was interested in engravings and his gift to Armagh Library included a large collection. The timing of the commission, and the immediate production of a print after it, suggests that Robinson was producing an image for circulation and publicising of his name at a time when the vacancy in Armagh was about to occur.

There is an interesting drawing of the 1764 portrait in a notebook attributed to Reynolds, in the Ashmolean Museum, Oxford (Fig. 8), which is particularly worthy of consideration in an Irish context.[29] The notebook includes several drawings of known Reynolds portraits, as well as a number of landscape views of county Wicklow. Reynolds was planning a visit to Ireland in 1785 during the viceroyalty of his patron the Duke of Rutland; although in a letter to the Duke of 20 July he complained that the pressure of work would make such a trip difficult.[30] However, there is no evidence that the visit took place and it is difficult to assess whether the notebook is autograph as so little is known of drawings by the artist.[31] While it is very much a sketch, the drawing has none of the uncertainty or changes of composition which one would expect of a preparatory study. Such preparatory sketches as are known to be autograph are diffident and show much reworking and alteration.[32] The notebook is probably the work of a studio assistant and the study of Robinson is after the finished portrait.

Richard Robinson appears to have shared with his brother, Sir Thomas, a great interest in architecture and, having decided to reside at Armagh, he immediately commenced an extensive building programme there.[33] Arthur Young in 1776 was enormously impressed by the work which the Primate had carried out during his first eleven years in office.[34] He employed architect Thomas Cooley (1741-84) to build churches, restore the cathedral and to design and construct a new palace, an observatory and a public library.[35] Robinson also encouraged the young local architect, Francis Johnston (1760-1829), to train under Cooley and Johnson continued to work for the diocese after his master's death.[36]

The third portrait which Robinson commissioned from Reynolds, at the age of sixty-six, in 1775 is very different from the earlier studies (Fig. 3).[37] The portrait was especially well received at the Royal Academy exhibition of 1775 when Horace Walpole noted that it was 'most admirable' and, in a letter from Strawberry Hill dated 7 May 1775 to a friend, Rev William Mason, recorded his impression of the picture and its impact:

Sir Joshua has indeed produced the best portrait he ever painted, that of the Primate of Ireland, whom age has softened into a beauty; all the painters are begging to draw him, as they did for Reynolds' beggarman.[38]

The picture was especially admired by Robinson's cousin and

3. Joshua REYNOLDS (1723-92): Portrait of Richard Robinson, Archbishop of Armagh. 1775. *Oil on canvas, 142 x 115 cm. (Musée des Beaux-Arts, Bordeaux).* In this canvas Robinson is depicted more as a country gentleman than as an Archbishop and, true to form, he was raised to the peerage as Baron Rokeby of Armagh two years after the picture was painted.

4. Joshua REYNOLDS (1723-92): Portrait of Richard Robinson, Archbishop of Armagh. 1779. *Oil on canvas, 142 x 115 cm. (The Barber Institute of Fine Arts, University of Birmingham).* Commissioned from the artist as a version of the 1775 portrait (Fig. 3), this picture hung at Robinson's country seat, Rokeby Hall, Co Louth.

SIR JOSHUA REYNOLDS AND RICHARD ROBINSON, ARCHBISHOP OF ARMAGH

5. Thomas COOLEY (1741-84) and Francis JOHNSTON (1760-1829): Rokeby Hall, Co Louth. 1785-94. The original design was Cooley's but, after his death in 1784, building was supervised by Johnston whom Robinson had encouraged to study under Cooley.

friend, the fashionable Mrs Elizabeth Montagu (1720-1800), the celebrated author and London society figure for whom the phrase 'Blue Stocking' was coined due to her literary and intellectual gatherings.[39] It was probably at one of her gatherings, frequently attended by Reynolds and Dr Johnson, that Robinson first met the painter. It appears that she so admired the picture that the Archbishop gave it to her.[40]

Robinson's bulky, statuesque, grey-clad figure is turned to look at the viewer and silhouetted against the predominantly green-brown outdoor scene. The landscape includes a church spire, similar to the many Archbishop Robinson had built throughout the archdiocese of Armagh, and said to be that at Grange near the city. Instead of the usual 'convocation dress', the Archbishop is presented informally in outdoor clothes of a slate grey suit with matching kid gloves and wearing a tricorn hat, waistcoat and cummerbund of charcoal. Portraits of eighteenth-century bishops informally

attired are very rare. There is an elegant refinement about the limited range of colours and, while his clothes are sober, there is a secular feel to the image which marks him out as a gentleman rather than a cleric.

Continuing to promote his public image, Robinson allowed John Raphael Smith to engrave the portrait in mezzotint in 1775.[41] As Reynolds's 1763 portrait can be read as an attempt to publish an image of a candidate suitable for elevation to the archiepiscopal see of Armagh, the 1775 portrait can be read as an attempt to portray the sitter as a gentleman suitable for elevation to the ranks of the hereditary peerage. Robinson was created Baron Rokeby of Armagh in the Irish peerage in 1777 and the gentlemanly image anticipates this. Robinson also inherited the family's English baronetcy on the death of his brother William in 1785.

When Robinson commissioned from Reynolds a second version of the same picture in 1779 (Fig. 4) it had a secular function, to hang at his

6. William MOSSOP (1751-1805): Richard Robinson, Archbishop of Armagh (obverse); the Armagh Observatory (reverse). Bronze medal. Dated 1789. (*National Museum of Ireland*). The medal was struck to commemorate the construction of the Observatory.

SIR JOSHUA REYNOLDS AND RICHARD ROBINSON, ARCHBISHOP OF ARMAGH

newly-built seat, Rokeby Hall, Co Louth (Fig. 5). Although Robinson never married, Rokeby Hall was bequeathed to a member of his family and was the seat of the Robinson family until the middle of this century. While the 1779 version passed to Robinson's heirs to whom he left Rokeby Hall, the earlier (1775) version passed, via his cousin Mrs Elizabeth Montagu, to the heirs to his new title of Baron Rokeby.

The Robinson family estates at Rokeby Park in Yorkshire had been sold in 1769 by his bankrupt elder brother, Sir Thomas.[42] It is not surprising that Richard Robinson set about restoring the status and finances of his family. Archbishop Robinson added further to his personal dignities when he was made Prelate of the newly established Order of St Patrick on its foundation in 1783.[43] The 1775 portrait, in the possession of his cousin Mrs Montagu, was subsequently altered to incorporate the powder blue ribbon and the Prelate's badge of the Order, replete with its mitre (Fig. 3).

Richard Cumberland, the dramatist, whose father, Dr Denison Cumberland was Bishop of Clonfert (-1772) and Kilmore (1772-74), left a vivid and revealing account of Robinson, whose guest he was during his father's period in the latter see:

> splendid, liberal, lofty, publicly ambitious of great deeds and privately capable of good ones, … He supported the first station in the Irish hierarchy, with all the magnificence of a prince palatine.[44]

Cumberland gives a marvellous description of one event during his visit which illustrates the splendours of the prelate:

> I accompanied him on Sunday forenoon to the Cathedral. We went in his chariot with six horses attended by three footmen behind. Whilst my wife and daughters, with Sir William Robinson, the Primate's elder brother, followed in my father's coach, which he lent me for the journey. At our approach, the great western door was thrown open and my friend (in person one of the finest men that could be seen) entered, like another Archbishop Laud, in high prelatical state, preceded by his officers and ministers of the Church conducting him in files to the robing-chamber and back again to the throne.[45]

Robinson was a consummate public official and as such was successful in carrying out the functions demanded of an episcopal appointment in the eighteenth century. Equally his portraits self-consciously present the image of sobriety and moderation which he wished the public to see. The three portraits are progressively larger in scale and more confident in presentation but they never exceed in flamboyance the status of the position he occupied when they were painted.

JOHN COLEMAN is a civil servant and art historian. He is Secretary of the Irish Association of Art Historians and Chairman of the Visual Arts Committee of the Royal Dublin Society.

ACKNOWLEDGMENTS
I would like to acknowledge the assistance of the following in preparing this article: Dr Peter Cherry, Trinity College, Dublin; Paul Doyle, National Museum of Ireland; The Knight of Glin; David Logan, Diocesan Secretary, Armagh; Dr David Mannings; Elizabeth Powes, Paul Mellon Centre for British Art, London; Dr Catherine Whistler, Ashmolean Museum, Oxford and Dr Lucy Whittaker, Christ Church Picture Gallery, Oxford.

7. John BACON THE ELDER (1740-99): Bust of Richard Robinson, Archbishop of Armagh. c.1776. *Marble, life-size. (Christ Church College, Oxford).* Successively Bishop of Killala, Ferns, and Kildare, Robinson achieved his ultimate ambition in 1765 when he was appointed Archbishop of Armagh and Primate of Ireland.

8. Attributed to Joshua REYNOLDS (1723-92): Portrait of Richard Robinson, Archbishop of Armagh. *Pencil drawing (detail), from a sketchbook. (Ashmolean Museum, Oxford).* This drawing is probably a copy of Reynolds's portrait (Fig. 2) rather than a preparatory sketch.

1. This article is based on a chapter from a thesis submitted to Trinity College Dublin in 1993 (John Coleman, *Images of Assurance or Masks or Uncertainty: Joshua Reynolds and the Anglo-Irish Ascendancy*, unpublished M Litt thesis, Trinity College Dublin, 1993 – hereafter referred to as Coleman 1993). On Reynolds's Roman caricatures, which included several Irish gentlemen, see Cynthia O'Connor, 'The Parody of the School of Athens; The Irish Connection', *Bulletin of the Irish Georgian Society*, Vol. 26 (1983), pp.4-22. There are a number of articles in Irish periodicals which provide biographical information on Archbishop Robinson. These are: C Mohan, 'Archbishop Richard Robinson, Builder of Armagh', *Seanchas Ardmhacha* Vol. 6 (1971), no. 1, pp.94-130; G O Simms, 'The Founder of Armagh's Public Library: Sidelights on Primate Robinson, Baron Rokeby of Armagh', *Booklore*, Vol. 1 (1971); G O Simms, 'Archbishop Robinson', unpublished lecture, 1971 (Hereafter referred to as 'Simms 1971a'); G O Simms, 'The Founder of Armagh's Public Library', *Long Room*, Spring 1972, pp.139-49.

2. Simms 1972, p.140. Reynolds also wrote on one occasion to Robinson recommending his nephew, Rev Joseph Palmer, for a possible living in the diocese.

3. For further details on these portraits see Coleman1993, p.125, note 235.

4. Mohan 1971, p.98.

5. John Ingamells, *The English Episcopal Portrait 1559-1835: A Catalogue*, London (Published privately by the Paul Mellon Centre for Studies in British Art), 1981, p.1.

6. Mohan 1971, p.95. On Rokeby Park see Giles Worsley, 'Rokeby Park, Yorkshire', *Country Life*, 19 March 1987, pp.74-79; 26 March 1987, pp.176-79; 2 April 1987, pp.116-17.

7. Simms 1972, p.145. J Foster, *Alumni Oxoniensis 1715-1886*, Vol. 3, London, 1888, p.1,214.

8. Simms 1972, p.145; Mohan 1971, p.98; Richard Mant, *History of the Church of Ireland*, 2 vols, Dublin 1840, Vol. 2, p.604.

9. Mohan 1971, p.97. With the appointment to Kildare also went the position of Dean of Christ Church Cathedral in Dublin. His appointment to Armagh in 1765 is thought to have been largely due to the influence of the Lord Lieutenant, the Duke of Newcastle, to whom Robinson later erected a memorial in Armagh (Mant 1840, Vol. 2, p.632).

10. Robinson sat to Reynolds in 1758 as Bishop of Killala (Algernon Graves and William Vine Cronin, *A History of the Works of Sir Joshua Reynolds*, 4 vols, London, 1898-1901, Vol. 1, pp.553 and 827). A portrait, thought by Ellis Waterhouse to be the one referred to above, was sold at Sotheby's in 1987 and again at Christie's sale on 12 July 1990 (lot 44) (Fig. 1).

11. Graves and Cronin 1898-1901, pp.553 and 827-29. He sat again to Reynolds in 1767 and 1771, which might have been for the several versions of the 1763 portraits, though there is no discernible evidence from the portraits to distinguish one from another and to justify further sittings. A payment is recorded in the artist's ledger after 1762 which may have been for one of these. There are two replicas at Christ Church College.

12. Rokeby Hall was constructed 1785-94.

13. It was recorded in Robinson's will, as by Sir Joshua Reynolds.

14. The artist's pocket book for 1774/5 is missing so that sittings cannot be verified.

15. There has been some dispute over which of the portraits at the Barber Institute in Birmingham or the Musée des Beaux Arts in Bordeaux was commissioned in 1775 or copied in 1779. I believe the Bordeaux version, which passed from Robinson to his cousin, the famous bluestocking Mrs Montagu, to be the original as the inscription on the 1775 engraving by John Raphael Smith notes that the original was in the possession of Mrs Montagu (*Elizabeth Montagu: Queen of the Bluestockings, Her Correspondence 1720-1761*, 2 vols, ed. Emily J Clementson London, 1906, Vol. 2, p.vii). The version in the Barber Institute was acquired in Ireland in 1943 at the sale of the collection of Maud Robinson of Rokeby Hall (*Catalogue of The Barber Institute* 1952).

16. It was one of 4 busts for which Christ Church College paid John Bacon £259.7s.1d in 1776 (*A Christ Church Miscellany*, Oxford, 1946, pp.83-4; Mrs Reginald Lane Poole, *Catalogue of Portraits in the Possession of the University, Colleges, City and County of Oxford*, 2 vols, Oxford, 1926, Vol. 3, nos. 190, 191 and 192). A bust of Robinson, possibly a replica of that by Bacon, appeared on a table to the left of the sitter in a full length portrait of his protegé the architect Francis Johnston (see the Irish journal *Martello* 1991, p.2).

17. Illustrated in *St Patrick's Cathedral, Armagh*, Derby, 1991, p.5.

18. Anne Crookshank and the Knight of Glin, *Irish Portraits*, Dublin 1969, no. 189.

19. Ingamells 1981.

20. Raymond W Houghton, David Berman and Maureen T Lapan, foreword by John Kerslake, *Images of Berkeley*, Dublin, 1986.

21. Brian Fothergill, *The Mitred Earl: An English Eccentric*, London, 1974. Brinsley Ford, 'The Earl-Bishop: An eccentric and capricious Patron of the Arts', *Apollo*, June 1974, pp.426-34.

22. Marcia Pointon, *Hanging the Head: Portraiture and Social Formation in Eighteenth Century England*, London and New Haven, 1993.

23. A sitting is recorded in the artist's pocket-book for 1763/4 and payments by the Bishop of Kildare are recorded in the artist's ledger for 1763 of £52.10s.

24. Simms 1971, p.19; H M Colvin, *The History of Oxford University*, Vol. 5, The Eighteenth Century, ed. L S Sutherland and L G Michel, Oxford, 1986, p.850; Rev Henry L Thompson, *University of Oxford, College Histories: Christ Church*, London, 1900.

25. 'Convocation dress' is the dress worn out-of-doors, while preaching, as court dress, or in the House of Lords. It comprised rochet, chimere and tippet. The rochet is a white, long-sleeved, whole-length tunic. The chimere is a black, sleeveless overcoat, open in the front, worn over the rochet (Ingamells 1981, pp.47-51). The tippet, a black silk scarf, worn over the chimere is not visible in the Robinson portrait.

26. There are several portraits of Irish bishops with books, including a three-quarter length portrait of George Berkeley (1728) by John Smibert (National Portrait Gallery, London) and James Latham's (1696-1747) animated double portrait of Bishop Clayton and his wife (National Gallery of Ireland).

27. Simms 1972, pp.142-43.

28. Richard Houston (c.1721-75) was a pupil of John Brooke in Dublin and went to London in 1746. Of the 153 known mezzotints by Houston, 22 are after Reynolds (T Clifford, A Griffiths and M Royalton-Kisch, *Gainsborough and Reynolds in the British Museum*, London, 1978, p.43).

29. D B Brown, *Ashmolean Museum Catalogue of Drawings*, Vol. IV, pt. 2, Early British Drawings, p.521, '1514 Reynolds, Sir Joshua, attributed to, a sketchbook'.

30. *Letters of Sir Joshua Reynolds*, ed. F W Hilles, Cambridge, 1929, p.131

31. The views include several of Co Wicklow. F W Hilles doubted that the drawings were autograph.

32. Timothy Clifford, 'Drawings by Gainsborough and Reynolds' in Clifford et al, 1978, pp.1-8.

33. Richard Robinson subscribed to the second volume of James Gandon's *Vitruvius Britannicus* (Edward McParland, *Vitruvius Hibernicus*, London, 1985, p.19).

34. Arthur Young, *A Tour in Ireland 1776-1779*, Vol. 1, Shannon (Reprint), 1970, pp.117-20.

35. Robinson also contributed towards the cost of the observatory, school, hospital, gaol, barracks and other buildings.

36. Johnston became his official architect after Cooley's death in 1784 (Edward McParland, 'Francis Johnston, Architect, 1760-1829', *Bulletin of the Irish Georgian Society*, Vol. 12, no. 3-4 (July-September 1969), pp.61-139.

37. In June 1775 Reynolds received £73.10s from the Primate for the portrait (Graves and Cronin 1898-1901, Vol. 2, p.329 and Vol. 4, p.1399). The artist was paid £36.15s. for a copy in 1779.

38. C R Leslie and Tom Taylor, *Life and Times of Sir Joshua Reynolds*, London, 1865, p.128.

39. His cousin, Elizabeth Robinson, married on 5 August 1742 Edward Montagu, second son of the fifth son of the 1st Earl of Sandwich (DNB).

40. Mrs Montagu sat to Reynolds and Ramsay.

41. John Raphael Smith (1752-1812), regarded as one of the best engravers of his time, produced 41 mezzotints after Reynolds between 1774 and 1784 (Clifford et al 1978, p.51).

42. Rokeby Park, Barnard Castle, Co Durham, a Palladian house, was built in 1735 by his eldest brother Sir Thomas Robinson (d.1777). Sir Thomas Robinson was an amateur architect who overspent on extravagant building schemes, and was forced to sell the family estate at Rokeby in 1769.

43. Peter Galloway, *The Most Illustrious Order of St Patrick 1783-1983*, Chichester 1983, pp.12-13.

44. R Cumberland, *Memoirs of Richard Cumberland*, (Supplement), London, 1807, p.37-38.

45. *ibid*.

THE MUDDLED MALTONS

1. James MALTON (d.1803): The Custom House, Dublin (detail). *Watercolour, 54 x 77 cm. Signed and dated, James Malton del. 1793. (National Gallery of Ireland).*
The Custom House, completed in 1791, was designed by James Gandon in whose office James Malton is believed to have worked.

Confusing details about the Malton family are unravelled by **Maurice Craig**.

The Malton family, father Thomas and sons Thomas and James, have always been confusing and have sometimes been confused. All three died within a short space of time, in 1801, 1804 and 1803 respectively, and the 'Dublin' Malton (James) who in 1799 completed his famous series of drawings of the principal buildings in Dublin, was not the one who lived in Dublin for sixteen years and died there. In particular, the birth-date of James Malton is unknown.

There is, however, a contemporary source of information which seems so far to have been overlooked. The *Memoirs of William Hickey* (ed. Alfred Spencer, 1913), covering the years 1749 to 1775, contain two references to the Malton family. In 1772, Hickey was, rather incongruously, sent to Thomas Malton senior to be instructed in drawing, geometry and perspective. He describes Malton as 'having then a wife and six children, three boys and three girls. The eldest son (about sixteen) when an infant had the misfortune to fracture his leg so badly as to make amputation of the broken limb necessary ... the eldest girl, at the time the father came to attend me, was thirteen years of age, looking older, and very pretty. The rest of the children were infants' (Hickey, *op. cit.*, pp.281-82). In 1775, Hickey writes that he went to lodge with the Malton family, in 'a neat, new house, at Chelsea, exactly opposite the avenue leading up to Ranelagh. This family then consisted of himself, at that time about forty years of age, his wife, nearly the same, and remarkably well looking, a shrewd, sensible woman, a daughter, Ann, just turned sixteen, with a sweet and interesting countenance, their eldest son Thomas, already mentioned, and who was a year younger than his sister, Ann: and besides four younger children, two boys and two girls.' Hickey later refers to 'the sprightly playfulness of the little ones' (Hickey, *op. cit.*, pp.326-27).

It will be seen that these two accounts do not agree. The eldest son, Thomas junior, has, in the space of three years, regressed in age from sixteen to fifteen, and has changed places with his sister Ann. The age of Thomas senior, which Hickey gives as 'about forty' was, in 1775, actually forty-nine. Thomas, junior, whose birth-date is given by the Dictionary of National Biography and all modern writers as 1748, was actually born, as Howard Colvin established from the Royal Academy Admissions register, on 22 August 1752, which would make him about six years older than the ages imputed to him by Hickey.

Can we, therefore, believe Hickey at all? On his own admission he led such a dissolute life that it is a wonder to us that he can recall so many events in such detail, and perhaps this makes him suspect. It is very clear, however, that he knew the family well, and at least he is consistent about the number and distribution of the children (three boys, three girls); and he seems to classify all the younger children as being very young in 1772 and 1775.

This has a bearing on our principal crux, which is the approximate birth-date of James. I have argued elsewhere (M Craig, *Malton's Dublin Views in Colour*, Dolmen Press, Dublin, 1981, preface), that James Malton is likely to have been born either in about 1750 or in about 1764. We now know the earlier date to be impossible for James, though it may just suit for Thomas junior. The testimony of William Hickey, confused and contradictory though it be, supports the later date. He can hardly have invented the fact of Thomas junior's wooden leg, and this, too, seems to be something not otherwise recorded. The *Memoirs* are by no means an obscure book, but they do not seem to have been consulted by writers on the history of art. So 'our' Malton, James, must have been born about twelve years after his brother Thomas, and, if so, was about twenty-seven when he started doing his *Dublin Views* and about thirty-five when the last of them was issued.

DR MAURICE CRAIG is an Honorary Fellow of Trinity College Dublin and author of a number of books including The Architecture of Ireland (*Batsford, London 1982*) *and* Dublin 1660-1860 (*4th edition 1992*)

1. James GANDON (1743-1823) after Charles Louis Clerisseau: An Architectural Vignette. *Dated 1773. Wash drawing, 30.5 x 23 cm (Private collection.)* Clerisseau's works, exhibited at the Royal Academy in London in 1772, were popular with English collectors and several artists, including Gandon, were employed in copying them.

A James Gandon Discovery

Hugh Maguire

has located a previously unknown drawing by the great architect of eighteenth-century Dublin.

Before leaving London for Dublin in 1781, James Gandon's varied career in London included the publication of two volumes of *Vitruvius Britannicus* and the copying of architectural vignettes by Charles Louis Clerisseau (1721-1820). Clerisseau had exhibited at the Royal Academy, London, in 1772, the same year in which Gandon displayed his unexecuted elevation for the Royal Exchange, Dublin.[1] Such was Clerisseau's popularity with the English that artists were employed to copy his works – Gandon was among these.[2] But, although he established something of a reputation as a copyist, few of the drawings are known to have survived; Dr McParland records only two.[3] However, a further drawing (Fig. 1) has recently come to light in a private collection in Dublin and contributes, if only in a small way, to our knowledge of Gandon's activity as a copyist.

The drawing, measuring 30.5cm x 23cm, represents the vestibule of a ruined temple with figures variously disposed in the foreground. No watermark is evident and attempts to establish a provenance have proved unsuccessful. As if to avoid an identity crisis the drawing is signed in three places, with *J Gandon Sculpt 1778* written in pencil on the bottom right perimeter of the drawing. A further *J. Gandon* is visible on a fragment of stone towards the base of the drawing and to the right of this the date *1773* is inscribed. *J. Gandon* is also inscribed in brown ink on the reverse. Both dates on the drawing are within the period when Gandon resided at 21, Broad Street, Soho, and correspond with the dates of two similar drawings by him illustrated by McParland. Given the carefully delineated border and the inscriptions, it is possible, in the absence of evidence to the contrary, that the drawing was exhibited at the Royal Academy, London. While the subject matter does not correspond to his exhibits of 1774, it may relate to that of the following year, when he exhibited *Ruins: the vestibula of a temple* (No. 124).[4] The two other surviving drawings in this manner represent a similar subject and incorporate comparable motifs such as the grouped figures and somewhat stylised, damaged Corinthian capitals. However, they are of a different format and, being more finished, are more clearly exhibited drawings.

By 1773, in addition to his Royal Exchange entry, Gandon had won a Royal Academy medal for architecture and executed Nottingham Court House.[5] Surprisingly, therefore, many of the details in the drawing appear quite amateurish and display a certain inability in the representation of three-dimensional space. It is not, for example, immediately evident where the base of the second column from the left is meant to be. Such inadequacy was associated with Gandon throughout his career and in 1786 his draughtsmanship was doubted; his use of perspective was referred to as 'egregiously deficient'.[6] However, these drawings were intended as works of design where 'his talent lay' rather than draughtsmanship.[7] They reveal a concern with what has been defined as the 'visual effect of the ensemble'.[8] As architectural vignettes or 'vedute', they evoke the Antique and induce wonder at the architectural glories of the past. In discussing the erection of testimonials, Gandon himself felt that 'great dimensions must impress the spectator with astonishment'.[9] His spectators in this drawing seem oblivious to the grandeur of their surroundings and, in spite of Gandon's NeoClassicism, are comparable to actors on Baroque stage sets, intended to animate the scene and emphasise the great scale of the surrounding architecture. The figures appear carefree and light-hearted in the manner of those in 'vedute' by Giovanni Paolo Panini (1692-1765) such as his series of *Roman Ruins* (1740, Dublin, National Gallery of Ireland).

Although Gandon's drawing displays an interest in the Antique, it would be futile to seek similarities with later architectural designs or executed work. However, the absence of windows and the use of urns in niches, as depicted in the drawing, were motifs later employed by him, if not always executed.[10]

His ability as a copyist is witnessed by his invitation to St Petersburg in 1779, as an architect, by Princess Dashkof.[11] Both she and the Empress Catherine the Great were familiar with the work of Clerisseau. The Empress collected his drawings and also appointed him as her architect. It is unknown if Gandon's invitation had been to fulfil the role subsequently played by Clerisseau. If so, it is clear that in the eyes of some contemporaries at least, Gandon was considered comparable to Clerisseau. With the possibility of Gandon being appointed an architect in St Petersburg and the Empress Catherine's great collection of Clerisseau drawings, it becomes likely that further drawings of this nature by Gandon may also have been in that collection.

DR HUGH MAGUIRE is a lecturer in the History of Art in the University of Otago, Dunedin, New Zealand.

1. E J McParland, *James Gandon: Vitruvius Hibernicus*, London 1985, pp. 20-21, figs. 20, 21.
2. Algernon Graves, *The Royal Academy of Arts: A Complete Dictionary of Contributors and their work from the foundation in 1769 to 1904*. London, 8 vols, 1905; reprint, 1970, p.197
3. 103 'Ruins of a temple; stained drawing.' 104 'Ruin of a temple; stained drawing.' Graves *op. cit.* 1776:
4. University of London, Witt Collection.
5. T J Mulvany, *The Life of James Gandon Esq.*, London, 1846; fasc. reprint, 1969, pp.23-24.
6. James Malton, *Letters to Parliament*, Dublin 1786, p.208.
7. *Ibid*. Compare the detailed design of an architrave in the Fitzgerald Kenney Collection, National Library of Ireland, MS, 22016.
8. McParland, *op. cit.*, p.195.
9. 'Hints for Erecting Testimonials' in *The Life of James Gandon Esq.*, Dublin 1846. pp.275-82, p.277.
10. Fitzgerald Kenney album, National Library of Ireland, MS 22,015 acc. 3492. Microfilm Positive 8884 design for urn. See unexecuted villa design illustrated in McParland, *op. cit.*, p.143. See reference to absence of windows in his Royal Exchange submission: Dublin City Library, Gilbert Collection MS 135.
11. Mulvany, *op. cit.*, pp.40, 41.

THE ARCHITECTURE OF
ST PATRICK'S CATHEDRAL, DUBLIN

Dublin's Cathedral dates from the thirteenth century but its original appearance is disguised by nineteenth-century restoration. **Michael O'Neill** *discovered drawings which record its earlier architectural character.*

St Patrick's Cathedral, Dublin was heavily restored in the course of three campaigns during the nineteenth and early twentieth centuries.[1] Anyone attempting to unravel the architectural history of the building must take these restoration campaigns into account. The first of these, which was begun in 1845 and carried on well into the next decade, was undertaken by the Dean of the Cathedral, Henry Pakenham.

The English architect Richard Cromwell Carpenter (1812-1855) was engaged to conduct the restoration.

Carpenter was one of the best and most successful architects of his generation ... His friendship with Pugin was of great significance in the development of the Gothic revival in the Church of England ... It was he who pre-eminently brought Pugin's innovations into the mainstream of Anglicanism. His work is distinguished by exquisite colour, harmony, scholarship and control.[2]

He was one of the 'approved' architects of the Cambridge Camden Society, later the Ecclesiological Society. A paragraph from his obituary in that society's journal is worth quoting:

Nor was Carpenter merely an architect; his acquaintance with symbolism and instruments of worship was great, and his resources in them never at fault. But, above all, his eye for colour was exquisite ... we think that he was superior to Pugin, safer and more equitable.[3]

The Ecclesiologist carried reports on the restoration plans in 1844 and 1845 and in the volume for 1850, a sixteen page supplement penned by Pakenham was included. A final report in the 1865 volume reviewed the later Guinness restoration.[4]

A series of drawings of the proposed restoration was published for Carpenter by Thomas Bury.[5] These drawings, including a valuable plan of the Cathedral, concentrate on the choir and Lady Chapel; it was planned to restore the latter as a chapel for the Knights of St Patrick. According to one commentator, Carpenter was 'likely to secure lasting fame by his designs'.[6]

This restoration campaign seems to have been hampered from the beginning by lack of cash. The initial subscription fund quickly ran out and with the beginning of the famine in 1846 contributions dried up. In 1850, the Lady Chapel was apparently still only one third restored, some stone work had been replaced in the choir, and the aisle windows had been rebuilt in lancet form.[7] This piecemeal approach to the restoration eventually forced Carpenter to resign the commission. In his obituary it is stated:

Carpenter likewise furnished complete and extremely beautiful plans for the restoration of St Patrick's, Dublin, which were unfortunately laid aside in favour of very questionable, bit by bit, and almost amateur, achievements'.[8]

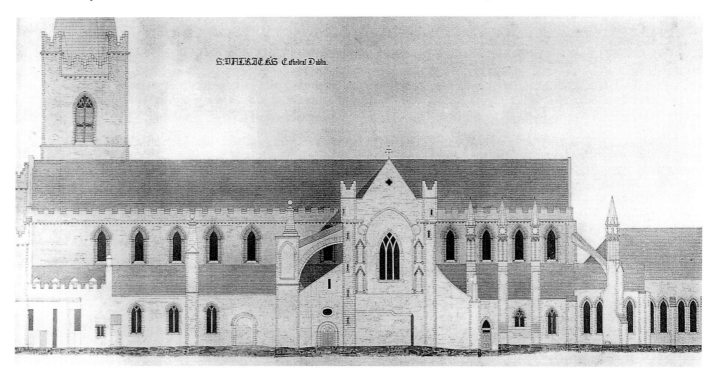

1. Richard Cromwell CARPENTER (1812-55): St Patrick's Cathedral, Dublin in 1845. South Exterior. This drawing from a series recently discovered in the Cathedral archives shows the condition of the building prior to the nineteenth- and early twentieth-century restoration campaigns.

The Architecture of St Patrick's Cathedral, Dublin

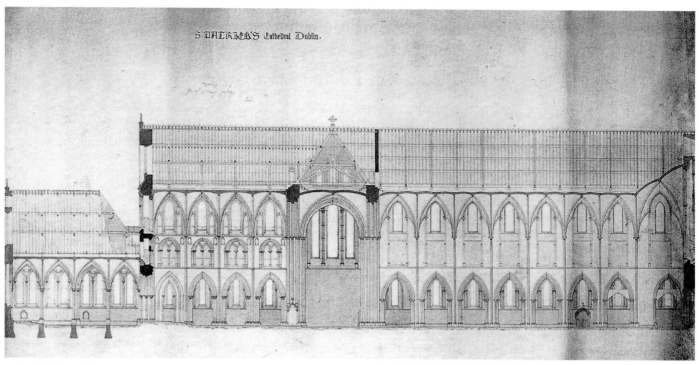

2. Richard Cromwell CARPENTER (1812-55): St Patrick's Cathedral, Dublin. South interior as Carpenter proposed to restore it. His 'complete and extremely beautiful plans were unfortunately laid aside'.

As well as the published series of drawings by Bury mentioned above, there is also a further series of plans and elevations by Carpenter which records the condition of the cathedral as he found it in 1845 and his restoration designs. These drawings had lain unknown and uncatalogued in the Cathedral until recently rediscovered and identified by the author. It is difficult to over-estimate the value of these records of the Cathedral prior to the restoration campaigns. On the one hand they enhance Carpenter's reputation as a scholarly and conscientious restorer. They are also invaluable in our attempt to understand the architectural history of the Cathedral, its English design sources, and its place in the context of Gothic building in Ireland.

Two elevations by Carpenter are illustrated: one records the south exterior elevation before restoration (Fig. 1), the other shows the south interior elevation as Carpenter proposed to restore it (Fig. 2). His schemes for the interior restoration followed very closely the original elevation (from what we know from the surviving fabric and from other views and accounts). The additional or replacement decoration he intended for the west front, the transept gables, and the work actually carried out to his design on the Lady Chapel, are close to features found at Wells and Salisbury for example, but are patently his additions to the fabric.[9]

It is interesting to compare Carpenter's interior elevation with what is now extant. Detached colonettes on bases supporting capitals were added to the clerestory of the choir by Sir Thomas Drew at the turn of the century. Carpenter had planned to retain the simple continuous rolls on bases around the main opening in each bay, a feature with a long English West Country pedigree. The most striking features in the nave are the combined upper storeys and the trefoil shape of the vault wall-rib. During the Guinness restoration a triforium arcade was 'added' to the nave elevation and the vault was restored in lath and plaster.

This very brief analysis of one of Carpenter's elevations shows the value of these drawings in aiding our understanding of the architectural history of the building. If the resources had been available to carry through Carpenter's scheme, St Patrick's may well indeed have stood as one of the pinnacles of his career as a restorer of great sensitivity and architectural imagination.

MICHAEL O'NEILL is engaged in post-graduate research on the architecture of St Patrick's Cathedral at Trinity College Dublin.

1. A recent discussion of the restorations may be found in M O'Neill, 'Marks of Unheeded Dilapidation' The nineteenth and early twentieth century restorations. St Patrick's Cathedral 800 series, Dublin 1991. See also Edwin C Rae, 'The Medieval Fabric of the Cathedral Church of St Patrick in Dublin', JRSAI, 109, 1979, pp.29-73, and J H Bernard, The Cathedral Church of St Patrick, (Bell's Cathedral Series), London 1903.
2. Macmillan Encyclopedia of Art.
3. The Ecclesiologist, XVIII, June 1855, pp.137-42.
4. The Ecclesiologist, IV, 1844, pp.190-91; V, 1845, pp.204-06; X, 1850, pp.326-27; Xi, 1850, supplement pp.1-16; XXVIII, 1865, pp.87-108.
5. Thomas T Bury, Restoration at St Patrick's Cathedral, Dublin. Seven plates, five drawn and lithographed by T Bury. R C Carpenter, architect. 1847.
6. The Ecclesiologist, V, 1845, p.204.
7. ibid., X, 1850, p.327.
8. ibid., XXVIII, pp.137-42.
9. M O'Neill, op. cit., pl.22 for the proposed restoration of the west front.

A FIRM OF DUBLIN CABINET-MAKERS
MACK, WILLIAMS & GIBTON

Angela Alexander *has located several items of furniture which were produced by this important firm between the years 1812 and 1829.*

1. MACK, WILLIAMS & GIBTON: Mahogany breakfront serving table bearing the trade label of the firm. Made for Lord Bellew, Jenkinstown, Co Kilkenny, c.1825-29.

2. Detail of Fig.1 showing one of the richly carved imposing sea-creatures which support the table.

The furniture examined in this article forms an important group produced by the Dublin cabinet-makers Mack, Williams and Gibton between 1812 and 1829. It gives, however, only a sample of the varied work of this long lived and successful partnership, one of many firms of cabinet-makers who were in business in Dublin in the nineteenth century, as indicated by trade directories of the period.

The work of Mack, Williams and Gibton is distinctly recognisable, possessing, as it does, an individual and particular quality in their choice of the finest wood, richly figured, their use of ornament and the quality and individualism of their carving. A detail of a massive serving table, (Fig. 1) showing a magnificent sea creature, one of four imposing creatures which support the table, has carving of the highest quality.[1] They have lion heads and their bodies are covered with acanthus scrolls which emerge from scaly twisted fish tails (Fig. 2). The table already bore the trade label of Mack, Williams and Gibton but when it was dismantled, a second label was discovered with 'Lord Bellew, Kilkenny' written on it. A photograph dating from around 1900, of the dining room at Jenkinstown, Co Kilkenny, a Gothic mansion built in the early nineteenth century to the designs of William Robertson, shows this table *in situ*.[2]

The partnership of Mack, Williams and Gibton was established in 1812 after the death of Robert Gibton who had founded the firm with John Mack in 1803. John Mack is first listed in the Dublin Trade Directories as a cabinet-maker at no.188 Abbey Street between 1784 and 1800, during which period he also advertised frequently in the *Dublin Evening Post* as an 'Upholder and Auctioneer'. In 1801 he supplied beds to Lettyville for the Dillon family of Clonbrock, Co Galway.[3] A document dated 18 March 1803,[4] which shows that Mack lived and worked at no. 39 Stafford Street, Dublin, registered his purchase of the adjoining premises, no. 40 Stafford Street, an indication that his business was expanding. A charming billhead, from Peter Eggleso to the Provost of Trinity College,[5] (Fig. 3) giving an idea of the elegant shop facades of Georgian Dublin, shows Eggleso's shop-front at no. 41 Stafford Street, next door to Mack's premises..

The earliest surviving accounts of the Board of Works[6] indicate that John Mack supplied them with furniture in 1802. Furniture was also supplied to the Board by Peter Eggleso and by Hall Kirchoffer, who was in business at no. 62 Henry Street from 1796 until 1812. By 1806, however, it is clear, from these

MUN|P|4|214

3. Bill-head of Peter Eggleso, no.41 Stafford Street, Dublin. Eggleso's shop – shown on the bill-head – was next door to John Mack's in 1803.

4. Bill-head of George Gillington, Dublin, dated 1837. The Gillingtons were contemporaries of Mack, Williams & Gibton in the Dublin furniture trade.

accounts, that John Mack had become the principal supplier to the Board, superseding the other two cabinet-makers.

The Board of Works was a government board with an appointed architect who was in charge of official architecture.[7] It was re-organised in 1802 but its system of patronage did not alter, and the Lord Lieutenant continued to spend freely. By 1811, complaints were made that Francis Johnston, who had been appointed in 1805 as Architect to the Board, had a lax control over estimates and costs were rising. The Board was disbanded in 1831 and reconstituted in 1836 by Act of Parliament. In 1807 John Mack received his official appointment from the Board and was allowed to place the King's Arms and Royal Tablets over the door of his premises, as seen in the bill-head of Peter Eggleso.[8] Furniture supplied to the Board furnished the State Apartments and other rooms at Dublin Castle, the Four Courts, the War Office, the Barracks Office, the Treasury and the Viceregal Lodge, now Aras an Uachtarain. The Board remained remarkably faithful to its suppliers and was a steady source of income to them. In 1802-1803, the account of John Mack totalled £265. 9s. 11d.; this increased to £2925. 7s.7d.in the 1803-1804 period, indicating a major refurbishing project. For 1804-1805, John Mack's bill amounted to £1782. 18s.5d. and in the last year of this surviving abstract account, 1805-1806, his total was £823. 0s. 11d. John Mack's position as principal supplier of cabinet and upholstery work continued through the Mack and Gibton partnership and throughout the Mack, Williams and Gibton alliance between 1812 and 1829.

From 1801 to 1806, Mack and Gibton are listed in the Directories at no. 188 Abbey Street and no. 39 Stafford Street, both the property of John Mack. From 1803, Mack and Gibton also advertised frequently as auctioneers, selling a variety of lands and properties. The partnership may have initially been formed to allow John Mack to expand his business; perhaps Robert Gibton brought a particular talent and expertise in the areas of design and craftsmanship. At this date John Mack is the

more established of the two and possesses capital. The partnership appears to have been formalised in 1805 from which date the Board of Works accounts are drawn to Mack and Gibton.[9] Robert Gibton is listed in the Directories at no. 21 Aungier Street from 1790 to 1793, and at no. 28 Aungier Street from 1794 to 1796. From 1800 to 1806 he is listed as cabinet-maker, upholder and auctioneer at 10 Stephen Street (sic). Robert Gibton's trade card appears on a deed box in the National Museum.[10] He publicises himself as a maker and seller of trunks, portmanteaus, gun cases and musical instrument cases and states that he is a new beginner. Robert Gibton's father, William, had died young and he had served an apprenticeship with one William Fernsly for a term of seven years.[11]

An apprentice was expected to have a good appearance and a good standard of education. He had to obey his master and complete an agreed term of years; the master in turn ideally fulfilled the role of a father and passed on his skills[12] in return for a fee which varied according to the status of the firm or the training offered. It was more expensive to serve a managerial apprenticeship than to obtain a straightforward craft training. Fees were high for upholstery training which was held in high esteem; the working conditions were cleaner than in a cabinet-maker's workshop and, although the work was not artistic in the way that a carver's was, it required specialised training to cut and handle expensive textiles. The job of cutting and nailing was done by men, while women were employed to carry out general sewing, including curtains, cushions and other soft furnishings, and did not serve an apprenticeship.[13]

This was a period of relative prosperity for Ireland. After the Union the early years of the nineteenth century were a comparatively peaceful and increasingly prosperous time.[14] Trade improved during the war between Britain and France which had begun on 1 February 1793. It abated briefly when the Peace of Amiens was agreed on 25 March 1802, revived in 1803 and continued until 1815. Between 1792 and 1815 the volume of exports to England

A Firm of Dublin Cabinet-makers: Mack, Williams & Gibton

5. Francis JOHNSTON (1760-1829): design for a wine cooler, c.1810 (*Private collection, Belfast*). The design is based on a plate from Sheraton's Cabinet Dictionary (1803).

6. A mahogany wine cooler in Aras an Uachtarain by Mack, Williams & Gibton incorporating the emblems of The Knights of St Patrick, c.1812. The design shown in Fig. 5 has been executed in a more vigorous and robust spirit.

rose by forty per cent with a sharp rise in prices as England needed more supplies for its army and navy. After the Napoleonic Wars, there was a sharp fall in prices resulting in an economic slump. A series of advertisements by the furniture makers Gillingtons of Abbey Street (Fig. 4) indicates the difficulties experienced by the trade during this period. Samuel and George Gillington refer to the 'present stagnation of Trade throughout the Country' and offer their stock at reduced prices.[15] Gillingtons survived this crisis and in 1837 they advertised expansion of their business, opening a second showroom at no. 34 College Green.[16] Others were not so fortunate; surviving correspondence refers to 'the misfortunes of Mr Eggleso' and in another letter there is a reference to Henry Eggleso, a bankrupt.[17]

On 16 May 1812, the following announcement appeared in *The Dublin Evening Post*:

7. A mahogany wine cooler bearing the crest and motto of the Smith family of Ballynegall, Co Westmeath. A virtuoso carver's piece, it is now in the National Museum of Ireland and on view in No 29 Fitzwilliam Street, Dublin.

In consequence of the Death of Mr Robert Gibton, a partner of the House of Mack, Gibton & Co., the remaining Partners beg leave to acquaint their Friends and the Public, that the Business of their House, in all its branches, will in future be carried on by them in the same extensive manner as heretofore, under the firm of Mack, Williams and Gibton, (son of their late Partner), and they respect-fully request their Customers will, as soon as possible, settle their Accounts, and that all those to whom the late firm are indebted, will furnish theirs, in order to close the late Partnership account.
May 5, 1812
39, Stafford St[18]

John Mack
Zachariah Williams
William Gibton

Mack and Gibton had expanded to include a younger partner, Zachariah Williams, in about 1810 as from this date they advertised as Mack, Gibton & Co. It must be presumed that Zachariah Williams served his apprenticeship with the firm. He sustained a close relationship with John Mack, being named as executor of his will alongside his wife Elizabeth Mack.[19] Williams continued to work suc-cessfully with William Gibton after John Mack's death in 1829, until the death of Gibton in 1842. In 1810 he married William Gibton's sister, Mary, and received a loan of £1,000 from John Mack and William Gibton, which he then invested in the firm to make provision for his wife.[20] Partnerships were not uncom-mon but they were rarely as enduring or successful. William Gibton would certainly have served his apprenticeship with the firm and his large set of tools, with his name impressed on each, survives.[21] In 1809 he was advertising as an auctioneer with premises in Bishop Street.[22]

There are scant surviving references as to how workshops were organised within the Dublin trade. How did Mack, Williams and Gibton run their firm? Who controlled the various elements which comprise a workshop, including supplying designs, dealing with clients, buying wood, training apprentices and running the upholstery room? The success of the firm with three full partners confirms that they had a well organised work-shop and their expansion throughout the period would have necessitated the business having distinct spheres of duty, with consultation occurring for important orders. When the sale of the stock of Peter Eggleso was advertised on 17 November 1803, after his death, the diversity of stock and upholstery materials included confirms that there was a demarcation of areas of responsibility and labour. The sale included, along with a collection of furniture:

several hundred yards of the richest furniture Calicots, elegant Paris Fringes, Lace, ornamental Brass Work and pier Glasses executed to the newest Parisian style, many hundred stone of the best seasoned Bed Feathers, a quantity of large English Blankets, a State Four-post Bedstead and Curtains finished for a nobleman abroad, in the highest style of elegance, Mahogany Logs, Timber, Veneers, a large quantity of Iron and Brass Work.[23]

A foreman may have been

8. A mahogany pew bench supplied by Mack, Williams & Gibton to the Board of Works for the Chapel Royal, Dublin Castle c.1812. Regency taste had changed in favour of furniture based on antique models with richly carved detail.

employed to run the workshop while the owner dealt with clients and perhaps design. In 1809 James Jesson announced that he had opened an Upholstery and Cabinet Warehouse and that he had been the late foreman to Mr Eggleso, of Abbey Street.[24] Eggleso and Power, advertising in 1812, refer to their 'ware-rooms having a selection of fine and well seasoned materials'.[25] This advertisement mentions 'The number of artists and mechanics, as well as the large capital necessarily employed in their concern, together with the extensive stock kept.' This reference to artists is significant as the sphere of design in relation to Dublin cabinet-makers is largely an unexplored area. Design was a fundamental and vital element in the work produced by Mack, Williams and Gibton. The furniture referred to here merges classical decorative motifs with architectural components. Drawing classes were available at the Dublin Society Schools to 'painters, carvers ... and others whose profession depends upon Design' including cabinet-makers.[26]

9. Design for antique marble seats from Tatham's *Etchings*, 1799.

The furniture produced by Mack, Williams and Gibton during this period shows an understanding of the change in taste in the Regency period and a knowledge of the increasing number of pattern books being published during this period. A wine cooler which is one of a pair, relates closely to an elegant drawing by Francis Johnston (Fig. 5).[27] This drawing is in fact based on a plate in *The Cabinet Dictionary*,[28] published by Thomas Sheraton in 1803. In this he applied to furniture motifs, such as animal elements, which were to become fashionable essentials of Regency design.[29] The wine coolers as executed by Mack, Williams and Gibton correlate closely to the design by Francis Johnston but the spirit has altered (Fig. 6). Their design is more robust, the vibrantly carved lions are more vigorous and fierce, the outline of the sarcophagus shape is more extravagant. Incorporating the emblems of the Knights of St. Patrick, they date from around 1812 to 1815 and are of the finest mahogany. A wine cooler dating from the same period, which is allied in taste and style, bears the coat of arms of the Smith family (Fig. 7), perhaps of Ballynegall, Co Westmeath, a house designed by Francis Johnston and largely furnished by Mack, Williams and Gibton.[30] The coat of arms and the family motto 'Delectat Amor Patriae' are placed within a quatrefoil. This wine cooler is stamped with an impressed number of Mack, William and Gibton, B3795.[31] and is a virtuoso carver's piece, similar in outline to the piece in Aras an Uachtarain, and especially comparable in the design of the lid with carved grapes and vine leaves. On this piece the contour of the sarcophagus is edged by tied bunches of bamboo which again terminate in paw feet. As previously, the mahogany is of the finest quality; the firm were always particular in their choice of wood and displayed it to its best advantage.

Mack, Williams and Gibton received a major commission from the Board of Works to provide furnishings for the Chapel Royal in Dublin Castle.[32] The Chapel, designed by Francis Johnston, with whom the firm continued to work closely in his official position as architect to the Board, was begun in 1807 and is an early example of

Gothic Revival, its exterior built in Black Calp Limestone. Inside is an elaborate confection of carving and decorative fan-vaulted plaster work by George Stapleton. A water-colour, dated 1842, attributed to George Petrie, shows the interior as originally laid out,[33] with projecting galleries for the Lord Lieutenant and the Archbishop, facing each other and covered in sumptuous upholstery. In the centre aisle are placed a set of mahogany pew benches (Fig. 8). A later water-colour by James Mahony, dated 1854, shows the benches placed across the centre.[34] These benches, which are numbered and bear an impressed mark B W 409 DC, complete the interior scheme and relate in design to the fixed seating placed at the bases of the private boxes, which, as shown in James Mahony's charming watercolour, had been removed by 1854. For such an important commission it can be accepted that Francis Johnston contributed to the design.

These pew benches disclose a knowledge of the work and publications of Charles Heathcote Tatham. In 1799, Tatham published *Etchings Representing the Best Examples of Ancient Ornamental Architecture Drawn from the Originals in Rome and Other Parts of Italy during the Years 1794, 1795 and 1796.*[35] Tatham made drawings of marble benches (Fig. 9), thrones,

10. Trade label of Mack, Williams & Gibton.

11. One of a pair of mahogany console tables, c.1812-15, in a private collection. They bear the impressed mark D5219 and the makers' label (Fig. 10) and are related in style to the table in Fig. 12. The flat panelled back supports are a favourite device of the firm.

stools, tripods and friezes in Rome. These drawings, sent in a series of illustrated letters to Henry Holland, architect to the Prince of Wales, provided inspiration in his work and formed the basis of Tatham's *Folio.* In *Etchings* almost half of the 102 plates are engravings of classical furnishings, including chairs, tables, stools and pedestals. The mahogany benches of the Chapel Royal have swirling acanthus leaf carving, the end supports terminating in a plumed effect, with the royal coat of arms placed within a shield. A version of Tatham's drawing also appeared in George Smith's publication of 1808, which shows the seats with four supports and alternative designs for scroll or paw feet.[36] The robust quality of the benches by Mack, Williams and Gibton is closer in spirit to the heavier, more resonant drawings by Tatham and the Regency designs of George Smith. Their vigorous character is in contrast to the elegant sweeping curves of the hall benches formerly at Townley Hall, Co Louth, also attributed to Johnston.[37]

These Regency benches underline the change in taste from the Neoclassical period, which favoured painted decoration. Sheraton had commented that most of the carved decoration on chairs was on gilt or painted chairs and consisted mainly of flat strap work and scrolls. The price of mahogany had risen in the

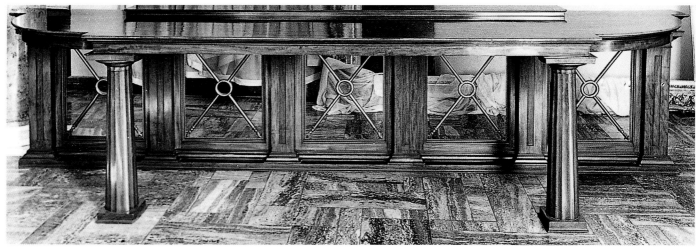

12. A magnificent mahogany hall table, c.1812, in Dublin Castle. Over 12 feet long, it bears the impressed number D2583 and a fragment of a Mack, Williams & Gibton trade label.

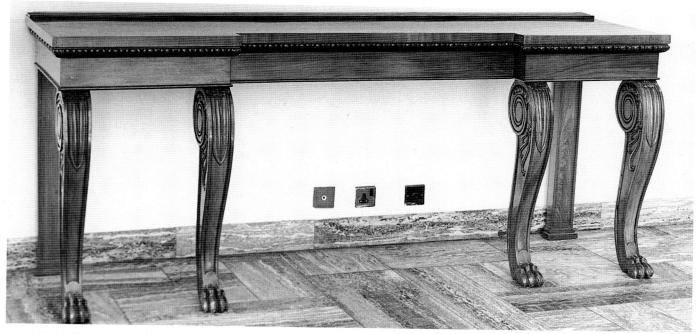

13. A mahogany serving table, c.1812-15, in Dublin Castle, bearing the trade label of Mack, Williams & Gibton. The frieze is carved in egg and dart and the elegant cabriolet supports end in paw feet.

14. One of a pair of mahogany wash-stands, c.1815, which also bear Mack, Williams & Gibton trade labels. These were part of a large order of furniture supplied to Ballynegall House, Co Westmeath, which was designed by Francis Johnston and built in 1808. The contents were sold in 1964 and the house stripped in 1981,

1770s and 1780s, which encouraged the use of softwoods. With the fashion for furniture based on antique models, with robustly carved detail, carvers were once again in demand, their numbers increasing in the first half of the nineteenth century. The use of carved animal monopodia and Greek and Roman elements was popularised by the published work of George Smith. In 1808

George Smith published his *Collection of Designs for Household Furniture*, which contained 158 coloured plates, mainly of furniture in the Greek revival style. Smith's designs were inspired by the furniture and interior decoration of Thomas Hope's house at Duchess Street, London. Hope had published his designs in 1807 and in these he assimilated all the motifs and patterns he had studied, in particular from Roman and Greek remains.[38] He combined the motifs and designs, which were to form the basis of the Regency style, to create highly original furniture, imposing in outline, with a daring use of ornament.

The Board of Works records show the following payments relating to work on the Chapel Royal:

Dublin 31 December 1814:
Castle Chapel Dr To Mack, Williams & Gibton
To Upholsterers Work £1,053.0.11
Dublin 11 March 1815:
Castle Chapel Dr To Mack, Williams & Gibton
To Upholsterers Work £522.1.8
Dublin 8 December 1815:
Castle Chapel Dr to Mack, WIlliam & Gibton
To Upholsterers Work £18.10.7[39]

From this date Mack, Williams and Gibton regularly stamped and/or labelled their furniture. The firm Gillow & Co of Lancashire had been the first to adopt a numbering system in 1785.[40] This may have been used for stock control or a piece may have received a number when the order was placed. A magnificent mahogany hall table, (Fig. 12) which remains in Dublin Castle, bears an impressed mark D2583.[41] This splendid architectural piece is over twelve feet long, the front pair of supports being fluted Doric columns, the panelled back incorporating crossed brass arrows centred by a circle. A pair of console tables in a private collection (Fig. 11) related in style, bear trade labels and the impressed mark D5219. The label (Fig. 10) states that

A Firm of Dublin Cabinet-makers: Mack, Williams & Gibton

Mack, Williams and Gibton are 'Upholsterers and Cabinet Makers to His Majesty, His Excellency the Lord Lieutenant.' This pair of tables relates in their use of architectural components to the Dublin Castle table. A pair of fluted columns, decorated with floral paterae, supports a frieze decorated with bead and reel and egg and dart; the back has flat panelled pilasters. The use of flat panelled back supports is a favoured device of the firm and reappears in the work of Williams and Gibton between 1829 and 1842. A mahogany console table in the style of Mack, Williams and Gibton with panelled galleried back and narrow shelf above a panelled apron and supported on two horned panther monopodia with claw feet, c.1830, was sold by Hamilton Osborne King at Tudor House, Dalkey, Co Dublin on 31 August 19934, lot 16.

Another handsome piece at Dublin Castle is a dining room serving table (Fig. 13). On this the frieze is carved with egg and dart, the elegant cabriolet supports terminate in paw feet. The design is polished, refined and elegant. The intent of this table is close in spirit to a pair of mahogany wash-stands also with labels from Ballynegall,[42] Co Westmeath (Fig. 14). The wash-stands have acanthus leaf carving on the curving cabriolet legs which are placed on block supports and date from around 1815. Ballynegall was designed by Francis Johnston for James Gibbons and built in 1808. It was a classical two-storey house, with an Ionic portico. The entrance hall had a screen of fluted, Ionic columns and the fine delicate plasterwork was by George Stapleton, who, as already mentioned, worked with Johnston for the Board of Works. Mack, Williams and Gibton supplied a large order of furniture to Ballynegall, indicating the working partnership between Johnston and the cabinet-making firm during this period. This furniture is part of another significant component in the history of Mack, Williams and Gibton, which was the important commissions they received to furnish country houses – but that is a story for another day.

ANGELA ALEXANDER is researching the work of nineteenth-century Dublin cabinet-makers.

ACKNOWLEDGEMENTS
I am grateful to the following who have given me information and encouragement since I began researching Mack, Williams and Gibton: Glascott Symes, great-great-grandson of William Gibton, allowed me to study family papers in his possession and discussed his knowledge of the firm; the Knight of Glin for his enthusiasm and many valuable contributions; David Griffin for information and suggestions. Sincere thanks to Geraldine Walsh who read the text; Mairead Dunlevy; Dr Edward McParland; Nicholas Robinson; Gordon Nichol; the Johnston brothers; Willie Flynn; all the staff at the Irish Architectural Archive, the Public Record Offices in Dublin and Belfast, Dublin Castle, Number 29 Fitzwilliam Street and the Manuscript Department, Trinity College, Dublin.

1. This table was sold at Tudor House, Dalkey, Co. Dublin, by Hamilton, Osborne King, 31 August1993, Lot 281.
2. This photograph is in the Irish Architectural Archive.
3. This reference was extracted from the Dillon manuscripts of Clonbrock, Co Galway, by the Knight of Glin.
4. Registry of Deeds B554/218/36690.
5. TCD Manuscripts, Mun/P/4/78/16.
6. Public Record Office(PRO) 2D/56/25.
7. Maurice Craig, *The Architecture of Ireland from the Earliest Times to 1880*, London 1982, p.285.
8. PRO. 2D/57/34.
9. PRO. 2D/52/83.
10. I am grateful to Mr Glascott Symes for bringing this to my attention.
11. The indenture between William Fernsley and William Gibton is in the possession of Glascott Symes.
12. Pat Kirkham, *The London Furniture Trade, 1700-1870*, Furniture History, England, 1988. A comprehensive history of how the London trade was organised.
13. A bill, dated 1814, from C Stephens, Upholsterer includes the item; 'To 8 Days Work for the 2 Women Sewing curtains &c @ 2.6. per Day-Total 1.' TCD Manuscripts, Mun/P/4/143/7.
14. Louis M Cullen, *An Economic History of Ireland since 1660*, London 1987.
15. *The Dublin Chronicle*, 17 April 1816.
16. George Gillington's trade label showing his shop-front is published in The Knight of Glin, 'Dublin Directories and Trade Labels', *Furniture History*, vol.XX1 (1985). Figure 10.
17. TCD Manuscripts Mun/P/4/196.
18. *The Dublin Chronicle*, 20 May 1816.
19. Registry of Deeds 846/90/566590.
20. Registry of Deeds 627/198/430368.
21. Collection of Glascott Symes.
22. *The Dublin Evening Post*, 29 June 1809.
23. *The Dublin Evening Post*, 17 November, 1803.
24. *The Dublin Evening Post*, 26 October, 1809.
25. *The Dublin Evening Post*, 16 May, 1812.
26. Anne Crookshank and The Knight of Glin, *The Painters of Ireland, c.1660-1920*, London 1978, pp.70-71.
27. This wine cooler is at Aras an Uachtarain, the second is from the National Museum of Ireland and is of unknown provenance. It can be seen in Number 29, Fitzwilliam Street, Dublin, which is open to the public. In photographs of Kilmore, Co Armagh, family seat of Francis Johnston, a wine cooler can be seen in the drawing room window. These photographs were published in 1909 in Robert M Young's *Belfast and the Province of Ulster in the Twentieth Century*. Young mentions that the sarcophagus was a replica of one in Dublin Castle and that there was another in the room, smaller and bearing the arms of the Johnston family. Young also claims that much of the furniture in the room was designed by Francis Johnston. An identical wine cooler was illustrated in *Country Life*, 21 October, 1993 having been sold at auction in England.
28. This drawing, in the collection of Anthony Malcolmson has been attributed to Johnston by The Knight of Glin.
29. Thomas Sheraton, *The Cabinet Dictionary*, London 1803(reprint, New York, 1970).
30. The Knight of Glin, David J Griffin and Nicholas K Robinson, *Vanishing Country Houses of Ireland*, Dublin 1988. This contains photographs of Ballynegall which was stripped in 1981. The contents were sold by Christie's in 1964. I am grateful to the Knight of Glin for suggesting the probable connection of this wine cooler to the Smith family of Ballynegall, Co. Westmeath.
31. The Mack, Williams and Gibton partnership regularly use a letter, most commonly D, but also A and B, with four numbers.
32. PRO.2D/52/88.
33. This watercolour is in a private collection. A colour photograph is in the Irish Architectural Archive.
34. James Mahony, *The Nave of Dublin Castle Chapel*, 1854, National Gallery of Ireland.
35. Charles Heathcote Tatham, *Etchings Representing the Best Examples of Ancient Ornamental Architecture Drawn from the Originals in Rome and Other Parts of Italy during the Years 1794, 1795, 1796*, London 1799.
36. George Smith, *A Collection of Designs for Household Furniture and Interior Decoration*, London 1808. 'Hall seats for recesses.', pl. 34.
37. These elegant hall benches are no longer at Townley Hall, Co. Louth. Photographs of the hall interiors showing these benches are in the Irish Architecture Archive.
38. Thomas Hope, *Household Furniture & Interior Decoration*, London 1807, (reprint, New York, 1971).
39. PRO. 2D/52/87.
40. Gillow, *A Record of a Furnishing Firm During Two Centuries*, London, 1901.
41. Part of a damaged Mack, William & Gibton label survives on this table.
42. These wash-stands were resold by Christie's and Hamilton & Hamilton, on 2 and 3 November 1987, at 19 North Great Georges Street, Lot 468.

A VICTORIAN LANDMARK
TRINITY COLLEGE'S MUSEUM BUILDING

The Museum Building in Trinity College (Fig. 1), which was erected between 1853 and 1857, is an important example of Gothic Revival architecture, and has been referred to as one of the landmarks of Victorian architecture in Britain and Ireland.[1] A number of years after its erection *The Dublin Builder* of 1866 referred to it in glowing terms:

> *a great work, most important in its influence on the arts in this country ... erected under the auspices of the late Mr Woodward and Mr Thomas N. Deane. To this remarkable building and this alone we trace an inauguration of a great revolution in public taste which has since taken place.*

The architectural principles on which it was designed owe much to John Ruskin (1819-1900) and Venetian influences: comparison of details such as the wall plaques and the windows with illustrations in Ruskin's *Stones of Venice* (1851) and in the British journal *The Builder* (1851) show remarkable similarity.[2] The building also contains Moorish features which can be paralleled in, for example, the Great Mosque in Cordoba, in Spain.

The building contains numerous examples of native limestones and marble as well as granite and imported stone. The purpose of

The polychrome architecture of Deane, Woodward and Deane necessitated the extensive use of coloured stone and marble. **Patrick Wyse Jackson** *identifies the sources which were used.*

this article is to describe and provide a plan of the stone types used in the building, to examine the costs of these materials, and to discuss the dealings between the client (the Board of Trinity College, hereafter referred to as the Board) and the architects in relation to these materials.

The Museum Building was designed by the Cork firm of Deane, Woodward and Deane. The firm had been founded in Cork by Sir Thomas Deane (1792-1871)[3] (Fig. 2), the first in an architectural lineage of father, son and grandson who were all knighted.[4] Before its removal to Dublin in 1853, the firm was responsible for the Cork Town Hall and the Killarney Lunatic Asylums, which were largely designed by Benjamin Woodward (1816-61) (Fig. 3).[6] The firm's 'signature' – a carved motif of the letters 'DWD' is often to be found in the buildings they designed (Fig. 5). After the move to Dublin, Deane became too involved in public matters and did not play as active a role in the firm as he had previously. The organisation of the business and the artistic and architectural input came from Woodward and from Deane's son, Thomas Newenham Deane[7] (later Sir Thomas) (1828-99) (Fig. 4), who

1. THE MUSEUM BUILDING, TRINITY COLLEGE, DUBLIN, designed by Deane, Woodward and Deane (1853-57) – view of south and east facades. An important example of Gothic Revival style, it is one of the landmarks of Victorian architecture in Britain and Ireland.

2. SIR THOMAS DEANE (1792-1871): Founder of the Cork firm of Deane, Woodward and Deane. Sir Thomas, his son and grandson were all architects and were all knighted.

3. BENJAMIN WOODWARD (1816-61): Woodward became a partner in the firm in 1851 and designed Cork Town Hall and the Killarney Asylums before they moved to Dublin in 1853.

4. SIR THOMAS NEWENHAM DEANE (1828-99): Son of the founder, he became a partner in 1851 and with Woodward designed many important buildings including the Kildare Street Club, Dublin and Brownsbarn,Co Kilkenny.

were both made partners in the firm in 1851. The younger Deane was a keen yachtsman and wished to join the Navy, but after paternal pressure he joined the family firm. Together Woodward and T N Deane were responsible for many other important buildings in Ireland and Great Britain: Brownsbarn, Co Kilkenny; Oxford Museum; the Kildare Street Club.[8] After the deaths of Sir Thomas Deane and Benjamin Woodward, the firm continued under T N Deane, who was succeeded by his son, Sir Thomas Manley Deane, who continued an architectural practice until 1924.[9]

In 1833 the Board of the College instigated a competition for a new Museum[10] to contain the geological and other collections which were housed at that time in a large room in Regent House, overlooking College Green.[11] Nearly two decades passed during which several architects submitted plans, while others, such as Decimus Burton, declined invitations to do so. Finally the designs submitted by Deane, Woodward and Deane were accepted in April 1853,[12] although a row with the Dublin architect John McCurdy over who designed the initial plans caused some concern to the College Board.[13]

The Museum Building was erected between 1853 and 1857. In this communication, details, mainly gleaned from the College Muniments [MUN ms] housed in the Manuscripts Department of the Library of TCD, relating largely to the building materials

The keen-eyed may spot cats, snakes, frogs, squirrels and birds, lurking among shamrock, daffodils, oak, ivy, lilies, and acanthus.

and fittings used in the Museum Building will be discussed. Additionally, considerable details relating to the various costs of the building are also available in the College Muniments, and these provide an insight into the economics of building in the mid-1800s. Other aspects of the building, such as its architectural style and origins, are chronicled in some detail by Eve Blau in her book *Ruskinian Gothic* (1982).

On 23 May 1853 a contract for the foundations worth £15.17s. 2d. was agreed by the Board and Messrs Cockburn and Son, builders,[14] and these were opened a few months later. The Revd Samuel Haughton (1821-97), the Professor of Geology, examined the excavations and reported a succession of made ground, ash pits and calcareous glacial drift.[15] He found no evidence for a raised beach which, had it existed, might have rendered the chosen site unsuitable, because of its proximity to the College Library, designed by Thomas Burgh and built in 1712-32. The contract for the building was worth £24,000 and Cockburns undertook to complete the work in three to four years.[16] The exterior was in place by 1855 (Figs. 6 and 7) while the interiors and fitting out the building was not finished until 1857.[17] On completion of the exterior Cockburns received the seventeenth instalment of £1000.[18] The exterior walls of the building are constructed of Calp Limestone (Fig. 6) which are faced externally with blocks, nine inches thick, of Ballyknockan

A Victorian Landmark: Trinity College's Museum Building

Granite[19] which was quarried some fifteen miles away south-west of the city in Co Wicklow. This stone is a fine-grained igneous rock composed of clear quartz, white feldspar, and black and silvery mica. The carved ornate string courses (Fig. 8), quoins (Fig. 9), columns and 108 capitals (Fig. 11) are in Portland Stone, and the tympanum, bearing the College crest, over the heavy wooden door, is in Caen Stone, an oolitic limestone from France. The exterior dressings, which cost £12,768. 3s.7d., contributed to just under half the cost of the building.[20] The total cost of the building amounted to £27,980. 6s.8d.[21]

The interior of the building is breathtaking (Fig. 12). The large central hall is a 'geology lesson' in itself and is dominated by a pair of skeletons of Giant Irish deer. Initially Deane and Woodward planned that the interior walls would consist of rubble masonry which were to be plastered over. However, early in 1855, they changed their mind and decided to use Caen Stone, which would only cost an additional £185.[22] The Board agreed to this change in plan and instructed the builder accordingly.[23]

5 Capital above a small Connemara marble column in the Museum Building with a shield device bearing the interwoven letters 'DWD' — the 'signature' of the architects.

Portland and Caen Stone was £6,021. 14s.11d.[26] The arches between columns over the balconies show a clever use of alternating natural yellow and stained red blocks, and the capitals and bases of columns are in Portland Stone. All the Portland Stone is heavily carved. This carving was done by a Mr Roe of Lambeth and by the remarkably versatile Cork-born brothers John and James O'Shea.[27] Woodward allowed the brothers considerable flexibility and they carved their designs in situ. It is said that they worked from material gathered from the College Botanic Gardens, in Ballsbridge.[28] The keen-eyed may spot cats, snakes, frogs, squirrels and birds, lurking among shamrock, daffodils, oak, ivy, lilies, and acanthus. The O'Sheas also worked on the Kildare Street Club and spent sometime working with Woodward at Oxford. After his death they worked in England and Wales for a number of years but there is no trace of them or their work after 1860.[29]

The staircase and floor of the balconies are in Portland Stone while the floor of the hall is paved with buff-coloured Yorkshire flags which

However, by May they rescinded the order on learning that only two of the expected three cargoes of stone had arrived. Sir Thomas Deane responded in strong terms and urged the Board to reconsider this action,[24] and Cockburn reported that the work could be completed for £270.[25] Evidently the Board overturned their decision of 4 May as Caen Stone was used to face interior walls. The total estimated cost of the internal stone dressings of

cost fifteen shillings per square yard (total price £324).[30] These flags interlock with rectangles of Portland Stone and squares of black slate or limestone. The whole floor is enclosed in a thin rim of purple Welsh Festiniog slate containing beautiful olive green reduction spots. The floor was relaid about a decade ago, and is now two and a half inches higher than the original. In many places black slate was not available and was replaced by

6. The Museum Building under construction c. 1855. Note the Calp Limestone rubble wall behind the arches and the use of thin wooden scaffolding.

7. The Museum Building under construction c. 1855. The keystone of one window arch being positioned. Many such blocks were carved in situ by the O'Shea brothers.

8. Exterior string course of Portland Stone on the Museum Building which is elaborately decorated with carved foliage.

9. Museum Building – quoin with rope effect and capital carved with shamrock sprigs.

black limestone. This rock is much softer than the former; it has unfortunately has become quite scratched and now appears grey in colour.

The twin-domed roof is composed of blue, red and yellow enamelled bricks, which are now rather faded. The roof is slated in blue and green Super Bangor Queen slates from the Cambrian Mountains of North Wales, which cost £290.[31] Portland Stone was used for the outer series of chimneys which are visible from the ground while the hidden inner ranks of chimneys are composed of Ballyknockan Granite.

The columns of Irish marbles, together with the paired central enamelled brick domes, add considerable colour to the interior of the building (Fig. 12). Of the stone used in these columns, only the Connemara Serpentine is a true marble, the others are polished limestones[32] of Lower Carboniferous age (360-333 million years Before Present.). All the stone was supplied by the firm of Mackinson at a total cost of £326. The fourteen full columns cost £13 each, the eighteen half-columns cost £8 each, and the ninety-eight feet of marble coping on the bannisters and balconies cost £122. 10s.[33] Insets of Irish marble were used in the wall veils on the exterior walls. These are one and a half inches thick. The suppliers had some difficulty in procuring complete seven and a half feet lengths of Irish marbles and in May 1855 Deane requested that the Board accept split

columns. He intimated that refusal would result in a long delay as complete examples of foreign stone would have to be ordered. While the Board said they would refuse to accept any imperfect columns, the desire to minimise delays resulted in a number of split columns being used. In addition the Board probably didn't wish to be seen to veto the use of native stone which they had been commended for promoting.[34]

The only non-Irish stone used in the columns is a dark reddish-black serpentinite from the Lizard area in Cornwall. This material was probably finished at a factory at Carleon Cove, near Ruan Minor, which was supplied with stone from five local quarries. A number of buildings still remain at this site, as does the slipway from where ships carrying their valuable cargo embarked on their sea journeys.[35] The use of the Lizard Serpentinite was probably due to the influence of Professor Haughton, who had investigated the geology of the area only a short time previously.[36] The stone was supplied by the London and Penzance Serpentine Company of Sydenham, London, at a cost of between £24 and £19 per column. The price difference depended on whether full or split columns were required. Mr H Gladwin, the agent for the suppliers, recommended that the latter be used, as it would allow for a better selection of stone which would be easier to transport and erect.[37]

In the Museum Building Woodward added

10. Floor plan of the ground and first floors showing the position of the marble columns, balconies and bannisters.

colour to the interior by utilising various limestones and marbles in thirty-two whole or half columns seven and a half feet in height and seventeen inches in diameter, and in bannisters, balconies, and string courses. Unfortunately there are no contemporary plans of the building which state the provenance of this decorative stone. Neither are the columns labelled as they are in the Oxford Museum, where several Irish examples are found, particularly in the Upper Arcade (north side). These include Cork, King's County (Offaly), Connemara, Armagh, Kilkenny, Clonony, Dunleary (Donegal), Galway, Castle Espie, Tullamore, and Enniskillen marbles.[38] It is tempting to assume that stone from these localities was also used in the Museum Building. However, comparison with stone used in other buildings (most notably the Office of Public Works, 51 St Stephen's Green, Dublin), and with details of marble available at the time[39] has allowed for the identification of the Museum Building stone; not all varieties cited above are represented and some additional marble types are present. Close examination of the Cork Red marble reveals that three varieties with subtle differences are present; the source for these has been confirmed by recollecting in disused quarries in the Cork area. The marbles are described below and a plan of the layout of the columns is presented (Fig. 10).

1. Lizard Serpentinite. A distinctive black metamorphic rock composed largely of olivine and pyroxene, with veins of red oxidised serpentine minerals. Locality: The Lizard, Cornwall.

2. Connemara Marble. A pale green marble rich in serpentine, chlorite and mica. Resulted from metamorphism of limestone 580-475 million years ago. Locality: Barnaoran, Co Galway.

3. Connemara Marble. A dark green variety of this distinctive stone which shows alternating folded layers of dark and green minerals. Locality: Clifden, Co Galway.

4. Baneshane Cork Red Marble. A red limestone (stained by iron oxides) with blebs of white calcite, and linear concentrations of red clay. Looks like corned beef. Locality: Baneshane, Cork.

11. Ornately carved pilasters and capitals with decorations of foliage, first floor window north facade. The Portland Stone of the Museum Building is now heavily encrusted with gypsum and soot.

12. View of the main hall of the Museum Building, showing the staircase, some of the splendid interior stone dressings and the flagged floor. 'The interior of the building is breathtaking'.

5. Midleton Cork Red Marble. Similar to Baneshane. This stone was very popular with late nineteenth century builders and architects. It was known in the trade as 'Victoria Red'. Locality: Midleton, Co Cork.

6. Little Island Cork Red Marble. A red limestone with patches of white calcite and small circular crinoid ossicles. Much sheared by Hercynian earth movements. Locality: Little Island, Cork.

7. Armagh Marble. A pale, relatively unfossiliferous, brown limestone. Locality: Armagh, Co Armagh.

8. Clonony Marble. A brown limestone with cavities infilled with white calcite; containing many fossils including crinoids and some cephalopods. Locality: Clonony, Co Offaly.

9. Galway Marble. A black relatively unfossiliferous limestone. Galway was, and remains, one of the major sources of black 'marble'. It has been worked since the 1700s. Locality: Menlo Park, Co Galway.

10. Mitchelstown Marble. A black 'reefal' limestone which contains many cavities infilled with white sparry calcite that contrast with the black micritic bulk of the rock. Locality: Mitchelstown, Co Cork.

11. Kilkenny Marble. A black limestone which was much sought for internal work. It is very fossiliferous, containing crinoids, corals and large productid brachiopods. Locality: south of Kilkenny City.

12. Castle Caldwell Marble. A pale grey fossiliferous limestone, rich in crinoidal debris. This marble is not well known, and does not appear to have been widely used in the nineteenth century. Locality: Castle Caldwell, near Belleek, Co Fermanagh.

Within a short time the building started to be adversely affected by the smoggy particulate-rich atmosphere of the city. After ten years the marble insets in the wall plaques had lost their polish.[40] It is now difficult to determine which marbles were used – only the Cork Red and Connemara marbles are still recognisable. The College Register for 2 May and 5 May 1860 records that advice was sought from a Mr Ransome on a process for preserving stone. It is not

A Victorian Landmark: Trinity College's Museum Building

known if Ransome's process was applied to the building. Today many surfaces in the Portland Stone are heavily encrusted with gypsum on which sooty deposits have adhered (Fig. 11), and similar, but not as extensive, contaminants encrust the Ballyknockan Granite ashlar. The effect has been to darken considerably the exterior of the building. Similarly, interior walls in the hall are coated with dark particulate matter, but not to the same degree as exterior walls, and the marble columns have retained a sheen.

Since 1953 the large rooms housing the Geological and Engineering Museums on the east and west ends of the building, as well as many other smaller rooms, have been divided both vertically and horizontally so that the interior of the building is a labyrinth of floors and staircases. Fortunately the hall and balconies have not been affected by these alterations. They remain as the Deanes, Woodward and the O'Shea brothers left them – and the feelings that must have overwhelmed John

Ruskin when he first stepped inside the large oak door of the building can still be experienced by all who work in, or visit, the Museum Building today.

DR PATRICK N WYSE JACKSON is Curator of the Geological Museum of Trinity College, Dublin. He is author of The Building Stones of Dublin: A Walking Guide (Country House, Dublin,1993)

ACKNOWLEDGEMENTS

This study is a continuation of research carried out for a display on the building and decorative stones of the Museum Building, which was erected in 1990, having been first suggested by Dr G D Sevastopulo. I am grateful to the following who have kindly provided information for this study: Dr E McParland (TCD), Dr E Robinson (London), Dr D J Siveter (Oxford), Mr J Martin and Mr M A Taylor (Leicester), Dr S van Rose (Natural History Museum, London), and Mr E Rankin (McDonnell and Dixon, Dublin). Dr J Feehan (University College Dublin) and Dr R Heselden (University College Cork) collected samples from the old quarries at Clonony, and Midleton, Little Island and Baneshane for which I thank them. Mr T Dunne located the photograph illustrated in Fig. 7. The photography is by Mr D Burke.

1. E J McParland, 'The College Buildings', in C H Holland (ed.) Trinity College Dublin and the Idea of a University, Trinity College Press, Dublin, 1991, pp.153-84

2. Note in particular the wall plaques which are copies of those on the Venetian palaces the Palazzo Dario (above) and the Palazzo Ducale (below).

3. For more biographical details of Sir Thomas Deane see The Builder, Vol. 29, (1871) p.804; Eve Blau, 'Thomas Deane', in A Placzek, (ed.) Macmillan Encyclopedia of Architects. Vol. 1, p.520. Collier Macmillan, New York,1982.

4. M McDermott, 'The Deanes: an architectural dynasty', in J Owen Lewis (ed.) RIAI Yearbook l975-1976. Royal Institute of the Architects of Ireland, Dublin,1976, pp.85-88

5. Eve Blau, Ruskinian Gothic: the architecture of Deane and Woodward 1845-1861. Princeton University Press, 1982.

6. For more biographical details of Woodward see The Builder, Vol. 19, (1861) p.436; Irish Builder, Vol. 3, (1861) p.563 ; C P Curran, 1940. 'B Woodward, Ruskin and the O'Sheas', Studies Vol. 29,(1940) pp.255-68; F O'Dwyer and J Williams, 'Benjamin Woodward' in T Kennedy (ed.) Victorian Dublin. Dublin 1980; E M Blau, 1982. 'BenjaminWoodward', in A Placzek (ed.) Macmillan Encyclopedia of Architects. Vol. 4. Collier Macmillan, New York 1982, p.419.

7. For more biographical details of T N Deane see The Builder, Vol.a 77, (1899) p.471.

8. Blau op.cit.

9. R M Butler, 1934. 'Sir Thomas Manley Deane,' Journal of the Royal Institute of the Architects of Ireland, vols. 30-31 (1934) p.171.

10. See McParland op. cit. and Blau op. cit. p.29 for details surrounding the genesis of the Museum Building.

11. R Ball, 1846. First Report on the progress of the Dublin University Museum: January 1846. (M H Gill, Dublin 1846). W B Taylor, History of the University of Dublin.(R.

Jennings, London 1819) – contains an engraving of the Dublin University Museum in 1819. Drawn and etched by W B Taylor; engraved by R Havell and Son.

12. The Builder, Vol. 11 (April 1853) p.228.

13. Blau op. cit, p.30; McParland op. cit., p.178. McCurdy became Superintending Architect for which he received a fee of £75 (MUN ms P/2/356/18).

14. MUN ms P/2/323a.

15. MUN ms P/2/324.

16. MUN ms P/2/330.

17. Some interior fittings, such as display cases, for the Geological Museum were designed by Woodward (MUN ms P/2/354). Some of these display cases are still in use in a smaller Museum situated on an upper floor added in 1953. Smaller fittings such as brass door handles were supplied by Hart and Son, Wych Street, London at a cost of 30 shillings each (MUN ms P/2/353/B).

18. MUN ms P/2/336/5.

19. This estimate of the thickness of the granite blocks is derived from a core taken in the west end of the Museum Building in 1991. This core is now housed in the Geological Museum.

20. MUN ms P/2/329

21. Cockburns were paid £27,680. 6s.8d. in late 1857, and stated they were owed £399. 18s. The Board claimed that £300 was owing (MUN ms P/2/351/6). This balance was finally paid in January 1858 (MUN ms P/2/356/7).

22. MUN ms P/2/339.

23. MUN ms P/2/342.

24. MUN ms P/2/340.

25. MUN ms P/2/342.

26. MUN ms P/2/329.

27. Dublin Builder (March 1856).

28. MUN ms P/2/329.

29. For more biographical information on the O'Sheas see Curran, op. cit.; E M Blau, 'O'Shea Brothers', in A Placzek, (ed.) Macmillan Encyclopedia of Architects. Vol. 3. Collier Macmillan, New York, 1982. p.329

30. MUN ms P/2/329.

31. MUN ms P/2/329.

32. Up until the 1840s the distinctive Connemara marble and the dark black Kilkenny and Galway varieties were the only marbles seriously exploited. After this date the industry went through through a period of expansion, and new sources of decorative marbles, such as the red varieties from Co Cork, and the brown varieties from Armagh and the Irish Midlands, were found. Sir Thomas Deane was active in promoting the use of Irish stone, and the National Exhibition of 1851 in Cork, and International Exhibition of 1853 in Dublin, had advanced the industry considerably. By the 1890s the stone industry had gone into serious decline, out of which it is only now recovering.

33. MUN ms P/2/329.

34. MUN ms P/2/341.

35. D Washington, 'When Serpentine was in vogue', Country Life, 8 April, 1971, pp.828-29.

36. S Haughton, 'Notes on the Serpentines of Cornwall and Connemara', Journal of the Geological Society of Dublin, Vol. 5,(1852-53) pp.136-39.

37. MUN ms P/2/328.

38. H W Ackland, and J Ruskin, The Oxford Museum. Smith, Elder and Co, London, 1859.

39. G Wilkinson, Practical Geology and Ancient Architecture of Ireland. John Murray, London 1845. G K Kinahan, Economic Geology of Ireland – a comprehensive account of all economic aspects of Irish geology of the 1880s. This volume first appeared as separate papers in the Scientific Proceedings of the Royal Dublin Society, and was republished complete in 1886-89 as Volume 18 of the Journal of the Royal Geological Society of Ireland.

40. E Hull, A treatise on the building and ornamental stones of Great Britain and foreign countries. Macmillan, London, 1872.

JOHN HENRY FOLEY'S O'CONNELL MONUMENT

The nature and content of Dublin's best-known statue are studied by **Paula Murphy.**

The O'Connell Monument for Dublin's Sackville Street (O'Connell Street) was the most important sculptural commission of the nineteenth century in Ireland,[1] and as such it is of interest to be examined in political and social terms. Executed by John Henry Foley, the monument is three-tiered with the figure of O'Connell, larger than lifesize, positioned on top of a circular support, the bronze drum of which carries representations of the people of Ireland approaching the figure of Erin (Fig. 1). At the base are four female Victories recording the means employed by O'Connell to achieve success: Patriotism, Courage, Eloquence and Fidelity. The overall design of the monument has its source in European public sculpture.

The bronze drum is the main area of interest in a social reading of this monument. The sculpted drum is a particularly creative development in the presentation of monumental statuary as it transforms the more habitually pedestrian pedestal area and offers scope to the sculptor's imaginative and technical abilities. Its use in the O'Connell Monument serves a number of purposes, one of which is to inform, beyond the spiritual nature of the portrait.[2] When Foley presented his sketch model to the O'Connell Monument Committee for approval in 1867, he pointed out in an accompanying statement that the design was intended to record the gratitude of the Irish people of all classes for the blessings of Civil and Religious Liberty obtained by the labours of O'Connell.[3] It is on the drum that the people of Ireland are represented, and Foley indicated that the wave-like pattern circling the plinth just below these figures was intended to symbolise the island nation, surrounded by water.[4] Foley's reference to 'all classes' of Irish people does not, however, include both genders. While poet, peasant, politician and priest, amongst others, are represented, women are excluded, and are only present on the monument in allegorical form, as symbol of O'Connell's attributes in the

1. John Henry FOLEY (1818-74): The O'Connell Monument, Dublin; detail of the bronze drum showing the figure of Erin, positioned centrally and pointing upwards to O'Connell as she tramples chains underfoot.

Victories and, more independently, in the figure of Erin. Positioned centrally on the drum and of more heroic proportions than her attendant mortals, Erin, with shamrock in her hair and her harp nestling in her drapery, stands boldly pointing aloft to O'Connell and trampling chains underfoot. This figure incorporates multi-symbolism of a maternal nature: Mother Ireland, as goddess from Celtic and nationalist mythology; Mother Church, the cult of Mary indicative of religious dominance; and, perhaps more significantly, Mother Earth, for so long the only real power of women in Ireland, confined and domestic.[5] It is of interest that bishop and peasant are placed closest to Erin while peer and politician are farthest away on the back of the monument.

If Foley drew attention to 'the blessings of Civil and Religious Liberty' in his statement, the monument was to focus more particularly on the religious element. While at the model stage the sculptor describes the figure of Erin as holding a record of O'Connell's achievements in her hand, this was altered in the final monument to refer specifically to Catholic Emancipation, detailing in prominent lettering 'An Act for the Relief of His Majesty's Roman Catholic Subjects' (Fig. 2). A further change was to the drum where the musician was to hold a score with the accompanying verse inscribed:

*Oh where's the slave so
    lowly,
Condemn'd to chains
    unholy
Who, could he burst
His bonds at first,
Would pine beneath
    them slowly.*[6]

These are the first lines of Tom Moore's melody entitled 'Oh! Where's the slave;[7] which was sung at the Moore commemoration held in Dublin shortly after the balladeer's death in 1852.[8] While a fragment of a musical score, the notation of which is not unrelated to the melody, is to be seen on the monument (Fig. 3), the accompanying lyrics were not included in the final work.

The O'Connell Monument is both of and for the people and

JOHN HENRY FOLEY'S O'CONNELL MONUMENT

2. John Henry FOLEY (1818-74): The O'Connell Monument, Dublin; detail of the bronze drum showing the scroll held by Erin which records 'An Act for the Relief of His Majesty's Roman Catholic Subjects'.

3. John Henry FOLEY (1818-74): The O'Connell Monument; detail of the bronze drum showing a fragment of the musical score of Moore's Melody, 'Oh where's the slave so lowly/ Condemned to chains unholy'.

Foley has in a skilful way combined reverence and accessibility. There is no doubt that O'Connell is firmly positioned above the people – the portrait statue on top of the drum where the people are represented – and that he is accorded heroic stature, as he is larger in scale than the figures on the drum. It is also the case that the Victory females might be read as protective guardians, introducing a note of separateness between the heroic and the humble. However, when compared with other monumental statuary in position in Dublin at the time, this monument reveals a new accessibility as the sculptural work and includes representation of the people, who are, effectively, supporting O'Connell. Peter Springer, in a lengthy study of the role of the support in monumental sculpture, indicates the way in which the pedestal is used to elevate the person portrayed and separate that figure from the viewer.[9] While he addresses two Dublin monuments, the Nelson Column and the O'Connell Monument, amongst many other works, he fails, in his argument, to identify the way in which the three-tiered format of the latter and its spread at the base, which Foley himself described as being in the form of an ancient Irish cross laid horizontally,[10] reaches out towards the observer in contrast with the lofty position of Nelson, soaring beyond contact.

Public monuments of this nature incorporated a functional element in that they were expected to be didactic and to exercise a moralizing influence. When Foley exhibited his sketch model for the O'Connell Monument in the City Hall in Dublin in 1867, an editorial in *The Freeman's Journal*, noted the current state of discontent and discord in Irish society and dared to hope that the 'work of art, a source of National pride, may exercise the humanizing influence that art is acknowledged to possess, and that, at least, all classes of Irishmen may, at the base of O'Connell's statue, lay down (their) personal and class animosities'.[11] It was not expected that there would be a long delay between the enthusiastic acceptance of Foley's design and his completion of the monument and that therefore it would soon be in place; the O'Connell Monument, however, was not erected and unveiled until 1882.

DR PAULA MURPHY is a Lecturer in History of Art in University College Dublin.

1. For details of the commission see Homan Potterton, *The O'Connell Monument*, Gatherum Series No 3, Gifford & Craven, Cork, 1973. Also the Archive in the City Hall, Dublin has an extensive collection of articles on the subject of the monument taken from contemporary newspapers. Ms Ch 6/ 1 and 6/2 are particularly relevant.

2. Foley's use of a sculpted drum support and the informative possibilities inherent in it were to directly influence Thomas Farrell in his statue of Cardinal Cullen erected in the St. Mary's Pro-Cathedral in Dublin in 1882.

3. Foley's statement to the Committee is reproduced, along with a report of the meeting, in the *The Freeman's Journal*, 14 December 1867.

4. *ibid.*

5. Representations of Erin and their meaning are explored in Belinda Loftus, *Mirrors:William III and Mother Ireland*, Picture Press, Co Down, 1990.

6. The verse is recorded in the report of the O'Connell Monument Committee meeting in *The Freeman's Journal*, December 14, 1867.

7. I am grateful to Dr Rionach Ui Ogain, of the Irish Folklore Department in University College Dublin, for identifying the melody.

8. David Hammond, (ed.), *A Centenary Selection from Moore's Melodies*, Gilbert Dalton, Dublin, 1979.

9. Peter Springer, 'Rhetorik der Standhaftigkeit, Monument und Sockel nach dem Ende des traditionellen Denkmals', *Wallraf- Richartz-Jahrbuch*, 1987/8, Vol. 48/49, pp. 365-408.

10. *The Freeman's Journal*, December 14, 1867.

11. *The Freeman's Journal*, December 17, 1867.

BANK BUILDING IN NINETEENTH-CENTURY IRELAND

*It is ironic that the Yeats Society Centre in Sligo (Fig. 1), originally built in 1899 by the Belfast Banking Company to the designs of the architect Vincent Craig, was designed in the 'Old English' style to emphasise its links with the Union.[1] An acceptance of the fact that architects can relay political messages through abstract compositions, relies upon the understanding that an architectural language exists and that architectural design

Politics and religion played their part when it came to the design of banks in the last century. **Emmet O'Brien** *considers the symbolism of the various styles.*

climate and that of Italy? Not in the least ... We are not Italians, we are Englishmen'.[3]

In addition Pugin argued that Gothic was an honest style, as every feature of a Gothic church, including semi-decorative elements such as gargoyles, had some functional purpose. Ruskin developed this thesis further, stating that Gothic was in fact a natural building process based on medieval technical practices as opposed to classical architecture

can have an abstract text with a symbolic theme. Abstract motifs such as Celtic interlace and decorative features from Irish Romanesque churches are often considered to have symbolic associations of a nationalist nature, because they originate in a period of rich artistic merit in Ireland's history and belong to an era free from foreign dominance. In advance of establishing the existence of political metaphor in Irish bank architecture, it is essential to consider the relevant theories which influenced Victorian design and the architectural idioms favoured by nineteenth century architects. In addition it will be of some value to investigate the political loyalties held by many of the banking companies at large in Ireland during the nineteenth century.[2]

The architects of nineteenth century bank buildings in Ireland were faced with a dilemma concerning design and style. This 'Victorian' dilemma emanated from a conflict of differing architectural doctrines. One school of thought promoted the idea that architects should utilise the various styles of architecture provided by history when composing their designs. On the other hand the architectural theologians of the era, in particular Augustus Welby Northmore Pugin and John Ruskin, preached the concept that function and national identity should dictate the style chosen. This theory resulted in a rise in the number of churches and public buildings in the Gothic style and a reaction aginst classical idioms. Pugin objects strongly to the use of the 'Italian' style in England: 'Is there any similarity between our

which often incorporated unnecessary elements derived from obsolete classical formats.[4] A number of Ruskin's ideas, including the replacement of machinery by craftsmen and the practice of allowing function to dictate design rather than simply imitating style, were eventually practised with the arrival of the Arts and Crafts Movement. The theories of Pugin and Ruskin would make some impression on every architect working in Ireland after 1850. Indeed it was the political and moral agenda emphasised by Pugin and Ruskin which led to the architects of Irish bank buildings introducing a sectarian dimension into their designs.

The Northern Banking Company became the first Irish joint-stock bank when it was founded in 1824. The practice of banking, before the Irish Banking Act of 1824, had been monopolised by the Bank of Ireland and a number of small private banks with limited power. It was the system of branch banking that led to the competitive nature of bank architecture. The majority of the eight hundred and nineteen branches opened between 1820 and 1920 were specifically built for banking.[5]

Francis Johnston, Thomas Deane and Charles Lanyon are examples of the high standard of architects commissioned by the nineteenth century bank companies in Ireland. These institutions were, for the most part, willing to spend large volumes of money to receive outstanding designs and the most impressive structures. The result of all this activity is that bank buildings exhibit more nineteenth-century styles than any other individual

1. SLIGO. The Yeats Society Centre, originally the Belfast Bank. Designed in 1897 in the Old English style by Vincent Craig, brother of Northern Ireland's first prime minister. In 1923, the Belfast Bank ceased business in the new Irish Free State.

2. DUBLIN. The Bank of Ireland, College Green, originally the National Bank. Designed by William Barnes and Isaac Farrell in 1842, this style recalls the Renaissance palazzos of Italy's merchant banking families.

building type at large in Ireland and these designs provide the architectural historian with a reasonably good summary of nineteenth century architectural fashion in Ireland.

The first bank branches to be built in Ireland were similar in design to Regency town houses. The Wexford branch of the Bank of Ireland designed by George Halpin and completed in 1832 (Fig. 3), is a good example of the first bank buildings erected in Ireland.[6] Indeed the domestic appearance of these early banks better qualify for the term 'bank house' rather than the expression 'bank office'. These structures represent that period of transience when the home-based private banker had not yet departed from the Irish business scene and a new corporate image was still to emerge for the branch bank. The Travellers' Club in London, designed by Charles Barry and completed in 1832, provided Irish architects with a suitable model for bank buildings. The astylar (classical without columns) exterior of this 'Italianate palazzo' style structure made it possible to create a design either high in ornamentation or simple and austere. As this style harks back to the Renaissance palazzo which played host to Italy's most distinguished merchant banking families, this factor alone confirmed the acceptability of this architectural form as the chief model for Irish bank buildings. Sandham Symes and William Caldbeck, the most prolific designers of bank branches in Ireland, both used the palazzo theme as the point of departure for the majority of their compositions. The National Bank's headquarters, College Green, Dublin designed by William Barnes and Isaac Farrell in 1842, with alterations by Charles Geoghegan (Fig. 2), and the offices of the Belfast Banking Company in Waring Street, Belfast, by Charles Lanyon are two excellent examples of the palazzo style bank building in Ireland.[7]

It was not until the Ruskin-influenced work of Thomas Deane and Benjamin Woodward that Gothic became acceptable for commercial uses. Previous to their Venetian design for the Crown Life Assurance Office of 1855-57 in Blackfriars, London, Gothic remained essentially the style of the church, the Conservatives and, in its picturesque form, the country house. Ruskin's *Stones of Venice*, published in 1853, insists that not only is Venetian Gothic suitable for commercial architecture, but that it is in fact the style of Venice, the greatest 'aristocracy of commerce'.[8] William H Lynn's Belfast Bank in Dungannon, completed in 1855, and Thomas Newenham Deane's Munster Bank, Dame Street, Dublin are notable examples of the Venetian Gothic style.[9] A common feature of High Victorian architecture was the engagement of different styles in

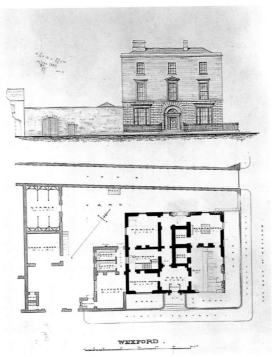

3. WEXFORD. Originally the Bank of Ireland. Designed by George Halpin and completed in 1832, this is similar in style to a Regency house and is a good example of the first bank buildings in Ireland.

a single design. These hybrid compositions are generally a combination of classical form with medieval trappings, an association which must have alarmed Ruskin. Many of the offices designed for the Provincial Bank in the Victorian period belong to this family of hybrids. William G Murray's Provincial Bank, College Street, Dublin completed in 1868, is a Neo-Palladian composition with Hibernian detailing (Fig. 4), while William J Barre's design for the Provincial Bank, Royal Avenue, Belfast incorporates a similar Neo-Palladian format with decorative features inspired by the Romanesque style.[10]

Late-Victorian architecture was emphatically influenced by the rebellion against academic Gothic led by Richard Norman Shaw, Edward William Godwin and John James Stevenson, which resulted in a new flexible style. Based for the most part on the seventeenth-century vernacular classicism of Holland, England, France, Flanders and Germany, this new idiom was loosely termed 'Queen Anne'. This group of architects was also responsible, in some part, for the introduction of a picturesque 'Old English' style. Philip Webb must also be ranked among the innovators of this new architectural epoch as his designs were highly influential. His Red House, built for the leader of the Arts and Crafts Movement William Morris, in 1859, shows the picturesque possibilities of mixing the 'Queen Anne' style with Gothic and Tudor building techniques. The architects of bank buildings in Ireland reacted to this philosophy of free selection by creating compositions in 'Queen Anne', 'Old English', 'Scotch Baronial' and even 'Arts and Crafts' styles. Nevertheless an indepth analysis of bank architecture in Ireland will not be attempted here. Instead it is the symbolic nature of these buildings, with particular reference to political metaphor evident in some of their designs, that will be the central theme of this investigation.

In 1839 an agreement was signed by the Ulster, Northern and Belfast Banks, binding them all to uniform levels of interest rates and preventing canvassing for each other's accounts.[11] Throughout the nineteenth century co-operation existed between the three Belfast-based banks, in order to protect their united interests against aggressive expansionists, notably the National and Hibernian Banks. As a result of the combined strategy of the three Belfast-based banks, they became a group apart from the other Irish banking companies based in Dublin and Cork. This division between the two banking communities in Ireland began as an economic rift, however the political nature of nineteenth-century Ireland added social and political differences to the already fractured equation. Daniel O'Connell and the Repeal

Movement's support for the National and Provincial Banks is proof of the political nature of banking in Victorian Ireland. The staffing of banks was a transparent exhibition of the religious and political bias of most companies. In general the majority of employees were Protestant and later Unionist, however the Hibernian and the Munster and Leinster Banks were Catholic and Nationalist. As a result of Fenianism, Cardinal Cullen's organisation of Catholic politics and the successes of Parnell, late nineteenth century Ulster witnessed a united Protestant bond between Anglicans and Presbyterians to protect their industrial interests in the Lagan Valley. Between 1851 and 1870 the membership of Orange Lodges in Belfast was trebled and the Home Rule Bills of 1886 and 1893 emphatically opposed in north-east Ulster. This political backdrop created substantial political suspicion between the various Irish banks.[12]

At the time of the Home Rule talks the Belfast-based banks are recorded as having told their staff to avoid political debate, however there is now no doubt that they all shared staunch Unionist convictions. All three banks had large numbers of leading Unionists on their advisory committees. Thomas Sinclair, the leader of the Liberal-Unionists in the 1880s, was a member of the Northern Bank's Advisory Committee and another leading Unionist, Robert Sherman-Crawford, was a member of the Belfast Bank's Board of Superintendance. Probably the most illuminating fact establishing the Unionist nature of these banks is that the Belfast Bank managed the Sir Edward Carson Unionist Defence Fund, an income which financed anti-Home Rule propaganda in Britain. The aggressive expansion of the overtly Catholic and nationalist Hibernian Bank into Ulster at a time when the Home Rule debate was at its most controversial was the final ingredient which separated bank companies under political and sectarian headings on a level never experienced before.[13]

There was also religious and political consideration behind the decisions of different boards of directors when employing architects. Between 1875 and 1910 Timothy Hevey, John O'Neill, William Byrne and Edward J Toye were all commissioned to design branches for the Hibernian Bank.[14] It was surely no coincidence that all three architec-

4. DUBLIN.. The Allied Irish Bank, College Street, originally the Provincial Bank. This Neo-Palladian composition with Hibernian detailing, by William Murray, completed in 1868, is a Victorian hybrid of styles which would have alarmed Ruskin, who favoured Venetian Gothic for commercial architecture.

5. DUBLIN. The figure of Erin, by James PEARSE and Edmund SHARP. The Bank of Ireland, College Green, Dublin, originally the National Bank. Carved for the National Bank's Head Office in 1889, this typically Celtic Revival image, with its inscription in Irish, 'Ireland for ever', harp, wolfhound and Irish crown, emphasises the Bank's patriotic leanings.

tural firms were also prolific designers of Roman Catholic churches. This was a conscious decision that confirms the Hibernian Bank's intention to promote itself as a nationalist institution serving the needs of the majority in Ireland. The Munster and Leinster Bank seems to have followed the same path of association as the Hibernian Bank. Both Walter Glynn Doolin and George Coppinger Ashlin, employed by the Munster and Leinster Bank in the late nineteenth century, were responsible for numerous fine designs for the Roman Catholic Church.[15] The Belfast-based banks employed architects almost exclusively from the Protestant community. The Belfast Bank commissioned Vincent Craig, the brother of James Craig, the Grand Master of County Down Orangemen and later the first Prime Minister of Northern Ireland, to design at least three branches between 1895 and 1905.[16] Godfrey Ferguson, the Secretary of the Church Army, an important arm of Anglicanism, was the chief architect of the Northern Bank.[17] In 1889 the Ulster Bank chose Thomas Drew, the son of a militant Orangeman, to produce designs for its most important branch of the Victorian period to be erected in Dublin.[18]

The most important question to be asked here is: did the political affiliations of the various banks influence the designs of their buildings? The Dublin and Cork based banks built branches in Italianate, Victorian Freestyle (hybrids), Romanesque and Gothic styles. However their buildings are often highly decorated with Hiberno-Romanesque motifs and 'Celtic Revival' ornamentation advertising their nationalist sympathies. These banks generally avoided the 'Old English' and 'Scotch Baronial' idioms inspired by previous eras of British architectural activity. In direct contrast, after initially using Italianate and Venetian Gothic forms, the Belfast-based banks favoured 'Queen Anne', 'Old English', 'Scotch Baronial' and 'Georgian Revival', all linked to Pugin's concept of employing an appropriate architectural image. To suggest that these architects were simply following British fashion and did not understand the innuendoes present in their own work would seem naive. The majority of these architects were trained by the best architectural firms in Britain and

Ireland, and would therefore be fully aware of current theories relating to stylistic appropriateness.

The socio-political leanings of most banks in Ireland began to influence their architectural briefs as early as the mid-Victorian years. Britannia, Justice and Commerce, carved by Thomas Fitzpatrick in 1860 for the headquarters of the Ulster Bank, left the public in no doubt as to the national identity of this institution.[19] In contrast Erin, carved by James Pearse and Edmund Sharp for the National Bank's head office in 1889 (Fig. 5), exhibits an entirely different sentiment. Here the patriotic leanings associated with the National Bank are emphasised by the artist's acknowledgement of the Celtic Revival.[20] Erin, represented by a female figure, sits in majesty – her harp, an Irish wolfhound, the Irish crown and various emblems of trade and commerce surrounding her. Although the central figure's cloth-

6. MONAGHAN. The Bank of Ireland, originally the Hibernian Bank. O'Neill and Byrne's design, completed in 1875, has similarities with Romanesque church design, and communicated the Hibernian Bank's unequivocally nationalist doctrine to the Ulster public.

ing is classical in treatment, the artists have employed a stylised manner for their forms. The ornate harp with its interlaced decoration and the Irish inscription on the pedestal 'Erin go bragh' (Ireland for ever), are typical examples of Celtic Revival design.

Stone carving was employed by many of the Dublin and Cork-based banks to highlight their sense of national identity. At the beginning of the 1860s the National Bank's architect, William Caldbeck, began to introduce details from Celtic and Romanesque sources into his designs. He maintained his classically proportioned model but changed its appearance with an admixture of motifs. The National Bank in Ennis, completed in 1864, is a good example of the Caldbeck hybrid.[21] It stands two storeys high with five bays, like an Italian tourist in Irish Romanesque garments. The doorcases are decorated with columns, foliate capitals and Hiberno-Romanesque chevrons. The round-headed windows of the ground floor meet to form an

arcade. Caldbeck's National Bank in Boyle, which opened for business in 1864, is similar in many respects to the Ennis branch.[22] On this occasion Caldbeck has decorated the entrances with shafts of polished limestone and foliated capitals. Above the entrances, providing the branch with a Victorian security system, are a pair of carved heads acting as keystones. The admixture of styles evident in the later work of Caldbeck is also apparent in William George Murray's designs for the Provincial Bank. Although the English-managed Provincial Bank was essentially a Protestant institution, it was aware of the complex nature of Irish politics. This might explain why Murray's most important design for the Provincial Bank, College Street, Dublin, completed in 1868, does not contain blatant visual metaphor of a Unionist or Nationalist nature and might at best be described as an Anglo-Irish creation.[23] At first glance Murray's design, incorporating a Corinthian order of columns supporting a central pediment, appears to be a Neo-Palladian composition. However the roped mouldings, panels of foliage and chevron carvings are far removed from the English Neo-Palladian style. The Provincial Bank in Dublin is a symbolic compromise exhibiting a visual truce between two very different forms, one English, the other 'Hiberno-Romanesque'.

The most remarkable example of political metaphor in Irish bank architecture is provided by the Hibernian Bank's offices in Monaghan (Fig. 6). Throughout the late Victorian period the Hibernian Bank had an aggressive policy of branch expansion, particularly with regard to Ulster. This policy, combined with the Nationalist and Catholic ethos of the Hibernian, led to a head-on collision with the Belfast-based banks in Ulster. The Hibernian believed that by advertising its political and religious convictions they would polarise the banking public and in doing so attract the substantial Catholic population. O'Neill and Byrne's design for the Hibernian Bank's offices in Monaghan appear to be the architectural realisation of the company's propaganda campaign. The Monaghan branch, completed in 1875, has many similarities with Romanesque church design.[24] It is a two-storey structure of rough stone located on an angular site facing Church Square on one side and Market Street on the other. Among the elements which are influenced by Romanesque church architecture are the portal with its columns and round-headed arch, the 'apsidal' treatment of the entrance-front complimented by the roof which turns the corner and the coarse texture of the stone. The curved facade is a very creative piece of design; it incorporates the projecting portal with its balcony and three segment-headed windows above linked by impost mouldings. The result of O'Neill and Byrne's work is an ingenious composition which precariously

BANK BUILDING IN NINETEENTH-CENTURY IRELAND

7. DUBLIN. The Allied Irish Bank, Dame Street, originally the Munster Bank. This florid composition, with its echoes of Venice and Irish Romanesque, was designed by Thomas Newenham Deane and completed in 1874.

8. BALLYSHANNON. The Allied Irish Bank, originally the Belfast Bank. This mongrel Scotch Baronial bank, probably designed by Samuel P Close in 1878, highlights the traditional cultural interaction between Scotland and Ulster and successfully advertises the Belfast Bank's political affiliations.

occupies the middle ground between the church and bank idioms, while brilliantly communicating the Hibernian Bank's nationalist doctrine to the public.

Timothy Hevey, a gifted architect who created many fine compositions for the Catholic church, designed the Letterkenny branch of the Hibernian Bank in 1874.[25] His work for the church and his involvement with the Catholic High Gothic circle of EW Pugin and George Ashlin must have made him an attractive choice for the Hibernian Bank. At Letterkenny his ornate Gothic design does not have the ecclesiastical aura of the Monaghan branch, however its blue rubble walls and red sandstone trim, combined with the columns in polished granite, are typical of the textured format chosen by church architects. The Celtic style monogram on the facade is the final clue to the public, leaving no uncertainty as to the political leanings of this institution.

The Munster Bank, which later became the Munster and Leinster bank, was recognised as being both Catholic and nationalist in its sentiments. Thomas Newenham Deane continued 'Deane and Woodward's' loyalty to the Venetian style when designing the Munster Bank's offices on the corner of Palace Street and Dame Street (Fig. 7).[26] Nevertheless this florid composition, completed in 1874, has also been dubbed 'Hibernian Monumental' by Douglas Richardson because of the wealth of Irish motifs employed especially in the interior.[27] The exterior has two colossal storeys of Ballinasloe limestone punctuated by ornate arcaded windows, which are in turn decorated with elaborate hood-mouldings and clusters of colonnettes. Completing this majestic design is a handsome modillion cornice supported by elegant corbels. Venice is not entirely responsible for providing the inspiration for the numerous columns, piers and colonnettes. These elements also exhibit references to Irish Romanesque architecture, which might be read as a prologue to the Irishness of the interior carving. The banking hall is surrounded by pilasters with carved capitals which support an arcade. The capitals play host to images of Irish fauna and flora

including herons, bulrushes and foxgloves. Above all, the most interesting visual statement is subtly placed above the capitals: here themes of plenty alternate with themes of poverty. Female heads with garlands of flowers in their hair are a reference to the good times, but in direct contrast are images such as the starving dogs reminding all that little time had passed in Ireland since the Famine. In Ireland after the Famine, nationalists,and indeed many ordinary people, perceived the Famine as representing the epitome of British oppression. Therefore its presence as a subject in the carvings in the Munster Bank is both a moral statement and a political comment.

At Ballyshannon in county Donegal the Belfast Bank's branch, probably designed by Samuel P Close in 1878, owes its inspiration to Scotland (Fig. 8).[28] This mongrel Scotch Baronial bank is a dramatic tower of coarse rubble armed with crow-stepped gables, bellcotes and a clock turret. There is no identity crisis surrounding the ancestry of of this edifice; its lineage highlights the tradition of cultural interaction between Scotland and Ulster. The relationship between Scotland and Ulster is one that Unionists relate to on many levels including religion, ancestry, economics and national identity. The Ballyshannon branch emphasises the common bond shared throughout the Union and successfully advertises the Belfast Bank's political affiliations.

Vincent Craig considered the bank building to be an opportunity to indulge in his own architectural adventures. The result of this attitude was three refreshing designs for the Belfast Bank at Sligo, Rathmines and Portrush that embody a broad knowledge of British architecture. In Sligo the Belfast Bank, now the Yeats Society Centre, is an excellent example of the 'Old English' manner practised by Norman Shaw and Nesfield.[29] Nonetheless, its location in a provincial Irish town poses questions about the appropriateness of its style. This vernacular was promoted as a suitable source by Norman Shaw for England as it was without doubt an English idiom. Yet at the time when Tudor plastering, brickwork, half timbering and tile-hanging was common in

England, the tower house was dominating Irish architecture. Therefore, while Norman Shaw and Nesfield were reviving a vernacular, Craig was in fact importing foreign style. If Craig is simply following fashion, the use of the 'Old English' style is naive; however, if the brother of Northern Ireland's first Prime Minister is employing it metaphorically then there is a conscious attempt to illuminate the 'union' between Ireland and 'mainland Britain'.

The twentieth century witnessed the revival of English classical forms through the work of Godfrey W Ferguson for the Northern Bank and the architectural partnership of 'Blackwood and Jury' for the Ulster Bank. In contrast, Edward J Toye opted for Italian sources for his Hibernian Bank branches and Arthur Hill was inspired by the classical purity of Beaux Arts design for his impressive Munster and Leinster Bank, South Mall, Cork. This underlines a conscious effort on the part of the architects employed by the Hibernian Bank and the Munster and Leinster Bank to avoid styles originating from English idioms.[30]

The Arts and Crafts movement of the late nineteenth century had a vision of an architecture free of imposed style which would develop naturally from its surroundings and from the needs of local people. This concept of employing vernacular

9. DUNGLOE. The Northern Bank. Demolished in 1972, this building, designed by Godfrey W Ferguson in 1896, was a rare example of Arts and Crafts architecture in Ireland.

building techniques, combined with William Morris's declaration that the only political ideology which would allow a true Arts and Crafts Society to emerge was Communism, presented an ideal for architecture which might avoid the obvious stylistic dilemmas resulting from nationalism. It is unfortunate that the Dungloe branch of the Northern Bank designed by Godfrey W Ferguson in 1896, no longer exists (Fig. 9).[31] Demolished in 1972, this building was a rare example of Arts and Crafts architecture in Ireland. Essentially rectangular in plan and two storeys high, it was constructed entirely of local materials including rubble walls with yellow cement dashing and rough granite for the base, quoins and window surrounds. Additional colour was supplied by the green slates and red tiles which covered the roof. Its organic flavour was created by the interaction of the pyramid roof, emphatic chimney, eyebrow windows, asymmetriclal fenestration and crow-stepped porch. At Dungloe Ferguson succeeded in avoiding historicism while designing a building with much character sympathetic to the ideas of William Morris.

EMMET O'BRIEN was awarded a Ph.D from University College Dublin for his thesis on Bank Architecture in Ireland, 1726-1910.

1. Tadgh Kilgannon, *Sligo and its Surroundings*, Sligo, 1926, pp.160-62. In 1923 the Belfast Bank withdrew from business in the new Irish Free State. The Royal Bank purchased the Free State offices of the Belfast Bank. The Royal Bank later became part of Allied Irish Banks. In 1965 all the Belfast Bank's branches in Northern Ireland became Northern Bank branches.
2. The principal source for information on nineteenth century bank architecture in Ireland is: Emmet O'Brien, 'The Architecture of Bank Buildings in Ireland 1726-1910', Ph.D Thesis, University College, Dublin, 1991. In association with the Irish Bankers Federation.
3. AWN Pugin, *The True Principles of Pointed or Christian Architecture*, London 1841, pp.64-65.
4. John Ruskin, *The Stones of Venice*, vol. II, London 1853, p.161.
5. See O'Brien, *op. cit.*, vol. II, pp.340-42.
6. 'Transactions of the Court of Directors', 28 April 1829, Bank of Ireland Head Office, Dublin, and Edward McParland, 'The Bank and the Visual Arts', *Bicentenary Essays: Bank of Ireland 1783-1983*, (ed) FSL Lyons, Dublin 1983, p.119.
7. Maurice Craig, *Dublin 1660-1860*, London

1952, p.322; *The Irish Builder*, 15 May 1889, p.208, and 15 March 1864, p.44; Paul Larmour, *Belfast, An Illustrated Architectural Guide*, Belfast 1987, p.14. The National and Hibernian Banks became part of the Bank of Ireland. The Royal, Provincial and Munster and Leinster Banks became part of Allied Irish Banks.
8. Nicholas Taylor, *Monuments of Commerce*, London, 1968, p.53.
9. RW Oram and PJ Rankin, *Historic Buildings, Groups of Buildings. Areas of Architectural Importance in and near Dungannon and Cookstown*, Ulster Architectural Heritage Society, Belfast, 1971, p.21 and 'The Munster Bank', *Dublin Evening Mail*, 8 April 1874.
10. *The Irish Builder*, 15 June 1862, p.165 and *The Irish Builder*, 1 September 1868, p.215.
11. The principal source for the economic history of the three Belfast based banks is Philip Ollerenshaw, *Banking in Nineteenth Century Ireland,* Manchester 1983.
12. The growth in Irish Protestantism and its effects upon industry in Ulster is discussed in RF Foster, *Modern Ireland*, London 1989, pp.373-400.
13. See Ollerenshaw, *op.cit.*, pp.157-63.
14. See the Alfred Jones Biographical Index in

the Irish Architectural Archive, Dublin, for the 'Timothy Hevey File', 'The William H. Byrne File', 'The John O'Neill FIle' and 'The Edward J. Toye File'.
15. *ibid.*, 'The Walter Glynn Doolin File" and 'The George Coppinger Ashlin File'.
16. *ibid.*, 'The Vincent Craig File'.
17. *ibid.*, The Godfrey Ferguson File'.
18. *ibid.*, 'The Thomas Drew File'.
19. *The Dublin Builder*, 1 October 1859, p.135.
20. *The Irish Builder,1* January 1889, p.14.
21. *ibid.*,15 February 1864, p.26.
22. *ibid.*, 1 October 1864, p.201.
23. *ibid.*,15 June 1862, p.165.
24. *ibid.*, vol. 17, 1875, p.34.
25. *ibid.*, 17 February 1875 pp.34-36.
26. The 'Munster Bank Premises Book', AIB Archives, College Street Branch, Dublin.
27. Douglas Scott Richardson, 'Gothic Revival in Ireland', Ph.D Thesis, Yale University, 1970, pp.416-17.
28. See O'Brien, *op. cit.*, pp275-76.
29. The 'Royal Bank Premises Book', AIB Archives, College Street Branch, Dublin. This was originally built as a Belfast Bank branch.
30. See O'Brien, *op. cit.*, pp.240-305.
31. See O'Brien, *op. cit.*, pp.286-87.

IRISH PAINTERS IN PARIS, 1868-1914

Julian Campbell *examines the registers of the École des Beaux Arts and the Académie Julian for the names of Irish students.*

Among the thousands of foreign students to study in Paris in the late nineteenth and early twentieth centuries, many were Irish. Only a handful of Irish pupils studied at the École des Beaux Arts, but dozens passed through the studios of Julian, which welcomed both foreigners and women students alike. The teaching at both institutions was highly academic, and some of the professors at the École also taught at Julian's. The existence of the registers of the École and the recent discovery of many of the registers of Julian's, has facilitated a much more precise study of the Irish pupils at these institutions. In both cases, I am grateful to publications by American scholars: H Barbara Weinburg, *American Students of Jean-Leon Gerome*, Fort Worth, 1984; and Catherine Fehrer, *The Julian Academy, Paris 1868-1939*, Shepherd Gallery, New York 1989, for drawing my attention to the presence of these registers, in the Archives Nationales de France, Paris.[1]

The following lists include the names of both well-known and lesser-known Irish students, as well as some completely forgotten figures. It is significant that amongst the earliest students at Julian's was a large contingent of women artists. The fact that many went on to gain successes at the Paris Salon is testament to the quality of the teaching they received. The presence of George Moore's name amongst hundreds of French students, in Cabanel's atelier at the École, was an exciting surprise, as was the opportunity to pinpoint the movements of elusive artists such as William Gerard Barry at Julian's. The registers also provide valuable information about the artists' date or place of birth, address in Paris, and so on. According to Dr Fehrer, registers of the women's ateliers at Julian's have recently been re-discovered.[2] So further research into these Irish students undoubtedly remains to be done.

IRISH STUDENTS AT THE ÉCOLE DES BEAUX ARTS[3]
Entries follow the following format: name, date of study, *atelier/teacher*, no. in studio, date of registration, address in Paris (city and country of birth, date of birth).
ST GAUDENS, Auguste, 1867, *Jouffroy* (Sculptor) no. 96, 8 September, 1867, 7R.3(?) Freres, (Dublin, Irlande, 1 Mars 1848).
MOORE, Georges, 1873, *Cabanel*, no. 270, 25(?) April 1874, Hotel Voltaire (Castlebar, Irlande, 24 Feb. 1852).
O'KELLY, Aloysius, 1874, *Gerome*, no. 383, 7 October 1874, 4 Rue Jacob (Dublin, Irlande, Jan 1851).
HOVENDEN, Thomas, 1874, *Cabanel*, no. 313, 28 October 1874, 15 Rue Jacob, (Cork, Irlande, 28 Dec 1844).
HOEY, Joseph (?) Nicholas, 1881, *Gerome*, no. 746, 17 May 1881, 6 Rue Boissonade (Dublin, Irlande, 18 Sept. 1842).
BONAPARTE WYSE, Lionel H., 1898, *Gerome*, no. 311, 30 April 1898, 23 rue Marget (Waterford, Irlande, 7 Sept. 1874).

IRISH STUDENTS AT ACADÉMIE JULIAN
Entries follow the following format: artist's name, date of study, *atelier/teacher*, date of inscription, address in Paris, nationality, or place of birth, by whom recommended (*An asterisk* * *denotes artists whose names are listed in registers*)
MOORE, George, 1873, 1875-76, *Lefebvre*, Hotel de Russie (corner of Rue Drouot) Galerie Feydeau, Passage des Panoramas.
KENNEDY, Kate J, c.1878-79, *Julian Robert-Fleury*, 19 Rue Paul Lelong.
PURSER, Sarah, 1878-79, *T Robert-Fleury*, Avenue des Ternes.
O'HAGAN, Harriet, 1875, *Robert-Fleury*
*SWINNERTON, Fern (?) 1879-80, 50 Rue de Douai, Dublin.
McKENZIE, William Gibbes.
JONES, Henry Thaddeus, c.1879-81, *Boulanger, Lefebvre*, Faubourg Saint-Honore, Cork.
*COGHILL, Egerton, 1881-83, *Bouguereau, Robert-Fleury*.
LAVERY, John, 1881-84, *Bouguereau, Robert-Fleury*, Hotel de Saxe, 12 Rue Jacob.
WEBB, Maria Dorothy, c.1883-84, *T Robert-Fleury*, 39 Bvd St Germain.
*BARRY, William Gerard, 1883-84, *Lefebvre, Boulanger*, 8 Sept 1883, 54 Rue Notre Dame des Americain (sic) Irlandais (par Townes (?)).
*CAIRNES, Harry Stein, 1884-87(?), *Lefebvre, Laurens*, 17 Rue Bleue, Anglais, (Cork).
STARKIE, Edith H, 1884-87, *Robert-Fleury, Lefebvre, Boulanger*.

*MOYNAN, Richard T, 1885-86, *Robert-Fleury, Bouguereau*, 620 Avenue Victoria, Anglais.
MACCAUSLAND, Katherine, c.1885-88, *Robert-Fleury, Lefebvre, Boulanger* (?).
DILLON, 1886-87, *Lefebvre*, Rue St Hyacinthe, Irlandais.
OSWALD, John H, 1888
McCANN, Louisa,1890, *Robert Fleury, Bouguereau, Lefebvre*, Hotel de Chartres, Rue Brea.
*BUTLER, O, 1890, 203 Bvd. Raspail, Anglais (Irlandais) (par Hitchcock).
*CHETWOOD-AIKEN, Walter C, 1890-93(?) *Bouguereau*, Bvd St Michel, 7 Rue Delhambre, Anglais.
*GEOGHEGAN, 1890, 16 Avenue Niel, Irlandais.
*DIGNAM, J, 1890, *Laurens*, rue d'armarille, Dublin (par O Butler).
*O'BRIEN, William Dermod, 1891, *Robert Fleury, Flameng*, 16 Rue Lemartine, Irlandais.
*SWAN, Edmund, 1891-92, *Bouguereau, Ferrier*, 57 St Andre des Arts, Dublin.
*SWAN, Edwin, 1891-92, *Bouguereau, Ferrier*, 57 St Andre des Arts, Dublin.
*HUGHES, John, 1892, *Laurens(?), Constant*, 31 Oct. 1892.
MORROW, George, 1893, *Laurens, Constant*, 4 Sept. 1983, 2 Rue d'Odessa, Irlande (par Duffy).
*MOONEY, R, 1893-94, 1895-97, *Bouguereau, Ferrier*, 4 bis rue des Beaux-Arts, Irlandais.
*DOOLEY, 1893-94, 2 Rue d'Odessa.
*TALLON, J A, 1894, 38 rue St Honore, Dublin.
*BRUCE-JOY, Albert, 1896, *Laurens*, 13 July 1896, 16 imp Du Maries, London.
GORE-BOOTH, Constance, 1898, *Laurens*.
*HENRY, Paul, 1898-99, *Laurens*, 203 Bvd Raspail/9 rue Campagne. Belfast (par Pierpoint?).
*McGINN, Francis A, 1898, *Laurens, Constant*, 203 Bvd Raspail, Dublin.
MORGAN, Miss Taylor, 1899.
*O'DONOHOE, Francis Joseph, 1900-01, *Constant*, 24 Sept, 1900, Hotel de la Forell, rue Delambu(?).
*McGUSTY, Henry Alexander, 1900, *Constant*, 12 Rue Foie de Raux (?).
*WYSE, Lionel H Bonaparte, 1900, *Laurens*, 23 rue Marget, Waterford, Irlande.
*LEECH, William John Brougham, 1901, *Bouguereau, Ferrier*, 9 rue Chaumel, Dublin.
HERDMAN, Maud, Omagh, Irlande (won Prix a l'Academie)[4]
LEMERCIER, Eugene E, 1907-10, *J P Laurens*
*WHITE, 1912, *Laurens*, Dublin.
*MAHONEY, Martin F, 1913, *Laurens*, 15 Delambu (Cork).

---

1. Registers of inscription of students at l'École des Beaux Arts, 1863-1875, and 1874-1945. Archives Nationales de France, AJ 52-245 and AJ 52-248. Registers at Académie Julian, Archives Nationales de France, 63 AS 1-9. These include many volumes, containing principally account books for no. 31 Rue de Dragon, 1890+, but also a list of 'élèves recommandés', c.1875-1919 (63 AS 1 (ii)), and a registration book for the ateliers of Boulanger and Lefebvre c.1881-85, and Laurens and Constant, c.1892-1900 (63 AS 9). Catherine Fehrer's book, *The Julian Academy, Paris 1868-1939*, also proved extremely useful. Further information was derived from the Catalogues of the Paris Salon, 1870-1914; J Campbell, *The Irish Impressionists, Irish Artists in France and Belgium, 1850-1914*, National Gallery of Ireland, 1984; and Edward Morris and Amanda McKay, 'British Art Students in Paris, 1814-1890, *Apollo*, 9 February, 1992, pp.78-84.

2. Catherine Fehrer, in correspondence with the author, 3 May 1993.

3. William Foy, c.1791-1859 was also a student at the École, c.1816.

4. I am very grateful to Dr Fehrer for informing me about this prize-winning student.

A FORGOTTEN ARTIST, WALTER CHETWOOD-AIKEN

The discovery of a pair of colourful and exotic Breton scenes in an Irish family collection in 1990 has led **Julian Campbell** *to review the career of a painter whose early death hastened his obscurity.*

Walter Chetwood-Aiken (1866-99) was a virtually forgotten artist until the appearance of two Breton paintings by him, *A Song to Spring* and *Le Pardon de Sainte Barbe au Faouet,* in the salesroom in Dublin, in June and in December 1990.[1] Both pictures had been in the family collection at Woodbrook, near Portarlington, Co Laois until 1970. With his unusual name and Anglo-Irish background, the handful of exotic, colourful paintings of Breton life and customs that he painted, and his early death, curiosity in this late nineteenth century artist was aroused. Chetwood-Aiken's career followed a similar pattern to that set by many Irish and English artists in this period: heading off to Paris, studying at the Academie Julian, feeling the powerful lure of Brittany, and gaining success at the Paris Salon and the Royal Academy with his original figurative compositions. Then, on the verge of a successful career, he died in Bristol aged only thirty-three, and his name seems to have passed into obscurity.

Walter C Chetwood-Aiken was born in Bristol in 1866. His father John (1835-1907) was a banker, who inherited the family estate at Woodbrook.[2] His mother

2. WALTER C CHETWOOD-AIKEN (1866-99): Le Pardon de Sainte Barbe au Faouet. *Oil on canvas, 185 x 101 cm (Private collection).* The composition is reminiscent of the work of Gauguin and, like A Song to Spring, this painting was also for many years at Woodbrook.

Lucy had been born in Cork in 1845. Walter was the eldest of five brothers[3] the second of whom, Edward Hamilton, was also an artist, later becoming a bank manager in Bristol. In 1988 Walter was painting at Burnham, Somerset. He may have studied in London before going to Paris around 1890. He studied at the Academie Julian from 1890 to 1893, in the atelier of Bouguereau.[4] At Julian's he was a contemporary of Dermod O'Brien and John Hughes. Astonishingly, Henri Matisse was also a student of Bouguereau's at this time, 1891-92.[5] Aiken also studied with the academic painter Cormon.[6] At Julian's he would have received a conventional academic training, with a strong emphasis on life drawing. However, inevitably he would also have become aware of the revolutionary developments in French art that were taking place outside the studio.

Probably in the mid-1890s, Aiken made his first visit to Brittany. He spent much of the period between 1895 and 1898 here, first at Concarneau, then exploring the region away from the beaten track. He made chalk drawings of peasants, and painted four or five large Breton canvases, in which many figures in traditional dress

1. WALTER C CHETWOOD-AIKEN (1866-99): A Song to Spring. *Oil on canvas, 70 x 168 cm (Private collection).* The picture hung at the artist's family home, Woodbrook, County Laois, until it was sold in 1990 and its rediscovery has led the revival of interest in the painter.

3. WALTER C CHETWOOD-AIKEN (1866-99): La Croix des Marins, Concarneau. *Dimensions and location unknown.* This drawing was made by the artist for reproduction in the Salon Catalogue of 1896 after his own picture exhibited that year.

4. WALTER C CHETWOOD-AIKEN (1866-99): Study of a Breton Woman. *Chalk on paper, 42 x 31 cm. (Bristol Museums & Art Gallery).* The artist was in Brittany from about 1895-98 and most of his known work derives from that period.

are included. He first exhibited at the Salon in 1896, then again in 1897 and 1898. His Breton paintings were shown again in England, at the Royal Academy, the Institute of Painters in Oil Colours, the Bristol Fine Art Academy, and the Liverpool Autumn Exhibition, 1896-99. (See list of works below).

His painting *Le Croix des Marins, Concarneau* was exhibited at the Salon in 1896.[7] It shows five Breton girls and a younger child, in traditional dress and bonnets, upon the quayside, with a mysterious banner or cross in the background. There is a slightly dream-like atmosphere as the figures move in quiet conversation. *A Song to Spring* ('a decorative panel', RA 1897) shows seven girls and an infant in a dappled orchard landscape. The white headdresses and collars, the delicate pink blossoms, are attractively composed along the horizontal canvas. The variety of shapes, the curling 'lapettes', and the colour of the impressive headwear, perhaps suggesting the individual status or village of each girl, add to the alluring decorative effect. The frieze-like appearance recalls Dagnan-Bouveret's *Breton Women at a Pardon*, 1887 (Gulbenkian Foundation, Lisbon). But, more significantly, Aiken's picture has echoes of Gauguin's *Vision after the Sermon*, 1888 (National Gallery of Scotland, Edinburgh),[8] in the cutting of the figures at shoulders or waists, and the decorative treatment

of the headwear, to create an exotic, symbolic effect.

Le Pardon de Sainte Barbe au Faouet et la fete du Saint Sacrament, 1897-98, is a large canvas, containing numerous figures processing in a sunny landscape. Aiken observes the white caps of the women, the fine vestments of the priest, with a red banner above him, and the distinctive bony faces of the men. The man in black behind the priest has different features; might this be a portrait of the artist? The *pardon* was an annual pilgrimage of peasants to receive forgiveness for their sins, and the one at Le Faouet was evidently an important one.[9] With the discovery of Brittany by artists, and a fascination for its customs and traditions, French painters such as Jules Breton, Lhermitte and Dagnan-Bouveret had all painted important pictures of *pardons*.[10] But such great compositions were unusual amongst Irish and British artists. *Le Pardon* is a narrative painting, yet with a brightness of palette and feeling for light that shows an awareness of Impressionism. The relaxed treatment of the landscape even has similarities with Roderic O'Conor, who was in Brittany in the same period, whilst the grouping of pious women around a central event again has echoes of Gauguin.[11]

Le Pardon received a 'mention honourable' at the Salon in 1898. Art critic Antonin Proust (father of the novelist) included Aiken's name amongst several artists to be commended,

A Forgotten Artist, Walter Chetwood-Aiken

and commented: 'each canvas shows its quota of effort, aspiration and draughtsmanship'.[12]

Both *Le Pardon* and *A Song to Spring* have ornate wooden frames, in which the titles are carved in Breton script[13]. These add to the impression of Aiken's fascination with Breton culture.

The two paintings are now in private collections. Aiken's brother Edward presented a painting of a French village, and nine chalk drawings of peasants, to the Bristol Museum and Art Gallery in 1932, in memory of his brother.[14] It is hoped that other pictures by him will re-appear in future years. Combining varied elements of Salon painting with Impressionism and Symbolism, Chetwood-Aiken's work has a distinctive quality of its own, and is worthy of further attention.

DR JULIAN CAMPBELL is a Tutor in History of Art at the Crawford College of Art in Cork. He selected the paintings for the exhibition 'Onlookers in France, Irish Realist and Impressionist Printers,' held at the Crawford Gallery, Cork in Autumn 1993.

ACKNOWLEDGEMENTS
I am very grateful to the following people for help in preparation of this article: Anthony Beeson, Desmond Fitzgerald, Marian Keyes, Vera Ryan, Sheena Stoddard, and the Courtauld Institute Library.

WORKS EXHIBITED BY CHETWOOD-AIKEN 1888-1899[15]

1888:   *Lover's Lane, Burnham*; Bristol Fine Art Academy, Winter Exhibition, no. 728, (Esplanade House, Burnham, Somerset).

1894:   *Twilight*, Royal Society of British Artists, no. 125, £12-12.

1895:   *Souvenir of Brittany*, Bristol FAA Winter Exhibition, no. 167, (The Glen, Stoke Bishop).

1896:   *La Croix de Marins, Concarneau*, Paris Salon, no. 451, né à Bristol (Angleterre), élève de M Cormon, (chez M Richie, rue de Fleurus 27 Paris).

1896-97   *A Breton Girl*, Institute of Painters in Oil Colours, no. 413, £10-10 (137 Gower Street, London WC).

1897:   *Danse au biniou*, Paris Salon no. 378, (Rue de Douai, 39, Paris) *A Song to Spring*, decorative panel, no. 27 and *Shadow of the Cross*, no. 285, Royal Academy (Royal Eye Hospital, Moorfields).

1898   *Le Pardon de Sainte-Barbe at Faouet et la fete du Saint-sacrament* (received 'mention honourable'), Paris Salon, no. 404, (Rue Notre-Dame-Des Champs, 70 bis).

1898   *A Breton Dance*, Royal Academy, London, no. 18 (The Glen, Stoke Bishop, Bristol) *A Breton Dance*, Liverpool Autumn Exhibition no. 1149, £150. *Shadow of the Cross*, Bristol FAA, no. 65

1899   *Le Pardon de Sainte Barbe etc.*, Royal Academy no. 413, Aiken, W C Chetwood (the late)

6. Walter C Chetwood-Aiken (1866-99): Study of a Breton Peasant. *Chalk on paper. 42 x 31 cm. (Bristol Museums & Art Gallery).* The artist died in Bristol and this drawing is one of a number of his works presented to the museum there by his brother in 1932.

1.   Christie's, Dublin, Sale of Irish Paintings, 6 June 1990 and 12 December 1990, respectively

2.   See Desmond Fitzgerald, in *Catalogue of Irish Paintings*, Christie's, Dublin, 6 June 1990, p.67.

3.   Census returns for Stoke Bishop, 1881 and 1891. The family home was at 'The Glen', Stoke Bishop. I am very grateful to Anthony Beeson, Fine Art Librarian, Central Library, Bristol for communicating this, and further biographical information to me.

4.   Registers of Académie Julian, in Archives de France, no. 63 as 1. Aiken commenced at the Académie on 13 January 1890. His address was Bd St Michel, then 7 Rue Delhambre. See also Catherine Fehrer, *The Julian Academy, Paris 1868-1939*, Shepherd Gallery, New York, 1989.

5.   Fehrer, *op. cit.*

6.   As listed in Salon catalogue, 1896.

7   It was illustrated by a drawing, presumably by Aiken himself, in the Salon *Catalogue Illustré*, in 1896, p.21.

8.   See Fitzgerald, *op. cit.*; also Gertrude Prescott Nuding, 'Irish Art on the Market', *Irish Arts Review, Yearbook 1991-92*, p.234.

9.   See also *Onlookers in France, Irish Realist and Impressionist Painters*, Catalogue of an exhibition at the Crawford Art Gallery, Cork.

10.   For example J Breton, *Le Grand Pardon*, (Salon, 1869); Lhermitte, *Le Pardon de Ploumanach*, (Salon, 1879), (Musée de Saint-Quentin); Dagnan-Bouveret, *Pardon en Bretagne*, (Salon, 1887), (Metropolitan Museum, New York).

11.   E.g. *Vision after the Sermon* and *The Yellow Christ* (Albright Knox Art Gallery, Buffalo).

12.   Antonin Proust, *The Salon 1898*, Paris and London 1898 (English trans. by Henry Bacon), p.14.

13.   I am very grateful to Dr Padraig O Riain, University College, Cork for translating these inscriptions from Breton to English.

14.   *A French Village*, 23" x 29". Bristol Museums and Art Gallery, (cat. no. K1164), and nine chalk drawings of peasants. I am very grateful to Mrs Sheena Stoddard, Assistant Curator of the Gallery, for communicating this information to me.

15.   Aiken's name is often listed variously from one exhibition catalogue to another; e.g. Chetwood-Aiken, Walter; WA (sic) Chetwood-Aiken; Aiken, W C Chetwood; Aiken; Chelwood (sic) Aiken, W. C. His address is given in parentheses.

THE ART OF BEATRICE ELVERY, LADY GLENAVY (1883-1970)

Beatrice Glenavy, whose beauty was captured in a celebrated portrait by Orpen, was exceptionally talented. Her life and work as painter, illustrator, sculptor, and stained-glass artist is recalled by **Nicola Gordon Bowe**.

Lady Glenavy's reputation as an artist is generally related to the few oil paintings that only rarely turn up at auction, monogrammed 'BG', usually smallish in scale, perhaps in an old gilded or painted frame. Smoothly and expertly painted, mostly between around 1932 and 1965, they usually depict a consistently idiosyncratic vision, quite at odds with her Modernist and Expressionist contemporaries. Still lifes in haunting, glaucous tones, set against deserted beaches, wooded moonlit glades, pinned *trompe l'oeil* on walls, or glimpsed through windows, they include shells, driftwood, swags of ivy, potted plants, paper cut out into figures or randomly crumpled, chains, beribboned flowers; a medley of keepsakes, some incorporate, like trophies, her own little painted plaster sculptures of mermaids fleeing; of plaques depicting Madonnas and children, or Georgette Heyer-like scenes of a lover and his lass, or a mermaid with a shipwrecked sailor. Strangely knowing, and festooned, doll-like heads, Staffordshire china figures (Fig. 8), tiny articulated artists' dummies, monkeys and stuffed encased birds, her own children's dolls (Fig. 9) and teddy bears seem more animate than the gesturing mythical figures frozen in Arcadian landscapes behind them. Some enact dreamlike classical tableaux of the chase in a Rex Whistler-esque idiom. Wearing poetically historicised costumes, lovers are reunited, abducted, surprised; they embrace or promenade arm in arm, accompanied by blowing zephyrs, leaping centaurs or prancing dogs. Evoking an 'enigmatic, at times almost Surrealist quality',[1] these 'elegant Regency pastiches'[2] reveal impossibly curvaceous figures, Regency bucks, poeticised Macaroni heroes and gracefully buxom heroines enacting romantic scenes in balletic poses, accompanied by happy children in timeless idylls. Other players include child Pans and Cupids, sea monsters, unicorns, ghostly coachmen, shepherdesses, musicians and hunting woodsmen, dramatically posed, fluidly, sinuously handled, but inhabiting as unreal a world as their still-life counterparts.

Although Beatrice Glenavy exhibited at the Royal Hibernian

2. Beatrice ELVERY (1883-1970), The Intruder. *Oil on canvas, 70 x 95 cm Signed, BG in monogram, c.1931 (Private collection).* This picture, 'a sort of Thessalian allegory of desire', was the focal point of the artist's first one-woman show which was held in Dublin in 1935.

Academy nearly every year from 1902 until her death in 1970, only a few of her works were generally seen at one time. In 1955, an exhibition at the Waddington Galleries in Dublin offered a unique opportunity to see thirty of her recent paintings. Critics praised her effortless technique and inventive sense of composition and decoration. One wrote of the 'remote and gentle world Lady Glenavy has created ... a static world, viewed ... through a sort of kindly, nostalgic haze ... in which the initial action or emotion were frozen,' in a 'welcome escape from the facile high-pressure clichés of so many contemporary painters'.[3] Another felt 'She does in pigment what Rupert Brooke did in words in *The Great Lover*', conveying an evocative and whimsical imagination, able to 'create ... a personal mythology'[4] of frolic and fancy, redolent of an 'enchanted age when people were sufficiently strong and confident to be lyrical rather than strident.' James White in the *Irish Press* recalled Poussin, the seventeenth century mannerists, the Surrealists and the artist's much younger contemporary, Patrick Hennessy (whose artistic approach she would later passionately defend).

Prior to that, Glenavy had only held one other one-man show, at the Dublin Painters' Society Gallery in St Stephen's Green in the spring of 1935. There, her showing of nearly sixty paintings with the progressively avant-garde group of 'young and liberally minded artists'[5] who had broken the stranglehold of the RHA, ironically celebrated her delayed election as an Academician (in 1934). This exhibition, centring on her large, dashingly provocative painting, *The Intruder* (Fig. 2), 'a sort of Thessalian allegory of desire',[6] heralded the welcome possibility for her to start painting more prolifically, now that her third child was eleven years old. She was critically acclaimed for her vivid, intense colour, her originality of conception and treatment, humour and unconventional (one might say Post-Modernist) blend of realism and romanticism. Her fundamentally academic approach, matched by an unaffected romanticism devoid of sentimentality, her seemingly effortless integration of composition, decoration and design, and her consummate ease of execution were qualities which had marked her work since its first critical acclaim at the turn of the century.

Beatrice Moss Elvery was born in Dublin into an enterprising, musical and artistic family. Her father, who ran the Dublin family waterproof business, came of Spanish silk trading and worthy

1. Beatrice ELVERY (1883-1970): Lectern, *1904. Cast bronze, 120 cm high. (Tullow Church, Carrickmines, Co Dublin).* The carved oak prie-dieu in the background was also designed by Elvery although made by Frank Browning and carved by Therese Moss. It dates from 1905. Cast in Paris, the lectern, in a proto-Art Nouveau style, is one of the very few pieces by the artist to have been made in bronze.

The Art of Beatrice Elvery, Lady Glenavy (1883-1970)

3. Beatrice ELVERY (1883-1970), The Bath. *Painted and stained glass, 30 x 30 cm. 1909. (Private collection)*. Intended as a representation of the Virgin and Christ Child, this was one of several such small stained glass panels which Elvery exhibited at the Arts and Crafts Society Exhibition of 1910.

4. Beatrice ELVERY (1883-1970), The Virgin Ironing. *Pen and ink design, hand-printed by the Cuala Press. 24 x 21 cm. Signed 'BE' in monogram. c.1910. (Private collection)*.

English stock; her mother, Teresa Moss from Kilternan, Co. Wicklow, was the seventh child of exceptionally enlightened parents and the sister of Phoebe Traquair an outstandingly inspired and versatile star of the Edinburgh Arts and Crafts movement, whom WB Yeats described as 'delightful, a saint and a little singing bird'.[7] Both sisters had attended the Dublin Metropolitan School of Art, as would Beatrice from the age of thirteen. Her disillusionment with the Antique room there, and laborious shading 'from the cast … an awful process done with chalk and a chamois-leather stump and breadcrumbs'[8] soon vanished when she modelled her first piece of clay. John Hughes, the gifted Professor of Sculpture, soon claimed her as his star turn, while William Orpen, aged eighteen and in his final brilliant year, was the School's painting hero, en route for the Slade School of Art.

Over the next eight years, 'in complete devotion to a beloved master',[9] she won many prestigious awards, mostly for her life drawing and modelling. Among her acclaimed designs were a tobacco jar, a chimney piece, handles for silver sporting trophies commissioned by West & Co., the Dublin silversmiths, and a presentation piece to the battleship HMS *Hibernia*. So impressive was the 'poetic abandon'[10] of her 'beautiful' modelling that the Royal Dublin Society Taylor Scholarship judges needed proof in 1901 that a *Bather* and a child's head in circular relief were her own unaided work. After her four hours in a locked room with an old woman model, they pronounced themselves 'staggered'.[11] Scholarships took her to South Kensington, where Edward Lanteri was perpetuating Jules Dalou's 'ideals and working methods'[12] in clay modelling, as influential on Elvery as on her master Hughes; and to Paris, where John Hughes had settled in 1903

and where he tried to persuade her to join Rodin's studio to learn to cut stone. Apart from heads, busts,[13] statuettes, a crucifix and holy water stoup,[14] and relief portraits and genre scenes modelled in plaster and often coloured, she painted romantic themes from Dante and Wagner and made a series of exquisitely tender small terracotta sculptures,[15] (Fig. 11) 'charming in their naiveté and grace',[16] mostly of mothers and babies, surely influenced by the Dalou-inspired new school of English decorative sculptors (e.g. Harry Bates and Alfred Drury) in their noble peasant simplicity. Lady Dudley, the dazzling young Vicereine, who enjoyed Beatrice Elvery's work and company so much that she used to send the viceregal carriage and pair to bring her to Phoenix Park, commissioned various pieces and sold them in London. This stopped when the back-street Dublin clay pipe maker, who fired them for Elvery in his kiln, went out of business.[17]

She could not ordinarily afford to get her work cast in bronze. This was particularly sad in the case of *Glendalough* (1904), a soulful, Symbolist head of a woman grieving for her lost children, whose bodies are entwined in her hair; this eventually remained uncast, in plaster.[18] However, in 1904, the artist did model a lectern for Tullow Church in Carrickmines (Fig. 1), beside the house in which the Elverys and their seven children had lived from around 1888 to 1896. Cast in bronze in Paris, its sinuously tendrilled roots, leaves and a peeping child's head recall the proto-Art Nouveau style of her older English contemporaries like Alfred Drury, Reynolds-Stephens, even the more Symbolist Alfred Gilbert.[19] So, too, does her dramatically veiled and winged *Mourning Victory* of 1908, cast in bronze for the Boer War Memorial at the (now Kickham) Barracks in Clonmel, Co

Tipperary. In both cases, she collaborated with her friend and fellow parishioner, the architect Richard Caulfeild Orpen, brother of the artist. Tullow Church also has a fine oak prayer desk and seat made by the Elverys' musical and woodworking lodger in Foxrock, Frank Browning, and carved from Beatrice Elvery's integrated flat, foliate design by her mother in 1905 (Fig. 1). The same church also has two stained glass windows designed and made by Beatrice Elvery: the earlier, a *Good Samaritan and the Prodigal Son* (1908), for which her younger painter sister Dorothy posed, also features her little sister Marjorie as an angel in the tracery and delightful mediaevalized mice and leaves in the border.

By 1904, she was trying to make ends meet by tutoring at the Dublin Metropolitan School of Art, illustrating children's books, drawing dissections and operations for doctors and archaeological finds for the museum, while designing for silversmiths. The ever-supportive Sarah Purser gave her 'a corrugated iron studio in the yard'[20] of her newly established stained glass cooperative, An Túr Gloine (the Tower of Glass – known as the Gas Works by Elvery). When Sarah Purser suggested she take stained glass classes at the Art School and be employed by her studio (at ninepence an hour), she was still deliberating whether to sculpt in Paris (to her parents' horror) or take up Orpen's offer to 'make a painter', instead of a sculptor, out of her; she was also a creditable musician. At the Arts and Crafts Society of Ireland's 1904 third exhibition in Dublin, she exhibited (from her studio at the Tower of Glass) ten pieces of sculpture. At the same exhibition, her Aunt Annie (Phoebe Traquair) exhibited two much admired pieces in the small, specially invited loan exhibition of works by artists living outside Ireland: a copper plaque triptych, *The Kiss*, and an ivory and enamel casket decorated with *Scenes from the Life of the Madonna*.[21] Elvery's painted plaster relief, *The Mother*, an affectionate but unsentimental image of a pensive young Irish peasant Virgin with her baby snuggled up to her shoulder, is comparable with the engaging plaster bas-reliefs by her older English contemporary, Ellen Mary Rope. This piece was singled out by critics and Elvery described as 'a genuine artist',[22] 'one of the rising school of modern Irish workers'.[23] From 1902 she had also been exhibiting with the Young Irish Artists in Dublin, with WJ Leech, Mary Swanzy, Eva Hamilton, Estella Solomons, and her sister Dorothy.[24] She had become one of the 'new age of Irish Women's suffrage'.[25]

She later deeply regretted her decision to take up stained glass ('which I loathed')[26] rather than painting, although she subsequently made about twenty-six windows over the next fifteen years or so,[27] the best of them on a small scale and in the best Irish idiom of the progressive English Arts and Crafts tradition. Her own two favourites were the two-light *Good Samaritan*

5. Beatrice ELVERY (1883-1970), 'We rode on, passing many other islands'. *Signed 'BE' in monogram. Book illustration for Violet Russell, Heroes of the Dawn, 1913.* After their marriage in 1912, Elvery and Gordon Campbell (later Lord Glenavy) went to live in Howth. With the birth of their children the artist had less time for art although some of her graphic work was published at this time.

(1908) for Tullow and her three-light *St. Columba and the Crucifixion* (1910) window for EW Godwin's little gem of a church on Tory Island, Co Donegal.

Beatrice Elvery, gifted, well-read, physically striking, unaffected, generous, sympathetic and witty, was soon absorbed into 'a clique, a côterie centred on the Arts Club in Dublin'.[28] Her celebrated cartoon, for Susan Mitchell's *Aids to the Immortality of Certain Persons in Ireland* (Dublin 1908) includes Douglas Hyde, George Moore, Hugh Lane, 'AE', Horace Plunkett and WB Yeats. Romantically imbued with the strong emotional appeal of nationalism, and deeply impressed by seeing Maud Gonne play Cathleen Ní Houlihan in an early performance of Yeats' play, she painted an 'allegorical picture of [her] seated, hooded figure ... with a child on her knee, presumably Young Ireland, stretching out his arm to the future, and behind her a ghostly crowd of martyrs, patriots, saints and scholars'[29] (Fig. 6). Maud Gonne bought this hauntingly powerful, Symbolist image for Patrick Pearse's School, St Enda's. Entitled *Eire*, it was reproduced in the Gaelic League's *An Claideam Soluis* 1907 Christmas supplement. Pearse used to come to her studio at the Tower of Glass to translate the stories of his *Iosagán agus Sgéalta Eile* (1907) into English for her to illustrate. She also painted enchanting children's panels for St Enda's (Fig. 7), one of which was reproduced in *An Macaom*, his school record, did illustrations for *Sinn Féin* magazine and participated in the 1907 Oireachtas Exhibition. At this and at the fourth Arts and Crafts Society of Ireland exhibition in 1910, she exhibited domestic small stained glass panels. These included *The Bath* (Fig. 3), an affectionate scene of a young rustic Virgin wrapping her child Jesus in a towel while a little angel plays with the bath tub, and *The Nativity*, where Mary in rolled-up sleeves does the ironing and bids two young visiting angels not to wake her sleeping, booted baby (Fig. 4). These were admired for their 'Folk Spirit'[30] and portrayal of 'simple loving country folk in Ireland'.[31] At the same time she exhibited twenty one small paintings in a figurative group show with Leech, AE and others, which were praised for their strong 'decorative impulse', 'candid zest', 'sincere feeling for beauty' and 'fine sense of linear form'.[32]

By 1910, she had decided to follow Orpen's advice, and abandon stained glass and sculpture for the Slade. At an Arts Club farewell dinner, Susan Mitchell wrote:

Our Pretty Beatrice departs
To win her Art more grace.
But she'll not fashion anything
More lovely than her face.[33]

This had been sculpted by John Hughes and Oliver Sheppard, eulogised by George Moore and Lady Gregory, and painted and

6. Beatrice ELVERY (1883-1970), *Eire. Oil on canvas, 91 x 71 cm Signed and dated, B Elvery 1907. (Coll. Lady Goff).* Impressed by seeing Maud Gonne play Cathleen ni Houlihan in an early performance of Yeats' play, the artist painted this allegorical picture where the child is intended as Young Ireland and the other figures as saints and scholars.

7. Beatrice ELVERY (1883-1970): *Symbolic painting, c 1907. Oil on canvas, 132 x 109 cm. Signed in monogram, 'BE'. (Private collection).* Painted for Patrick Pearse's school, St Enda's, Rathfarnham, Co Dublin; the inscription translates 'and the Child grew and waxed strong, full of wisdom and the Grace of God was in Him.'

drawn by Sarah Purser, Dermod O'Brien and Orpen. She, in turn, drew devastatingly perceptive, humorous caricatures, usually brilliantly self-deprecatory, for her family and friends. On his return to Dublin in 1909, Orpen and she became close friends; witness volleys of notes and caricatures signed 'Bridgit' and 'Digit' respectively, and his two magnificent portraits of her, both painted in 1909 (Fig. 10). They depict a mischievous temptress with flaming red hair, exotically attired in his plumed hat, her smiling features emulating Augustus John's portrait of Dorelia as *The Smiling Woman* of the same year.[34] Orpen recalled:

'There was one [young artist in Ireland] who stood out alone – Beatrice Elvery, a young lady with many gifts, much temperament, and great ability. Her only fault was that the transmission of her thoughts from her brain to paper or canvas, clay or stained glass, became so easy to her that all was said in a few hours. Nothing on earth could make her go on and try to improve on her first translation of her thought. The thing was impossible; she was bored at the very idea … I remember meeting her in Dublin one morning and asking her to lunch with me. She said, "Yes, but make it half-past one, will you? I have to do a large window this morning". I called to take her out to lunch, and during those three hours or so she had designed a huge stained glass window, three enormous 'panels' … a hundred figures or so were in the design'.[35]

A tongue-in-cheek caricature by Elvery, *Alas for Glass*[36] shows a weeping Sarah Purser with her manager AE Child, Richard Caulfeild Orpen and Lady Aberdeen (for whose charitable tuberculosis work Elvery had been drawing) bewailing her departure.

Subsidised by an aunt, she persevered for a term at the Slade, dismissed by Tonks as too clever, too academically slick, and unencouraged by Steer. She painted portraits for a living from a tiny studio flat in a Bloomsbury women's hostel.[37] Aged twenty-six, her younger painterly sister married and pregnant, she began to feel that 'having a baby seemed the only possible satisfaction and fulfilment; but as there was not much that I could do about it, I had no choice but to continue with my 'Art Work'.[38]

In 1912 she married Gordon Campbell, a brilliantly articulate sporty young barrister, recently called to the English Bar. Popular in London pre-war progressive literary circles, he had shared rooms with DH Lawrence and was particularly close to John Middleton Murry, Kathleen Mansfield, SS Koteliansky, Mark Gertler and the DH Lawrences. After a drenched honeymoon in Donegal, they moved into a rustic terraced house in South Kensington and Beatrice Campbell had to learn house-keeping. She returned to Dublin in 1913 for the birth of her son, Patrick (later to become 'Quidnunc' of the *Irish Times* and a

THE ART OF BEATRICE ELVERY, LADY GLENAVY (1883-1970)

8. Beatrice ELVERY (1883-1970), Still-life of Staffordshire Figure with Fruit and Flowers. *Oil on board, 64 x 75 cm. Signed 'BG' in monogram. c 1935. (Private collection).*

well-known wit and columnist), and took a cottage on Howth, where she was joined by the Murrys. Although she continued to exhibit painted fantasies at the RHA, and some of her graphic work was published, such as her heroic line illustrations to *Heroes of the Dawn* (1913) (Fig. 5) by AE's wife, Violet, looking after her baby son and a daughter, Brigid, born in June 1914 just before War was declared, left time only for drawings. In 1915, Gordon Campbell's work in the Ministry of Munitions allowed them to move to a larger house in St John's Wood, where their stimulating, hospitable Sunday evenings set a pattern they would continue on their return to Dublin in 1918.

After bombing raids in London, evacuations, German submarines in the Irish Sea on summer trips home, the War ended, and Gordon Campbell began a successful career at the

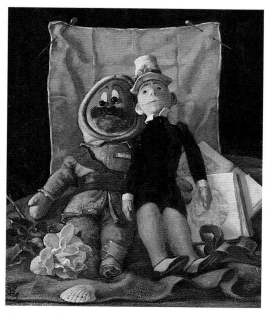

9. Beatrice ELVERY (1883-1970), World War I. *Oil on canvas, 51 x 36 cm. Signed 'BG' in monogram. c 1930. (Private collection).*

Parliamentary Bar. They both wanted to return to Ireland, however. In 1919, he was called to the Bar in Dublin, and in 1922 became an eccentric but invaluable Secretary to the new Free State's Ministry of Industry and Commerce. His wife, as Beatrice Campbell, did some theatrical designs and resumed her narrative pen and ink illustrations. Most of these were for Lily and Elizabeth Yeats' Cuala Press[39] – calendars, Christmas cards and prints illustrating (principally traditional) folk and faery scenes, or what she called her little holy drawings' by contemporary Irish poets such as Padraic Colum and Monk Gibbon. Her poignantly observed, strongly graphic 'homely' images are unique in the iconography of the Celtic Revival in Ireland in their uncontrived, modern treatment, akin only to the earlier graphic work of her lifelong friend, Jack B Yeats.

Life was not easy: both her father-in-law (created Lord Glenavy in 1921 as Chairman of the Free State Senate and a former Chief Justice and Lord Chancellor) and her husband were targets in the Civil War. Continual raids and house moves culminated, in 1922, in the razing of their newly acquired house, Clonard, in Kimmage. The 'wonderful feeling of owning nothing'[40] was transitory when they realised their compensation claim had been ludicrously small, and funds were low. Many friends and family left Dublin, which was a changed place since before the War. They kept up their London friends, regularly visiting and being visited; a vertiginous car tour in Kerry in 1923 with the George Bernard Shaws was immortalised in a series of the wittily trenchant caricatures Beatrice Campbell continued to draw until around 1930. In 1924, the Campbells' last child, Michael, another future writer, was born and she began to paint small, almost pointilliste, exactingly lifelike watercolour portraits in muted tones with symbolic attributes. Often taken from photographs, these included children, self-portraits with her baby, family and friends, like James Stephens. In 1921, she and the Jack Yeatses exhibited prints and Christmas cards hand-coloured by the Cuala Press with the Arts and Crafts Society of Ireland; several of her vigorously linear graphics were also printed for the United Arts Club.

Both Campbells' love of the theatre drew them to the Dublin Drama League, in whose productions they both acted. In 1926 she set-designed and produced (with their friend Shelagh Richards) Ki Kuchi Kwan's *The Housetop Madman* in the Abbey Theatre. For the League's offshoot, the New Players, she and Norah McGuinness set-designed and painted, and she acted in Denis Johnston's production of *From Morn to Night*. In 1928 she painted the scenery[41] for Gordon Campbell's first pseudonymous 'ironic comedy', *Treaty with the Barbarians*, which became a *cause célèbre* at the Peacock Theatre. By now she was 'painting and drawing like mad, never have I had so many orders and I'm trying to get through them all before the carpenter has some sea chests for me to paint! Sure I'll be rich at this rate!'[42] On these deep wooden chests, painted ultramarine, she had opted

10. William ORPEN (1878-1931), Bridgit -a Picture of Miss Elvery (detail). *Oil on canvas, 110 x 84.5 cm. Signed and dated, Orpen 1909. (Pyms Gallery, London).* Orpen first met Beatrice Elvery at the Metropolitan School of Art in Dublin in about 1896 when they were both students but this portrait was painted after Orpen's return to the school as a teacher in 1909 when the two became close friends. He called her 'Bridgit' while she referred to him as 'Digit'.

11. Beatrice ELVERY (1883-1970), Mother and Child. *Terracotta, c.20 cm high. Signed, B Elvery. c.1904. (Private collection).* At the South Kensington School of Art, Elvery came to appreciate, through her teacher Lanteri, the ideals of the French sculptor, Jules Dalou, whose style she adopted in a series of small terracotta sculptures.

to depict 'amusing sailors and women, in thick paint' since, apart from her stunned admiration of Stanley Spencer's *Resurrection* in the Tate, she could not stomach most contemporary London Group trends.[43] She was up to her eyes in work. In one week alone, she reported to her sister, 'I have painted eight tables, thirty-six chairs, a sign, and a wall decoration for a tea shop'.[44]

Her sculpture was limited to two garden figures cast in concrete: a pipe-playing *Pan* and an inscribed, more geometrically conceived bird bath depicting a kneeling child tending a bird (modelled from her daughter as a toddler). *Pan* was shown at the 1932 Dublin Aonach Tailteann exhibition along with her *Virgin Ironing* stained glass panel, four Cuala Prints and a spiritedly painted chest and wooden crib.[45] What really excited her was her painting, *The Intruder* (Fig. 2), on which she had been working for some time. Its completion coincided with her husband's succession to his father's title in 1931, and her own election as an Associate of the RHA in 1932. This richly coloured, bucolic but stage-set fantasy of a sylvan picnic interrupted by a female centaur was acclaimed at the 1933 London Royal Academy, when it was seen to recall Pisanello and caricatured by George Morrow in *Punch* as 'The Home Wrecker'. At the disapproving 1932 Dublin RHA, only Richard Caulfeild Orpen admired its 'playful subtlety – gorgeous colour: that strange and beautiful type of figure which you have devised which renders your subjects symbolic'.[46] That year she decided to paint a picture entitled *Motherhood* (or *Birth Control*), showing two women burying a baby by the light of a kitchen lamp, to dispel her RHA critics' accusations that she painted from photographs; but her greatest pleasure was 'painting still-life arrangements with romantic backgrounds of forests and distant figures. I would like to have painted still-lifes like some of Gertler's pictures ... The profundity and mystery, the beauty of the paint, the queer sense of eternity'[47] were qualities she deeply admired in the work of one of her dearest friends.

In 1934, her election as an Academician marked the beginning of the last phase in a richly varied, prolific artistic career, to be sustained in her paintings for a

THE ART OF BEATRICE ELVERY, LADY GLENAVY (1883-1970)

further thirty or so years. She belongs, with her aunt Phoebe Traquair and an old friend like AE, in the company of 'the last romantics', those who 'chose for theme/Traditional sanctity and loveliness'.[48]

DR NICOLA GORDON BOWE *is a lecturer in the History of Art and Design in the National College of Art and Design. She has published and lectured widely on early twentieth century decorative arts and is editor of* Art and the National Dream: Vernacular Expression in Turn of the Century Design *(Irish Academic Press, Dublin, 1993).*

ACKNOWLEDGEMENTS

Ian Smith, the late Bill Holden, Sir Robert and Lady Davis-Goff, Alan and Mary Hobart (Pyms Gallery), Mary Kelleher (RDS), Anthony Hobbs (NCAD), Bernard Williams (Christie's, Glasgow), Philippa Corkill, Dr Moore Tweed, Brian Sibley, Pat Cooke (Pearse Museum), Captain M O'Connell (Kickham Barracks, Clonmel), James and Therese Gorry, Peter Murray (Crawford Gallery, Cork); Anthony O'Brien, Marjorie Reynolds, Seán Ó Ceárnaigh, Beverly Bolton.

NOTE

A major retrospective exhibition of Beatrice Glenavy's work is to be mounted by the Crawford Art Gallery, Cork within the next two years, which will travel to Dublin and Belfast

1. Kenneth McConkey, *A Free Spirit – Irish Art 1860-1920*, London 1990, p.73
2. S B Kennedy, *Irish Art and Modernism 1880-1950*, Belfast 1991, p.56.
3. *The Irish Times*, 30 September, 1955.
4. *The Irish Independent*, 30 September, 1955.
5. Kennedy, *op. cit.*, p.20.
6. Kennedy, *op. cit.*, p.355.
7. WB Yeats quoted in Colin Smythe (ed.), *Seventy Years: Being the Autobiography of Lady Gregory*, Gerrards Cross 1974, p.435; cited in Elizabeth Cumming, *Phoebe Anna Traquair 1852-1936*, Scottish National Portrait Gallery, Edinburgh 1993, p.9, the definitive publication on Traquair.
8. Beatrice Lady Glenavy, *Today we will only Gossip*, London 1964, p.23.
9. Glenavy, *op. cit.*, pp.33-34.
10. RDS *Annual Proceedings*, vol.139 (1902-03), pp.94-95.
11. Letter (undated) from Lady Glenavy to Alan Denson in Alan Denson, *John Hughes, Sculptor 1865-1941, A Documentary Biography*, Kendal 1969, p.439.
12. Susan Beattie, *The New Sculpture*, New Haven and London 1983, p.16.
13. 'I grew to dislike busts because there never seems to be any place in an ordinary house to put them. Statuettes are just as bad and I came to the conclusion that sculpture should either be huge and out in the open air against the sky or something small that you could hold in your hand like a Tanagra figure', Glenavy, *op. cit.*, p.38.
14. Painted by her talented sister Dorothy in two versions of a painting for which their young neighbour, Samuel Beckett, posed as a *Child at Prayer* (Dorothy Kay Bequest, National Gallery of South Africa, Cape Town).
15. Seven of these were described as sketches in the third exhibition of the Arts and Crafts Society of Ireland in 1904. Beattie (*op. cit.*, p.193) writes: 'Smallness of scale may be seen as one of the most powerful tools used by the New Sculptors in their search for flexibility and freedom from the institution-alised image of their art'. The artist's largest work is her Clonmel *Mourning Victory* (1908).
16. *The Studio*, January 1905, p.365.
17. 'Because people were starting to smoke cig-arettes' instead, Glenavy, *op. cit.*, p.38.
18. See Nicola Gordon Bowe, *The Arts and Crafts Movement 1886-1930*, Edinburgh 1985, catalogue no.90 and 'Symbolism in Turn-of-the-Century Irish Art', *GPA Irish Arts Review Yearbook* 1989-90, p.137.

19. The lectern is illustrated in GO Simms, *Tullow's Story*, Dublin 1983, p.80 and listed in Bowe, 'Aspects of the Art Nouveau style to be found in immovable objects in Ireland', *Art Nouveau/Jugendstil Architecture in Europe* (HD Dyroff ed.), UNESCO, Bonn 1988, p.133. See also Paul Larmour, *The Arts and Crafts Movement in Ireland*, Belfast 1993, p.108.
20. Glenavy, *op. cit.*, p.38.
21. Both aunt and niece favoured images of motherhood, the innocence of childhood and lovingly observed details of small ani-mals and plants.
22. TW Rolleston, 'Art Work at Irish Exhibitions', *Journal of the Arts and Crafts Society of Ireland*, vol.I, no.4, 1906, p.282.
23. *Irish Builder*, 13 January 1906.
24. Dorothy Elvery in 1910 married Hobart Kay and left for South Africa, where she became a well-known painter. See Marjorie Reynolds, '*Everything you do is a portrait of yourself*', *Dorothy Kay, A Biography*, Rosebank (South Africa), 1989. Reviewed in *Irish Arts Review Yearbook 1991-92*, pp.267-68.
25. McConkey, *op. cit*, p.142.
26. Letter from Lady Glenavy to Alan Denson, 24 August 1956, Denson, *op. cit*, p.381.
27. See Nicola Gordon Bowe, David Caron and Michael Wynne, *A Gazetteer of Irish Stained Glass*, Dublin 1988. 'I might have become a good painter and I might never have taken to making stained-glass windows, an activi-ty which never gave me any pleasure', Glenavy, *op. cit.*, p.38.
28. Glenavy, *op. cit.*, p.71. The club was then in rented rooms in Lincoln Place, and from 1910 in St Stephen's Green.
29. Glenavy, *op. cit.*, p.91.
30. Manning Robertson, 'The Craft Revival in Dublin', *Architecture*, February 1926, p.328.
31. 'The Oireáchtas Salon: the Crafts', *An Claideam Soluis*, 10 August, 1907, p.7.
32. Untraced cutting.
33. Quoted in Patricia Boylan, *All Cultivated People, A History of the United Arts Club Dublin*, Gerrards Cross 1988, p.39.
34. The more racy portrait, described by Orpen as *The Colleen*, is illustrated in his *Stories of Old Ireland and Myself*, London 1924 ,at p.70; the other, described as *Bridgit*, was subsequently owned by John's former mis-tress Mrs Val Fleming; it is reproduced in Pyms Gallery's *Celtic Splendour*, London 1985, p.51.
35. Sir William Orpen, *Stories of Old Ireland and Myself*, London 1924, pp.69-70.

36. Preserved in one of the artist's own scrap-books, now part of the Glenavy Estate.
37. 'I did not think I had much chance of becoming a great queen or a great courtesan and the possibility of becoming a creative artist of any importance seemed just as remote. I decided to stay at home', Glenavy, *op. cit.*, p.39.
38. Glenavy, *op. cit.*, p.38.
39. For whom she had already drawn a number of prints and cards and a painted book cover before her marriage. Some depicted scenes she had already executed in stained glass.
40. *The Elvery Family: A Memory. Dorothy Kay*, ed. Marjorie Reynolds, Cape Town 1991, p.89.
41. Once the two oldest children were away at school, she used her daughter's bedroom as a studio for the considerable amount of the-atrical work she did in the 1920s.
42. Letter to her brother Malcolm in Nyasaland, *The Elvery Family, op. cit.*, pp.109-10.
43. 'Having walked round miles of London Group pictures, all back yards and bananas and tin cans, I decided that if you aren't Cezanne, and can't give an aesthetic intel-lectual extasy (sic) with your bananas, you'd better leave them alone, and paint some-thing amusing or attractive ', Letter to her sister Dorothy Kay, *The Elvery Family*, *op. cit.*, p.111.
44. *The Elvery Family, op. cit.*, p.127, Letter to her sister Marjorie Tweed.
45. She does not appear to have sculpted again; only provided simple, classical designs: for the sailing ship on her friend Tom Casement's gravestone (1939) in Dublin, and memorial plaques to Oscar Wilde, John Hughes and AE on their Dublin houses.
46. Letter from RC Orpen to Lady Glenavy, 19 October 1932. Private Scrapbook of the artist. The painting was exhibited in *Irish Women Artists from the Eighteenth century to the Present Day*, National Gallery of Ireland, cat. no.112, where it is reproduced in colour (plate 19). It is analogous with Rex Whistler's Tate Gallery murals, *The Pursuit of Rare Meats* (1927).
47. Glenavy, *op. cit.*, p.148.
48. WB Yeats' lines from 'Coole Park and Ballylee', 1931 (*The Winding Stair and Other Poems*, 1933) gave the title to John Christian's huge reappraising exhibition of *The Romantic Tradition in British Art from Burne-Jones to Stanley Spencer* (Barbican Art Gallery, London 1989).

MARKIEVICZ AND THE KNIGHTS OF ST PATRICK

*T*he Investiture of the Right Hon. The Earl of Mayo as Knight of St Patrick 1905 by Casimir Dunin Markievicz (b. 1874 d. 1932) is not to be regarded primarily for its artistic merit, but rather as a document of historic and social importance. The picture depicts Dermot Robert Wyndham Bourke, 7th Earl of Mayo, just after his investiture with the appropriate insignia and robes as a Knight of The Most Illustrious Order of St. Patrick. He is seen subscribing to the Statutory Declaration at a Chapter of the Order. The Order of St Patrick was the national honour of Ireland for a hundred and forty years and was founded on 5 February 1783; to all intents and purposes it demised in the 1920s. The origins of the Order were politically dubious, and although supposed to be a symbol of evolving Irish independence, it was frequently used as a bribe. During the nineteenth century, it became the most prominent feature of the Irish social world centred on the Viceregal Court at Dublin Castle.

Casimir Dunin Markievicz, the artist, was born in the Ukrainian part of the Polish Commonwealth then under Russian rule; Dunin, a distinguished Polish patronymic, was his middle name. Markievicz met Constance Gore-Booth, the unusual and self-willed daughter of a west of Ireland landlord, when they were art students at the Académie Julian in Paris. They married and returned to Dublin.[2] The Edwardian period 1901-1910, was a happy time for the young couple. They plunged into social activities, taking particular pleasure in amateur theatricals, and appearing in various venues such as the Gaiety Theatre. The years ahead when the lovely Countess Markievicz would be a gun-toting revolutionary, striding about the battleground in martial attire, could hardly have been imagined in 1905. Nevertheless, there is a hint of her future role in this picture where she is seen sitting amongst the court ladies, demurely elegant in a green stole, the only touch of green in the entire picture. Casimir Markievicz, however, enjoyed the social life of Dublin; he especially appreciated, as this picture shows, the Viceregal court, which in its splendid setting, theatrical ritual and colourful costumes, was comparable to any leading European court of the day.[3] As Peter Galloway comments, 'The Order of St. Patrick was, in essence, a small part of the whole Anglo-Irish establishment. The Investitures were a social feature of the Viceregal court as much as the Garter ceremonies were a feature of the English court. The Viceroy in Dublin, with his castle, his court and his servants, and surrounded by his aristocracy, was in every respect a miniature replica of the King in London. His State Entrance to the city at the beginning of his Viceroyalty and his solemn investiture with the Grand Master's Insignia by the Lords Justices, paralleled the Coronation'.[4] Markievicz's 'sno-

A painting of the investiture of the Earl of Mayo as a Knight of St Patrick in 1905 provides a glimpse of life at the Irish Viceregal Court. The scene is set by **John Maiben Gilmartin**.

bisme', his psychological insight and his acquaintance with avant garde artistic movements on the continent, may be seen in various aspects of this picture and in his technique, which has expressionist overtones. Nor is it surprising to learn that Markievicz was an accomplished theatre set designer.

On either side of the blue covered table, the Knights of St Patrick are seated, wearing their insignia and their sky-blue mantles. The assembly is gathered before the King's representative, the Viceroy, Lord Dudley, Grand Master of the Order, who is enthroned beneath a crimson canopy of state. St Patrick's Hall in Dublin Castle is the splendid eighteenth-century setting for this assembly of the 'Ancien Regime' meeting, unknowingly, for one of the last investitures before the revolution which was to sweep it all away.[5] These ceremonies were always held late in the evening at half past ten or even eleven o'clock. They were glittering and impressive occasions, for those privileged to be present. The reason for the late hour was that the ceremony looked better in artificial light, or so Sir Bernard Burke decided when in 1871 the Order was secularized and the investiture replaced the religious ceremonies formerly held in St Patrick's Cathedral as their main event.

In the foreground is an officer of the 6th Inniskilling Dragoons, identifiable by the castle of Enniskillen on his primrose yellow collar. Pierce Gun Mahony, the Deputy Usher of the Black Rod, attired in a tabard and ruff, stands behind him holding the black Rod of Office. Mahony was later to be one of the hapless victims in the sinister story of the theft of the insignia of the Grand Master of the Order of St Patrick, an event which occurred two years later.[6] Then the diamond insignia of the Grand Master, and the gold chain collars seen here worn by Lord Dudley and the knights, disappeared from the safe in the Office of Arms in Dublin Castle, never to be seen again. The subsequent political rumpus over these missing crown jewels shook the Establishment and altered the lives of some people present at this ceremony; these were P G Mahony, F R Shackleton and the Ulster King of Arms, Sir Arthur Vicars. In violet robes and official triple chain, Sir Arthur Vicars stands on the right of the Viceroy. On the left of the Viceregal dais stands the tall debonair figure of the Rt Hon George Wyndham, Chief Secretary for Ireland, and ex officio Chancellor of the Most Illustrious Order of St Patrick; he was a close friend and cousin of Lord Mayo. Here Wyndham is reading out the Solemn Declaration to which new members of the Order of St Patrick had to subscribe, repeating it word for word after the Chancellor. Lord Mayo does this, standing in his blue mantle just to the right of the Viceregal dais. Lord and Lady Mayo were major figures in the cultural life of early twentieth century Ireland. Lord Mayo founded the Arts and Crafts Society of Ireland, while his wife Geraldine, Countess of Mayo directed the Royal Irish School of Art Needlework. She was a protégée of Mrs Percy Wyndham, a prominent London aesthete and the mother of George Wyndham. As well as being a politician, Wyndham was a prominent member of the aesthetic and aristocratic elite called 'The Souls'. The adornment of Church of Ireland altars with finely

1. Casimir Dunin MARKIEVICZ (1874-1932): The Investiture of the Right Hon. The Earl of Mayo as Knight of St Patrick, 1905 (detail). *Oil on canvas, 260 x 325 cm. Signed and dated. (Private Collection)*. In St Patrick's Hall in Dublin Castle, the Viceroy, Lord Dudley, is enthroned beneath the canopy of state, surrounded by members of the Viceregal Court.

2. Casimir Dunin MARKIEVICZ (1874-1932): The Investiture of the Right Hon. The Earl of Mayo as Knight of St Patrick, 1905.

embroidered altar frontals was one of Lady Mayo's achievements.

The Earl of Dudley was a man of riches and opulent tastes, whose Viceroyalty was marked by lavish display.[7] His son and heir, Viscount Ednam, stands on his right as a page, while a second page, Master Troubridge, is on his left. Two aides-de-camp stand behind, the one on the left wearing the uniform of the 1st Life Guards. The dashing Hussar who stands at the left of the Viceroy, is Sir Bryan Leighton, Bt., a remarkable and colourful Edwardian adventurer. His uniform is that of the Westmoreland and Cumberland Yeomanry. Also on the dais, in the uniform of an officer of H M Civil Service, First Class, wearing a blue riband and holding the Sword of State, is Sir Anthony MacDonnell, the Under Secretary for Ireland. Standing behind in court dress and holding a Viceregal mace is Guillamore O'Grady, Esq. On the opposite side, behind George Wyndham, likewise in court dress and hold-

> *The lovely Countess Markievicz is seen sitting amongst the court ladies, demurely elegant in a green stole.*

ing the second Viceregal mace, is S M Power, Esq. At the end of the blue draped table is the Insignia Procession. This group is depicted facing the Vice-regal dais, consequently we have a rear view which makes identification difficult. According to a contemporary account,[8] this procession also included the Bearer of the Mantle (of the new knight), E Louis Spiers, Esq., 3rd Royal Dublin Fusiliers and the Bearer of the Sword, F R Shackleton, Esq, 3rd Royal Irish Fusiliers. However, the mantle having been donned and the sword already girded on the new Knight, the party is here reduced to four. These are Henry Claude Blake, Athlone Pursuivant, and beside him Sir Henry Farnham Burke, son of Sir Bernard Burke and Secretary and Registrar of the Order of St Patrick and Somerset Herald in the English College of Arms. The Helm and Crest are borne by J R Blake, 3rd Royal Welsh Fusiliers, while the Bearer of the Banner

MARKIEVICZ AND THE KNIGHTS OF ST PATRICK

is Lord Mourne and Newry, identifiable by his uniform as an officer of the 1st Regiment of the Life Guards. The banner, which is semi-furled, displays the quartered arms of Dermot Robert Wyndham Bourke, 7th Earl of Mayo. The Roden quarter is displayed prominently, with the argent and sable wreath with four golden hawk's bells on a field azure. Nearby on duty stands an officer of the 6th Inniskilling Dragoons.

The assembled Knights of St Patrick seated at the table make a historic portrait gallery. On the Viceroy's right, seated at the top of the table may be seen HRH The Prince of Wales, later King George V, who had come specially to Dublin for the occasion.[9] On the same side, in descending order, may be seen Lords Carysfort, Monteagle, Erne, Iveagh, Lucan, Clonbrock (almost hidden), and finally Lord Enniskillen. Facing these peers across the table, starting on the Viceroy's left, are the Lords Listowel, Dunraven, Ormonde, Rosse, Roberts, Bandon, Waterford, and finally Lord de Ros. The ladies of the court provide a decorative foil to the Knights. They are seated immediately behind, painted in a impressionistic technique which softens the overall effect of harsh, fauve-like colours, but does make identification difficult. More strongly delineated than any other amongst the court ladies, Countess Markievicz is seated last but one, on the Viceroy's left side. She has a determined, though detached, look. Opposite, first amongst the ladies on the Viceroy's right hand, sits Lady Dudley. Standing by her is a blue-clad page, the young Lord Glentworth; the fair-haired lady on her right is Geraldine, Countess of Mayo.

The assembly contains many other figures, most of whom may be identified by their military or civil service uniforms, as belonging to the various military ranks or civil service grades. Further research, however, needs to be carried out before the full historical significance of this unique court picture can be completely appreciated.

As for Casimir Markievicz, his Irish world started to dissolve before the Rising of 1916. He and his wife retained a mutual esteem but went increasingly separate ways. The new independent Ireland of the 1920s would have held little attraction for Markievicz and he returned to live in Poland, where he died in 1932, five years after his wife's death in Dublin.

JOHN MAIBEN GILMARTIN is an art historian and lecturer in the Dublin Institute of Technology School of Art and Design.

1	Officer of a Highland Regiment	23	Page, Lord Glentworth
2	Officer of H.M. Civil Service 4th Class	24	Lady Dudley
		25	Lady Mayo
3	Mace Bearer Guillamore O'Grady	26	Pierce Gun Mahony
		27	6th Inniskilling Dragoon
4	Sir Anthony MacDonnell	28	Lord Enniskillen
5	Hon. M O'Brien ADC	29	Lord Clonbrook
6	Hon G Ward, ADC 1st Life Grds	30	Lord Lucan
7	Sir Bryan Leighton, Bt. ADC	31	Lord Iveagh
8	Mace Bearer S M Power	32	Lord Erne
9	Rt. Hon George Wyndham	33	Lord Monteagle
10	Officer H M Civil Service 4th Class	34	Lord Carysfort
		35	The Prince of Wales
11	Officer of the Royal Navy, Hon C A Ward	36	Lord Listowel
		37	Lord Dunraven
12	Dean of the Chapel Royal	38	Lord Ormonde
13	Officer of H.M. Civil Service 1st/2nd Class	39	Lord Rosse
		40	Lord Roberts
14	A County Lieutenant	41	Lord Bandon
15	Officer of H.M. Civil Service 1st/2nd Class	42	Lord Waterford
		43	Lord De Ros
16	Page, Master Troubridge	44	Sir Henry Farnham-Burke
17	The Viceroy, Lord Dudley	45	Athlone Pursuivant H C Burke
18	Page, Lord Ednam	46	J R Blake 3rd Royal Welsh Fusiliers
19	Lord Mayo		
20	Ulster King of Arms Sir A Vickers	47	Lord Mourne & Newry
		48	6th Inniskilling Dragoon
21	Officer of H.M. Civil Service, 4th Class	49	Countess Markievicz
		50	Officer of H.M. Civil Service 4th Class
22	Officer of H.M. Civil Service, 4th Class		

ACKNOWLEDGEMENTS
I should like to express my thanks to Glenn Thompson and to Stanislaus Deskur KM, Krakow, for their valuable help.

1. The picture was exhibited at the Royal Hibernian Academy in 1906, no. 111. *The Irish Builder and Engineer*, 5 May 1906, pp.353-54, RHA.Exhibition, second notice, has the following comments , 'The Investiture of The Rt Hon. The Earl of Mayo as Knight of St Patrick, by Count Casimir Markievicz is scarcely worthy of the artist's reputation, in fact it is amateurish looking and the faces are hardly recognizable. Of course the ceremony itself, although a brilliant one, full of colour, is yet not easy to successfully group as a picture. It is apt, like all such scenes , to become hard and diagrammatic in execution'.

2. *Polski Stownik Biograficzny* Vol. xx, Krakow. 1984, p.26.

3. Raymond F Brooke, *The Brimming River*, Allen Figgis, Dublin, 1961, p.95.

4. P Galloway, *The Most Illustrious Order of St Patrick*, Chichester, Phillimore, 1983, p.84.

5. J Gilmartin, 'Vincent Waldre's ceiling paintings in Dublin Castle', *Apollo*, January 1972.

6. F Bamford and V Bankes, *Vicious Circle*, Max Parrish, London, 1965, p.26.

7. Galloway, *op. cit.* p.36, 'Lord Dudley was rich, and hated any form of economy. He maintained a brilliant and extravagant Court, spending £80,000 of his own money during his first year of Office'.

8. *The Irish Times*, Saturday 4 February 1905.

9. 'King George V, then Prince of Wales, did indeed visit Dublin in 1905, from 31 January until 4 February, but he was not accompanied by The Princess of Wales'. Letter to John Gilmartin from the Deputy Registrar, Royal Archives, Windsor Castle, 15 January 1991.

This gives a detailed account of the ceremony. However, in a few details the picture and the report do not tally. Sometimes Correspondents were not admitted and had to rely on accounts given to them. For instance, in *The Irish Times* report Sir Arthur Vicars is described as wearing a tabard while in the picture he wears the violet mantle and chain appropriate to this office.'

CASIMIR DUNIN MARKIEVICZ
PAINTER AND PLAYWRIGHT

The notoriety of his Irish wife, Constance Gore-Booth, has eclipsed the artistic reputation of this Polish painter, writes **Wanda Ryan-Smolin.**

As husband of one of Ireland's most famous historical figures, Markievicz's name has become indelibly stamped on the nation's consciousness (Fig. 1). Because of his relationship with Countess Markievicz the details of his life with her have often been outlined but his work as a painter of considerable talent has been virtually ignored both here in Ireland, where, to judge by his exhibitions, his output was prodigious, and in Poland. Various factors have conspired against his receiving adequate recognition. In Ireland, where he lived for eleven years, his work has been understandably overshadowed by his wife's political career while in Poland he is remembered chiefly as a playwright and producer. The extremely nomadic nature of his life and the diversity of his interests which led him to give up publicly exhibiting his work after he left Ireland have all contributed to his present obscurity. The fact that he was not an avant garde painter and was not directly inspired by Impressionism or by the Modern Movement which followed has also tended to render him unworthy of attention. He is by no means the only artist to have been discriminated against in this way and the quality and standard of his work, while undeniably rooted in nineteenth-century tradition, stands as sufficient evidence of his worth and ability as an artist.

Born Kazimierz Jozef Dunin-Markiewicz[1] in the village of Denhofowka in the Ukraine, he was a younger son and one of nine children of Piotr Dunin-Markiewicz, a Polish landowning nobleman.[2] The family had estates at Zywotowka and Rozyn near Kiev and were well-off. He initially studied law in Kiev before deciding in 1894 to move to Paris and devote himself to painting instead. In Kiev he had attended from about 1892 a private school of art (under the directorship of M I Muraszki) and took lessons from the Polish painters S Bohusz-Siestrzeńcewicz and W Mazurowski. In Paris he joined the École des Beaux-Arts and the Académie Julian. Also studying in Paris at this time was Jadwiga Splawa Neyman who came from a neighbouring family in the Ukraine. Together they rented an apartment in the Latin quarter, married and had two children (Stanislaw and Ryszard). Their marriage was not a success and ill health forced Jadwiga to return to her family in the Ukraine where she and her younger child died in 1899.

1. Casimir and Constance in fancy dress for the Dublin Castle Ball of 1905.

Markievicz remained in Paris where he was gaining a reputation for his painting. The first work he exhibited there was *The Travelling Beggar* which appeared at the Salon des Independants in 1896. He again exhibited there in 1898, showing several portraits and a triptych *Bread*[3] which depicted, in side panels, peasant figures sowing wheat and harvesting, and a peasant interior with a loaf of bread on a cloth in the central panel. In the same year as his first wife's death he met Constance Gore-Booth. She was then a student at the Académie Julian and found much common ground with Markievicz whom she affectionately referred to as Casi. Among Casimir's close friends of the time were Polish painters Leopold Piotr Andrzejewski and Boleslaw Szankowski who later became court painter to the Kings of Saxony and Rumania. Szankowski painted separate portraits of both Constance and Casimir and the former was presented to the Municipal Gallery in 1909 by Casimir and his son Stanislaw.

At the Official Paris Salon of 1900 Casimir achieved a measure of notoriety when he received a medal of honour for his painting *Amour* based on the Polish legend of the Eve of St John. Following its success in Paris, which prompted a visit to Casimir's studio from the Grand Duke Vladimir Alexandrovitch, President of the Imperial Academy in St Petersburg, it was exhibited in both St Petersburg and in Krakow in 1901. This highly accomplished life-size allegorical work depicted the figure of a nymph mourning over the dead nude body of a man and a figure of a spirit emerging from a stump of a tree. According to the legend, a rare fern flowers at midnight on the Eve of St John and those who are brave enough to go to the enchanted forest and pick it are granted any wish, provided they show no emotion or fear, otherwise they are struck dead. In the painting the man wished for love, but when love in the form of a beautiful nymph appeared he could not conceal his delight and therefore died. The mystical nature of the subject, and even its manner of execution, shows Markievicz's interest in Symbolism which was then at its zenith in Europe. It also helps to explain the close friendship which was later to develop between him and AE whom he encouraged to paint and whose art, like his poetry, was influenced by Symbolism. The painting has been lost for many years[4] which is particularly regrettable in view of the fact that it was offered as a gift to the United Arts Club in Dublin in 1924. After it had been several months in the Club's possession, the donor, Mrs Longworth Dames (friend of Michael Collins and member of the Club from 1912), discovered that the work was not hanging and wrote to the committee to suggest that if they did not intend to display it they should consider returning it to her. Their unbelievable decision, given the quality of the painting, was to send it back.[5] It is conceivable that the display of nudity in the painting made it distasteful to certain members of the committee.

Another painting exhibited at the 1900 Salon was a portrait of *Baron Von Greifenfels*; this indicates a growing interest in portraiture which was to become more important in subsequent years. The full length life-size portrait of his future wife, *Constance in White* (Fig. 2), had been painted in Paris in the previous year. This romantic portrayal of Constance in a long flowing gown, standing in profile in an interior, admirably captures that beauty which in later years W B Yeats was to immortalise and lament in his poem *In Memory of Eve Gore-Booth and Con Markievicz*. It was, according to Stanislaw Markievicz, a feature in their Dublin home and luckily found its way to the National Gallery of Ireland,[6] unlike many of Markievicz's other paintings which were either dispersed or destroyed as a result of Constance's later turbulent life. They married in London in 1900, and with their joint incomes[7] were able to set up home in Paris in a large apartment containing a studio in the rue Campagne Premiere in Montparnasse.

They spent the summer of 1901 at Lissadell, where their daughter Maeve Alyss was born in September. It was probably on this visit that Casimir decorated the dining-room with a series of unique murals which represent not only larger than life-size stylised images of the artist and Constance's younger brother, Mordaunt Gore-Booth, on pilasters at either side of the fireplace, but also life-size costume portraits of the butler, gamekeeper and forester on pilasters at either ends of the room (Fig. 3). The scheme (which also includes an excellent painting of a dog) was to have been completed with a sixth portrait of the house-

keeper but she was too shy to sit for the artist and so her pilaster was left bare. The wit and theatricality of these paintings are an apt prelude to the artist's later career as playwright and set designer. Lissadell also contains a number of other striking portraits of family members by Markievicz.

Some months after Maeve's birth the couple returned to Paris leaving the baby in the care of a nurse. In the following spring they went to stay with Casimir's family at Zywotowka for several months and there continued to paint, setting up a small studio in the park on the estate. Some of Markievicz's best work was done at this time. Among extant oils and drawings by Markievicz in Polish private collections are family portraits and landscapes of this period, some of which indicate something of the diversity and richness of his oeuvre. The portrait of his sister, *Wanda Markiewicz Malkiewicz*, and *Landscape with Bridge* are good examples. The pair returned to Paris in October 1902, where they hosted a costume ball for a hundred and fifty people, spent Christmas in Lissadell and again travelled to the Ukraine in the spring. They stayed there until autumn 1903 when they returned, together with Casimir's six-year old son Stanislaw, to live permanently in Ireland. They went first to Lissadell and then to Dublin where they settled in St Mary's in Frankfort Avenue, Rathgar. Neighbours in Rathgar included Maud Gonne and AE (George Russell). AE first met Markievicz in 1902 when he was visiting Constance's brother, Sir Josslyn, at Lissadell. Through AE, Markievicz was introduced to Dublin's artists and intellectuals who frequented his Sunday salons. He also became a popular figure on the Dublin social circuit which centred on the Viceroy and Vicereine, the Dudleys, who entertained at the Viceregal Lodge and Dublin Castle.

In October 1903 Casimir, Constance and AE held their first group exhibition in Dublin at the Leinster Hall, Molesworth Street. The majority of Casimir's twenty-four paintings were of landscapes and townscapes of his homeland[8] and were clearly painted earlier at Zywotowka and brought by him to Ireland. In the following year, in August 1904, the three again held an exhibition at the same venue.

2. Casimir MARKIEVICZ (1874-1932): Constance in White: Portrait of Constance, Countess Markievicz (née Gore-Booth) (1868-1927), Artist and Revolutionary. *Signed, 'C.de Markievicz 1899'. Oil on canvas, 205 x 91 cm. (National Gallery of Ireland).* To mark the 75th anniversary of the Countess's election to Parliament this painting now hangs in Leinster House.

This much larger exhibition was entitled *Paintings from Two Countries* and in it Casimir showed more than eighty works which, as the title suggests, included views and genre scenes from both Ireland and the Ukraine. The titles such as *A Cossack's Wife*, *Peasants Marketing on the Dnieper*, *The Strike*, *Sunflowers*, *Sligo Fishermen*, *Benbulben*, *Black Biddy's Cottage* and *Irish Nocturne* give an indication of the subjects that interested

3. Casimir MARKIEVICZ (1874-1932): Murals, larger than lifesize, of members of the Gore-Booth family in the dining-room at Lissadell, their home in Co Sligo.

4. Beatrice ELVERY (Lady Glenavy) (1883-1970): In the good old times before the licence. Members (of the United Arts Club) arriving for a House Dinner, 1910. *Watercolour, pen and ink on paper, 15 x 21 cm. (Private collection).* Lady Glenavy's depiction of Casimir as the figure at the door with a gun captures the Members' general perception of the Polish artist as a towering giant.

the artist at the time. Markievicz also exhibited his most prized works *Amour* and *Bread* at the exhibition for which he asked £330 and £150 respectively. Other works in the exhibition were priced much more modestly at between £2 and £5. *Portrait of AE* and *His Honour Judge Seymour Bird* were the only portraits in the exhibition and these were not for sale.

Regular salons held in private houses were the fashion of the

period and Markievicz, who had already earned a reputation as a bon viveur in Paris, frequented many of these, including the salon of Dr and Mrs Denis Coffey who was Registrar of the College of Medicine and later became first President of University College, Dublin. Although the Markieviczes both had some private means, they clearly needed to augment this with money earned and to this end Casimir solicited a number of prestigious portrait commissions. His rather dry portrait of George Coffey, now in the Hugh Lane Municipal Gallery, was painted at this time as was his *Investiture of the Right Hon. The Earl of Mayo as Knight of St. Patrick* (1905) a group portrait including some of the most influential figures of the period and which must have done much to enhance his reputation in Dublin (See article by John Gilmartin in this issue). His portrait of the Chief Justice of Ireland, *Lord O'Brien of Kilfenora*, which today hangs in the Dining Hall of King's Inns,[9] was painted in 1906 and exhibited at the RHA[10] in that year. 'Peter the Packer', as he was nicknamed for allegedly packing juries, lived near by and the Markieviczes were frequent guests at his house.

These were, of course, exciting times in Dublin for both art and literature and Hugh Lane's efforts to establish a Municipal Gallery of Modern Art finally bore fruit in 1905 with the opening of the Harcourt Street premises. The intense concentration on artistic matters created by Lane's activities formed a suitable climate for the establishment of a new Arts Club in Dublin. Around this time a circular proposing the setting up of an Arts Club for all those interested in art, music and literature was issued by a committee of eight which included Casimir Markievicz, George Russell, Dermod O'Brien, Ellen Duncan, who headed the committee, and others. AE had, as early as 1902, written to Sarah Purser of his hopes of establishing such a club, 'The Gore-Booth girl who married the Polish Count with the unspellable name is going to settle near Dublin about summertime. As they are both clever it will help to create an art atmosphere. We might get the materials for a revolt, a new Irish Art Club'. AE found rooms for the new Club when it opened in 1907 in the same building in Lincoln Place where he worked for Sir Horace Plunkett's Irish Agricultural Organisation Society. The Markieviczes, along with AE, Lady Gregory, Hugh Lane, William Orpen, W B and Jack Yeats, were among the first artistic and literary people to join. Casimir, by all accounts, was very prominent in the Club where he gave lessons in life drawing in the early days. But his bohemian ways did not endear him to everyone and especially, it would appear, not to Lady Gregory and W B Yeats. Beatrice Elvery's caricatures of the early days (Fig. 4) wonderfully capture the divergent personalities of the club members and the general perception among them of Casimir Markievicz as a towering giant whose primary interest was in the consumption of alcohol. However it was more than his 'bohemianism' which alienated him from Yeats and Lady Gregory.

Always interested in the theatre, Markievicz had begun to write and produce his own plays and formed his own Independent Dramatic Company in 1908. It produced his first play, *Seymour's Redemption* (about a politician who renounces public life in favour of illicit love), in March of that year. His next play *The Dilettante* was staged at the Abbey in December and was followed on the same night by *Home Sweet Home*, a collaboration with Nora FitzPatrick. All of these plays were comedies and although they achieved popular success in Dublin,

CASIMIR DUNIN MARKIEVICZ, PAINTER AND PLAYWRIGHT

they provoked the disdain of W B Yeats who did not approve of the Abbey being used by groups producing 'mere entertainment'.[11] Despite the much recorded hostility towards Markievicz from Yeats and Gregory, their social lives were inevitably linked in the small Dublin art world of the time. Proceeds from one of the offending plays went towards the purchase of a Corot painting for Hugh Lane's Gallery. Though Lane, too, did not always see eye to eye with Markievicz, he nevertheless included two of his paintings, *Study of Trees* (1908) and *Portrait of AE* (1904) in his 1913 Gift to the Gallery. Lane's judgement in paintings is legendary and his choice of Casimir's portrait of AE (Fig. 5) for the Modern Gallery is evidence of his discernment. It is certainly one of the most painterly and sensitive of the artist's work and portrays in its pose and props of easel and pince-nez the earnest enthusiasm of AE, mystic poet and painter. *The Study of Trees* with its low view point, cloud-dappled blue sky and slight stylisation, departs somewhat from Casimir's more earthy impasto-laden landscapes such as the *Russian Cottage* (Fig. 6) in the Crawford Gallery, Cork of 1909.[12] *The Study of Trees* was probably purchased at the exhibition held in Leinster Hall in August 1908 to which Casimir, Constance and fellow Club members, Dermod O'Brien, William Leech, and AE all contributed.

In 1910 Markievicz's most successful play in Ireland, *The Memory of the Dead*, was performed at the Abbey. The plot centres on the 1798 Rising. In 1911 George A Bermingham's *Eleanor's Enterprise* was put on in Belfast by Markievicz's company which also put on in Dublin, Eva Gore-Booth's *Buried Life of Deirdre*, her *Unseen Kings*, Edward Martyn's *Grangecolman* and Markievicz's own *Rival Stars*, about an artist and his socialist wife whose political involvement leads to estrangement and infidelity. This, like many of his plays, has some obvious parallels with his own life. At the same time Casimir founded a new company, The Dublin Repertory Theatre, with Evelyn Ashley. The main objective of this company was to bring the best of new European plays to Dublin. Francois Coppee's *For the Crown*, Maeterlinck's *Monny Vanny* and George Bernard Shaw's *The Devil's Disciple* were among the company's productions. Always noted for pursuing extreme realism in his productions,[13] Markievicz's staging of *The Devil's Disciple* must have caused considerable comment when he recruited Trinity students to play the British soldiers and Fianna boys and nationalists to play the crowd.

However, events in the real world, particularly those surrounding the arrest of James Larkin in August 1913, were shortly afterwards to put a stop to Markievicz's Dublin career. The manager of the Gaiety Theatre (which was the main venue for the Repertory Theatre Company in whose plays Constance frequently

acted) wrote to Evelyn Ashley in September, telling him that '... owing to the prominent part which the Countess has taken in the labour disputes I honestly do not think that her appearance on the stage would be good for business'. Ashley in his reply stated that he too felt 'that the involvement of the Count and Countess could only do the Repertory Theatre movement irreparable injury'. When these opinions became known, labour boycotted

5. Casimir MARKIEVICZ (1874-1932): Portrait of AE, 1904. *Oil on canvas, 61 x 51 cm. (Hugh Lane Municipal Gallery, Dublin)*. One of the most painterly and sensitive of of Markievicz's works, this portrait was given to the Gallery by Hugh Lane, whose discernment in painting was legendary, in his 1913 Gift.

the Repertory and Casimir resigned his co-directorship.[14]

In September 1913 he exhibited for the last time in Dublin with Frances Baker and AE – he left in December. The United Arts Club had been an important part of Markievicz's life in Dublin and he had frequently entertained friends there including Breffni O'Rourke, Gerald Doyle, Grace Gifford, Seamus O'Sullivan (James Starkey) and Oliver St John Gogarty.[15] Casimir's attractive portrait of Ellen Duncan (Fig. 7), a leading figure in the early Club, dates from this period.

Casimir, who was a champion fencer, was also founder and

president of the Dublin Fencing Club which met at Merrion Row. His painting *The Fencer*, a portrait of M Charles Dain, maître d'armes, whom he brought over from France to direct the club was one of Casimir's best known paintings of his Dublin period and is still remembered in fencing circles.[16]

When he left Dublin in 1913 he first went to Albania as a war correspondent then to his family estate in the Ukraine where he painted landscapes and continued to write satirical plays – though now in Polish rather than English. His *Wild Field* was staged in Warsaw by A Szyfman in 1914. At the outbreak of the First World War Casimir was staying at Rózyn and joined the Russian Army. He fought in the Carpathian mountains and was decorated for bravery. Seriously wounded in the winter of 1914/1915, he spent time recovering in a military hospital in Lwow. His son Stanislaw moved to the Ukraine in June 1915 and later became an interpreter of French and English in the Russian Volunteer Fleet at Archangel. In 1917 Casimir was in Moscow where he was appointed artistic director of the New Polish Theatre. Among the plays that he directed there were S Wyspianski's *November Night* and his own *Memory of the Dead*. Towards the end of 1917 he moved to Kiev where he was co-director of the Polish Theatre and professor of painting at the Polish School of Fine Art. At the end of 1918 as the effects of the Russian

6. Casimir MARKIEVICZ (1874-1932): Russian Cottage, 1909. *Oil on canvas, 36.5 x 53 cm. Signed 'Dunin Markievicz 1909'. (Crawford Gallery, Cork).* An earthy, impasto-laden landscape.

7. Casimir MARKIEVICZ (1874-1932): Portrait of Ellen Duncan (detail). *Oil on canvas, 111 x 76 cm. Signed with monogram. (Private collection).* Mrs Duncan was a leading figure in the early days of the United Arts Club, which had played such an important part in Markievicz's life before he left Dublin in 1913.

Revolution were becoming more acute in Kiev, Casimir moved to Warsaw where he lived for the remainder of his life.[17]

In Warsaw in 1919 he produced Childau's *Romance* and G B Shaw's *Major Barbara* and his own plays, *The Marriage of Martha, Lilies of the Fields* and *The Memory of the Dead*. Towards the end of the year he was appointed economic and legal adviser at the American Embassy in Warsaw, a position he held until his death in 1932. Although this full-time post prevented him from taking a very active role in the theatre, his plays continued to be shown in Warsaw, Vilno and Poznan and he still managed to write four new plays (*The Rogue's Conversion*, 1922; *The Miracle of Mr Tosh*, 1927; *Love or the Fist*, 1929 and *A Matter of Honour*, 1932). In 1928 Markievicz published a novel, *The Power of Flesh and Blood*, the action of which is set in Ireland. This was followed by another novel (*In the Embrace of Melpomene*) in 1931. During the last years of his life Casimir continued to paint (mainly portraits) but gave up exhibiting altogether and any works from this period which survived the Second World War are in private collections.

WANDA RYAN-SMOLIN has an MA degree in the History of Art from the Jagellonian University in Krakow. She was on the staff of the National Gallery of Ireland (1981-89) and lecturer in the National College of Art and Design (1988-91).

1. Later in Paris he began to use the French spelling of his name Casimir Dunin Markievicz and normally signed his paintings *C de Markievicz* or *Dunin Markievicz*.
2. *Herbarz Polski i Imionospis Zasluzonych w Polsce Ludzi Wszyskich Stanów i Czasów* (Polish Heraldic Dictionary) Lwów 1855 (reprint London 1963). Vol.1, pp.143 and 144, vol.2, p.137
3. This painting was later exhibited in Dublin in 1904.
4. Illustrations exist in private archives.
5. See Patricia Boylan *All Cultivated People, A History of the United Arts Club*, Gerrards Cross, 1988, pp.135, 147. The Club's minute book which records the donation describes the painting as large but does not give a title. It seems likely that the picture in question was *Amour* as several of the biographies of Countess Markievicz note

that a Mrs Longworth bought the painting though they also state that she presented it to the Polish Embassy in London - this may have been her subsequent action but to date this has been difficult to establish.
6. It was purchased by the Gallery from Mr P Egan in 1952.
7. See A Haverty, *Constance Markievicz. An Independent Life*, Pandora 1988, p.51
8. See A Marreco, *The Rebel Countess. The Life and Times of Constance Markievicz*, London 1967, p.88.
9. See W. Ryan-Smolin, *King's Inns Portraits*, Dublin, 1992, p.52.
10. Markievicz exhibited every year between 1905 and 1910 at the RHA. All but one of his ten exhibits were portraits.
11. See Joseph Hone, *W B Yeats 1865-1939*, London 1962, p.286
12. *A Russian Cottage* from the Tulira Castle

collection was also bequeathed by Edward Martyn to the Hugh Lane Municipal Gallery.
13. This included the use of live donkeys, chickens etc. on stage.
14. See J Van Voris, *Constance de Markievicz. In the Cause of Ireland*, p.110.
15. See Boylan, *op cit.*
16. I am grateful to Shirley Armstrong Duffy for showing me an illustration of this portrait which is recorded as having appeared in *The Irish Review* (date unknown).
17. He visited Dublin briefly in 1919 and again in 1927 with his son, when he came to the bedside of his dying wife.
18. The last two of these were co-written with his friend M. Fijalkowski on whose estate at Nowy in the Kutnowski region Markievicz is buried.

THE ENGRAVED GLASS OF FRANZ TIEZE

Mary Boydell *finds a consistency of style in the decoration employed by this Bohemian glass-maker who worked in Dublin.*

When writing about Franz Tieze, the Bohemian glass engraver, due homage should be paid to the remarkable Pugh family of glassmakers who were responsible for bringing Tieze to Dublin. Richard Pugh from Wales came to Cork in the late eighteenth century where he was employed by the Cork Glass Company. Descendants of his family later came to Dublin where they set up a small glass-works in Liffey Street in 1854.[1] After a few years, in 1863, they moved to larger premises in Potter's Alley where fine quality glass was made until 1890. From the middle of the nineteenth century there had been a growing demand in these islands for Bohemian glass, which was on display in shops and at the numerous exhibitions of the period both here and in England. This style of well-engraved glass became most fashionable and in order to compete, the Pughs engaged some Bohemian craftsmen one of whom was Franz Tieze (Fig. 1).

Franz Tieze was born in 1842 in North Bohemia where he learned his craft. He came to Dublin via London in 1865. Seven years later he married a local girl. Tieze died in 1932, having spent the last twenty one years of his life in Simpson's Hospital for the blind.[2] The major part of his work as a glass engraver in Dublin was devoted to working in the service of the Pugh glassworks, though he eventually undertook work for various Dublin glass retailers who often imported their blanks or unadorned wares from England.

In the context of this article the attribution of glass engraved by Franz Tieze is mainly based on the firm evidence of engraved glass which was purchased by the National Museum of Ireland – and its predecessor – directly from the Pugh glassworks or from the Pugh family following the closure of the firm in 1890.[3] In addition, a noted example of his work was purchased by the Museum from Frederick Vodrey, a retail glass and china merchant of Moore Street and Mary Street. This comprised a jug and two goblets (Fig.2) exhibited by Vodrey at the 1883 Cork Exhibition and purchased by the Museum in the same year. The glass is engraved with a classical scene inspired by the Parthenon frieze which was also used by other continental engravers of the same period.[4]

Few glass engravers' sketch books are known and it is indeed most fortunate that Tieze's is one of the few. It was in the Dudley Westropp collection and, following his death in 1954, it was sold by auction[5] in 1956 to a London glass dealer from whom it was purchased by the Victoria and Albert Museum.

The drawings in the sketch book cover a wide range of subjects from deer in

1. TUMBLER (*ht.11.5cm*) with a design of deer in a woodland setting, engraved by Franz TIEZE (1842-1932). Bought from the Pugh glassworks, Dublin, after its closure in 1890, by the National Museum of Ireland.

woodland settings and hunting scenes on the early pages to formal designs including ferns, flowers and grasses. The Irish nationalist symbols of shamrock, the Round Tower, harp and wolfhound are featured; and a design for glassware for the 93rd Regiment of Foot, which was stationed in Ireland from 1876 to 1879,[6] is included. There is even a sketch for decoration on a chamber pot.

Included with the sketch book, when it was sold in 1956, was a jug engraved by Tieze in the Bohemian style with a scene of deer in a woodland setting drinking by a pool. This was a popular subject with engravers of the nineteenth century from Bohemia. Also sold with the jug and the sketch book was a print which probably was the inspiration for the design on the jug; unfortunately the print has not been traced. The jug (damaged) is in the Victoria and Albert Museum, London.

As another indication of the nature of Franz Tieze's art, he sold to the Dublin Museum (now the National Museum of Ireland) a glass medallion for a brooch engraved with Venus seated on a cloud with cupids on either side.[7] According to the Museum records, this was engraved between 1870 and 1875; possibly it was for his wife on the occasion of their marriage in 1872. Tieze received five shillings for this brooch in 1911. Sadly this was the year in which he was admitted to hospital having lost his sight.

One of the commonest motifs on glass by this engraver is the maiden-hair fern. This was not an unusual subject to choose for decorative use during the second half of the nineteenth century but was seldom used by glass engravers other than Tieze. The cultivation of ferns by ladies in the drawing room and in Edwardian cases was a fashionable pastime. In the *Journal of Design* for 1850 there is an actual sample of material with the maiden-hair fern with tendrils which is referred to as the 'Designers sprig'. A decade or so later this fern was also much used as a decorative motif on silverware made in England. In general when Tieze engraved the maiden-hair fern it was botanically almost correct.[8] A pair of carafes and tumblers in the National Museum show how well the engraver has made use of this motif: it seems actually to embrace the form of the vessel like ivy on a stone or branch of a tree (Fig.7).The shamrock is used in an equally effective manner. His stylised use of flowers in general is shown on two claret jugs of the same form.[9] On each is engraved a similar bouquet of flowers on the lower section of the jug. Amongst these is a spray of botanically correct blue bells. A rough drawing for this engraver's sketch book.[10]

By the middle of the nineteenth century the Round Tower, Irish harp, shamrock and Irish wolfhound had come to symbolise Irish nationalist aspirations. The Belleek factory, and the makers of the popular bog oak ornaments, among others , used these as a trade mark or as a decorative feature. The shamrock had been in use as an Irish emblem earlier.[11] The harp as depicted by Tieze is based on the 'Brian Boru' harp in Trinity College Dublin, which was well known since it had been exhibited at the Dublin International Exhibition of 1853. During the second half of the nineteenth century the Round Tower was commonly illustrated in the numerous publications on the subject of Irish antiquities; however, when Tieze engraved the Round Tower on glass it is usually shown incorrectly with the door at ground level (Fig.4). The wolfhound is based on the greyhound. There are two possible reasons for this peculiarity. The wolfhound had become almost extinct by the end of the nineteenth century and Tieze would have been unlikely to have seen one in Dublin; however Whyte and Sons of Marlborough Street, who had a small financial interest in the Pugh glassworks,[12] also had a share in the ownership of Master McGrath, the famed greyhound who won the Waterloo Cup on several occasions. In addition they had a portrait of this greyhound, along with a listing of the shareholders, hung in their showroom and, to add further to the doggy interest, in the 1873 advertisement for their glass and china they added 'Sole agents for any good medicine for dogs'.[13] By the end of the nineteenth century Tieze was most effectively incorporating flying insects within engraved design; these appear mainly to be based on insects with transparent wings similar to dragon flies or 'daddy long-legs' (hymenoptera), unlike Belleek pottery and porcelain decorators who favoured butterflies (lepidoptera). Motifs based on grass-like foliage are,however, common to both as shown on the popular Belleek 'Grass Pattern' Tea Ware.[14]

Besides working for the Pugh glassworks and for Vodrey, Tieze also engraved for William Whyte's glass and china shop in Marlborough Street. As late as the 1890s, following the closure of the glassworks, he was using Whyte's note paper for making sketches of glass designs

2. A JUG AND TWO GOBLETS (*ht.26cm and 15.5cm*) shown at the 1883 Cork Exhibition by the Dublin glass firm of Frederick Vodrey. The design, engraved by Franz TIEZE (1842-1932), is a classical scene inspired by the Parthenon frieze. (*National Museum of Ireland*).

and for taking rubbings from completed engravings.

Thomas Leech of Dame Street, another glass and china shop, also had glass engraved by Tieze.[15] In 1883 Leech advertised that 'glass was exhibited on a special table under Miss Pugh's charge'.[16] Firm evidence has recently come to light that Tieze engraved for Percival Jones, another glass and china merchant of Westmoreland Street.

On Whyte & Sons notepaper with incomplete date, 189..., are sketches based on various grasses[17] and these are used to great effect on a jug which is definitely known to have originated in the glassworks of Thomas Webb of Stourbridge.[18] Besides the grass motifs, the engraving includes flying insects and bulrushes (Fig. 5). Around the upper cup-shaped pouring lip are garlands of flowers and the ubiquitous tendrils. Two ice plates dating from the same period are engraved with stylised ferns, grasses possibly based on the plantain, couch grass and the garden flower Solomon's Seal (Fig. 6) Again flying insects are included in the design. Another jug, magnificently engraved with floral and grass motifs and dating from about 1890, is shown in Fig. 8.

Glass engravers seldom sign their work. It was therefore of the greatest interest to find in 1980 Franz Tieze's initials on the underside of the bowl of a goblet engraved with shamrock and a monogram.[19] The engraving also included the date 1916 which had been added later by a different hand. Subsequently the signature 'Tieze' was found well hidden within the shamrock decoration on a wine glass.[20] This prompted a closer look at other examples of engraved glass attributed to Tieze and revealed that a jug, also engraved with sprays of shamrock, was signed 'Tieze', not only once but twice, and again hidden within the decoration.[21] Both the wine glass and the jug are engraved with the same design comprising the Round Tower, Irish harp, a stylised Irish wolfhound and surmounted by the toast 'Erin go Bragh' within a ribbon. The sprays of shamrock which surround this group incorporate tendrils – a characteristic of Tieze's engraving when using this motif. One knows from the structure of the jug that it dates from after 1870. The manner in which the lettering is engraved on the wine glass and the ribbon which surrounds it closely resembles that on a jug in the

3 CARAFE (*ht. 24cm*) one of a pair signed 'Tieze' and discovered in England. The band of footless parrots on oval perches is a motif not previously found on glass attributed to Franz Tieze. (*National Museum of Ireland*).

National Museum of Ireland which also features a portrait of Charles Stewart Parnell.[22] On the occasion of the 1885 Dublin Artisans' Exhibition, Parnell visited the Pugh stall on 3 September and it was noted that he spent a few minutes there. Pugh's display included a portrait of Parnell. This portrait and the facsimile of his signature were taken from a photograph.[23] One wonders if Parnell appreciated having his portrait on glass since figurative work was the weakest aspect of Tieze's engraving technique.

Following the publication of the signed goblet, wine glass and jug, a pair of signed carafes were found in England and were subsequently purchased by the National Museum of Ireland (Fig. 3). These are of particular interest, since the engraver uses motifs which hitherto had not been found on glass attributed to him. These comprise, around the body of the glass, a band of fanciful footless parrots with decorative crests on oval perches. Above and below this band are thistle-like flowers and scroll-like leaflets from which issue groups of ferns. Some of the thistle motifs support sprays of grass; and to add to the fanciful effect two large tendrils spring from the vase on either side of the grasses. The neck of the carafe is engraved in a more orthodox manner with a fruiting vine. The glass in the two carafes is exceptionally thick in section, thus suggesting that they were intended for cutting rather than engraving. Were they perhaps specially engraved for a parrot fancier or even a Mr Parrot?

The most recently found examples signed by Tieze are a part set comprising four small jugs and seven small tumblers. These glasses were a wedding present to Joseph

4. CONE-SHAPED 'BRANDY' BOTTLE (*ht.33cm*) engraved by Franz TIEZE (1842-1932) with popular nineteenth century nationalist symbols and round tower – this was usually shown by Tieze incorrectly, with the door at ground level. (*Private collection*).

Mitchelburne Symes and Adelaide Gibton on the occasion of their marriage on 9 June 1897 at the Mariner's Church, Dun Laoghaire. Family tradition is that they were purchased from Whyte & Sons of Georges' Street, Dublin. A cheque book stub survives made out to Whyte & Sons, dated 9 April 1897 for the sum of £22.17s. Would it be too much to surmise that this was the amount paid for the complete set of commissioned glass? A grandson of Joseph Symes, when a child, used on occasions to accompany his grandfather to Whyte's; he remembers how his grandfather enjoyed these visits and the kindly attention of Miss Jones, the saleswoman. Each piece is engraved with fern-type sprays and the family crest surrounded by two sprays of maiden-hair fern. The crest is that of a head with helmet with the visor up and three feather-like plumes springing from the rear of the helmet (Fig 9). These plumes are engraved in a similar manner to those on the signed pair of carafes in the National Museum. Unlike the other signed examples of this engraver's skill, these are signed prominently below the decorative design on the lower section of each glass. This group of glasses is of the utmost importance, being an example of Tieze's work which shows that at the age of fifty-five he was still in his prime.

There is little doubt that Tieze was a very skilled craftsman as shown in his engravings of subjects such as deer in woodland settings, hunting scenes and garlands of flowers. All these subjects he would have studied while learning his craft in Bohemia. He also shows his skill when engraving

5. WATER JUG (*ht.23cm*) from the glassworks of Thomas Webb of Stourbridge, engraved by Franz TIEZE (1842-1932) with grass motifs, flying insects and bulrushes. (*Private collection*).

6. GLASS ICE PLATE (*diam. 15cm*) late nineteenth century, (detail), one of a pair engraved by Franz TIEZE (1842-1932) with stylised ferns, Solomon's Seal, grasses based on the plantain, couch grass and flying insects. (*Collection, Mary Boydell*).

THE ENGRAVED GLASS OF FRANZ TIEZE

7. TUMBLER (*ht.8.5cm*) one of a pair with carafes, engraved by Franz TIEZE (1842-1932) with a motif of maiden-hair fern; one of his commonest motifs, it was seldom used by other glass engravers. (*National Museum of Ireland*).

8. JUG (*ht. 21cm*) magnificently engraved by Franz TIEZE (1842-1932) with a variety of floral and grass motifs; Tieze excelled with such delicate subjects. (*Private collection*).

9. TUMBLER (*ht. 9cm*) part of a set and signed 'Tieze'. The plumes at the back of the helmet are similar to those on a signed pair of carafes in the National Museum of Ireland, and show that at the age of 55, Tieze was still in his prime as an engraver. (*Collection, Glascott Symes*).

learning his craft in Bohemia. He also shows his skill when engraving inscriptions in German Gothic lettering and in monograms, of which there are numerous studies in his sketch book. As already noted, his figurative work is weak. When he came to London at the age of twenty, and then on to Dublin, however, he would have had to adapt his engraving skills in order to meet the changing fashion in taste. He thus had to develop his skills to encompass a wide variety of new subjects such as classical scenes from the Parthenon frieze, and designs based on ferns and grasses. In Dublin, fashion demanded that he included harps, round towers, wolfhounds and an abundance of shamrock. There was also a demand for the engraving of commemorative motifs of particularly Irish interest on glass of retrospective design or manufacture.[24] With the broadening of subject matter

which he was required to master, his most imaginative work is undoubtedly to be seen in the late examples based mainly on botanical motifs decorated with insects.

MARY BOYDELL is a writer and lecturer. She is President of the Glass Society of Ireland and a member of the Glass Circle and of the Glass Association.

ACKNOWLEDGEMENTS
In the preparation of this paper, grateful acknowledgement is due in the first place to Mairead Dunlevy for her inspiring encouragement. Dr J O'Connor of the Natural History Museum of Ireland and Dr Charles Nelson of the National Botanical Gardens offered invaluable help with possible sources of motifs for plants and insects, and the staff of the National Museum of Ireland were most helpful in providing access to examples of Tieze's engraving. A most important aspect of this paper was made possible by Mr and Mrs Glascott Symes, who brought their hitherto unpublished set of glasses to my attention.

1. Mary Boydell, 'Flint Glass Manufactory, Liffey Street,' in *Technology Ireland* no.28, Dublin, July-August 1973.
2. Mary Boydell, 'Recently Discovered Signatures on Glass from the Pugh Glassworks in Dublin', *The Glass Circle No. 7*, 1991, pp.50-52.
3. Private correspondence between Richard Pugh and the National Museum of Ireland, now in the Acquisition Ledgers .
4. Catriona MacLeod, 'Bohemian Glass-ware at the Cork Exhibition 1883', *Studies*, Dublin, Winter 1978, pp.300-42. Illustrated.
5. Catalogue of Sotheby's sale, London, 25 June 1956, Lot 62.
6. I am grateful to Michael Ball of the National Army Museum, London for this information.
7. Illustrated in Catriona MacLeod, *Glass in*

The National Museum of Ireland, by Thomas & Richard Pugh, Dublin, 1983, p.81.
8. See illustrations: MSD Westropp *Irish Glass*, 1920, (revised ed. Mary Boydell, Dublin ,1978, plate 2); Mary Boydell, 'Some Dublin Glass Makers', *Dublin Historical Record*, XXVII, 1974, no.5, p.59; McLeod 1983, note 7, p.41.
9. Illustrated in Westropp 1920, plate 2.
10. Sketch book, p.79. Illustrated in Mary Boydell, 'Engravers of Bohemia working in Ireland and England', *Proceedings of the International Association for the History of Glass*, Liège, 1981, p.337.
11. Richard Degenhardt, *Belleek*, New York, 1978, pp.35 and 115.
12. M. Boydell, 'Some Dublin Glass Makers', *Dublin Historical Record*, XXVII, 1974, p.45.
13. *Hackett's Dublin Almanac*.

14. Degenhardt 1978, p.104.
15. MacLeod 1983, p.59.
16. Advertisement in *Christmas Sunshine* (unidentified contemporary Dublin journal)
17. Tieze's sketch book, Victoria and Albert Museum, London,p.87.
18. I am most grateful to Charles Hajdamach, Director of the Broadfield House Museum of Glass, Stourbridge, for identifying the manufacturer of this jug..
19. Sotheby's sale in Ireland, Slane Castle, 12 May, 1980, Lot 206, ill. See also Boydell 1981, p.338, ill.
20. Illustrated in Boydell 1991, p.51.
21. *ibid.*, p.51.
22. Illustrated in McLeod 1983, p.51, pl.xix.
23. *ibid.*, p.51.
24. This aspect is being researched by Peter Francis.

'SOMETHING INDEFINABLE' IN THE WORK OF DEBORAH BROWN

Hilary Pyle *traces the career in painting and sculpture of a well-established artist from Northern Ireland.*

Deborah Brown has been one of Northern Ireland's leading artists since the early 1960s, highly regarded both at home and abroad. When her sculpture experienced a complete turnabout a decade ago, moving from pure abstraction to the figurative style which she had abandoned twenty-five years before, few were taken by surprise. Her work still contained that indefinable something that was the nature of her art. She herself maintained that the abstraction was still there, and that the figurative element was but an extra dimension – the visible human element.

This cool objective approach to her work has been typical of the artist since the beginning of her career. She has always tended to question what she was doing, and to embark on the project only after much experimentation in sketchnotes, sketch maquettes and discussion with herself as to the reason why she was pursuing a certain idea. Her early paintings were constructed on principles evolved by herself,[1] comparable for their thoroughness with the cubist exercises of Mainie Jellett and Evie Hone (whom she did not at the time know) in her search for the personal form of abstraction that she eventually reached in 1958. Yet, at the same time as seeking a style in such a disciplined fashion, she is certain that 'Art has one rare quality which sets it apart from other forms of work and that is the element of something indefinable, something which is beyond explanation. Technique and aesthetics can be talked or written about but this extra quality cannot.'[2]

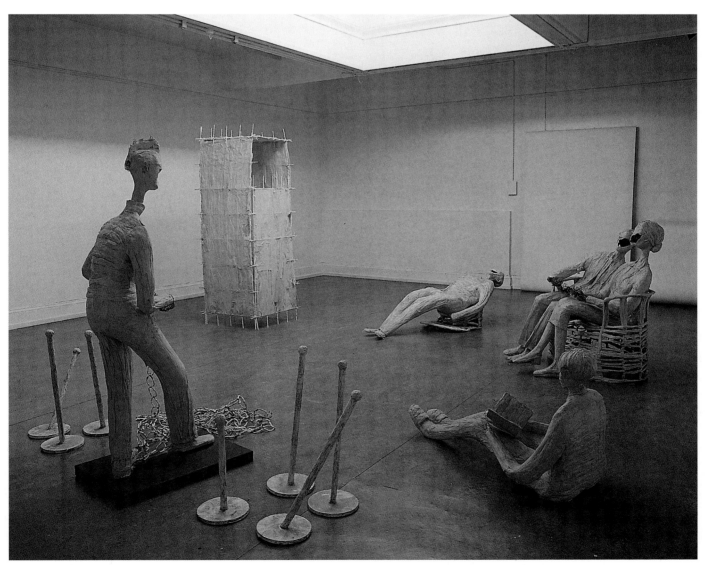

1. Deborah BROWN (b.1927): Waiting (1982) *Paper and wire, life-size. (Hugh Lane Municipal Gallery of Modern Art).* An environmental piece with a Godot-like mood: the shapes of the five life-size figures, who show no interest in one another, draw the eye towards the empty Punch and Judy tent – but nothing happens.

'SOMETHING INDEFINABLE' IN THE WORK OF DEBORAH BROWN

Born in Belfast in 1927, the only child in a family with business interests but with a devotion to the arts, her first memorable visual experiences are of Cushendun (literally 'beside the river Dun') by the sea, at the foot of Glendun in county Antrim. Here she spent most of her childhood particularly during the War years. Her companion was Heather Harper, later to become a soprano of international standing. Deborah Brown herself played the cello, and contact with the musical Harpers aroused a conflict within herself as to whether she should choose art or music as a profession. 'Between them the two families created a very intellectual background,' Anne Crookshank has written, 'isolated in one of the world's most

2. Deborah BROWN (b.1927): Purple Forms (1962). *Tempera on paper, 36 x 30.7cm. (Private collection).* In her early paintings, the artist searched in a disciplined fashion for her own personal form of abstraction which she eventually reached in 1962.

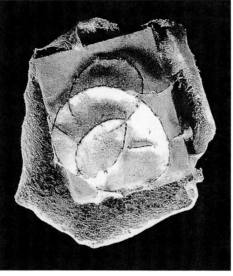

3. Deborah BROWN (b.1927): Barbed Wire (1971) 41 x 52cm. *(Arts Council of Northern Ireland Collection).* Despite the ferocity of the Barbed Wire Series which the artist made in her central Belfast studio at the height of the troubles, she is not a political artist.

beautiful districts, where the harshness of the rocks and the cliffs and the sea is only equalled by the splendid lushness of the valley and the wide isolation of the bogs.'[3]

Brown herself was aware of the mysterious, 'sometimes frightening feel' of the Antrim coastline. She was unconsciously studying the patterns of rocks, and the fields folding and weaving their way down to the shore. When with her father by the river, she met Humbert Craig, the landscape painter. 'This was my first introduction both to the word and to an artist'. But it convinced her that she must make painting her career. Craig talked to her while he interpreted the mood of the glen, introducing her to colour mixing and to aesthetic ideas.

Later she was able to realise that the origins of her sculpture were deeper than she had imagined. 'In the spring, the greatest joy in my life was to work with a horse-drawn plough. Here was an early experience in the exciting feeling of something being created in direct contact with myself. The sense of the iron handles of the plough and the reins in my hands and the brown shining earth unfolding as the horses strained forward.' A later

parallel would be the 'fiddling' or drawing with wire, and the sawing at sheets of fibre glass, communicating intimately with her material till she happened on the unexpected shapes which grew into sculpture.

In 1946, after attending classes held at Sidney Smith's studio, Deborah Brown went to Belfast College of Art to study painting. She transferred the following year to the National College of Art in Dublin, where she appreciated the sound academic training, and enjoyed studying the History of Art. Recently she has been thinking that her tendency to work in white may have its roots in the act of drawing from plaster casts during the first two years; just as the strong discipline in her training as a musician may have had its effect on her painting in later life. She remembers fellow student Michael Morrow, in the courtyard of the College, performing from transcriptions he had made of medieval music, playing instruments borrowed from the National Museum. On a visit to London she encountered the 'wonderful linear movements' of Botticelli.

Most influential in her early training was her period in Paris after she had left the College in 1950. Here abstract art began to have a personal meaning for her, and she realised that every mark she placed on her canvas had a significance in itself. Her first landscapes, though realistic, were simplified to become impressions of image and atmosphere, worked in prominent brushstrokes.

On her return to Belfast, and her first one-woman show at the CEMA gallery, her initial aim was to identify with the local ethos. She was always conscious of her Irishness. This expressed itself not only in a love for the Cushendun landscape, but also in an interest in Irish legend, an interest which has been lifelong. In the Irish legends, she says, she first found herself. They conserved the humanity not immediately apparent as her work was growing more abstract. Brown's legendary paintings of the mid-1950s were popular with collectors. She stresses, though, that the legends she used, drawn from her reading of Lady Wilde and W B Yeats, were simply jumping off points for inspiration, to set line and colour in motion, in what were figurative, but non-illustrative paintings. Her colours were strong, primary reds and blues, vivid as stained glass. The influence of the sea, observed or in legend, on her work, caused the ceaseless rhythmic movement in counterpoint to an apparent stillness which she has continued to capture. Detailed notes on a preliminary sketch show how she worked out colour and rhythm while studying a Fra Angelico. In these paintings she became aware that subject itself was not an end, but that it represented a conduit through which she could confront the materials which were what really absorbed her.

'Something Indefinable' in the Work of Deborah Brown

These early paintings have their own relationship with more recent works; because at some stage she cut up rejected oils, preserving minute passages which she looks at now and again when awaiting inspiration. These 'suggesting figures' or gestures in paint, she regards as ancestors to her recent sculptures. Abstracted from a larger space, the liberated brushstrokes of those early years have a look of the work of Jack Yeats, for whom she had an admiration at the time. This may have been what attracted Mary O'Malley to her work when she saw it on exhibition. She invited Deborah Brown to make props and scenery at the Lyric Theatre, Belfast, an enjoyable task because she liked working on a large scale, painting loosely and losing detail. This was ephemeral work; but the artist felt it helped her out of the legendary period into the pure abstraction that was her goal. Her aim was to create atmosphere.

Her musical sense, too, was contributory to her move away from the figurative: 'I think music made me understand abstraction. Like a composer striking a chord and working from that chord, I put the first brushstroke on the canvas and worked into shapes, as if they were notes. That led me into what I call visual language, that pure visual language where you start from the first brushstroke and the first mark'. Listening to music may bring ideas to mind, and suggest how a work may be built up; but, for all its importance to her, she has never wished to translate music into paint.

By 1958 she was a purely abstract painter, still ceaselessly experimenting. 'From then,' she wrote in her Ferranti article, where she analysed her aims and her views on art, 'my subject was the first mark or series of marks placed on the canvas. The marks represented nothing but marks; I believed them to be sufficient in themselves and there was no reference to symbol, object, legend or narrative. These paintings were my first essays in a type of painting where brushstrokes, lines, tone values, etc. were used to create an experience felt through the visual senses.'

She had been looking at international moderns for some years. A fascination with Rothko, whom she imitated for a time, perhaps accounts for the meditative quality of her work in these early abstracts, and for the ease with which she had been able to project a sense of an invisible interior to her painting. Seeing Pollock's work about 1958 made her attempt spontaneous painting, breaking down any final inhibitions about the abstract, though she found these pictures too derivative of Pollock to take them seriously. Some Fontanas exhibited at the Belfast Museum eventually led her to physically explore her hidden interiors by cutting through the canvas to expose new elements. Her lasting admiration for the paintings of William

4. Deborah BROWN (b.1927): Seated Figure (1981) (back view). *Tissue paper and wire, 36 x 17 x 13cm. (Private collection)*. After a visit to America in 1980, Deborah Brown began to make figures in wire and tissue paper, in recollection of the wire models she had made for the Lyric Theatre, Belfast, in the 1950s.

Scott is reflected in the way she, like him, works away at persistent images (though hers may be abstract ones), exploring the visible presence and the nothingness of them, their outer and their inner character at one and the same time.

Over a period of about three years she experimented with stroke and movement using oil over tempera, then introducing brown paper collage. Her image might be no more than a few revolving white brushstrokes on unprimed canvas – executed exquisitely – yet it conveyed a sense of progression into the canvas, as through a veil. She experimented with papier maché, with leather, nails and stitched canvas collage. In 1962 she brought the spatial dimension inwards in a physical way, piercing through the actual support, rather crudely in that the hole was not fashioned but appeared to have been spontaneously broken: but as always she preserved a delicacy of manner along with a visible determination to pursue her obsession with the wonder of space.

In 1964 she began to move the picture plane outwards, building up papier maché forms, sometimes like bats' wings, which floated on white canvas. In the following year some of her papier-maché wall pieces were akin to sculpture. These first essays in three dimensions had an energy and a strangeness beyond the integral beauty.[4] The artist might paint the canvas on which her forms were mounted in the warm or pale colours she so obviously enjoyed; yet she maintained at the same time that the colours were irrelevant to what she was doing. The canvases were flat supports for the spatial shapes floating above them. They were capable of reflecting light and shadow, but were still the passive component in works that soared with life.

During this period of the 1960s Deborah Brown was still exhibiting, in Belfast, and then Dublin, and joining group shows in Bristol, London, Glasgow and Paris. While still committed to her three-dimensional direction, she undertook a commission for eight canvases for the interior of the new Ferranti building at Hollinwood, in Manchester (completed in 1965). These works paralleled what she was doing in papier-maché in a gentler way, deriving ultimately from her last brush paintings of a few years before. The relaxed abstract forms in each floated in and out of the harmoniously coloured rectangular space on the canvas, hung at the end of a corridor, or filling the wall of an office with a mood of visual poetry. The commission was an inspiration on the part of the architect, John Seward.

In 1966 Deborah Brown began to work in fibre glass, her principal material for the next decade. It was a very unhealthy medium to work in, and required using a mask though she now admits that she was not fully aware of its dangers. With fibre glass she was seeking to pierce through the picture surface not only physically (which she had continued to do whether in painting or in sculpture) but visually, making its enigmatic transparency the core of the work. Anne Crookshank, whose sensitive interpretation in the introduction to the 1982 retrospective catalogue has not been equalled, describes this phase vividly. 'Her early use of fibre glass was in flat, often concave, shapes placed in relation to a coloured canvas background.

5. Deborah BROWN (b.1927): Badgers (detail) (1990). *Bronze, over lifesize.* In this detail from a larger than lifesize group of badgers, the artist has captured delightfully the enjoyment and amusement she finds in her encounters with animals.

These reliefs, which were slightly transparent, have now weathered into an alabaster-like constituency, with the quality of stone. Naturally she became involved in the transparency of the medium and to achieve maximum effect the reliefs swelled away from the background so that the light could be trapped, shimmering within the forms. The next step was the free standing form where the light shines and reflects off the resin like crystal but with a random glance like light catching water. The wing forms of her largest fibre glass pieces dance and change as one walks round them, but some of the most enchanting examples are the tiny twists of resin which seem to remain fluid and alive permanently. As a result of her use of this very flexible material, her fibre glass work has an infinity of moods, though the calmness and peace which are the prime qualities of all her work remain the features one remembers best.'

Among the three dimensional fibre glass works are two of 1972 simply entitled *Barbed Wire I* and *Barbed Wire II*. At the time, the artist was working in her studio in Donegall Street in Belfast. The troubles were at their height. She was surrounded by barbed wire. But even though the barbed wire was horrific, she felt that it looked quite beautiful too. Torn paper sticking to it, and clinging crumpled plastic, gave it a fascinating character in her eyes. Despite their ferocity compared with other contemporary work, she insists that these works have nothing to do with the political situation, but were the results of a chance encounter, a fleeting visual moment.

The effects of the events in Belfast were bound to come out unconsciously in some way. Deborah Brown has described the repeated evacuations from offices because of bombs, the glass 'pouring out of windows into the streets like waterfalls', and the machine gun attacks 'like a lot of flies coming from the top of the street' on Bloody Friday, when she was trying to make her way through the middle of the city. But she is not a political artist, and has succeeded in preserving a calm detachment in her art despite being deeply moved at the horrors she has seen.

Many of her works of the 1970s are tiny, sometimes contained in perspex boxes. But she worked on a larger scale too, her works finding their way into the collections of, in the main, connoisseurs, artists and architects. Her fibre glass won major awards in the Irish Exhibition of Living Art, in the Open Painting exhibition, and in the Limerick Exhibition of Visual Art (EVA). One of the last of these fibre glass works of the 1970s was the *Glass Fibre Form mounted on stainless steel* of 1976, now in Radio Telefís Eireann. But Deborah Brown felt by now that she 'had reached a sort of coldness' in her abstraction, her creativity reduced to a matter of lines and space. She sensed that her attraction to the material while it was new, with the light shining through it, was making her work facile. While outwardly serene, inwardly she felt she needed something new to struggle with. The fact that the fibre glass gradually loses its freshness and transparency in itself was disturbing.

She worked little over the next few years, and always with a sense of dissatisfaction, beginning to feel that she had worked herself out. She attributes her return to sculpture and to figuration to a 'chance encounter', a dejected little figure whom she saw sitting on a bench on a very wet day, when she was on a visit to America in 1980. On her return home, she still could not work abstractly to her satisfaction. One year later, recalling the wire models she had made for the Lyric in the 1950s, she was fiddling with some wire, and 'the wee woman' who was hovering in her mind came out, the small *Figure sitting on bench with tree* of 1981.

To wire she added tissue paper. *The Rehearsal* that followed, with figures four feet high, was the turning point. Again based

6. Deborah BROWN (b.1927): The Ram (1984). *Papier-maché and wire, 172.7 x 122 x 50.8cm. (Private collection).* A large confrontational form, which fits into a chimney-breast as though made for it. The artist recalls how the animal fled into a stone shelter when she approached, then reappeared in the darkened aperture of the doorway, his mask-like face framed by stones, defying her to come closer.

7. Deborah BROWN (b.1927): Distant Buildings, Sand and Water (1947). *Oil on board, 25.6 x 30.7cm. (Private collection).* Deborah Brown was inspired by 'the mysterious, almost frightening feel of the Antrim coastline'. In this charming early work, we see the sound academic background which she has always valued.

8. Deborah BROWN (b.1927): Sheep on the Road (1990-93) *Bronze, lifesize. (Stranmillis Sculpture Park, Arts Council of Northern Ireland).* In this, Deborah Brown's largest and most ambitious commission in bronze, the lifesize figures present a simple image that is both fleeting and eternal.

The Rehearsal outside, where the kinglike figure could rock in the wind.

Waiting (1982) has five life-size figures arranged in a semi-circle around a Punch and Judy tent – 'but nothing ever happens.' A figure sitting on the floor reads, others are seated, and a tall standing figure with punk hairdo drags chains with him. Their mouths are gaping holes, interpretabl as tragic or comic laughter: the whole has a Godot-like mood.

Yet the artist insists that there is no underlying intention or meaning. Like her abstracts these are forms made for the sake of making forms, the object the exploration of her materials simply for the sake of so doing. The figures are detached, taking no notice of each other, simply creating the notion of 'Waiting', and their different shapes are designed for the purpose of drawing the eye in towards the empty box. The paper covering the wire armatures has a freedom akin to the brushwork in her paintings. The shoes have been made with the definitive delicacy that is the signature of all her work, and, mingled with the sense of the fun encountered in the act of making, there is a discernible mood of seriousness.

Another environmental piece, *The Vendor*, was shown in Rosc '84, as was *The Ram* (also 1984), a large confrontational form, fitting into a chimney breast as though made for it. Again Brown stresses the element of chance encounter in the work. 'I have always enjoyed watching the behaviour of people and animals,' she has written in the Rosc catalogue,[6] referring to her paintings of the fifties. 'Now I have come back to shapes made by things around me. In my papier maché sculptures the people or animals are as I have, by chance, encountered them. The gesture of a hand, the tilt of a head, drooping or hunched shoulders, the shape of a back, the placing of feet, these are the things I emphasise, combining them with the shapes I first notice. One side of a face may be left hollow or blank, a piece of wire as a foot conveyed life by its gesture. With animals it is more fleeting, when I tried to photograph a ram he disappeared into a stone shelter and just as I was about to give up the attempt he reappeared in the darkened aperture of the doorway and stood posing for me framed by the stones, his masklike face defying me to come closer.'

on her experiences with the Lyric Theatre, there were three figures, one 'slightly like a king', or, because he was abstract, 'like a stone, with a wire head, and something that just suggests a crown', A second figure stooping towards him, and a figure sitting on a chair (the producer), completed this environmental work. The artist intended the piece for a darkened room, with the figures highlighted in a mysterious way, in the same way that *Waiting,* her second environmental piece, now in the Hugh Lane Municipal Gallery,[5] should be seen. She also considered siting

For some years she worked in wire and paper. Then she turned to papier maché, enjoying the flexibility of the material which allowed an element of spontaneity. Both media have their practical drawbacks though; and she has had to make the decision to convert the fragility and evanescence which fascinates her into the permanence of bronze. It has meant mastering a totally new technique. She has had to come to terms with having to create multiple images, though the artist insists that each cast is individual, chased and completed by herself to become a unique work in its own right.

'Something Indefinable' in the Work of Deborah Brown

Brown's major problem has been the translation of holes, which are integral to her idiom, into bronze. Hollow spaces or piercings in the papier-maché model for her first bronze, a goat made for Lord Belmore, had to become a form of honeycomb. Rather than being opaque or transparent white, textured by the armature beneath, they are a warm burnished brown, often with suggestions of holes, rather than with piercing all the way through. She still likes to work initially in papier maché, emphasising certain areas by adding wax, and then casting the result in a very lightweight wax prior to the final *cire perdue* stage. The final casts are graceful living men or beasts, nothing to do with narrative or drama, but meditations in form and space rather, the detail reduced to a minimum despite the accuracy with which their essential character has been observed.

While she prefers to work on a large scale, she regards a small piece as a challenge, and she responded with alacrity to the request to make a piece not larger than six inches in any direction for the 'Little Sculpture' exhibition in the Solomon Gallery, Dublin, in 1993. *The Wreck* is a small bronze environmental piece, with a figure standing at the end of part of a boat. The jagged edge, and the abstract spaces caused by the interaction of the forms, and echoed in the surface of the broken hull, cause tensions in the tiny sculpture. Deborah Brown always seeks to create visual tensions. Whether textural or spatial, the tension can be as important to the artist as the material which still absorbs her.

In 1993 also she completed her largest and most ambitious commission in bronze, the lifesize *Sheep on the road* which she had been working on over three years for the Arts Council sculpture park at Stranmillis, Belfast. A farmer herding his flock, at the brow of the hillock in front of the main building, is a startingly simple image, a man doggedly repeating the daily task, a fleeting moment on a road, yet an eternal image.

At the moment the artist is preparing, as entrance to the sculpture court in front of her house, a small gate which encapsulates more than any recent work, her essential preoccupations. A series of panels on square bronze bars feature scenarios from Irish legend, and notably legends of the sea. Coomara, the Merrow, with his cocked hat, is there, and Jack Dogherty who tried to get the better of him. One panel shows Jack releasing the drowned seamen, whom Coomara has collected in his house under the floor of the sea, out of the soul cages in which they are imprisoned. Then 'something indefinable' transforms the narrative on to that visual plane where Deborah Brown can enjoy yet another spatial encounter.

HILARY PYLE *is a distinguished art critic among whose most recent publications are the definitive* Catalogues Raisonnés *of the oil paintings and watercolours of Jack B Yeats.*

1. Conversation with the author at her studio, 14 December, 1993.
2. 'Why' by Deborah Brown. *Ferranti Journal*, 121 (autumn 1966) 2.
3. Introduction to *Deborah Brown: a selected exhibition of works completed between 1947 and 1982.* (Arts Council Gallery, Belfast; Orchard Gallery, Derry; Hugh Lane Municipal Gallery of Modern Art, Dublin, 1982) [5].
4. Reviews by H P, *Irish Times*, 27 October 1964 and 3 November, 1965.
5. *Images and Insights.* Hugh Lane Municipal Gallery of Modern Art, Dublin (1993), pp.144-5 (col. repro).
6. *Rosc '84* catalogue, p.66.

SELECT ADDITIONAL BIBLIOGRAPHY
Artist's Choice: paintings and objects from the personal collections of Deborah Brown, Edward Maguire, Tim Goulding, Neil Shawcross, Cecil King and Patrick Scott. Ulster Museum, Belfast 1973.

John Hewitt, *Art in Ulster: 1*, Belfast, 1977.
Michael Catto, *Art in Ulster: 2*, Belfast, 1977.
Anne Crookshank, *Irish Art from 1600 to the present day* Dublin, 1979; *Irish Sculpture from 1600 to the present day*, Dublin, 1984.
T P Flanagan, 'Deborah Brown at home', *Ireland of the Welcomes*, 34, no. 5, Sept-Oct 1985.
Irish Women Artists from the eighteenth century to the present day, National Gallery of Ireland, Dublin, 1987.

DEREK HILL AT ST COLUMB'S
AN ARTIST AND HIS COLLECTION

The one-time Donegal home of the painter, who for almost fifty years has derived inspiration from the Irish landscape, is visited by **Brian Ferran**.

In beautiful countryside beside Lough Gartan outside Church Hill, which is about ten miles northwest of Letterkenny, Co Donegal, there is situated an elegant red former glebe house and an art gallery. It is surrounded by a lovingly created garden and the environment captures the spirit of its former owner, Derek Hill, a serious artist, an author, a generous host and a witty and well-informed raconteur.

It is ten years since the Glebe Gallery, with its arts collection, opened its doors to the public. It is almost fifty years since Derek Hill, the donor of this generous gift to the Irish people, settled in his Donegal home where he has worked as an artist of international celebration. His garden, his home and its contents were gifted to the Irish State and its people in 1981. Although he has lived here for most of his life, Derek Hill is still considered an English artist in Ireland but, when he is in England, he is thought to be an Irish artist. However, his gift to the Irish nation leaves in no doubt his commitment to his adopted home. Both the gallery and the house are now open to the public and this picturesque idyllic environment gives great pleasure to its numerous appreciative visitors whose number increases annually. The house, which overlooks Gartan Lake, is called St Columb's because it was close by there that the saint was born and raised. It is appropriate that from this site Derek Hill travels to every corner of the globe. He was, and still is, an intrepid traveller who has collected paintings, interesting artefacts and objects which he brought back to his Donegal home. In 1954, Derek Hill moved to Church Hill, Co Donegal and, in the same year, set off for Anatolia with Freya Stark. His visits to mosques on this trip increased his interest in Islamic art and architecture and he has maintained this interest, seeking out treasures of Islamic architecture. This research was published in two volumes: *Islamic Architecture and its Decoration* and *Islamic Architecture in North Africa* (Faber and Faber). Evidence of this interest is now enjoyed in the collection of tiles and plates from Turkey contained in the collection.

Derek Hill was born in Southampton in 1916. After school at Marlborough College, he studied stage design in Munich in 1933. Afterwards, he spent eighteen months working in Vienna with Josef Gregor, the Director of the National Theatre Collection in Vienna and an expert on the Russian theatre. As a result, he spent six months in Russia, travelling to Leningrad and Kiev. He studied ballet, opera and theatre with Tairov and Meirhold and developed an interest in early Russian icons. From Russia, he travelled further east to Vladivostok and then on to Japan, China, Bali and Siam, nurturing his great love of travel. He also studied in Paris under Paul Colin.

Though he returned to England in 1937, and began designing for a ballet by Frederick Ashton at Sadler's Wells, he did not stay long and returned to Paris where he took a studio and began to paint. Edward Molyneux, the Paris couturier, encouraged Derek Hill to paint and allowed him free access to his own collection of paintings. Derek Hill returned to England when war broke out and worked on a farm as a conscientious objector. During this time, he met many of the leading English painters and began to collect their paintings: Lawrence Gowing, Mary Kessell, Victor Pasmore and the Euston Road School. He exhibited for the first time at the Nicholson Gallery in London in 1943.

Although he had visited Ireland often before, in 1946 he stayed for a year painting on the West coast, in Galway, Mayo and Achill. Louis le Brocquy and he painted together on Achill Island. However, after this year he returned to England and designed sets and dresses for *Il Trovatore* at Covent Garden. He did not stay long, however, and the following year he went to Italy and spent the next five winters there until 1952. His meeting with Bernard Berenson resulted in these long stays at his villa outside Florence and further encouragement to continue painting.

2. Derek HILL (b.1916): The Glebe, Church Hill, 1960. *Oil on board 23 x 34 cm. (Collection of the artist).* The Glebe House was known locally as St Columb's because of the celtic saint's association with the area.

Derek's fascinating collection embraces more than three hundred art works and was assembled over a period of more than forty years; it reflects his lifelong interest in travel, theatre, art history and art practice. He is a painter known for his portraits of 'the great and the good' and for his landscapes of Italy, England, France and, most particularly, of Donegal.

He had first visited Donegal in 1949 as the guest of Henry McIlhenny and stayed at Glenveagh Castle. He was painting in Italy at the time and Henry McIlhenny was also there, studying Renaissance sculpture. During this period, he had come to

1. THE GLEBE HOUSE, formerly St Columb's, Derek Hill's Donegal home overlooks Lough Gartan. Built as a rectory in 1828, it was gifted by the artist to the Irish State and its people in 1981 and is now open to the public. The Glebe Gallery, in the former stables, is on the right, behind the beech trees.

know and admire many Italian artists: Antonio Music, Renato Guttuso, Dalla Zorza, Bruno Saetti, and particularly Giorgio Morandi. Small, but impressive, works painted by these artists are included in the collection and are on view in the changing displays at the gallery.

In his book, *Derek Hill: an appreciation* by Grey Gowrie, published by Quartet Books in 1987, the author confidently claims that the artist is 'the best painter of Irish landscapes since Jack Yeats'. The Donegal locale most favoured in his paintings is Tory Island, either painted at close range from his rented hut at one end of the island, or from the mainland looking out to the

3. Derek HILL (b.1916): *Dr Tony O'Reilly. Oil on canvas, 38.1 x 33cm. (Collection of the artist).* Derek Hill has established a reputation as a portrait painter of great technical skill. In 1994 Tony O'Reilly was made a Pro-Chancellor of Dublin University which had earlier conferred an Honorary Litt.D. on Derek Hill.

horizon. For years, he has devoted weeks in all weathers to painting in this isolated location where he has established a close and affectionate relationship with the local population. Derek Hill always shares with others his knowledge, his experience and his skills and it was this commitment to sharing which led him to initiate James Dixon into the world of painting.

James Dixon was a fisherman living on Tory Island who had been fascinated at seeing Derek Hill paint in the open air and was encouraged by the artist to take up the activity. He provided him with paints and paper but he insisted on providing his own brushes which he made from the tail of his donkey. In the last years of his life, Dixon painted many works of originality and

charm. Derek Hill became, inadvertently, the advocate and promoter of a small group of Tory Island primitive artists whose works were exhibited from Burtonport and Derry to Vienna and Paris. In the mid 1960s, Derek persuaded Alice Berger Hammerschlag, who then ran the New Gallery on the Grosvenor Road in Belfast, and Kathleen Bell, to present an exhibition of works by Tory Island artists. James Dixon travelled to Belfast for the crowded exhibition opening and an excitement was generated by the public discovery of something extraordinary.

Derek Hill brought the talent of James Dixon to public attention in the same way as Ben Nicholson had espoused the works of the old St Ives fisherman, Alfred Wallis, in the late 1920s. Wallis had begun to paint shortly after his wife's death in 1922 'for company' as he put it. Ben Nicholson and his friends for twenty years sustained Alfred Wallis with their interest and encouragement. Most of them owned his works and, in like manner, Derek Hill and his friends became the proud custodians of works by James Dixon. The works owned by Derek Hill now form part of the Glebe collection and are amongst its many highlights. The painting entitled *West End Village, Tory* is particularly impressive. As with the many artists who gravitated to Cornwall in the 1940s and 50s, Tory Island became Derek Hill's Penrith or Land's End. Derek moved further into the Atlantic Ocean to his island retreat with its ever-changing moods of sea and sky and the rhythm of the sea and wind pounding on the rocks and on the earth. These elements became the subject of his art and, informed by an intimate understanding of the history of painting, he interpreted the moods of this hitherto unpainted landscape. Often the artist was marooned for weeks watching the unrelenting storms which became recurrent themes in his painted landscapes. These are removed from the classical landscapes of Tuscany, painted in the artist's youth, but the palette colours and the tone are consistent, and the vigour of the brush strokes communicates a passion for the materials of painting and for landscape motifs. These landscapes are symphonies of grey and green, of browns, ochres and mauves. Although they are original in their subject matter, they could not exist without the artist's familiarity with details of Degas and of Corot paintings. It was appropriate that, in 1952, Derek Hill should have organised the Degas exhibition for the Edinburgh Festival which was subsequently shown at the Tate Gallery.

In 1951, he re-visited Glenveagh and, while there, discovered that St Columb's, which was close by, was for sale. It had been built as a rectory in 1828 to serve the Church of Ireland parish of Gartan and nestled beautifully into meadows which sloped down to the lake shores. It had been used as a small fishing hotel for over fifty years. When he returned in 1953, he bought it. He loved the elegant proportions of this square house, with its rust-red exterior, protected from the wind by a circle of beech trees. It gave him a home in Co Donegal which afforded him the opportunity to paint the landscape of the area and extensive gardens which he could plant and nurture. Gracie McDermott, who had worked in the hotel since she was a young girl, returned to live there as Derek's housekeeper. Her warmth and humour and her good cooking and baking created a hospitality and a welcome for Derek's many friends.

In the same year, Derek Hill took up the position of Art Director at the British School in Rome, a position which he held for five years and during which time he met many other young

DEREK HILL AT ST COLUMB'S: AN ARTIST AND HIS COLLECTION

artists, including John Bratby, Derrick Greaves, Michael Andrews and Joe Tilson – all beginning their artistic careers – as well as more established artists: Henry Inlander, John Craxton and Keith Vaughan. Examples of these artists' work are included in the collection and some, like John Craxton, with whom he shared an interest in music, poetry and travel, were intermittent visitors to his Donegal home. Howard Hodgkin, Anthony Caro and Victor Pasmore also came.

When Derek Hill bought St Columb's in 1953, he restored the house with the help of his brother John, an interior designer and director of the design firm Green & Abbotts in London. John provided many useful ideas as well as furniture and wallpapers, unusual at the time, often by William Morris, which had been bought by his firm. He, too, was a good painter and totally in sympathy with his brother's plans and aspirations. The stable block which is now the gallery became a studio and extra accommodation was added for guests, as well as a sitting room for his housekeeper. This space has now become a big open space gallery, on two floors, which houses the collection and touring exhibitions.

In the house, the brilliant blue of the front hall, made from blue bag, was chosen to match the blue in the two Chinese scrolls which Derek bought in Peking in 1936. Each room is arranged in an theatrical manner reflecting his early training in stage design in Munich and Paris. This is best exemplified in the morning room. Throughout the house there are fascinating artefacts, ranging from Wemyss ware wash-basins and jugs to a shamrock decorated pig. In the dining room, the mid-nineteenth century inlaid circular table depicts the arts – music, painting, drama, architecture, sculpture and poetry – and was discovered in Belfast's old Smithfield Market and brought to St Columb's. It sits happily in a dark green room, enriched by the Turkish paper set into the alcoves, an unusual Belleek earthenware plate and cover, a Tiffany lamp and other bowls and objects displayed on the sideboard.

The kitchen has changed little since the days of the hotel but it is now painted in bright primary colours, from the kitchen dresser to the colour-coded water pipes. The eclectic collection of plates and ceramic dog sculptures epitomises Derek Hill's love of interesting objects, irrespective of their value. A plate by Pablo Picasso which depicts a bullfight sits on top of the dresser alongside a pair of locally made plaster dogs. The paintings on the kitchen walls are mainly by Tory Island painters: James Dixon, and his brother John, James Rodgers, Patsy Dan Rodgers, Michael Finbar Rodgers, Ruairi Rodgers and Anthony Meenan. The younger painters still live on the island and continue to paint its wild landscape and daily life.

In the drawing room, Derek Hill's theatrical design again manifests itself. The pale lilac walls create a dramatic effect, either night or day, and are echoed in the purple glasses and vases punctuating the room. It is a room in which to sit with friends in front of a roaring fire in a fireplace which came from Lough Veagh House in the 1950s, to read the newspapers or to converse. The golden glow of the carpet creates warmth in contrast to the Turkish paper in the alcove. Above the fireplace is Victor Pasmore's painting, *Evening Thames at Chiswick*, painted in the 1940s and, on either side, two small paintings by Antonio Music, *Horsewomen and Horses* and *Umbrian Landscape*, painted in 1948. These were the first pictures Music sold in a public exhibition when they were exhibited at the Venice Biennale in 1948. Opposite is *Donegal Late Harvest*, painted by Derek from the

4. Derek Hill painting in his studio in 1958.

bridge on the way to Church Hill from St Columb's.

The stairwell and walls are covered with paintings which include Henry Inlander, Renato Guttuso, Joe Tilson, Victor Pasmore, Joan Eardley and Sidney Nolan. William Morris's designed wallpaper, *Apple*, surrounds the landing window and the same designer's *Blackthorn* covers the walls and ceilings of the study which is filled with books and periodicals. A John Bratby painting, *Waves in Italy*, (1954) hangs above the fireplace which is decorated with William de Morgan tiles. John Bratby's painting, *Jean in Bed with Jaundice*, hanging in the Morris bedroom is one of Bratby's finest works. This bedroom, with mahogany half-tester bed, is decorated in another William Morris design, *Golden Lily*. Beautifully woven Morris curtains hang at the window. The guest bedroom is light and airy, in soft pinks and creams. The master bedroom is decorated in the blue and grey paper made by Green and Abbotts, dominated by a simple black metal brass bed which Derek bought locally. A

5. Derek HILL (b.1916): Quiet Wave. *Oil on asbestos which was found outside his Tory Island hut, 17.8 x 35.5cm. (Collection of the artist).* Derek Hill is fascinated by the ever-changing moods of sea and sky as storms pound the coastline.

6. Derek HILL (b.1916): Lake Averno, Naples. *Oil on board 30.5 x 20.3cm. (Collection of the artist, and formerly in the collection of J B Priestley).* A classical Italian landscape, a symphony of brown, ochres and mauves. Hill spent five winters in Italy from 1947 to 1952 staying with Bernard Berenson at his villa outside Florence.

7. Derek HILL (b.1916): Tory Island with Tau Cross, 1991. *Oil on canvas 30.5 x 20.3cm. (Private collection).* The isolated island of Tory is the subject of more than a hundred paintings by Hill.

Colin Middleton painting hangs in the bedroom; Middleton used to come and fish in Lough Gartan and his ashes were scattered by his wife on its water. His painting hangs in the company of a Giorgio Morandi etching of a house among trees and a work by Edward Molyneux, his first guiding muse and the principal advocate of Derek Hill becoming a painter.

In the 1960s and early 1970s, as an Arts Council Exhibitions Officer, I presented a series of open submission exhibitions and, in 1973, the judges were Norbert Lynton, John Walker and Ian Campbell. The selection and allocation of awards usually took

8. Derek HILL (b.1916): Golgotha II: Tory Island Sunrise c.1978. *Oil on canvas 25.4 x 48.2cm. (Private collection).* Tory and the Atlantic which washes its rocky shores have been the subject and inspiration of some of Derek Hill's finest landscapes.

9. Derek HILL (b.1916): Tory Island from Tor More *Oil on canvas, 30.5 x 20.3cm. (Ulster Museum Belfast).* Tory Island is exposed to the unrelenting sea and bitter winds.

10. Derek HILL (b.1916): Church Hill, 1956. *Oil on panel, 17.8 x 24.2cm. (Private collection).* The immediate neighbourhood of the artist's home provided him with constant inspiration.

two or three days and work progressed from early morning to late evening. Relaxation periods gave the opportunity to enjoy conversation with distinguished practitioners. In the course of one conversation, John Walker, who was on his first visit to Ireland, asked me if I knew an artist called Derek Hill who, he thought, now lived in Ireland. Before I could make reply, he went on to tell me that, when he was a student at Birmingham College of Art in the late 1950s, Derek had purchased one of his paintings. It was the first painting he had ever sold. This intuitive skill in identifying talent, combined with a genuine desire

11. Derek HILL (b.1916): Tory Island Village. *Oil on canvas 71.1 x 91.4cm. (Museum of Birmingham, Alabama)*. Tory Island is a rock three miles long and a quarter of a mile wide, situated in the Atlantic nine miles from the Donegal coast. In this retreat, where he is often marooned for weeks in a rented hut, Derek Hill has close and affectionate links with the islanders.

to give useful patronage to young artists, has informed his collection and widened his circle of friends. Many of the works he purchased and the artists he supported are, in subject matter and execution of their work, more avant-garde and audacious than Derek. Nevertheless, he has sustained a passion for the imagination, when it is supported by unerring craftsmanship, from his devotion to Joan Eardly and the Tory Island painters to his current enthusiasm for Philip McFadden's sculptures.

He admires artists who are consistent in their vision and the works he collected by Roderic O'Conor, Pierre Bonnard, Oscar Kokoshka, Sir Edwin Landseer, Walter Sickert and Jack Yeats all re-affirm this admiration. They are also painters with whom he shares a love for the medium of oil paint.

Although he has a considerable reputation as a portrait painter of great technical skill, he has recently become reinvigorated by

12. Derek HILL (b.1916): Duncan Grant, (1885-1978). *Oil on board, 20.3 x 25.4cm(Private collection)*. The sitter was a Scottish-born painter, decorator and designer of textiles, pottery and theatre; a member of the Bloomsbury Group and exhibitor at the New English Art Club. This delightful portrait was a present for his ninetieth birthday.

landscape painting. He was encouraged by the view, eloquently expressed by Grey Gowrie in his book, that he is, above all, a landscape artist of great sensitivity. This text, presented in an extended interview format, is more self-revealing than self-serving.

In Derry, in the early 1960s, I first met Derek Hill when, with a small group, we came together to form a trust for the purpose of collecting contemporary art works for exhibition in schools, hospitals, libraries and public places in Derry, Donegal, Tyrone and Fermanagh. This North-West Arts Trust has continued its work since then and it was through the efforts and tenacity of Derek Hill that the resources were found to purchase works. Some years passed before I first visited Derek's home and experienced this magic environment and found enjoyment in the paintings he had collected. At the time, I was enthused by the works of artists like Keith Vaughan, Joe

Tilson, Graham Sutherland, Victor Pasmore, and John Bratby; there, at his secluded home in Donegal, Derek Hill had examples of works which I had known mainly from reproduction. Additionally, most of these artists were his personal friends and it was enjoyable to listen to his anecdotes about each one.

After the untimely death of Alice Berger Hammerschlag in 1969, we were again part of a small group of her friends who had come together to form a trust which would continue the work she had initiated in support of young and emerging artists. This resolve to help young artists was a commitment which Derek Hill shared with Alice Berger Hammerschlag and this trust, which carries her name, has continued to make annual awards since then.

In 1970, I was privileged to organise a retrospective exhibition of paintings by Derek Hill. The exhibition comprised some seventy-five works which charted his subject matter and growing confidence, from the early works painted in Paris in 1939, to images painted more than thirty years later on Tory Island. The exhibition was shown in Belfast, Dublin and Derry to an appreciative audience although it did receive some unfair critical comment. In his catalogue introduction, James White, who was then Director of the National Gallery, wrote:

> In Waves of Tory, *therefore, we are presented not merely with a study of the majestic ocean but with a resounding statement of the relentless force which batters the remote island and isolates it, often for months on end, from contact with the mainland nine miles away.*

13. Derek HILL (b.1916): Stone Wall near Classiebawn. *Oil on canvas 33 x 25.4 cm.* Derek Hill painted this while staying at Earl Mountbatten's estate at Classiebawn, Co Sligo. The vigour of the brushstrokes communicates Derek Hill's passion for the materials of painting and for landscape motifs. Grey Gowrie considers him the best painter of Irish landscapes since Jack Yeats.

Derek Hill won a prize for painting from the Contemporary Art Society in London in the 1950s and he became a board member of the society in the 1960s. Derek Hill is larger than life and is interested in every cultural event. His absorbing interest in opera, for example, continues to attract him to performances all over the world and I believe that he has attended almost every performance staged at Wexford since its inauguration. He has been a member of the Wexford Opera Council since 1956. Much more could be written on all his achievements and his benefactions. In conclusion, and because the words are still so apt, I repeat the three concluding sentences of James White's text for the 1970/71 catalogue:

Well though I am aware of my duty to estimate him as a painter, I cannot but believe that a knowledge of his highly talented life will enlarge appreciation of the pictures. For in the end it is by the pictures that he will be judged; and if he is judged by the standards which are applied not only to contemporary work but to the works of past time he will be seen to be an artist of stature.

Long may he continue to enrich us.

BRIAN FERRAN is Chief Executive of the Arts Council of Northern Ireland and a practising artist.

A major retrospective exhibition of over a hundred paintings by Derek Hill from public and private collections was held at Colnaghi's, 14 Old Bond Street, London in 1994, accompanied by an illustrated catalogue with introductions by Grey Gowrie and John Julius Norwich.

1. Evie HONE (1894-1955): Stained glass window of the Saints of the Society of Jesus grouped round a figure of the Sacred Heart. The largest of the five windows, 'her finest work in Ireland', executed in 1945/46 for the Jesuit philosophate at Rahan, Co Offaly, and now at Manresa House, Dublin.

A NEW SETTING FOR EVIE HONE'S RAHAN WINDOWS

Some of the artist's finest stained glass has been relocated in a purpose-built site to the satisfaction of
Anthony Symondson.

The well-known windows painted by Evie Hone for the domestic chapel of the Jesuit philosophate at St Stanislaus College, Rahan, Tullamore, Co Offaly, are the most enlightened expression of artistic patronage by a religious order in Ireland of the present century. In 1944 the Very Revd Donal O'Sullivan SJ, the Rector, appointed Michael Scott to re-design the interior of the chapel. The chapel was a rectangle facing north. It was lighted by four narrow windows facing east and had a large window facing south, opposite the sanctuary. Scott provided an apse behind an arch with an altar of oak, a crucifix of sycamore wood five feet in height above it, and figures of Our Lady and St Joseph carved by Laurence Campbell, a Belfast sculptor. The result was held at the time to be a 'great transformation'.[1]

Fr O'Sullivan's involvement in modern art needs neither emphasis nor introduction to Irish readers.[2] What is, perhaps, less known is the origin of his interest. The source lies in Michael Scott, a pioneer architect of the Modern Movement who became the leading Irish Modernist. In 1934-37 he and his partner, Norman Good, had built the large public hospital at Tullamore.[3] It was as a result of this work that O'Sullivan gave him the commission for the domestic chapel.

Scott's involvement in Modernism was not confined to architecture. He was also an Irish pioneer in the promotion of modern art.[4] Scott became O'Sullivan's mentor and formed his opinions on art.[5] These were at first broadly summed up by an admiration for l'École de Paris and the work of Braque, Picasso, Rouault and Manessier. Later 'his preference was for abstract works in the international hard-edge style considered avant-garde at the time.'[6] Scott persuaded O'Sullivan to commission Evie Hone, then at the zenith of her powers, to fill the chapel with a unified scheme of stained glass.

The commission was, however, partly motivated by altruism. In 1944 An Túr Gloine, the Dublin glass-painting co-operative of which Hone was a member, was dissolved. This led to her setting up her own studio at Marlay Grange, Rathfarnham, across the yard from the Dower House in which she lived below the Dublin mountains.[7] The Rahan windows were her first independent commission and laid the foundations of her mature achievement.

Five windows were designed and executed between 1945 and 1946. The first was the Nativity, erected in the sanctuary to the right of the altar. It was followed in the same year by a larger window of the Saints of the Society of Jesus grouped round a figure of the Sacred Heart (Fig.1).[8] In 1946 came the Pentecost window, erected next to the window of the Jesuit Saints at the southeast end of the chapel, followed by the Last Supper and concluded by the Beatitudes.[9]

From the completion of the scheme the windows attracted serious critical attention. They were acclaimed as 'the finest work produced in modern Catholic art'.[10] A more considered opinion was that of Geoffrey Houghton-Brown, an English Catholic muralist, who, in a letter to O'Sullivan, declared, 'The windows by Evie Hone in your chapel are the best I have seen in Ireland; and better, I think than any modern work in England'.[11] In company with her windows at Kingscourt, Co Cavan, Hone judged them to be her best work. C P Curran agreed in his seminal essay on the artist's stained glass, published in 1955, and regarded them as 'her finest work in Ireland'.[12] Curran's opinion has, if anything, gained conviction to the present day.

When the windows were completed opinions varied on their success. Their artistic merit was not questioned. It was the realisation of the windows in their setting that induced reservations and objectively the position of the windows was not considered ideal. It is of interest that neither O'Sullivan nor Hone believed that Rahan would be the windows' permanent destination. Hone recognised that subsequent removal was possible and to some extent this is said to have influenced her design.

The philosophate was closed in 1962 and thereafter St Stanislaus College became a retreat house. The Jesuits left in

2. Interior of the prayer room at Manresa House, showing three of the four Gospel windows by Evie Hone (1894-1955) and on the right, her window of the Jesuit Saints (Fig 1). Furnishings are deliberately sparse. The cross, in Irish ash, on the west wall represents Christ at the centre of the Four Evangelists. 'The deeply coloured glass pulsates in solemn, even anguished, intensity'.

A NEW SETTING FOR EVIE HONE'S RAHAN WINDOWS

3. Exterior of the prayer room (1992) at Manresa House, Dollymount, Dublin, showing the position of the Evie Hone windows in deeply recessed frames. The design by Roderick McCaffrey is rooted in Irish vernacular classical tradition.

4. North wall of the prayer room at Manresa House, showing the connecting glass bridge and narrow pool.

1991. A major decision as the house faced closure was the future destination of the windows. Many applications for them were received, notably from Mullingar Cathedral and the Milltown Institute of Philosophy and Theology, Dublin. Serious consideration was given to re-installing them in the parish church at Rahan, the shrine at Knock, housing them at Clongowes Wood College, Co Kildare, and depositing them in the Irish Museum of Modern Art, Kilmainham. The final decision was to put them in a new building designed as a prayer room at Manresa House, Dollymount, Dublin, where they would form part of the Jesuit retreat house. The availability of the windows coincided with the need for an additional prayer room.

The retreat house at Dollymount is a concrete, steel and glass building of four storeys with an articulated circular chapel designed as a functional statement of the International Modern Style by Andrew Devane of Robinson, Keefe, Devane, in 1966-67. It expresses the scientific austerity of the time. Roderick McCaffrey, of the same practice, was commissioned to design the prayer room (Fig. 3). His approach is far less ideological and is rooted in the Irish vernacular classical tradition.

McCaffrey proposed an independent building which would have the two-fold function of providing a new setting in which the windows would be seen to greater advantage as works of art and a space reserved for prayer. It was not intended that the room should be used for the celebration of Mass, thus eliminating liturgical criteria. The windows determined his design.

The prayer room had to form part of the existing building, yet be separate from it. This has been achieved by the formation of a narrow pool with low fountains approached from the main structure by a glass bridge (Fig. 4). It was originally intended to surround the room on all sides by water but this proposal was abandoned.

The plan of the building is fan-shaped. The south wall is in the form of an extended arc composed of a trabeated frame in which the windows are placed in their original order. A panoramic effect has been achieved which enables them for the first time to be encompassed as a visually accessible whole. The east and west walls are placed at inverted angles until they square to form a narthex with a northern convex wall

designed to complement the arc opposite.

From inside the retreat house the room is approached from a ramp leading to the bridge which is asymmetrically positioned to gain access to the right of the narthex. The first windows seen on entering are of the Jesuit Saints and Pentecost (Fig. 2). The floors are stepped, creating a viewing platform in the upper level (forming the narthex), descending by a tier of three steps to the principal space beyond. This ensures that people seated in the lower level do not obstruct the view of the windows.

There are two ceiling heights. The upper floor, at the entrance, has the lower ceiling. Here the walls are broken at ceiling level by a narrow band of windows, with light diffused through horizontal timber louvres. The main space expands in capacity towards the trabeated arc and has a higher ceiling corresponding to the main floor level.

It is in the exterior of the building that Irish vernacular references are to be found (Fig. 3). It is a statement of classical abstraction. The walls are finished in grey, roughly rendered plaster, broken to east and west by recessed panels; they are designed to create a negative effect to counteract the powerful external trabeation of the window frames facing south. The grey plaster finish unifies the exterior with the smoothly rendered main block. Air ventilation is provided beneath the windows, using traditional Irish ventilation grilles. A heavy, simply moulded cornice gives scale and weight to the external walls on all sides.

The furniture and decoration of the room is deliberately understated (Fig. 2). The walls are painted white with a dull surface in order to allow the colours of the glass to shine with their own force. Great care was taken with the choice of colour for the carpet: a rich Roman purple was judged to complement the prevailing tonal balance of the windows. The furniture is sparse. Irish workmanship and themes are once more applied. The solitary ornament is a variation on St Brigid's cross hung on the west wall to the right of the window of Jesuit Saints. Executed in ash, it comprises a central cross which represents Christ and has four peripheral crosses which represent the Evangelists. The cross's design is intended to reflect Irish Romanesque themes which are among Hone's own precedents. The Blessed Sacrament is reserved in a small gilded tabernacle which can also be used for Exposition. It is placed in the marginally widened wall which separates the four Gospel windows from the Jesuit Saints. Simple stools and chairs of light wood, upholstered in Irish tweed of neutral colour, complete the scheme.

The objective of providing a building with a two-fold function does not result in a conflict of interest or intention. No European art gallery could have achieved a more successful result in exhibiting Hone's windows to such advantage. As works of art they have come into their own in a new setting in a way that was never achieved at Rahan. The deliberate darkness of the room enables what Nicola Gordon Bowe has described as the 'loosely painted, deeply coloured glass (which) pulsates in solemn, even anguished intensity'[13] to declare itself in the mutations of natural light which are now freely available. The precise axis veers to south-west. Problems are created by this position. Some of the windows are very dark. Trees in summer will affect the unbroken diffusion of light. The best light at Manresa comes from east-south-east where there are no trees and the reflecting light of the sea might well add an extra quality. In its present orientation the best time to see the glass is in the falling light of a late autumn afternoon or at 4pm in winter. Avoid the harsh noon light of summer.

In its function as a prayer room the glass is equally successful. The room has a numinous intensity which is neither compromised nor dominated by such powerful works of art. It possesses the twofold distinctions of unity and repose which are essential to a space made for such a purpose. The generous volume created by the long convex frame and inverted walls generates a spirit of freedom conducive to religious and artistic contemplation.

My only serious criticisms are of the use of water and artificial light. While the pool is a solution to the problem of connecting an independent building to the parent structure, two reservations present themselves. Maintenance of water is problematical, especially when it is situated near trees. It could quickly become clogged with leaves and litter. More seriously, the fountains present difficulties. Silence is an essential quality in a retreat house. Although some retreatants have appreciated the play of running water others, including myself, have not. I found the noise distracting, manipulative and invasive. Water adds no advantage to the building.

I am thankful that the original proposal to turn the room into an island, thus enabling the reflection of water to dance upon the external surface of the glass, was abandoned. Stained glass is a static art form where movement is governed by the natural motion of light as it unfolds throughout the day, rather than being disturbed by an orchestrated play of shadow. Equally, I have reservations about the external lights which enable the windows to be illuminated at night. These were requested by the clients in order to extend the use of the room. Artificial light is too hard and immovable to bring out the subtle qualities of stained glass. In this case the windows are deadened when so illuminated. The lighting may well prove to be counter-productive.

Overall, the new addition to Manresa House is a remarkable achievement. It keeps the windows in the possession of the Society of Jesus. It gives them a new and deeper life than they had before. The commission represents a considered response to the protection of works of art of international significance. It keeps faith with history and the artist's intentions. Architecturally, McCaffrey has achieved an ingenious and sympathetic response to a difficult brief. Potentially it gives an opportunity for the windows to be seen by more people than before. What is surprising is that this has been accomplished for as little as £150,000. As patronage, the building of the prayer room is every bit as enlightened in its own way as the original commission.

ANTHONY SYMONDSON is a member of the British Province of the Society of Jesus. He is studying theology at the Milltown Institute of Philosophy and Theology, Dublin. He has contributed to a volume of essays edited by Chris Brooks and Andrew Saint, Building the Victorian Church, *Manchester University Press, 1994.*

ACKNOWLEDGEMENTS
I am grateful to Mr Roderick McCaffrey and Mr Martin Donnelly of Robinson, Keefe, Devane, for valuable information and for generously providing illustrations for this article. I must also thank the Revd Cyril Barrett SJ, the Revd Ronan Geary SJ, the Revd Brendan Murray SJ, the Revd Senan Timoney SJ, the Revd Brendan Woods SJ and my Rector, the Revd Frank Sammon SJ for help, information and constructive criticism.

1. *Irish Province News*, Vol. IV, July 1944, pp.850-51. The crucifix and figures are now in the chapel of the Jesuit Residence, Cherryfield Lodge, Dublin 6. The head of St Joseph was modelled on O'Sullivan. In 1934-35 Scott had used Campbell for three architectural reliefs for the façade of the Theatre Royal, Dublin. When the theatre was demolished they were acquired by the architect Richard Guy who built them into the façade of his own house at Blackrock, Co Dublin. S B Kennedy, *Irish Art and Modernism*, 1991, pp.194-96, n.8, p.361.

2. Donal O'Sullivan (1904-77). Rector of St Stanislaus College, Rahan, 1940-47. In 1955 he served on the committee which mounted a memorial exhibition of the work of Evie Hone in University College, Dublin. On the death of Mgr Pádraig de Brún in 1960 he was appointed Director of the Arts Council, a post he held until 1973. He developed an interest in Swedish design which led to the establishment of the Kilkenny Design

Workshops, of which he was a founding director. Among many exhibitions of contemporary art he brought to Dublin was the first Irish exhibition of the work of Francis Bacon. 'His closest collaborator and friend in the Arts Council', wrote James White, 'was Michael Scott the architect for whom he had unbounded admiration. Together they would sway opposition and dare projects that others might find forbidding.' Obituary, *Irish Province News*, Vol. XVII, 1 January 1978, pp.28-32.

3. Sean Rothery, *Ireland and the New Architecture*, 1991, pp.146-49.

4. Michael Scott (1905-89) served on the organising committee of the Irish Exhibition of Living Art 1946-50. S B Kennedy, *op. cit.*, p.133, Appendix 3, p.375.

5. Conversation with the Revd Cyril Barrett SJ.

6. Brian Kennedy, 'The Arts Council', *Irish Arts Review Year Book*, 1990-91, pp.119-20. While recognising O'Sullivan's promotion of modern painting and positive aspects of his

Directorship, Dr Kennedy describes the criticism and frustration provoked by his collusion with Scott. I am grateful to Fr Barrett for drawing my attention to this article.

7. Nicola Gordon Bowe, David Caron and Michael Wynne, *Gazetteer of Irish Stained Glass*, 1988, p.26.

8. *Irish Province News*, Vol.V, 4 October 1945, p.109.

9. *Irish Province News*, Vol. VI, 2 June 1946, p.183; 3 July 1946, p.226; 4 October 1946, p.256.

10. *Irish Province News*, Vol.V, 4 October 1945, p.109.

11. *ibid.*

12. C.P. Curran, 'Evie Hone; Stained Glass Worker, 1894-1955', *Studies*, Vol. 44, 1955, pp.129-42; subsequently republished, with omissions, in Stella Frost, ed., *A Tribute to Evie Hone and Mainie Jellett*, 1957, pp.23-37.

13. Bowe, *op.cit.*

RICHARD KING'S KEVIN BARRY MEMORIAL WINDOW

This stained glass commission of 1933 reflects the style of Harry Clarke in whose studios it was produced. **Ruth Sheehy** *reports.*

The Kevin Barry memorial window (Fig. 2)located in the old Council Chamber (now known as the Kevin Barry Room) in Earlsfort Terrace is an early important and particularly fine work by the stained glass artist Richard King (1907-74). He entered Harry Clarke's studio in 1928 and remained there until 1940. His training in stained glass under Clarke was to prove fundamental for the initial stage of his artistic development and was a strong influence on his work of the 1930s. After Clarke died in 1931, King became principal designer at the Studios. He ultimately became manager of the Studios in 1935 and held this position until 1940. It was during his period as principal designer that the Kevin Barry window was commissioned. He was only twenty-six at the time.

In the years which followed Barry's death in 1920, the students of University College Dublin decided to erect a suitable memorial to him. By 1921, £100 had been raised and the Kevin Barry Memorial Committee proposed to collect another £400 from the College in 1923-24. The commission was given to Richard King in 1933 and the window was unveiled by The O'Rahilly on 1 November, 1934.

The window is signed with the name of the Studios and with King's own name in the bottom right hand panel which is extremely unusual at this stage because artists in the Harry Clarke Studios were not permitted to sign their work after Clarke's death. The fact that the commission was specifically given to King may account for his signature.

The political and historical content of the window reflects the Nationalist outlook prevalent in Ireland after the establishment of the Irish Free State in 1922 and concerns the protest by the Irish against British Rule. The panels are arranged in chronological sequence and read from left to right and from top to bottom. All the historical

1. RICHARD KING (1907-1974): Kevin Barry Memorial Window, 1933, (detail) showing Red Hugh O'Donnell who died in 1602, subsequent to the defeat of the rebellion at Kinsale.

subjects depicted are carefully interwoven and symbolically linked to each other as well as fitting into the main theme. The head and shoulders of the large Kevin Barry figure appear in part of the panel devoted to Robert Emmet and the 1798 Rebellion. This is an effective device to link Barry with the other figures of Irish history who preceded him. The panels of the window read as follows: Cuchulainn and Queen Medb; The Battle of Clontarf; Red Hugh O' Donnell (Fig. 1); Patrick Sarsfield; Lord Edward Fitzgerald & Wolfe Tone; Robert Emmet & The 1798 Rebellion; The Easter Rising of 1916 and the arrest and subsequent interrogation of Kevin Barry in September 1920.

Kevin Barry was an eighteen-year-old first-year medical student at University College Dublin. He was also a soldier of the First Battalion, Dublin Brigade of the Irish Volunteers at the time of his arrest. On 20 September 1920 he was involved in an ambush of a British Army lorry outside Monks' Bakery in Church Street during which three British soldiers were shot and killed. Barry was subsequently charged with the murder of one of these soldiers, Private Matthew Whitehead at a Court Martial on 20 October and was sentenced to death. He was hanged on 1 November 1920 in Mountjoy Prison. The fact that his execution took place on the Feast of All Saints increased the perception of him as a hero and martyr. This aspect is emphasised in the window by the purple shapes which resemble flames surrounding the main Kevin Barry figure. The imagery here is originally drawn from Harry Clarke where the idea of fire and flames around the head of a figure signifies a mystical, spiritual or supernatural event.

The design, technique and colour of the Kevin Barry window are undoubtably inspired by Harry Clarke's *Eve of St. Agnes* (1923-24)[2]

RICHARD KING'S KEVIN BARRY MEMORIAL WINDOW

(Hugh Lane Municipal Gallery, Dublin) and *Geneva* (1929) windows. The *Geneva* window in particular, with its format of eight square-shaped panels similar to that of the *Kevin Barry* window. The influence of the two Clarke windows on the *Kevin Barry* window can be seen in various ways: the decorative border of tiny heads outlining each panel seems to derive originally from the *Eve of St. Agnes*; the manner in which the scenes are divided in the Wolfe Tone and Robert Emmet panels owes its inspiration to both Clarke windows while the figure of Robert Emmet is reminiscent of the figure of Emmet in the Lennox Robinson and W B Yeats panel of the *Geneva* window. The influence of the *Eve of St. Agnes* is demonstrated by the highly decorative and stylised treatment of many of the figures especially in the top six panels; detailed patterns are seen in the costumes of many of the protagonists and in the backgrounds behind Robert Emmet and Wolfe Tone.

The stained glass technique is also similar to that of the two Clarke windows in the way in which the panels are divided by the sections of lead. In some cases, two layers of glass have been plated together to give a relief effect and to highlight the main scene in each panel. The debt to Clarke is further exemplified by the colour scheme which is characterised by a prevalence of blues, reds, greens and golds. This combination of brilliant colour and the incredible virtuosity in design gives the *Kevin Barry* window a jewel-like quality. The fact that the window is painted, stained and acided contributes to the overall richness of its appearance. King's knowledge of the Celtic Revival is shown by the wealth of detail in the ornamentation around the edges of each panel and by the Irish inscriptions on the bottom right of the window.

There is, however, a distinction to be made between Clarke and King: the fascination with the decadent, the grotesque and the macabre which is so much a feature of Clarke's Symbolist art is not to be found in the work of King who did not have the same interests nor the same complex imagination. The *Kevin Barry* window is nonetheless, an extraordinary achievement. The skilful interpretation of historical fact and symbol handled with craftsmanship is evidence of his considerable gifts even at this very early stage in his career.

RUTH SHEEHY is Slide Librarian in the History of Art Department, Trinity College Dublin.

ACKNOWLEDGEMENTS
My thanks are due to Dr Christine Casey, Dr David Caron, Mr Seamus Helferty, Mr Donal O' Donovan and Mrs Catherine Marshall for their assistance.

2. RICHARD KING (1907-74): Kevin Barry Memorial Window, 1933. *183 x 86cm (University College, Dublin)*. Rich in imagery and Celtic Revival ornament, the jewel-like window clearly shows Clarke's influence.

1. Donal O' Donovan, *Kevin Barry and His Time*, Glendale Press, 1989, p.193
2. *ibid*. The window was unveiled in 1934 by Richard O' Rahilly who was a member of the Kevin Barry Memorial Committee.
3. Information from George Walsh Jnr. All work produced by the Harry Clarke Studios had to bear the name of the Studio rather than the significance of the individual artists. According to present evidence, it seems quite likely that the *Kevin Barry* window may be the first signed stained glass by King.
4. S B Kennedy, *Irish Art and Modernism 1920-1949*. Ph. D Thesis, Trinity College, 1987, Vol. 1. p.33
5. O' Donovan, *op.cit.*, pp.42, 79-166
6. Nicola Gordon Bowe, *The Life and Work of Harry Clarke*, Irish Academic Press, 1989, p.55
7. Richard King, William Dowling and George Walsh assisted with the completion of the *Geneva* window because Harry Clarke was ill at the time. Clarke permitted his pupils to sign their names under the lead of the panels of the Geneva window on which they had worked.
8. Bowe, pls. 36, 46
9. *ibid.*, p.229. The figure of Robert Emmet in the *Geneva Window* is based on Lennox Robinson's play *The Dreamers*.
10. *ibid.*, pls. 36, 46
11. *ibid.*, p.63
12. *ibid*, pp.5, 57

MICHAEL CULLEN: A PAINTER PAINTING

Over the last few years, the surfaces of Michael Cullen's paintings have become quasi-reliefs, unlikely constructions which embody rudimentary figurative subjects in veritable mountain ranges of jagged and vertiginous impasto. Colour, straight from can and tube, unmixed, is piled on as if with a trowel and left there undigested, unmediated, for us to make of it what we will. The economy of elaboration, though, is contradicted by the sheer, unstinting generosity of delivery. Alpine peaks and valleys of snowy whites, visceral reds, flesh pinks, sunny yellows, sky blues, through which patches of raw burlap are still clearly visible, bespeak a rare largesse, a sensual overload. The dual message we receive is that the painting is there in a concrete, physical way, there vehemently, but it is also there with difficulty. The effect is usually uningratiating. Each painting has an indigestible roughness about it. And then, without warning, you can come upon pieces that are lusciously, edibly beautiful.

The notion of the painter's painter is a cliché, but that is what Cullen is, in more ways than one. Even if you don't like his work, you have to acknowledge the level of his ambition and achievement. Painting permeates his life and for him life is art. He has consistently understood the importance of the big picture, not for its own sake, but the need to test ideas on a large scale, to summarise, to punctuate. And his work is continually informed by other art, by his knowledge of painting and painters.

He was born in Kilcoole, near Greystones on the Co Wicklow coast, in 1946. After secondary school, he found work as a silkscreen printer. Even then, however, he thought of himself as a painter, employed for his skills as a printer. When it became clear that his employers regarded him as more of a factotum, they soon parted company. It was a pivotal moment because it established his own priorities.

He went to Dublin, where he had a fairly unsettled life, moving every few months or so, and he attended classes at the National College of Art and Design during 1962. He was involved with the Hell Fire Club Gallery, working for Edgar Battle, an arrangement that provided him with a studio and even with art materials. Lured by the promise of living cheaply, he made his way circuitously to Spain in 1969, settled for a while, painted landscapes, and the following year moved on to London. There he briefly

A knowledge of painters and painting informs the work of this artist but official recognition has eluded him for too long argues **Aidan Dunne.**

1. Michael CULLEN (b. 1946): Running Clown (1987) *Oil on paper, 70 x 50cm.* The artist as clown or performer is a stock figure in Cullen's work. Heavy black, white or red lines hold compositions together.

attended the Central School of Art to do life drawing.

Deciding to become a fulltime student at the National College of Art and Design, he returned to Dublin. However, it was a turbulent time in the NCAD's history and after a contentious final year, both Cullen and his friend Michael Mulcahy were failed. A year afterwards he was eventually granted his diploma after reassessment. In 1973 meanwhile, sans diploma, he went to Spain and Morocco with Mulcahy. In some ways it was a disastrous trip. He came down with hepatitis and, with few resources, had to suffer in poor conditions for months. Nevertheless, the work he made abroad and after his return home marked a turning point, marrying his natural representational facility to a concern with the more abstract aspects of picture-making – though it must be said that he is extremely uncomfortable with the word 'abstract'. The Moroccan work establishes his interest in flat pattern, which continues to be a cornerstone of his approach to pictorial organisation.

Since 1977 he has been based in Henrietta Street in Dublin, where he maintains a comfortable high-ceilinged studio in a big early Georgian house, although, an enthusiastic traveller, he has moved around a great deal and lived abroad for periods of time. He went to the United States and Mexico in 1980, bussing across vast distances. With Eithne Jordan he went to Berlin in 1984 and, bar 1988, which he spent at Annaghmakerrig in County Monaghan, he was there until 1989.

He has also spent time in the South of France, in a small village, near Montpellier in Languedoc (an experience which released floods of white light into his painting), and in 1993 he returned to Mexico, staying initially in Zacatecas, then in Chiapas (later the centre of the Zapatista uprising) for about six months in all. At home or elsewhere, work has always been primary: 'It's the painting that has to be sustained', he said to Margaret MacNamidhe in relation to travel, 'you have to get in there and cultivate ideas.' And while location is important, it rarely takes over: 'Think of Yeats creating a Byzantium in Sligo.'

When he first went to America he carried a camera and took photographs to work from. On this latter trip he didn't even bring a camera. He made himself work harder by keeping a kind of visual diary in sketchbooks, drawing everything along the

MICHAEL CULLEN: A PAINTER PAINTING

way. From his excursions he certainly imports colour. The comparative dullness of his earliest landscapes, which carried over into much of his first North African work, has gradually yielded to an enduring fascination with bright, full colour.

He has consistently made self-portraits. More, his work has consistently explored his own personal world and, as he is a painter, that world includes the studio and its surroundings. As Henry Sharpe noted in his 'Making Sense'catalogue, in the work from his time in America in 1980, which was marked by a new boldness of colour and stylistic cohesion, Cullen is an habitual presence in the canvases, but he 'is always curiously peripheral – the eternal tourist at the edge of things, unengaged, looking on.' He developed a shorthand visual notation for self, a graphic cut-out with his characteristic John Lennon glasses. The American paintings boast big open spaces, comic-book cacti, puffs of cotton-wool clouds, two-lane blacktops, all incarnated in livid pinks, blues, reds, rendered in a conspicuously stylised linear shorthand. 'Knock! Knock! Intrusion' (1979), a big quadriptych painted before his departure, sees him groping for an appropriate representational style, populating a succession of Francis Bacon-like arenas with tokens of animal and human presence. Everything is there, but the form is inchoate, tight, almost stilted. In a sense, America provided the solution.

After America, he adopted and began to relax into an idiomatic style derived from his own mark-making preferences and the example of Philip Guston. Guston, the Abstract Expressionist painter, had devised a cartoon-like, comic book figuration in his work based on gross caricature. Similarly, Cullen opted for a degree of caricature and to some extent embraced a form of comic book picaresque.

He plays anthropomorphic games with a menagerie of animals, and puts his human actors through various dramatic paces, implicating them in different theatrical frameworks: the circus, the farce, the tragedy, the charade. Stock figures include the artist as himself, the artist as clown, the model, usually a nude woman, often a nude man as well, death in the form of a skeletal figure, and, vitally, the *canaille*, the rabble. The notion of the *canaille* (it derives from the Italian *canaglia* or dog pack) becomes important, from the massed audiences of the circus spectacle to the more sinister mobs of the Berlin work.

As it happens, the animals he likes to depict include dogs, not in threatening packs but as fairly domesticated individuals, and specifically his own cross-bred Cubist dog, a cousin of the dog which Picasso included in his variations on Velasquez's *Las Meninas* (evidently a portrait of one of his own dogs), and at this stage a kind of mascot which, with its vast eye, is like a cross between Cerberus and a Cyclops.

Then there are zebras, particularly useful because of their stripes (for he is extremely fond of stripes as a graphic device), parrots and chimpanzees, both of whom, again, stand in for the artist.

Prior to his departure for Berlin in 1984, he produced an outstanding body of work, exhibited at the Lincoln Gallery in May

His paintings are theatrical, in the sense that they maintain a consistently high level of calculated artifice.

and June. The show marked an impressive synthesis of his various thematic and stylistic preoccupations up to that time. Free brushwork, casual compositions and a bright palette engender a mood of exuberance. Areas of raw canvas are visible, adjacent to layer upon layer of pigment. Alternatives, changes of mind, speculative passages are all left there on the surface.

Colours are used in their primal state, brushed on and, if mixing is desired, mixed roughly on the canvas itself. Brushmarks are left hanging, pigment dripped and splashed copiously. Heavy black, white or red lines hold compositions together. The painting's status as stage is emphasised by an exceptional number of truncated figures, by characters wandering casually in and out of the wings, by ladders that lead out of the frame.

Figures and locations, though spare and mannered, are treated quite naturalistically. That is, each picture contains one more or less coherent space viewed from one point. A central facet of Cullen's work as it developed throughout the 1980s was his progressively more flexible view of pictorial space. 'The Cubists,' he acknowledged in an interview with Gerry Dukes, 'made the break-through by dismantling or deconstructing the landscape, the object, the person, translating the three-dimensional space into a two-dimensional plane ... In many of my paintings I play the surface off against the implied space, simultaneously invoking and revoking some of the major features in the tradition of European painting.' When we look at *I'm Popeye the Painter Man* or *Life is a Bitch and Then You Die*, we are confronted with walls of paint as opposed to windows that we can look through. 'You see in a medium,' Cullen has remarked in the same interview, 'not through it.'

Cullen, that is to say, enjoys the post-Cubist freedom to ignore conventional rules of perspective, trading this freedom off against the limitation of an acknowledged flatness. Besides the space itself, however, he has also taken liberties with naturalistic representations of figures and objects, radically reorganising structures in a directly Cubist manner, and with something of the freedom of late Picasso in terms of flexibility, pace and levity. In fact, Picasso ranks with Guston in terms of influence: just think of Cullen's comparable adoption of the studio as world.

While these developments are decisively consolidated in the work made in Annaghmakerrig in 1988, there is also the long spell in Berlin to consider. Though from a more or less rural background, Cullen has spent most of his life in cities, and living in Berlin, he became interested in the idea of the city itself as a complex entity, a vast organism with an indifferent life of its own, its myriad layers of space and activity never entirely apprehensible to an individual consciousness. 'The metaphor of the walled city has always appealed to me, the idea of an enclosed, labyrinthine city, like Blake's Jerusalem.'

Berlin is a big, landlocked city with a formidable, terrible history. When Eithne Jordan and he moved there, it was still divided. Cullen's vision of the city is every bit as bleak, but really the bleakness, the grim view of life and death, is the painter's own, here borne out by the facts, rather than something specific

2. Michael CULLEN (b. 1946): Painter About to Paint a Painting. (1991-92). *Oil on linen, 210 x 210cm.* This theatrical studio scene, filled with anticipation, is a homage to Cullen's favourite Yeats painting, *About to Write a Letter*, in the National Gallery of Ireland.

3. Michael CULLEN (b. 1946): Studio Interior.(1991) *Oil on canvas, 48 x 48cm.* Cullen's work consistently explores his own personal world and surroundings. Picasso's influence is seen in his reorganisation of structures in a Cubist manner.

4. Michael CULLEN (b. 1946): Studio Scene with Painter Painting and Model (1991). *Oil on burlap, 38 x 41cm.* Images of artist and model could indicate his views on how the sexes relate.

5. Michael CULLEN (b. 1946): I'm Popeye the Painterman. (1992) *Oil on burlap, 223 x 228cm. Hugh Lane Municipal Gallery.* The artist, inspired by the hatted images of Van Gogh in his self-portraits, is deliberately self-mocking.

to or inspired exclusively by Berlin. He habitually arouses our expectations only to thwart them: frequently, at first glance, we anticipate luscious paintwork, a Matisse-like luxuriance, but, though the beauty is there, to gain access to it we also have to deal with something more disagreeable, a certain truculence of presentation by which things insist on being just what they are.

Often the image becomes virtually invisible, woven into the texture of the brushmarks. Black takes over his palette. Red

6. Michael CULLEN (b. 1946): Zebrine Triangles with Painter and Two Models (1992) *Oil on burlap, 55 x 72cm.* Cullen loves to play anthropomorphic games with various animals; he is particularly fond of the graphic device of stripes.

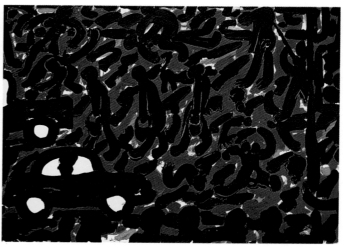

7. Michael CULLEN (b. 1946): Nude and Skeleton (1989) *Oil on paper, 32 x 46cm.* One of a number of paintings which explore graphically the artist's realisation that vitality and physical voluptuousness are inextricably bound up with the certainty of death.

8. Michael CULLEN (b. 1946): Berlin Inferno (detail) (1987) *Oil on paper, one of 16 panels, each 90 x 100cm.* From a rural Wicklow background, Cullen was fascinated by the complexity of Berlin, where he spent a long period. Its enclosed labyrinthine vastness and its grim and terrible history inspired this series.

comes next, and grey. A grid of streets and buildings regulates his compositions. People and buildings alike become anonymous silhouettes. The ubiquitous canaille presses in threateningly. The atmosphere is comparable to that in Fritz Lang's film *Fury*, a powerful indictment of mob rule in which an innocent stranger is the victim of a lynch mob.

'He sees Berlin,' Dorothy Walker wrote in 1986, 'as a walled city as in medieval times, having a certain siege mentality, a heightened feeling of delight in survival.' The circus of city life proves a bleak entertainment. The archetypal metropolis, hugely indifferent to the individual human subject, is the scene of conflict, murder, rape, hysteria. The mood is summed up when we see a crucifixion proceeding matter-of-factly while passers-by get on with their business, the city's pulse doesn't even skip a beat. Our 'Clown Witness' is summarily dealt with, as Gerry Dukes says, 'buffeted, marginalised, knocked down, badged in motley....In one image, *Masturbating Clown and Panzer*, we are given an extraordinary image of powerlessness and anomie. The material carapace, the armour of urban egotism, cannot be penetrated and the allowed fool makes contact only with himself.'

After France, white light banishes the blackness, the Teutonic gloom. That brilliant light irradiates *Popeye* and the painter on the point of painting. In *I'm Popeye the Painter Man*, 'Popeye' himself has a Cubist head, split between full-view and profile, Van Gogh's hat, massive hands and exposed genitals. His blonde model, sprawled out on a bed or couch, is naked, with pneumatic breasts and exposed pudenda. Although the title plays on the association, and a certain bouncy joviality of mood (the parodic masculinity-feminity, activity-passivity of the artist-model relationship parallelling that of Popeye and Olive Oyl), together with the marine background, reinforces it, Popeye the Sailor Man is not the reference's final destination. That is the notion of the painter as performer who will make the eyes pop out of your head, the spirit of Van Gogh in the South of France.

Painter About to Paint a Painting is a homage to an illustrious predecessor, Jack B Yeats' *About to Write a Letter*, Cullen's favourite Yeats painting. Both title and image set up a mood of anticipation. Despite differences in format and tone, there are obvious compositional similarities between the two works. Cullen's picture is a studio scene. An artist, again kitted out like Van Gogh, with huge, bulbous fingers and a tumescent penis, is poised before a framed canvas on an easel. A massive blue dog occupies the foreground. His vast eye blends with his open mouth as he gazes and barks at a nude woman model, who is either posing or on the verge of fleeing. Certainly the dog is consuming the woman with his ferocious eye. The painter has a mirror image, the silhouette of a man emerging from a screen on the right. His erection confirms that the anticipation is also sexual, or perhaps equates a strictly sexual anticipation with the painter's approach to the 'virgin' canvas or his posing model. By the 1990s, Cullen routinely deconstructs and reconstructs his figures, taking extreme liberties with proportion, space and scale.

His paintings are theatrical, in the sense that they maintain a consistently high level of calculated artifice; they apparently encapsulate dramas enacted for our benefit and they make explicit use of such performance settings as circus ring and stage. It might be interesting to look at them in the light of some of the ideas of Clement Greenberg or, more pertinently, of the art theorist Michael Fried, relating to the concept of theatricality in painting. Broadly speaking, Fried outlines a rationale for modernist painting and the importance of formal considerations (freed from a representational task, it must be said), that is distinct from, but has some parallels with, Greenberg's notions of painting's movement towards self-identity and purity.

Oddly enough, in its original setting, which was an analysis of late eighteenth-century French painting during the time of Diderot, the term 'theatricality' applied not to the kind of work that you might expect – the history paintings, the overly calculated narrative bourgeois genre scenes awash with sentimentality – but to the perceived excesses of the Rococo, to an overly decorative and complicit art. Diderot championed Jean Baptiste Chardin and Jean Baptiste Greuze.

Initially, Diderot saw in the latter's subject paintings a degree of self-absorption and naturalistic detail that served as an antidote to the artificiality and moral laxity of François Boucher. Fried develops this notion of an absorption, a self-awareness that allows the spectator a fuller, truer access to the world of the painting. More and more, painters address the history of painting. As Steve Connor puts it: 'in Hegelian terms ... the dialectical engagement of the new with the old ... (brings) an intensified self-consciousness at each stage of renewal.' Painting progressively becomes itself, though without Greenberg's point of terminal purification.

> *Cullen uses an essentially Cubist approach to deconstruct spaces and objects, but then confounds our expectations.*

Cullen's work encapsulates the apparent paradox between the opposing pulls of theatricality and absorption. According to Diderot's criteria it is, on the one hand, theatrical in its knowingness. It rehearses decorative strategies and motifs with shameless affection. It advertises a luscious physicality of detail, but in a stylised manner. It is often animated by and dramatises sensual and sexual desire.

It is also self-absorbed, however, burrowing deeply into art history for its subject matter, its terms of reference. Its physicality relates not only, not even primarily, to the subject matter but also to the 'thereness' of the painting itself. Pigment heaped irregularly onto burlap, though it might be disposed along approximately representational lines, continually drags the image back from any illusory picture space to the real space of the surface. Furthermore, as with Jackson Pollock's paintings, where the dripped paint lies emphatically on and not at all within the surface, we are not really allowed any access to the shallow space of juxtaposed planes that characterises Cubism and the uniform shallow space evident in the work of some Abstract Expressionist painters. Cullen uses an essentially Cubist approach to deconstruct spaces and objects, but then confounds our expectations: every mark is a superimpostion. We cannot get behind the canvas. Despite the undeniable, central representational element, Frank Stella's minimalist dictum,

MICHAEL CULLEN: A PAINTER PAINTING

'What you see is what you get', could well apply.

What of the paintings' representational status? For most of the time they are representational in a curiously self-referring way: the studio, the accoutrements of picture-making, the artist in the studio, the artist and his model, allegories of the painter and his public – in the same way, admittedly, images of artist and model could be read as standing for more general views of relationships between the sexes – and then stock subjects like the vase of flowers, the bowl of fruit (that might almost have 'still-life' stamped on them), and the landscape.

The image of the artist is often extremely self-reflexive: the Van Gogh archetype in the *Painter Cuts Ear Off* (1992) (a title that reads like a newspaper headline), *I'm Popeye the Painter Man* (1992) and *Study: Painter on his Way to Work (after Van Gogh)* (1991), the pointedly tautologous *Painting Painter* (1989) and *Painter Painting* (1992) (two of many), the ironic *Painting Monkey* (1984), the hermetically self-contained *Masturbating Clown* (1989). There is a conceptual flatness to these subjects, just as there is a literal flatness to their representation.

Then there are comprehensive re-workings of paintings, as with *Painter About to Paint a Painting*, correlative to Yeats' picture; *Luncheon on the Grass: study after 'Le Dejeuner sur l'Herbe' by Edouard Manet* (1992); *Study: 'La Grande Odalisque' (after Ingres)* (1991), as well as pictures by Van Gogh, Picasso (a series of *Crying Woman* (1990), related to Picasso's *Weeping Woman*), and Velasquez's *Las Meninas* in *Music from Annaghmakerrig: Painting Painter'* (1990), Jan Van Eyck's *The Arnolfini Marriage* as well as many other references and quotations. He has also reworked stock subjects, like *The Three Graces* (1983), and the crucifixion. In all it amounts to a systematic interrogation of the history, and the mythology, of painting.

In many respects Greenberg could well have approved of most of his output since the mid-1970s. The paintings are representational, but Greenberg has nothing against representation per se, and they are intimately concerned with the formal questions that so preoccupied him, with flatness, with painting's self-identity. But they deny the grail of an eventual closure, a final purity. They are expressly open, irreverent, demotic, picking up on ideas beyond the fine art canon, notably the idiom of broad caricature, the freedom of the cartoon, but they are not postmodernist works in the sense of assuming a stylistic promiscuity.

We should not forget that Cullen points to his own life and surroundings as his major source: you must paint what you know, he has said more than once, what's around you and what's going on around you. And it is true that each exhibition mirrors events in his own life, obviously so in the case of his move to Berlin, or in terms of the intimations of mortality in the *Dance of Death* series with its allusions to Dante (*In a Dark Wood* (1998)) which saw the artist, heading for his mid-forties, facing up to his own mortality. In these paintings a sense of vitality and physical voluptuousness is inextricably bound up with the certainty of death, most graphically in the several *Nude and Skeleton* (1989) paintings. Similarly his exhibitions *A Screaming Silence* (1990), *A Painter on His Way to Work* (1991)

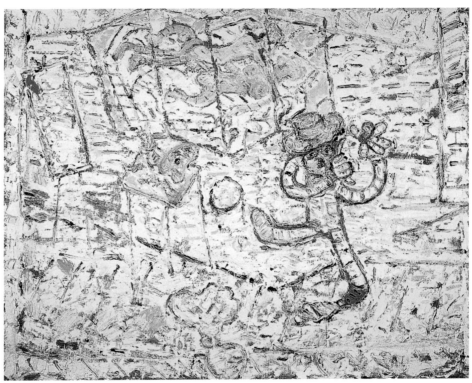

9. Michael CULLEN (b. 1946): A Day in the Life of a Painter. (1991) *Oil on linen, 137 x 166cm.*

and *Le Peintre Solitaire* (1992) coincide with tumultuous personal events. There is no distance between life and art.

While, for example, irony is employed, there is no ironic distance between painter and style. 'A painter's style is the product of his life experience,' Cullen said in conversation with Gerry Dukes, 'of the academic and practical knowledge of art and its media, of the cast of his mind and the sleight of his hand. It seems a hopeless, even hapless enterprise to try to pin down something so fluid and fugitive.' Cubism is straightforwardly employed for the pictorial possibilities it opens up. It seems that a persuasive argument can be made that his paintings function within a Western, modernist tradition in an unusually perceptive and constructive way. But it would be as well to leave the last word to the painter himself, or at least to a sentiment that he thought worth quoting. It was written by Sandro Chia: 'It is not a good idea to analyse painting...The most elevated, intelligent and subtle approach to painting is to say whether you like it or not.'

AIDAN DUNNE is a freelance art critic and writer.

1. Cormac BOYDELL, Green Spiral ceramic plate, *32 cm diam.* Boydell's work, based in the wild landscape of Allihies in West Cork, is overtly terrestrial and elemental.

THE CREATIVITY OF CONTEMPORARY IRISH CRAFTS

Patricia Jorgensen *finds a wide choice when it comes to selecting the finest Irish glass, ceramics, metal, and woodwork.*

2. Salah KAWALA, Screen Wall. *Glass in metal, 500 x 1250 cm.* This immense wall, designed by Roisín de Buitléir, was commissioned for the Blasket Island Centre.

The disparity between 'Fine Art' and 'Craft' is a relatively recent phenomenon, a rift caused partly by the aftermath of the Industrial Revolution of the nineteenth century and by changing values of patronage since then. By considering the practice, and illustrating the work of some selected artists in the areas of glass, wood, ceramics and metal, it is hoped to show that this is an arbitrary and artificial dichotomy. The creative impulse is mysterious and complex but the recognition of the end result is simpler: a work of art is an object that achieves a presence beyond the present. It emits an energy that results from certainty of technique and the artist's force of spirit, both of which communicate directly with the viewer in a bond that is strong, that is both sensory and intellectual.

Such force is evident, albeit very differently, in the work of two glass artists,

3. Killian SCHURMANN, Goblets. *Handblown glass, 25 cm high.* Trained in Germany, Schurmann fashions his medieval style goblets in the traditional way.

Salah Kawala and **Killian Schurmann**. Kawala, born in Egypt, benefited from considerable artistic and intellectual education and training there, followed by an eclectic and peripatetic career which eventually landed him in Dublin. The spiritual philosophies of Islam inform his approach. He emphasises that expertise involves concern for both technical and aesthetic solutions: use and beauty go together. He has the Muslim awareness of the ephemerality of things: art has always something provisional about it. He suggests that the artist's greatest achievement is the mastery he gains over himself, for it is there that art transforms itself into a spiritual and contemplative discipline. He expresses such sensibilities in a very original way, using heavy plate glass and glass rods. By cutting, fusion and moulding, Kawala transforms them into objects as

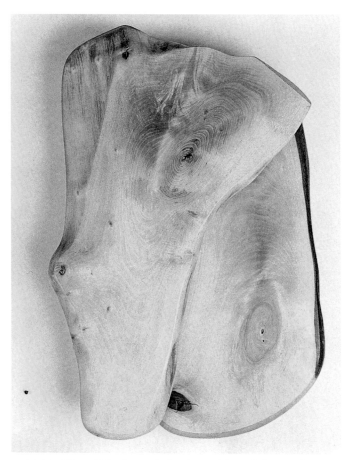

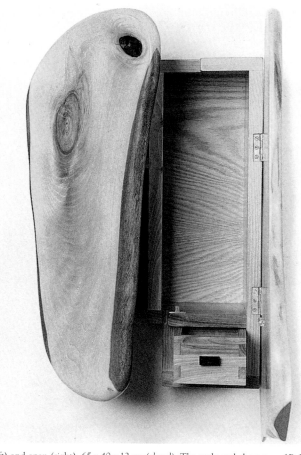

4. Michael BELL, Wall cabinet in Irish walnut with bog oak drawer pull shown closed (left) and open (right). *65 x 40 x 12 cm (closed)*. The scale and character of Bell's pieces are determined by the woods he finds.

diverse as spiralling square-section light fixtures, free-standing dramatically to wall height; stalactic tables and icy curved chairs, as well as commissioned pieces such as an immense screen wall of glass in metal for the Blaskets Centre, on which he is collaborating with Roisln de Butléir. Given that glass is thought to have originated in Egypt, it is appropriate that this Egyptian artist pushes it to such original lengths, always insisting that design emanates from the material.

Killian Schurmann actually makes the glass with which he works, literally at white heat, and some of his pieces are fashioned in the traditional way. There, however, tradition ends, for he is a breaker of boundaries. Extending the limits of his material possibly results from a long and strict technical training in Germany, and from being the son of artists. But extensive travel throughout Europe and in the United States has also influenced

5. Michael BELL, Branched and woven rope chairs in beech, adzed elm, and natural fibre rope. *Seat , 45 cm high*. Fantastical tree pieces excavated from forest and swamp inspire these textural chairs.

him, and he has rejected the comparative ease of studio glass making for the rigours of the experimental. He does make a basic 'production' line, but to call the result 'wine glasses' hardly does them justice. These are medieval scale goblets conjuring up the feastings of knights and ladies in tapestried splendour, yet such is their validity that they are at home on a kitchen table today. Presently experimenting with the concept of glass and nature – incorporating abstractly coloured slabs into gardens to observe the effects of weathering – Schurmann also continues to explore colour infusion, in monumental vessels from whose interior atavistic figures emerge as spectres onto the surface.

Wood, although not pliant like clay, metal, or glass, can be worked in several ways: carved, joined, turned or woven. There has been a growing awareness of its potential among Irish artists in recent years. Wood-turning , especially, has developed spectacularly, with many fine practitioners. **Peter Sweetman** is one of them. With a core philosophy as hard as his material, he deprecates the tempting facility of wood-turning: 'The "Salad Bowl" mentality', while enthusiastically expounding its challenges. In retrospect, Peter Sweetman's route to wood-turning seems predestined. After abandoning a photographic career, he worked for three years felling trees and also did a course in tree surgery. He acquired a deep knowledge and love of trees and a collection of special woods. Having seen the work of Michael O'Donnell, he attended a course and, as he says, he was hooked. Sweetman is adamant about the benefit of coming to his profession as he did, through learning about trees. He talks of 'respect for material' and again, 'playing into your material', dictums which form the basis of his design philosophy. 'The artist's job', he explains, 'is exploring and excavating the wood to liberate its quality'. His pieces invite touch. He welcomes this as a sign of successful communication: 'wood needs cuddling'. In 1993, he spent some time in Northern Transvaal with the Venda people. It is hoped that this will lead to a joint exhibition with Venda wood carvers to be mounted in Johannesburg and Dublin in 1995.

Michael Bell's initial relationship with wood seems primordial. From forest and swamp he excavates fantastical tree pieces. Their shape, texture and grain inspire the forms of the chairs he makes by combining them with other cut and joined woods. Scale, and character too, are determined by the original findings, varying from seats of throne-like proportions to fire-side stools. His approach is not unlike that of the 'objet trouve' school of sculpture and not inappropriate, given the sculptural results. Not all his work, however, is in this robustly textural mould. Alongside rope-lashed branch and plank is joinery of impeccable quality in fine hardwoods, so crafted that only a subtle tonal difference in pin or dowel may express the construction. It is the combination of meticulous traditional methods, learnt as an apprentice, with a feeling of

6. Killian SCHURMANN, Glass on limestone base, *25 x 20 cm.* This piece is one of a series based on sheep and animal heads.

7. Salah KAWALA, Out of the Blue. *Glass, 61 cm high.* In his Dublin workshop, this Egyptian artist creates dramatic spiralling forms.

creating for the future that characterises Michael Bell's furniture. Then there is his expressed belief that 'design comes through respect for material, and make should always be subordinate'.

Woven wood is ancient and international in furniture making and, particularly in the Far East, in exquisitely fashioned domestic utensils. In Ireland, we have a fine history of basket-making, a tradition very much alive, and heightened, in the work of **Alison Fitzgerald.** She is a botanist by profession and her first contact with willow came when she was living next door to beds grown for experimental purposes. An awareness of the familiar 'Sally Gardens' of Ulster led to her desire to learn basket-making. From a modest start ten years ago, her skills are now developed to a unique level. Her designs retain the dignity and integrity of tradition. Her handling of the raw material, at once sensitive and bold, and the sheer excellence of make, gives her work that 'edge' which is a hallmark of true art.

Clay seems to have an almost mystical hold on artists. Its inherent pliability as a material must be countered by a rigid discipline and control in the making. This applies particularly to porcelain clay, which **Vivienne Foley**, the foremost exponent of the medium, acknowledges: 'I enjoy the technical challenge of this difficult clay as well as its translucency, purity and fired strength'. Evidence of success is her increasing export to Japan. But her questing spirit is not still: 'I have always loved the historical mystique of porcelain as a precious material. My aim is to extend its possibilities and achieve a contemporary feel, underpinned by a classical fineness'. These ideals, and her feeling for excellence, are embodied in vases, bowls, and dishes, enhanced by unusual glazes, often textured, some metallic. Colouring is mainly neutral, creating an overall effect of restrained luxury.

Foley's approach at first appears very different to that of **Cormac Boydell** whose work, based in the wild landscape of Allihies in West Cork, is overtly terrestrial, primary and elemental.

8. Peter SWEETMAN, Brown oak vessel, *30.5 x 38 cm*. Wood-turner Sweetman has a deep knowledge and love of trees and special woods.

9. Laura O'Hagan and Orla Kaminski of Tileworks, Hand -painted ceramic platter with inlaid copper wire, *31 cm.diam*. Richly coloured, textured and tactile.

He is a pioneer, exploring, breaking and building on new ground. Yet he is close to Foley when he says; 'Ceramics is very much a love of the nature of materials, how they relate to one another and how they transform through fire'. Recalling formative influences, Cormac Boydell acknowledges a debt to his parents for teaching him 'how to avoid boredom by listening deeply to music', and to Oisin Kelly's inspired instruction when he first worked with clay. A degree in geology and four years work in the Australian bush played their part too; 'in retrospect I see my work with the earth in geology as being little different from my work with clay'. He sees the colours and textures of the Allihies landscape in his work; 'not intentional, but something absorbed and re-expressed'. And he makes an important point towards understanding his work: 'I seldom derive ideas intellectually from my surroundings, because I find that the process of making is often second hand to the idea and that the work suffers in vitality'. And vitality is the keyword to his work. These are egregious pieces brimming with life force and tactility. They are not for the fainthearted, they are to be embraced wholeheartedly – or left alone.

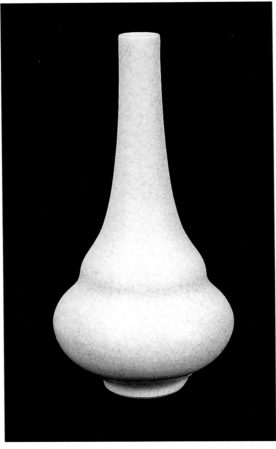

10. Vivienne FOLEY, Vase. *Dolomite crackle glaze stained with gold, z25 cm high*. Foley's neutral colours create an overall effect of restrained luxury.

The name '**Tile Works**' offers no hint of the richness and diversity of the work of artists **Laura O'Hagan** and **Orla Kaminska**. Both are graduates of the National College of Art and Design, Dublin. Initially, they went separate ways and gained their individual experience. They reunited, setting up a partnership in a studio workshop to make site-specific architectural art such as relief decoration for floors and walls. Their work has extended to three dimensions: tables, chairs and interior accessories including mirrors, platters and boxes. Materials are basic, technique is sophisticated. The starting point is mostly 'job lots' of unused biscuit-fired tiles and mouldings, to which reflective and coloured glass, buttons, beads and other collected bric-a-brac may be added later. These ceramic shards are decorated, glazed and fired, then cut, shaped and assembled to a pre-designed plan. The result is richly coloured, textured and tactile: a contemporary mixed-media rococo.

In Ireland, metal art is generally taken to mean sculpture or jewellery. Both these categories fuse in the work of metalsmith **Kevin O'Dwyer**. His silversmith and enamelling apprenticeships followed three years training in biotechnology. This may explain the organic forms of so much of his work. The helix figure occurs repeatedly. His double helix bangle in forged silver, exhibited at the 'Vice-Verse: Jewellery as Sculpture' show (Dublin 1990) is an outstanding example. This motif evolved further in spiral based candlesticks. When his work became more concerned with volume expressed in free forms, as in the fantastical tea-set series, organic forms survived in waves and spirals of metal, free-wheeling from the object into surrounding space. A self-confessed perfectionist and a meticulous craftsman, O'Dwyer attaches great importance to the initial design idea: 'Without that, nothing can happen', and to the importance of research on form, and its development into series. He also stresses the need for technical and ergonomic experiment to achieve a harmony of form and function. O'Dwyer's work is preoccupied with space – the interplay of positive and negative, and he uses contrasting surface treatments to produce visual tension. This is evident in his recent work, a collection of silver tableware directly inspired by the buildings of Chicago. His long association with that city – he lived there while training – has imbued him with a passion for modern architecture. Architectural forms are translated into a 'silver city' of related pieces, which are witty as well as functional.

Belfast artist **Derek McGarry** also returned from the United States to Ireland, to take his post as Head of the Metal and Jewellery Department at the National College of Art and Design, Dublin. Although coming to it from a different angle, he shares O'Dwyer's interest in volumetric space. In McGarry's early sculptural pieces this was expressed through linear forms. These have evolved into solids in his collection of silver brooches which won the Goldsmiths Award at the 1993 'Ten Jewellers' exhibition at the Irish Craft Council Gallery in Dublin. Rigorous and concentrated postgraduate studies in America covered the theoretical, technical and experimental aspects of metalcraft. These, plus tutorial experience, have equipped McGarry well for the challenging duality of teaching and creating. His designs are primarily mathematical and spatial. In sculpture, he re-arranges elements from which an infinite number of variations can be achieved, using a limited vocabulary of two- or three-dimensional images. Another system involves reorganising elements within set boundaries. Such concepts may appear rather arid, but they offer interesting possibilities for modular jewellery. Derek McGarry is exploring these. He is also enthusiastic about colouring and patination of metals. Given past achievements, exciting future developments can be anticipated from this artist – and from his disciples.

All these artists expressed common concerns. They demon-

11. Alison FITZGERALD, Woven wood baskets. Ireland's fine traditon of basket-making is heightened in the woven willow of this young botanist.

strated a high level of professionalism and dedication in their work. They also share a willingness to co-operate with each other and, most importantly, an awareness of promotion and marketing. The applied arts in Ireland are now of international standard, offering growth potential and investment opportunity for the astute collector.

PATRICIA JORGENSEN is a freelance artist and designer

WHERE TO SEE AND BUY

The Crafts Council of Ireland, Powerscourt Townhouse Centre, South William St., Dublin 2. Tel: (01) 6797368. A list of over 600 registered craftworkers is available from the Council who also produce a useful directory, price £2, the Craft Map which directs the visitor to various craft studios around the country.

Designyard, the Applied Arts Centre at Temple Bar, 12 East Essex St., Dublin 2. Tel. (01) 6778453. Contemporary Irish jewellery is on sale and exhibition, while the Commissioning Gallery deals with work in wood, glass, ceramics, textile and metal, including corporate gift projects.

12. Derek McGARRY, Modular brooch, *steel and neoprene, 2.5 x 7.6 x 7.6 cm*. The participatory pieces within the structure can be interchanged as the wearer pleases.

13. Vivienne FOLEY, Vessel. *barium/cobalt glaze over reactive slips, 34cm diam* . In her Co Clare studio, Foley is a leading figure in the field of hand-thrown porcelain.

BOOK REVIEWS

Belleek, The Complete Collector's Guide and Illustrated Reference

BY RICHARD K DEGENHARDT

Wallace – Homestead Book Company, Radnor, Pennsyvania, 1993 £50

Belleek Irish Porcelain: An illustrated guide to over two thousand pieces

BY MARION LANGHAM

Quiller Press, London, 1993 £50

Mairead Dunlevy

HOW THINGS HAVE changed! Twenty years ago antique dealers sold Belleek with ease, boasted of their knowledge of patterns such as *echinus, thistle* or *Neptune* but did not know when exactly the pottery was established – 1857, 1859 or 1863? There was such a superb pride in Belleek then that, amazingly, everybody accepted without question the confidence of those businessmen who recklessly established a modern Staffordshire-style pottery in a famine-stricken village, remote from commercial markets, four miles from the nearest port (Ballyshannon), with an undeveloped road system and no railways.

In contrast, to-day, when it is difficult to find good early Belleek pieces, two major reference books have been published. Superbly illustrated, together these volumes give the collector, and the student of antiques, comprehensive guides to the wide variety of porcelains produced in Ireland's most successful pottery of recent times. Both show that early pride was justified.

This is the second edition of Richard K Degenhardt's *Collector's Guide.* The scholarship and range of the first edition made it the 'bible' for the past fifteen years for antique collectors interested in the subject. This second edition is now expanded, updated and with many new illustrations from private and public collections. Dick Degenhardt's passionate love affair with Belleek porcelain has resulted in a well-referenced catalogue which includes a comprehensive history of pottery and a good bibliography. His dedication to this study has resulted in his sourcing – and saving for posterity – early photographs, indentures and unique archival material, much of which he illustrates. In his scholarly text, he gives the history of the pottery through to its recent change in ownership to George G Moore of Dundalk and California. His work is valuable also in

BIRD VASES: *moulded and hand-painted fine porcelain about 1895 (From Marion Langham, Belleek Irish Porcelain).* Young ladies were taught ceramic design and hand-painting in The Queen's Institute, Marlborough Street, Dublin. The aim was to prepare them for work in Irish ceramic industries, such as Belleek. These fine vases are painted in The Queen's Institute style.

that he gives much new information on those who developed patterns in the second and later periods of Belleek – Frederick Slater, Madame Broniuxz and Eric and Cyril Arnold. It was the latter who later started his own porcelain works at Bundoran, Co Donegal.

Marion Langham's most welcome new volume complements Degenhardt's. Her experience in cataloguing the Belleek collection of that enthusiast from Texas, Horace Manning Mann, and her own work as an antique specialist may be why she divides her subject logically according to categories such as tea-sets, vases, mirrors, candlesticks. Declaring that her aim is to present 'a pictorial tribute to the porcelain produced' at Belleek she achieves that through her marvellous photographs which are superbly reproduced. Lady Langham and Dick Degenhardt both exude in their texts that unique warmth and friendship which has always distinguished the workers at Belleek.

Both volumes concentrate on porcelain whose 'creamy texture, gossamer

appearance and translucent quality', according to Degenhardt won for Belleek an international reputation, and the ultimate sign of success, as it was copied contemporaneously by some American potteries. Belleek won that reputation fairly, due to the quality of its porcelain and of its designs.

The Belleek pottery factory in Co Fermanagh was built by 1860 and opened officially in 1863. The district was eminently suitable for a modern industrial pottery. It had the essential porcelain clays, as well as turf for fuel and the fast-flowing river Erne which could be harnessed for energy. These elements were recognised in 1857 by a number of men of vision – a caring landlord, John Caldwell Bloomfield; a brilliant architect and pottery manager, Robert Williams Armstrong; a nationalist, ceramic enthusiast and businessman, W H Kerr and a capitalist, David McBirney – who soon introduced industrial work practices to the area. Their determination to succeed can be seen in their building of a small railway to bring the clays from the quarry and in their persistence when the clays proved inferior and required much more preparation than would have been permitted by any Staffordshire accountant. Cleverly, however, the pottery ensured that their products would be marketable through copying some of the most successful items produced by Worcester, Goss, Crown Derby, Wedgwood, Brownfield, Milton, Copeland and Coalport. Nowhere did Belleek do this more blatantly than in their range of parian porcelain figures. Milton's *Solitude* became Belleek's *Prisoner of Love*. Their *Clorinda* and *Dorothea* became Belleek's *Affection* and *Meditation*. The *Crouching Venus* is based on a *Venus* of the first century AD from the Royal Collection which is now in the British Museum. It is there described as a copy of that by Doialses of Bithyria of 250BC. Modern copies were made by both Sevres and Wedgwood. Belleek, therefore, followed in a great classical tradition when it produced this piece.

Belleek's famous and popular *Clytie* was based on a Roman marble, known as *Antonia*, in the British Museum. Marion Langham tells us that *Clytie* depicted a water nymph who fell passionately in love with Apollo and was turned into a sunflower by the gods in their compassion when her love was unrequited. The Roman marble was reproduced in plaster for the decoration of eighteenth-century libraries, when it was known as *Flora*. A reduced version in parian porcelain, produced by Copeland and selected as a prize by the Art Union of London in 1855, was then copied by Belleek.

Aware of market problems, Belleek was cautious about developing their own parian ware but there were two well known pieces with important promotional connections. *Erin arising from her slumbers*, designed by Irishman William Boyton Kirk, shows the young maid, 'Erin', standing on the flagstones of the River Erne at Belleek while unveiling a classical urn to represent the opening of the Belleek pottery.

A bust of Lord James Butler, Third Marquess of Ormonde, was first exhibited at the Dublin Exhibition of 1872. Butler was probably singled out for this particular honour because he was Vice-President of and a prime mover in the Exhibition. Both Armstrong and

MIRROR AND BOUDOIR CANDLESTICK: *moulded and applied decoration, (From Marion Langham, Belleek Irish Porcelain)*. The Victorian appreciation of the family flower garden is shown in the faithful representation of the applied flowers on these boudoir pieces.

McBirney were on its Industries and Manufactures Committee and Belleek had a large and prominent stand there.

Being astute businessmen, when Belleek became confident they registered their own unique designs for tea-ware and ornaments with the British Board of Trade to protect their designs from others preying on them immediately. Those new designs were targeted directly at particular markets. Aiming at the fashionable audiences of London and Dublin, Belleek used the motifs which in that Victorian period were considered 'artistic' – marine, floral and vegetable. Hence tea-services moulded in shell shapes, hawthorn or artichoke patterns were produced. The insatiable Victorian interest in ornaments led also to Belleek's successful production of concepts which we find difficult to appreciate to-day – 'flying fish' posy-holders, pineapple oil lamps with hairy lion feet and vases shaped like onions or celery or of such unusual shapes as three Lough Erne salmon standing on their tails.

For the American market a Chinese range was produced. Tea-pots with silk handles and moulded with china-men on the lids as well as tea-pot stands moulded in the shape of Chinese dragons were given approval. To satisfy the Irish nationalist spirit, Belleek registered a Celtic interlace design in 1879 and, in

the age of Parnell, began to use the shamrock motif.

Belleek's marketing policies worked but the pottery was also successful in capturing the imagination and loyalty of Irish people – and of Belleek enthusiasts worldwide. It is likely that this was engineered also by Armstrong as the folklore which wove its web around the Pottery placed Belleek within the lore of other major European potteries. The story that Bloomfield, the landlord, first discovered that he had porcelain clays on his estate when he became aware of the glistening whiteness of a newly white-washed cottage can be compared with that of Augustus the Strong who, it is said, accidentally found porcelain clay near Meissen when, on a rainy day, his horse had difficulty with the plasticity of the clay underfoot. Another familiar story was that of Annie Langley Nairn – Mrs Armstrong – who for her Belleek designs collected shells on the strand at Bundoran. This lore must be balanced with the amount of shell shapes promoted by the pottery which were part of the ceramic designers' repertoire for over a century previously.

Both of these excellent volumes refer principally to the expensive porcelains which were the prestige products of the pottery. Yet the company's success on the home market was due to its successful competition with Staffordshire in its supply of 'delph' (earthenware) tea-ware, toilet jugs and basin for washstands, ware for the cottages and homes of Ireland, for hospitals and invalid rooms and for creameries. Some earthenware items are illustrated – seemingly accidentally – but the authors fail to concentrate sufficiently on Belleek's industrial ceramics and on the myriad fledgling potteries which surrounded the main factory.

These two volumes, though, will help the collector of Belleek porcelain in identifying pieces and they will, hopefully, encourage others and give them confidence to seek out and research Belleek.

A useful and informative *Price Guide to Belleek Irish Porcelain*, by Marion Langham, price £6 is available from the author at Claranagh, Tempo, Co Fermanagh, N Ireland.

Mairead Dunlevy is Director of the Hunt Museum in Limerick, on secondment from the Art and Industrial Division of the National Museum of Ireland.

BOOK REVIEWS

Town and Country
BY MARK GIROUARD

Yale University Press, New Haven and London, 1993.
pp.271, £25 (h/b)

Jane Fenlon

MARK GIROUARD is one of the best known and most successful writers in the field of architectural history. It is an area which he covers in the broadest sense. For instance, his discussions, ranging across the bones of a building or feature, are then put in context in a manner that is rarely matched by other authors. Overall, his writing of social history, linked with his descriptions of the uses of buildings, have set the standard. His approach to his subject, in his own words 'relating architecture to its background' is now generally accepted as the norm. Therefore, it is all the more difficult to appreciate that when his most successful book, *Life in the English Country House*, was published, as recently as 1978, it was regarded as innovative.

In his introduction to this book, *Town and Country*, the author reviews for us his feelings about architectural history and also gives us some insights into his writings on the subject. Amusingly, his experience with the best selling *Life in the English Country House*, elicits the following comment from him: 'When people come up to me and say how much they enjoyed my book, I resent the certainty with which I know what book this will be'. As one of those who did exactly this and received a suitably frosty response, this reviewer can now better appreciate his viewpoint on the matter. Above all, his introduction reveals to us a writer who is steeped in his subject and who followed his predilection from a very early age.

Divided under four broad headings, the twenty-one articles in this book cover subjects as diverse as the growth of the town of Whitby in Yorkshire, a reconstruction of Elizabethan Chatsworth and the plumbing at Tullynally Castle, Co Westmeath. With the exception of the last offering, 'The Georgian House', all of the articles have previously been published, more than half in *Country Life*. This does not detract from their production in book form, except of course for those who are avid readers of that magazine. It is a most enjoyable read, packed with diverse information. For Irish readers, the section 'Irish Interlude', consisting of five essays, has obvious attractions. There is an interesting discourse on Waterford, which reveals a collection of fine eighteenth-century buildings, including a double galleried Catholic chapel of 1764, one of the best kept architectural secrets in this country.

For anybody who is not familiar with this author, this book provides a rare chance to sample a varied collection of his work. It will serve as a perfect introduction to a writer whose lucid style provides us with easy access to the many nuances of architectural history.

Jane Fenlon, Ph. D., is currently working as Development Officer for the Irish Georgian Society.

THE STAIRCASE AT CARRIGLAS MANOR, CO LONGFORD. *(From Christine Casey & Alistair Rowan, The Buildings of Ireland: North Leinster)*. Designed by Daniel Robertson and dating from 1843, 'the interiors of Carriglas have much of the charm of Regency Gothic continuing in the early Victorian age'.

The Buildings of Ireland: North Leinster
BY CHRISTINE CASEY AND ALISTAIR ROWAN

Penguin Books, London, 1993
pp.576. 143 plates, 68 figures. £30

Jeanne Sheehy

IN ENGLAND 'Pevsner' is an institution. Since the first volumes of *The Buildings of England* began to appear in the early 1950s, no traveller with any pretensions to culture can be without the appropriate volumes, and they are the first recourse of researchers for information on architecture and design. Even with the comparatively rich resources – county histories, record offices, photographic records, over a century-and-a-half of scholarly work – available in Britain, it is a remarkable feat of scholarship and

BOOK REVIEWS

sheer slogging industry. The personality of Nikolaus Pevsner comes through powerfully in the early editions – his enthusiasm for modernism, of which he was a leading champion, and his gradual acceptance of the qualities of Victorian architecture. Pevsner legends abound – like the story of the packets of sandwiches made at the beginning of a spell of working in the field, and labelled for each day they were to be eaten. The English series has long since been completed, many volumes have come out in revised and expanded editions, and the work continues in the hands of a generation of architectural historians inspired and trained by Nikolaus Pevsner. Volumes have also been appearing in *The Buildings of Scotland* series since 1978, and in *The Buildings of Wales* series since 1979.

In 1970 work began on *The Buildings of Ireland*, under the direction of Alistair Rowan. In some ways the enterprise was an easier one than *The Buildings of England* – the format was already there, and had only to be followed, and Ireland is a much smaller country, and is less densely populated. There are far fewer buildings. In other ways the task has been vastly more difficult. There had been very little research on Irish architecture, except in patches for the medieval and Georgian periods. There was no systematic listing, except for the work already being undertaken by the *Ulster Architectural Heritage Society*, in the north. The beginnings of *The Buildings of Ireland* are part of a renaissance of architectural history to which other contributory factors have been the decision of the editors of *A New History of Ireland* to include art and architecture, and to fund the necessary research; the teaching of architectural history in the universities; and the founding of *The Irish Architectural Archive*.

The first volume of *The Buildings of Ireland*, *North West Ulster*, appeared in 1979. *North Leinster* is the second volume to come out. It is of inestimable value in all sorts of ways, and at several levels. It provides a compact and authoritative account of the history of Irish architecture, including pre-historic remains, and a useful introduction to further reading. The gazetteer is the first systematic listing of individual buildings and monuments, from 'pleasant, ordinary old farmhouses, vernacular mills

and C19 industrial or agricultural stores ... briefly noted as good examples of a common type', through churches, houses and public buildings, to well known and grand architectural monuments such as Bective Abbey, Bellinter, Killeen Castle or St Mel's Cathedral, Longford. The volume brings together scholarship to date, and makes its own substantial contribution – because the listing is so comprehensive it provides a useful base for broader analysis and interpretation, a valuable resource for scholars. It should also reveal to people, from Ireland, and from abroad, the rich delights of Irish architecture. As the authors say in the foreword: '... all our experience has served only to reinforce the conviction that Irish buildings matter, and that a huge resource for pleasure and instruction – perhaps even for inspiration – lies almost at the door of every Irish person. Our architectural heritage is here to be enjoyed and, if properly respected (which is not always the case today), must illuminate and enrich our understanding of the course of Irish history, and should make us proud of the ingenuity and creativity of earlier generations of builders and architects'.

There are causes for great pleasure to be found in this volume, the basis for years of happy exploring. There are also many causes of depression at the destruction and mutilation of so much of our architecture. It is perhaps vain to lament the burning, in 1922, of Summerhill, but the philistinism that led to the razing of its magnificent ruin in the 1950s is by no means dead. One of the delights of this book is to discover the abundance, and quality, of Irish church architecture, and church furnishing. One's pleasure is marred, however, by the treatment of many of these buildings. Churches of the Church of Ireland are being closed, and rotting from neglect. The Catholic Church has left very few interiors unmarred by re-orderings with wall-to-wall carpets and hideous chunks of granite and bleached wood, ripping out and destroying the craftsmanship of earlier times, the testament to the religious feeling of our ancestors.

The *North West Ulster* and *North Leinster* volumes of *The Buildings of Ireland* will do much to dispel our ignorance of the treasures we possess, and

make us value them as they should be valued. Work is in hand on *East Ulster*, and on *Dublin: City and County* – but there is urgent need for something to be done about the remaining twenty-one counties.

Jeanne Sheehy is an art historian, author and Lecturer in Oxford Brookes University.

The Follies and Garden Buildings of Ireland

BY JAMES HOWLEY

Yale University Press, 1993.
Over 350 illustrations, including measured drawings, photographs, sections, ground plans as well as paintings and engravings. £35stg.

Desmond Guinness

FOLLIES HAVE always fascinated me ever since as a child I first saw the copy of the Coliseum that floats above the self-satisfied town of Oban, with its tidy shops full of tartan souvenirs, on the west coast of Scotland. How galling it must have been for generations of sensible, economical Scots to be forced to witness such mindless folly and extravagance every time they went out to take their tea and scones. A more rarefied folly that I also saw as a child was built by the eccentric Lord Berners who was a friend of my mother's; he created one of the few follies of the twentieth century near Faringdon, to the designs of the Duke of Wellington. A notice warned visitors that 'persons committing suicide from the top of this tower do so entirely at their own risk.'

When I came to live in Ireland forty years ago, the Conolly Folly aroused my interest and amazement. Built in 1740 'to answer a vistow from the bake of Castletown House' and designed by the prolific German architect Richard Castle, it was in a sorry state. A local wit remarked that if the top fell off it would lose its point. Lightning had probably struck it more than once. It was to become the first practical restoration project of the Irish Georgian Society and has been our emblem ever since. An American benefactress, Mrs Rose Saul Zalles, purchased the Conolly Folly from the Carton Estate and gave it to the Irish Georgian Society at a ceremony in Washington, DC presided over by H E William Fay. He uttered the

BOOK REVIEWS

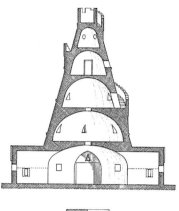

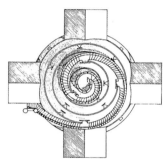

THE WONDERFUL BARN, LEIXLIP, CO KILDARE. *(From James Howley, The Follies and Garden Buildings of Ireland)*. Built in 1743, and one of the most unusual and highly functional follies in Ireland: a recent proposal to engulf it with a modern housing estate is being challenged.

immortal words; 'Finally I think we can say, that the marriage between Ireland and America, has been consummated'. The fact that the obelisk was a phallic symbol had not escaped the notice of our ambassador!

James Howley's knowledge of his subject is remarkable. He is a serious scholar, but not without the humour that this particularly peculiar subject demands. He manages to avoid a repetitious catalogue by skilfully grouping these varied structures into 'families'. This was a brainwave; it works particularly well because it enables the author to divide the book into sections. Each section is preceded by a fascinating essay on the meaning, symbolism or origins of the various building types: Obelisks, Grottoes, Hermitages, Towers and so forth. These essays are carefully considered, well written and a model of their kind. One disadvantage results from the 'family' arrangement, heavily outweighed by the advantages, which is that instead of treating it as a whole, the descriptions of a place like Larch Hill, where there is a veritable feast of follies, are spread throughout the book. With regard to

Larch Hill, near Kilcock, Co Kildare, James Howley will be glad to know that there is a new owner there now who is going to put back the lake, with its triangular island called 'Gibraltar', and use it for fishing. Another recent venture that will delight him is the recreation of the Heather House at Florence Court, Co Fermanagh by the National Trust, made possible thanks to the survival of an old photograph of the original, dating from the 1860s. The Heather House was built in the mid-eighteenth century and has been attributed by the Trust to Thomas Wright, the astronomer, mathematician and architect.

The number of follies all over Ireland is impressive and far exceeds expectations. Their hope of survival is precarious due to their being built in isolated places. The Irish Georgian Society has seen its work at several different places attract the attention of vandals. A recent proposal to engulf the Wonderful Barn at Leixlip, Co Kildare – a distinguished and unique structure roughly in the shape of a corkscrew – with a modern housing estate is being fought and the objectors were delighted that James Howley has

devoted seven pages to the Wonderful Barn; they have made good use of his book in their efforts to save its setting.

One Irish folly enjoyed the spectacle of an annual ceremony. The Browne-Clayton monument was erected on the Carlow/Wexford border by General Robert Browne-Clayton in 1839; a narrow staircase winds up to the top. It commemorates his victory over the French on 21 March, 1801. On the anniversary of this event the tricolour was seen fluttering from the top at first light but at precisely ten o'clock in the morning, the hour at which the tide of the battle turned in his favour, it was hauled down and the Union Jack hoisted in its place. The General had five hundred and fifty camel and three hundred horse and dromedaries under his command! In the next edition this remarkable tale should be included, and perhaps some day the ceremony will be re-enacted on the appropriate date; dromedaries anyone?

Desmond Guinness was co-founder and for many years President of the Irish Georgian Society. He is the author of a number of publications on Georgian buildings in Ireland.

Great Irish Houses and Castles

PHOTOGRAPHS BY JACQUELINE O'BRIEN

TEXT BY DESMOND GUINNESS

Weidenfeld and Nicolson, London, 1992.
300 col. plates, £29.95 (h/b)

Rosemary ffolliott

TO THOSE WHO LOVE houses few things are more exciting than to see other people's houses, particularly the interiors. This book takes a splendid tour through over sixty of Ireland's largest mansions, with emphasis on fascinating interior photographs that show details of stuccowork, decor and contents – a feast indeed. Inevitably, of course, with a book that has had so many worthy predecessors in the same field, a substantial number of those houses are old friends, since it is impossible to omit the like of Carton, the two Castletowns, Kilshannig, Leixlip, Bantry or Glin, amongst others, but happily not all are so familiar. It is a pleasure to see Carriglas, the recently restored Marino Casino, Cashel Palace, Strokestown and Ballywalter, not to mention the enchanting and also recently renovated Swiss Cottage – though exactly how the Hindu-Gothic *gateway* at Dromana or the Mussenden *Temple* at Downhill qualify as a 'great Irish house' is rather a puzzle! Admittedly they do make very attractive photographs.

The lay-out is a new departure for books of this kind, since the houses are arranged in approximately chronological order. Given the Irish passion for altering and 'improving' residences (far cheaper than demolition and rebuilding from scratch), the chronology can be only approximate, but a very good attempt has been made, and it does render the social changes that underlay the development of successive styles comprehensible to the layman. A sensible division is made into seven sections, beginning with impressive castles such as Dunluce and Trim, and ending with the high Victorianism of Glenveagh. Each section is prefaced by a short, general historical introduction, after which the various houses are dealt with individually. The book closes with a section on the decorative arts, painting, furniture, silver, glass, pottery and so on, an informative postscript to many of the interiors shown.

Variety and interest are added to the external shots by the inclusion of a considerable collection of aerial views, an

THE GOTHIC LIBRARY AT SLANE CASTLE. *(From Desmond Guinness & Jacqueline O'Brien, Great Irish Houses and Castles).* Originally designed by James Wyatt and completed by Francis Johnston, Slane is one of the earliest 18th century houses in Ireland to have been built in a medieval style; although damaged by the recent fire, the magnificent ceiling miraculously survived.

ideal way either to illustrate a property in its, often spectacular, rural setting, or to allow study of a complex conglomeration of buildings such as Howth Castle, Kilruddery or Russborough, though in some such instances one does long for a ground-floor plan with which to compare the air photograph. However, no book can have everything and there are good plans in Mr Guinness's earlier work, *Irish Houses and Castles.* Heartbreakingly sad is the picture of the gaunt, burned-out ruin of Powerscourt, standing blank-eyed and roofless above its magnificent garden, a terrible warning to all owners. (Since the pictures of

Slane Castle were taken before the disastrous fire in 1991 they do not provide that sense of shock).

The volume is big, handsome and showy, beautifully produced, inviting the old game of choosing one's dream house. The text fulfils its purpose well but, like most, will probably be read only once whereas the three hundred illustrations, all in colour, are an unending reservoir of delight and doubtless will be looked at over again, and yet again.

Rosemary ffolliott is co-author of The Houses of Ireland *(Thames & Hudson, London, 1975) and a former Editor of* The Irish Ancestor.

BOOK REVIEWS

Drawings from the Irish Architectural Archive

BY DAVID J GRIFFIN AND SIMON LINCOLN

Dublin, 1993
pp.80, £12.95

C E B Brett

SINCE ITS INCEPTION in 1976 as a very modest voluntary venture, the Irish Architectural Archive has grown into an important semi-public institution. This handsome paperback volume elegantly records the achievement of its courageous promoters over its first eighteen years. It falls into three parts. First, an account of the history, work, and problems of the Archive by one of its founders, that man of many parts, Nicholas Robinson. Instructive as it is, it is full also of entertaining sidelights: on salvage from skips, on the application of Vauban's techniques of fortification to headscarves, on the exact dividing-line between research and good lunches with archivally-minded friends.

Second, there is a concise (but sufficient) summary of the principal elements in the collections – now comprising over 250,000 photographs, 50,000 architectural drawings, and an extensive library, covering all thirty-two counties of Ireland (and many buildings elsewhere too).

Third, there is a selection of forty-four original drawings from the collection, almost all reproduced in colour, with scholarly explication and footnotes. The quality of the reproduction is very high, as it needs to be when very large drawings must be reduced to a width of six inches. They cover most of the major names, and quite a few of the minor names, in Irish architecture between 1675 and 1950. The Sections, often showing projected decoration and furnishing on a tiny scale, are especially delightful: as Nicholas Robinson remarks in another context, 'the appeal of a doll's house obviously goes deep.'

The printing, presentation and layout are excellent: only once did I get a nasty jar when, on page 67, I tried to reconcile an interior view of the proposed Dublin South City Markets with the caption below, which referred to a perspective view of the Holy Cross church on the Crumlin Road, Belfast: in fact, to be found on the next page. And one small quibble on the text, at the risk of incurring the charge of reviewer's oneupmanship: it

seemed a trifle ungracious not to refer to Howard Colvin's *Unbuilt Oxford* of 1983, in which he both illustrates and explains the extraordinary plan by Deane and Woodward to add a storey in the style of a French chateau to the St Aldate's front of Christ Church, Oxford.

The book is to be as strongly recommended as the institution it celebrates.

Sir Charles Brett is President of the Ulster Architectural Heritage Society and Vice Chairman of the Arts Council of Northern Ireland.

The Swiss Cottage BY SEAN O'REILLY, 1993; **Glenveagh Castle** BY WILLIAM GALLAGHER, 1993; **The Casino at Marino** BY SEAN O'REILLY, 1991; **Medieval Church Sites of North Dublin** BY MARY MCMAHON, 1991; **The Glebe House and Gallery** BY FRANCIS BAILEY, 1990

Government Stationery Office, Dublin, 1993.
Each £2 (p/b).

Barbara Dawson

THE OFFICE OF PUBLIC WORKS has recently published five small books on buildings of historical interest around the country. These include the Swiss Cottage in County Tipperary, the Glebe House and Gallery in County Donegal, Glenveagh Castle in County Donegal, the Casino in Marino, just outside Fairview in Dublin, and Medieval Church Sites of North Dublin. The books are designed as information guides for visitors and, as such, are easily readable and well illustrated. None of them exceeds sixty pages and all are generously illustrated with colour photographs. The books highlight the restoration work which has been carried out on architectural sites by the Office of Public Works. Such publications add to the interest and enjoyment of a visit to these places of cultural and historical interest.

Glenveagh Castle is perhaps one of the most spectacularly situated national monuments under the care of the Office of Public Works. In its lofty position, over the shores of Glenveagh Lake, its castellated battlements grandly survey the stark countryside of County Donegal. Its gardens are well protected by the glaciated valley. The sheltered area provides a micro climate in which beautiful and exotic trees and shrubs, not found anywhere else in Ulster, flourish. Built in

the nineteenth century by the notorious John Adair, the castle is a perfect example of a Victorian romantic desire for a highland retreat, a fashion set by the Queen and Prince Albert when they acquired Balmoral in the Scottish Highlands. The history of John Adair as a landlord and his relationship with the tenants of the Glenveagh area was a brutal and unhappy chapter in the history of the castle. His wife, and later widow, Cornelia Richie, whom he met and married during one of his many business trips to New York, lived happily in the castle after his death and did much to soften the harsh memory of her husband.

The castle had only three owners before coming under public care and so never fell into disrepair and ruin like many other Irish buildings. In 1936 the estate was purchased by the McIlhenny family from Philadelphia and remained in their hands until the death of Henry McIlhenny in 1986. Mr McIlhenny, a former curator of the Philadelphia Museum of Modern Art, set about softening the harsh and, what he considered, inelegant interior of the castle. He bought much exquisite eighteenth century Irish furniture and silver and built up a collection of Victorian art at a time when it was considered rather unfashionable. After his death, many of the furnishings and paintings were left to the Philadelphia Museum of Art, including a pair of Landseer paintings, which are now replaced by original engravings. While it is lamentable that so many of the original furnishings have left the castle, the gardens are considered Mr McIlhenny's greatest legacy to the nation. With the assistance and advice of Lanning Roper, with whom he became acquainted while at Harvard, and the English gardener, Jim Russell, Henry McIlhenny turned Glenveagh into one of the most important gardens in Europe. The rare and unusual vegetation is organised in informal secluded walks, converging on stunning vistas of the landscape. Today the castle is open to the public from Easter until the end of October.

Another publication in the series highlights the fact that Glenveagh Castle is not the only estate under the care of the care of the nation in Donegal. Equally important and interesting is the Glebe House and Gallery, formerly the

THE SWISS COTTAGE, CO TIPPERARY. *(From Sean O'Reilly, The Swiss Cottage).* This early 19th century 'cottage orné' had fallen into disrepair and was restored in the 1980's in part through the generosity of Mrs Sally Aall. It was transferred to the State in 1989.

home of the artist Derek Hill. This book gives a succinct and interesting account of Derek Hill as an artist and liberally illustrates his work and indeed the interesting interiors of the house, locally known as St Columb's. Although a few miles distance from Glenveagh, the gardens experience a completely different climate. Unlike Glenveagh, which stands on the edge of a lake which never freezes over, in an area which is sheltered from the harsh northerly winds, St Columb's, by contrast, is situated in a frost pocket of the valley and is exposed to the winds from every angle. However, despite this, the gardens are spectacular, enhanced by mature broad-leafed trees.

The Office of Public Works' programme carried out at the Casino at Marino restored this cultural gem of eighteenth-century architecture to its original state. It is part of the First Earl of Charlemont, James Caulfeild's, legacy to the city. Designed by William Chambers, the Casino is complemented by Lord Charlemont's town house, Charlemont House, in Parnell Square, now the home of the Hugh Lane Municipal Gallery of Modern Art.

All five publications convey an interesting and historical account of the

subject. One or two of the photographs in the books are deprived of a caption, which is somewhat frustrating, but otherwise the books are carefully laid out, informative and well written.

Such books as these should be translated into other European languages, providing our foreign visitors with additional information on our architectural heritage, leading to greater enjoyment on their visits to our national monuments.

Barbara Dawson is Director of the Hugh Lane Municipal Gallery of Modern Art, Dublin.

Letters from Georgian Ireland: The Correspondence of Mary Delany (1731-68)

EDITED BY ANGÉLIQUE DAY

Friar's Bush Press, Belfast.

£17.95 (h/b), £9.95 (p/b)

Sybil Connolly

A selection of the delightful correspondence of Mrs Delany has recently appeared in paperback. Sybil Connolly, a leading fashion designer who was inspired by Mrs Delany and her flower collages to design a range of china and fabrics for Tiffanys and who wrote a foreword to the book, here

introduces this most artistic wife of an eighteenth-century Dean of Down:

MARY DELANY RESISTS definitions. Her correspondence (1731-68) reproduced in Angelique Day's absorbing book shows her to be an acute student of human nature, a champion of high morals, a vivid and charming stylist and many other things besides. No one description tells nearly enough and indeed it is hard to decide which of her qualities to place in the centre.

The great attraction for readers of this book is that the style of her writing is part of a self-portrait. Mrs Delany reveals a woman, and that woman becomes a friend. In her letters she addresses the reader in her natural everyday language thereby presenting herself exactly as she was. She gains a friendly communication with her audience and I suspect that this is what she wanted. Abstract notions live and breathe under her pen; the letters are formal, luxuriant in images, spontaneous, in order reigning from the epigrammatic to the rambling and associative. One of the mysteries of good letter-writing, and part of its attraction, is how a note is struck in the reader, which can echo so sincerely one's own thoughts and experiences, that it seems as though one had written it oneself.

As a chronicler of her time, there was very little of importance that escaped her attention. In doing research on the history of printed materials in Ireland, I was amused to come across a reference to Mrs Delany. She is described as 'Mrs Delany, the diarist and maker of flower mosaics' and her remarks refer to 'Drumcondra' printed linens done from metal plates (a method never before practised) and invented by one Francis Nixon of Drumcondra. Mrs Delany found them 'excessively pretty.'

The years spent at Delville, Dr Delany's house in Dublin, were one of the happiest periods of Mary Delany's life. She had a lovely home, a beautiful garden and the constant affection of Dr Delany who encouraged Mary to persevere in her artistic work – embroidery, shell-work, writing, painting and drawing filled the hours of day-light, books were read aloud in the evening, enabling Mrs Delany to keep up to date with what was new in literature. Dr Delany never ceased to marvel at the variety of his wife's talents; he was prompted to remark to a friend 'she works even between the cooling of her tea.'

Mrs Delany made a point of entertaining at home and going out into society; she felt it was a duty incumbent on us to live socially, although she confessed to enjoying the occasional 'sweet solitary day.' She was convinced that happiness came through building up one's interests, as to rely solely on outside diversions was not to lay the foundations of a happy old age. Her letters are full of life-enhancing advice, as relevant today as it was two hundred years ago.

Sybil Connolly is a leading fashion designer who has written books on Irish houses and gardens.

Jack B Yeats, his Watercolours, Drawings and Pastels
BY HILARY PYLE
Irish Academic Press, Dublin 1993 pp.214, £65

The Art of Jack B Yeats
BY T G ROSENTHAL
Andre Deutsch, London, 1993 pp.308, £35stg

James White

IF I WERE ASKED by someone who knew absolutely nothing about Ireland to give them an introduction, I would hand them this catalogue by Hilary Pyle, so that they could peruse the pictures and notes provided with them. My reason for this statement is that as a rule catalogues of works of art give the relevant details but rarely that sense of the life of the subject or the quality of the theme.

In the 729 works included here, almost every other one bears a description which enlivens the photograph accompanying it. For instance, about No. 446, 'The Baker Rode a Piebald' we read 'A humorous, cartoon-like frolic of a horse flying over a wide landscape, while his baker mount, holding fast, his coat and apron flying in the wind, wears his bread basket on his head. In greens and browns.' In No. 639, 'The Widow Woman' we read 'The widow woman sits behind the counter in her shop, ready to hand out porter and gossip and pieces of her mind and to take in the filling of the till.'

Having read each entry with growing enjoyment I felt that I had been introduced to a cross-section of life in the West of Ireland such as I had never appreciated fully before, even though I

have spent quite a part of my early life there. But Hilary Pyle's understanding of Jack B's world is remarkable, as those who are familiar with her *Biography* of 1970 will fully appreciate.

This book is an absolute necessity for the art student because Yeats's oil paintings grew out of the works here described. There is a most excellent introduction outlining his watercolour methodology and for good measure the 233 sketch books are listed with their date and, where possible, the region in which he made the sketches. There are also 25 colour reproductions included, and the last one is a joyous discovery for me, a full page crayon of George Bernard Shaw playing the spoons in the traditional Irish manner, hilariously jiving, with his face a collage from a newspaper, but equally alive and amusing.

I have to confess that I approached T G Rosenthal's book with a feeling of 'surely not another'. But I ended up by really having enjoyed it. It is a beautifully produced volume, coffee-table size, which on world bookshelves at £35 sterling is going to seem a very good buy, considering that it contains 244 large reproductions of the oils, of which 111 are in full colour.

It places the artist in his Irish milieu, not only in terms of his painting but also of his writing in relation to Joyce, Synge, Masefield, his father John Butler Yeats and Tom MacGreevy , but not Beckett, whose *Hommage* of 1944 is reproduced as part of the introduction, but whom Jack B did not admire as he thought Beckett to be immoral, Rosenthal tells us. He gives quotations from his novels and plays and draws our attention to the fact that he published his last book *The Careless Flower* only ten years before he died. 'Thus he wrote for almost as long as he painted and for any true understanding of his work we should read the books as carefully as we look at his art'.

For such a splendidly produced volume the writer's text is comparatively short. But he does give a good summary of the events of Yeats's life, setting out all the relevant facts which led to the works of art and enabling the casual reader looking for a brief introduction to be well informed. Consequently one can regard it as taking its own place in the Jack B literature as a work ideally suited to the needs of those in search of infor-

mation without having to become immersed in the full documentation.

Rosenthal also pays a full tribute to the work of Hilary Pyle, who supplied him with the Bibliography, Chronology, Lists of Exhibitions and notes on the plates. His final appreciation of the artist, with which I am in complete agreement, reads 'Mere fecundity does not imply, let alone bestow, greatness. Yeats, however, managed to combine the two. The meticulous draughtsman of the last century became the heavy impasto, almost abstract virtuoso of the late paintings. The shrewdly observant reporter who accompanied Synge became the watercolourist who haunted and brought to life the race tracks and the boxing booths and the fairgrounds. The friend of Masefield created a world of jetties, harbours, sailors and pirates, more nautical and piratical than we have ever seen before. Above all the oil painter gave us four decades of continually developing canvases which constitute not only the most powerful group of paintings ever done in Ireland but, as with his friend Kokoschka, a colossal contribution to the humanist tradition of European painting, not only in this century but for the whole of Europe's art history.'

James White is a former Director of the National Gallery of Ireland. Among his most recent publications is the biography of Gerard Dillon (Wolfhound Press, Dublin 1993).

Jack B Yeats: a Catalogue of the Oil Paintings
BY HILARY PYLE
Andre Deutsch, London, 1992 3 volumes, £450

Homan Potterton

THE PUBLICATION OF Hilary Pyle's long-awaited catalogue raisonné of the oil paintings of Ireland's favourite artist, Jack B Yeats, has for years been one of the most keenly-anticipated events in the sphere of Irish art. Miss Pyle's knowledge of Yeats – both of his art and of his world – is unmatched; her superb biography of the painter was first published almost a quarter of a century ago; she has had unstinted access to all the artist's papers and sketchbooks still in the possession of his family; and it has long been known that over the years – or decades – since the catalogue was first ready for the press, according as pictures changed hands or were published or exhibited, she has assiduously up-dated her manuscript. In addition to her scholarship, Hilary Pyle is also exceptionally thorough in her marshalling of facts and, furthermore, she writes beautifully.

Although publication of this monumental work – descriptions of 1194 paintings and illustrations of most – was a colossal task it was still always a mystery why no publisher was easily forthcoming to undertake the project: 1194 paintings, after all, means almost the same number of owners (all likely purchasers of a catalogue) and Yeats's unflagging popularity on the art-market must mean a continuing interest in such a book. The sales of a Yeats catalogue raisonné, therefore, must almost be guaranteed.

In the light of this, it will seem mean-spirited to say that the pseudo-lavish, twenty-one pound (avoirdupois), four hundred and fifty pound (sterling), three-volume, limited edition (1,550 copies) boxed set which Andre Deutsch has now brought out is a disappointment. It is pretentious, unnecessary in its grandeur, and very far from being the beautiful collector's edition the publishers pretend it to be. More to the point, the volumes are exceptionally unwieldy and cumbersome so that to consult any of them requires a feat of physical endeavour that would tax even the most hearty. Furthermore, Miss Pyle's excellent text is very ill-served by such features as the grey smudges that are intended as thumbnail reference illustrations to some – but not all – the paintings (volume 3 contains proper plates); and the acres of blank paper which are necessitated by a layout of one catalogue entry to a page in most – but not all – cases add to the tedium. By contrast, the much more modest volume devoted to the works on paper (published by Irish Academic Press and reviewed elsewhere in this issue), is an example of publishing excellence (and good sense).

All of this is a great pity, but as the text remains the copyright of the author and the paintings themselves the copyright of the artist's estate, let us hope that all 1550 copies of this boxed monstrosity will soon find their way to the libraries of the rich and super-rich and that the way will thereby be paved for a more sensible edition produced by a

Jack B YEATS (1871-1957): Caballero. *Oil on canvas, 35.5 x 45.5 cm. (From Hilary Pyle, Jack B. Yeats: a catalogue of the oil paintings).* Painted in 1949, the picture was purchased in 1954 by the American Yeats collector, Dr Eleanor Reid. It was sold at Sotheby's, London in November 1993 for £32,000.

more sensible publisher.

Volume one begins with a chronology of the artist's life: a handy reference tool that documents his activities almost year by year. Next is the Introduction, a concise weaving together of the painter's movements, the influences which prevailed at different stages, the development of his art, his symbols, and in many cases quite a copious analysis of individual pictures in context. The change in style from the early West of Ireland watercolours to what the author refers to as 'the prolific forties' (when he painted as many as eighty canvases a year) to the excitement of the late works is described before other issues – such as the relationship with his extraordinary family, in particular the poet W B – are discussed. 'Nationalism' and 'J M Synge' are other headings here but missing is any extended attempt to place the painter or his art in an international context. That is perhaps because he defies any such examination: a line from the 'Chronology' for the penultimate year of his life reads bluntly, 'Letter from Oskar Kokoschka' and possibly that is all that it is necessary to say in this respect. The role of the dealer, Victor

Waddington, with whom Yeats first exhibited in Dublin in 1943 (when he was already seventy-two) is mentioned without being expanded upon. Waddington marketed Yeats in a way that no other Irish artist before him had been and without that one wonders if Jack would have emerged as 'Ireland's greatest painter' quite so soon or, indeed, if his reputation would ever have been as secure as it has been now for nigh on half a century. Miss Pyle's catalogue descriptions are definitive. Full of background information, much of it gleaned from Jack's own papers, and descriptions – often quite lyrical – which nicely convey the author's empathy with her subject.

As early as 1904, at the time of Jack's exhibition in New York (which was a disaster – 'the personal charm of sketches made by a tourist ... amateur ...' was how the *New York Times* described it) the artist irritated his New York patron, John Quinn, by his carelessness: 'his drawing is very bad in some of his pictures,' Quinn wrote to AE, and later, 'he ought to take more pains with his work; to exhibit fewer pictures'. This carelessness with technique persisted throughout his career

BOOK REVIEWS

resulting, as Miss Pyle points out, in the 'frequent deterioration of his pictures'. She excuses him, however: 'an arbitrary ... approach to technique had been essential because Yeats's mind – at all periods – teamed with ideas which spilled out erratically'.

Hilary Pyle's catalogue permits of a fairly thorough assessment or re-assessment of Yeats's work. Its bulky format reminds one of the huge nineteenth-century monographs that were produced in honour of 'great' contemporary Salon artists whose reputations at the time seemed quite secure but who later fell out of favour. Inconceivable though it may seem, is there a possibility that a similar fate might also await Jack B Yeats? If that happens then we will have all the more reason to be grateful for the years of diligence which Miss Pyle has devoted to this marvellous achievement.

Sir John Lavery
BY KENNETH MCCONKEY
Canongate Press, Edinburgh pp.232. £30 (h/b)

Ciarán MacGonigal

JOHN LAVERY was the brilliant portraitist of the Belle Époque, the Society Man, the Irish nationalist, and a Glasgow Boy. He was also the most French of the Franco-British painters at the turn into the twentieth century.

Kenneth McConkey gives us a very handsome and well laid out book on Lavery and with infinite patience and skill traces Lavery's life in every significant aspect. One of the areas which comes to the fore is the fact that whereas a painter may paint to order he cannot like to order, and this comes through in quite a number of the portraits by Lavery.

Lavery was technically very skilled and could as a result undertake many, probably too many, commissions. That being said, it is interesting to note that the accusation of technical perfection levelled against the two Irish knights of painting, Lavery and Orpen, is one which would not be applied today to say, David Hockney. Where Lavery is dismissed for his pictorial accounts of his travels in Egypt and Morocco, Hockney is lauded for his travels to Egypt and China. The painter's response to a subject is his own, different to, let us say, that of the photographer, and that

response includes the societal element in the painter's time.

Sadly for Lavery, much of what he has recorded has changed so much that the social motifs are as remote to us today as those of the dinosaur period. Much of what Lavery essays could be thought of as a history of a lifestyle, and the painterly element is overlooked, social nuance being sought instead by art historians and critics.

In McConkey's book I find the repetition of the Hazel paintings towards the end of her life tedious and do not do justice to Lavery's talents as a colourist. I think the Van Dyck interior at Wilton is a great painting of its period, as much for the sensation of continuity expressed in the composition as for the handling of the pigment. By treating the sitters as part of the furniture or as ancestral portraits hanging on the walls, Lavery the Irish painter gives life and historical perspective to a great English family.

The brio with which he painted this and other interiors, notably for the Sassoons and Lady Cholmondely, renders them masterpieces of their period. So, too, are the jockeys whom he painted with great feeling; the aeroplane sequences, as well as the London bombings, are also very telling and skilful.

His Irish pictures, I find, leave my withers unrung. His dead Collins may be an icon, and the Blessing of the Colours an emotional reaction, but not for me, thank you! They don't involve me in the core feeling which Lavery undoubtedly had for an emerging Ireland; I am left admiring but cold. Even the use of Hazel as an emblematic Ireland I find too contrived and artificial. That being said, the image has joined the other Irish icons as a standard reference point for an Irish iconography.

His portraits of Lord Carson and Cardinal Logue (which is full of simian menace) are very revealing, and one wishes that the Ulster Museum group of Lavery's work could be seen in Dublin.

The author chronicles Lavery in a most painstaking way, but without, I fear, a sense of the society in which Lavery lived. This is an essential part of the bifurcating nature of Lavery the painter, which may not be politically correct today but is a key to understanding how and why Lavery did what he did.

I can remember being told by my

father that when John Lavery died during the war, Eamon de Valera gave the RHA, through my father, £6-10s for funeral expenses to get a car and petrol coupons to attend the burial in Co. Kilkenny of this great Irish artist.

McConkey has delivered a worthy account of Lavery's life and work. The book is a splendid reference work, with good indices and lots of illustrations, and is thus an essential for the library of any scholar. At the same time the author delivers the painter in a clear and comprehensive way to his reader, and tidies up many of the grey areas surrounding this often underrepresented painter and chronicler of the early twentieth century.

Ciarán MacGonigal is Director of the Royal Hibernian Academy Gallagher Gallery, Dublin.

Frank McKelvey. A Painter in His Time
BY S B KENNEDY
Irish Academic Press, Dublin 1993. pp.96. 13 colour and 25 b&w ills. £29.95 (h/b)

Rosemarie Mulcahy

DR S B KENNEDY, Curator of Twentieth Century Art at the Ulster Museum and author of *Irish Art and Modernism (1880-1950)* (reviewed in *Irish Arts Review Yearbook*, 1993, Vol. 9, pp.167-69) is eminently equipped to write this monograph, which was commissioned by Irish Academic Press as part of their rapidly expanding Irish Art list. Francis Baird McKelvey (1895-1974), son and grandson of decorators, was Belfast-born. He had a consistently prizewinning career at Belfast College of Art between 1909-17. A *Study of an Old Woman*, dated 1916, is evidence of his early skill – which was to be sustained – and of promise of feeling rarely fulfilled, alas, in later academic portraits, of which no fewer than six were included in *Irish Portraits by Ulster Artists* (1927, Belfast Museum & Art Gallery).

Frank McKelvey was one of the Northern Painters of the newly created Northern Ireland State along with Humbert Craig, Charles Lamb and Paul Henry, who 'compared to the best known of their (republican) Southern counterparts, Keating and MacGonigal, were more concerned with the landscape itself and were not at all interested in socio-political interpretations of it.'

Throughout his long working life he painted the landscapes, coastal views and farmsteads around Belfast, and in the counties of Antrim and Donegal. Intermittently, over a period of twenty years he recorded the buildings of 'Old Belfast', now in the Ulster Museum. Perhaps, his most personal and appealing pictures are the farmyard scenes with hens, in which he captured the dappled play of light and evoked an atmosphere of rural tranquillity. One of these might with advantage have been reproduced in colour. From his late twenties, McKelvey was highly regarded in Belfast, Dublin and Glasgow. From the age of twenty-three he exhibited each year at the RHA. Victor Waddington gave him his first Dublin one-man show in 1937, and again in 1939, which was very favourably reviewed for 'insistent appeal' and 'power and vitality'. In 1930 he was included in major exhibitions abroad, *Works by Irish Artists in New York* and *Irish Art in Brussels*, and again in New York in 1950.

This book is handsomely produced, with comprehensive notes, bibliography, list of exhibitions and index. There are thirteen colour plates, mostly of landscapes, which span a period of forty years, and although not altogether uniform in technique, show little development.

Dr Rosemarie Mulcahy is an art historian and author whose latest publication is The Decoration of the Royal Basilica of El Escorial *(CUP 1994)*

Gerard Dillon: An Illustrated Biography
BY JAMES WHITE
Wolfhound Press, Dublin,
1993. £29.99 (h/b)

Martyn Anglesea

THIS BOOK WAS written at the request of the artist's sister Molly, by a critic who has since 1942 been an enthusiastic champion of Gerard Dillon and his work. Knowing this, the reader would expect the author to be biased. So he is, and I find no fault with this. Molly Dillon supplied James White with many of Gerard's scribbled notes and copious written memoirs of her own. They are quoted to the full, letting the artist speak for himself. The best biographers modestly keep themselves in the background. The early chapters are an object-lesson in sectarian

sociology. Gerard Dillon, born in April 1916, was the youngest of eight children of a post-office sorter who lived in a tiny house in Lower Clonard Street, in the Catholic Falls Road area of Belfast.

His father and two of his brothers were pro-British and served in the British army, whereas his mother was a bigoted Catholic nationalist who hated all that the British Empire, including Northern Ireland, stood for. The family rows must have been dire. In fact one of them is quoted at length. Gerard's child-hood was dominated by his mother's private mythology of 'wee women saints and holy souls'. His liberation from this claustrophobia, though never complete, came through his apprenticeship as a house-painter and his various escapes, first to pre-war London, then to Connemara, and to wartime, neutral Dublin where his self-taught talent as an imaginative painter was recognised. White does not flinch from alluding to a piece of his own art criticism of the time causing Dillon annoyance by using the expression 'stage Irish'. (I seem to remember Herbert Read describing the work of one of Dillon's favourite painters, Marc Chagall, as 'schmaltz'). The narrative flags somewhat in the middle chapters, degenerating into a pedestrian list of exhibitions and

reviews. Emphasis is, however, placed on Dillon's fascination with unusual media such as sewn leather, found objects and monotype. It recovers in the concluding chapters which detail Dillon's loss of his convenient quarters in Abbey Road, North London, his subsequent priva-tions, the loss of his brothers and the decline of his health. At this time the poignant figure of the broken-hearted pierrot appears frequently in Dillon's paintings. When Dillon moved to Dublin to share a house with Arthur Armstrong for the last three years of his life, a final idyllic fulfilment seemed to ensue. For the first time in his life, Dillon accepted practical tuition when he learnt to etch at the graphic studio, and a delightful, self-written account is quoted of the painting demonstrations he gave to schoolchildren in the National Gallery, organised by James White. The book is nicely produced and makes an attractive present. There are a few errors in proof-reading, and one irritating thing about its design is that the captions for the illustrations are awkwardly placed and hard to find. Despite these flaws, I greatly enjoyed reading it.

Martyn Anglesea is Curator of Watercolours in the Ulster Museum Belfast

GERARD DILLON (1916-71): *A figure in a Bedroom.* Oil on board, 28 x 38 cm. *(From James White, Gerard Dillon: an illustrated biography).* 'James White has, since 1942, been an enthusiastic champion of Gerard Dillon and his work.'

BOOK REVIEWS

Irish Paintings
BY BRIAN P KENNEDY

Town House and Country House, Dublin, 1993.
pp 141. 66 col. plates. £25.95 (h/b)

Peter Murray

BRIAN P KENNEDY's previous writings have dwelt largely in areas of passing interest to the general reader. His account of the cultural politics surrounding Alfred Chester Beatty and Ireland is a valuable source for future historians, but is unlikely to be widely read. His subsequent history of government arts policy in Ireland did make the headlines, but this was caused by the Arts Council shredding several hundred copies which had remained stubbornly unsold, thus raising the spectre of official censorship. In fact, the Council director's irritation with the offending volumes was due more to their poor marketability than with the contents therein: he was seeking more office space.

Perhaps chastened by these experiences, Dr Kennedy has now produced a volume which is eminently marketable and entirely non-controversial. One hundred and forty-one large pages feature magnificent colour reproductions of Irish paintings from the past three centuries. The author is careful to specify that several of these 'Irish' paintings are by English artists such as Malton and Wheatley and that their Irishness resides principally in the fact that they were created in this country. The traffic in talent was of course, two-way, with Barry, Danby, Mulready, O'Connor and Maclise all heading for London after their initial studies in Ireland. Kennedy selects sixty-four paintings and Evie Hone's stained glass window at Eton to represent the surprising breadth and richness of the visual art that we can justly call Irish. The seventeenth- and eighteenth-century portraits, by Wright, Morphy, Jervas, Latham and Fry are particularly impressive. There is a good balance struck between portraiture and landscape, between historical and contemporary scenes and between urban and rural. Only one or two inclusions seem a bit dodgy, and they are all twentieth-century. Francis Bacon while he was alive strenuously resisted attempts to label him an Irish artist, but as he is included here we must assume he had a deathbed conversion. Sean O'Sullivan's portrait of Eamon de Valera captures well the Irish leader's patrician disapproval of the world, but it is not a remarkable painting. There are no abstract paintings included, which is a great pity. This book is a feast of visual delight even for those familiar with the paintings, while the standard of photography and printing is excellent. These Hong Kong printers do a good job; let us hope that some of them settle here in 1997.

Fifty Treasures from the Hunt Collection
BY PATRICK F DORAN WITH A FOREWORD BY THE KNIGHT OF GLIN

Hunt Museum Executive, Limerick, 1993. £35

Ronald Lightbown

IN THE EARLY 1960s John Hunt was a figure I would occasionally see. Silver-haired and faultlessly dressed in a style that only those over fifty will remember, he would produce from his pocket some exciting object, a Renaissance jewel or medieval fragment and speak of it with quiet-voiced enthusiasm. His like is no longer with us. The 1960s saw the end of the years during which collectors like Hunt could buy major medieval, Renaissance and Baroque objects at prices which now, looking back, seem derisory. He exemplified one great truth about collecting, that when those claiming enlightened taste reject whole classes of works of art on arbitrary critical grounds, as was very much the case from the 1920s to the 1950s, one or two collectors like Hunt, whose feeling for the past is archaeological and antiquarian as well as aesthetic, can quietly buy during the general neglect, and by assembling great collections, retrieve some of the losses created by past vandalism or by ideological rage. The dramatic rise in art prices, the abandonment of all prejudice against periods like the Baroque or the Victorian, the recovery of an appreciation of design craftsmanship and ornament, make it unlikely that his achievement will be soon repeated.

Hunt was fortunate in collecting as works of art objects many of which were in his day still left to archaeologists and antiquarians. Some of these owed their first dispersal to the Reformation, others to the suppressions and secularisations of churches and convents begun during the French Revolution and the Napoleonic Wars and continued by some governments, for instance that of Spain, during the nineteenth century. For works of this kind Hunt, as a devout Catholic, had an especial feeling. In leaving his collections to Ireland, a country rich in major works of art made before 1150 AD but poor in relics of the periods that followed until the eighteenth century, Hunt was inspired by the wish to introduce to Ireland, and particularly to young Irish people, examples of arts not well represented in public collections here. The Hunt Collection, when finally assembled and displayed, will give Ireland, as was the intention of its founders, a rich and varied impression of European sculpture and the decorative arts from many epochs.

The paintings and works of art illustrated in this selection presented by Professor Doran show that Hunt's taste extended beyond the traditional interests of nineteenth century collectors, which to some extent he inherited, to Renoir, Gauguin, and the art of Mexico and Benin. He was, in fact, very valuably for a collector, both behind and abreast of his own times. Professor Doran has wisely chosen to illustrate the catholicity of his taste by presenting fifty coloured plates, each with a short descriptive text, of works of art ranging from a beautiful silver coin of Syracuse, issued c.405 BC to a painting by Jack B Yeats. However, it is the Dark Age and medieval metalwork, including some important Irish pieces, and the ivories of the same period, most notably some major English pieces, that are the great distinction of the collection, as Professor Doran has recognised by the number of plates he has allotted to them, about a third of the whole. His publication is intended to introduce the collection to a non-specialist public, and begins admirably its wider publicisation. A short introduction gives some account of John Hunt and the contribution of his wife and family to the collection, and of their educational aims in presenting it to Ireland. It is now to be finally installed in the eighteenth-century Limerick Custom House, and in a separate study the Knight of Glin gives an interesting account of this fine building, designed by Davis Ducart.

R W Lightbown is an art historian and author of a number of books on medieval jewellery and Renaissance painting and was for many years on the staff of the Victoria and Albert Museum, London.

Michael SCOTT (1905-89): The Irish Pavilion at the New York World's Fair, 1939 (From Michael Scott 1905-1989 one of the titles in Gandon Editions 'Works' series). The plan of the building was based on the shamrock and the sculpture (by Frederick Herkner) was inspired by W B Yeats's line, 'Your Mother Eire is always young.'

The Works Series on Modern Irish Art

EDITED BY JOHN O'REGAN

Gandon Editions, Oysterhaven, Co Cork.
12 vols., pp 32 each. av. 16 col. plates. £3.99 (p/b)

Peter Murray

I HAVE BEEN ASKED to review in two hundred words no less than twelve small books produced by Gandon Editions on individual Irish artists and architects. It is quite impossible. In order to get some idea of the delights and revelations contained in this excellent series you will have to go out and buy them yourself, which would be no bad thing. The mini-monographs published to date feature Patrick Hickey and Andrew Folan, both printmakers of note; sculptors Vivienne Roche and James Scanlon, painters Patrick Hall, Charles Brady, Michael Cullen, Mary Fitzgerald. Patrick Graham, and photographer John T Davis. The architect Michael Scott richly deserves his volume, as do O'Donnell and Tuomey for their Irish Pavilion devised and constructed in collaboration with artist Brian Maguire. It is described as moral architecture and to find out more you must buy volume 8. I get the impression that the Works series is directed more by the editor's personal

taste than by a rigid editorial board policy. This is a matter of some relief and indicates that an art publisher with some vision is at work here. It is heartening to see origination and printing of this quality carried out in Dublin and each one of the small paperback books is characterised by the elegant and precise design which is the hallmark of Gandon Editions.

Dr Peter Murray is Director of the Crawford Municipal Art Gallery , Cork.

Megalithic Art BY MUIRIS O'SULLIVAN; Early Celtic Art in Ireland BY EAMONN P KELLY; Metal Craftsmanship in Early Ireland BY MICHAEL RYAN; The Road to Freedom: Photographs and Memorabilia from the 1916 Rising and Afterwards BY MICHAEL KENNY

Country House in association with The National Museum of Ireland, Dublin, 1993
4 vols. each, £4.95 (p/b)

Rachel Moss

MEGALITHIC TATTOOING, Celtic fertility symbols, Irish prisoner art from 1913 to 1923, and the fallacy that Vikings attacked Irish monasteries solely for their

art treasures: these are some of the topics covered in four slender texts recently published by Country House in association with the National Museum of Ireland. Written by some of the most respected authors in their individual fields, they provide the introductory reader to these areas with clear and succinct texts, covering both artistic and historic themes. All four books are well produced, accessible to a general audience and are well illustrated with high quality photography.

The illustration of Michael Ryan's volume, covering an era of Irish art long ignored by authors, is particularly good, with some excellent details of the minute work which exemplifies what has become known as the 'Golden Age' of Irish art.

The volumes on artistic themes deal with materials, technique, influences, and chronology of styles, singling out specific works for closer attention. Muiris O'Sullivan and Eamonn P Kelly also take a closer look at the enigmatic symbolism of Megalithic and Celtic art, which has intrigued generations of archaeologists and art historians. They do not break any new ground, but it is not the intention to do so. Instead, a brief but thorough discussion is presented on each topic, whetting the appetite for further study. Short glossaries are also provided for those who confuse their lentoids with their lintels.

Michael Kenny provides an objective chronology of the events leading up to the 1916 Rising, the War of Independence, culminating in national independence in 1922. The merit of this volume, apart from the concise narrative of events which led to Ireland's independence, lies in the illustrations that punctuate the book. It contains a wealth of rare contemporary photographs and memorabilia from the collection of the National Museum, much of which is rarely available to the public eye.

Limitations of size mean that these volumes are restricted in their academic value. Instead, they are intended more for the generally interested reader, or as a student's introductory text. The reasonable price of the books, at £4.95 each, means that they are also financially accessible to this type of readership.

Rachel Moss is a post-graduate student at Trinity College Dublin

BOOK REVIEWS

Onlookers in France

BY JULIAN CAMPBELL

*Catalogue of an exhibition of Irish Realist
and Impressionist Painters at the Crawford Gallery,
Cork 1993*

Vera Ryan

ONLOOKERS IN FRANCE: *Irish Realist and
Impressionist Painters* was selected and
catalogued by Julian Campbell as guest
curator at the Crawford Gallery. The
exhibition was an important opportunity
for him to present his ongoing research
on Irish artists in France, although it was
sensibly and successfully pitched for general appeal. It was an intimate,
attractive exhibition of nearly three
dozen works, done between the 1870s
and the First World War, many of them
small scale and painted in the plein air
conservative tradition so important to
nineteenth-century Irish art. Familiar
pictures from public collections, for
example Roderic O'Conor's *Breton Girl*
(1890) hung with lesser known or
recently rediscovered works like
Nathaniel Hill's *Sunshine, Brittany*
(1884) and William Hennessy's *Fete Day
in a Cider Orchard, Normandy* (1878).

A strength of the selection was how
many facets it showed of Irish art activity in France in the later part of the
nineteenth century. The grim social
realism of Augustus Burke's *At the
Chapel Door* (1876) contrasted with the
picturesque Osbornes and Hones and
gave this interesting artist, born before
the Famine into a landlord family in
Galway, a good showing.

Stanhope Forbes' wonderful *Fair
Measures: a Shop in Quimperle* (1883)
hung very harmoniously with Gerald
Barry's *Time Flies* (1887), both contrasting youth and old age, but it and the
Chetwood Aiken picture did beg the
interesting question of national identity
and the nineteenth-century Irish artist.
Are Forbes or Aiken Irish? The pursuit
of an answer brings up interesting historical issues and helps set the artist in the
context of their own time.

An emphasis on work of local interest
motivated the inclusion of Gibson's
minor but interesting watercolour of
buildings destroyed during the Franco-
Prussian war. Gibson, a great benefactor
to the Crawford Gallery was the only
amateur included. Edith Somerville's
drawings of Colarossi's in 1886 convey

the atmosphere of this atelier where
women were welcome; the French atelier, a great leveller without colonial
implications, was so important to all
foreign artists.

Sarah Purser's Degas-like *Le Petit
Deieuner* (1885) gained from its proximity
to Sarah Cecilia Harrison's jewel-like *Self
Portrait* (1890). More realist than impressionist and, like most of the work in the
exhibition, formally non-innovative,
these two splendid portraits and Leech's
The Barber Shop (c.1910) held their own
among the plein air pictures. I was sorry
Orpen's *The Bedroom, Cannes* (1900) was
not included here, especially since the
title of the exhibition came from Orpen's
book. However, Aloysius O'Kelly's *Girl in
a Meadow* was adequately evocative of
Millais, who was exhibited in the RHA in
the 1880s, to remind us of the strong
influence British art had on many artists
who looked to France.

The scale of the exhibition and the
choice of pictures greatly encouraged
focus on paint handling. The sense of
the picture as object complemented the
stimulating plurality of ideas presented
in *Onlookers in France*.

As well as exhibiting important pictures from private and public collections,
it gave context to half a dozen or so
Crawford ones. It was a valuable and
appreciated exhibition.

*Vera Ryan is a Lecturer in the Crawford Art
College, Cork.*

The Life and Works of
Augustus Saint Gaudens

BURKE WILKINSON

*Dover Publications Inc., New York and Colin Smythe
Ltd., Gerrards Cross, England. £9.95*

Paula Murphy

A SCULPTOR'S LIFE is a tough one,
according to the American sculptor,
Augustus Saint Gaudens, because he
has to deal constantly 'with moulders,
contractors, derricks, stone-men, ropes,
builders, scaffolding, marble-assistants,
bronze men, trucks, rubbish men, plas-
terers and what-not else, all the while
trying to soar into the blue'. This
description indicates the extent to
which a monumental sculptor engaged
in public work is not an independent
artist. The quotation is taken from

Burke Wilkinson's life of the artist, but
the original words have their source in
Saint Gaudens's own *Reminiscences* published in 1913. In fact Wilkinson is
obliged to quote frequently from this
early publication, so much so that it
begs the question – why not read the
original text rather than the secondary
source? However the biographer is prepared for such a query and defends his
exercise by pointing out the way in
which Saint Gaudens becomes secretive
about revealing details of his private life
after his marriage in 1877, less to guard
family intimacy and more to hide the
existence of a mistress. We must assume
therefore that the biographer considers
it his duty to uncover the whole truth.

Saint Gaudens was one of the last of
the great monumental sculptors working
in a nineteenth-century tradition that
combines romantic naturalism with
heroic symbolism, and was perhaps best
known for his public commemorations
of American military heroes. The
authenticity of his richly exotic French
name, often questioned, is confidently
asserted by the author, and its original
source in the name of an early Christian
martyr ascertained. If the sculptor identified with Rome and classicism, it is in
fact a French influence that is more evident in his work, the result of a lengthy
period of training in Paris. Wilkinson
describes the mysterious facility that is
to be found in both his low-relief and
fully three-dimensional statues, and
identifies him, again in the tradition of
the time, as a modeller rather than a
carver. The late nineteenth century witnessed an exciting, if sometimes
awkward, period of transition in sculptural developments between the old
and the new, and in this context it was
the modellers who would lead sculpture towards modernist expression.

Saint Gaudens was born in Dublin in
1848 to an Irish mother and French
father. The family emigrated to
America, however, in the year of his
birth, and ultimately the Irish-American
angle is not over-emphasised in the
book. Of particular interest to the Irish
reader is information related to Saint
Gaudens's execution of the Parnell
monument, the head of which was rescued from a fire in the sculptor's studio
in 1904. If the proportions of the monument appear somewhat awkward today,

and this despite the fact that the sculptor built a scale model of O'Connell Street with which to work, it is of interest to discover that Saint Gaudens originally intended the obelisk to be some thirteen feet higher.

Wilkinson incorporates art historical detail into what is best described as a chatty biography, charting a life in art. Occasional reference to the author's research activities fit uncomfortably into the narrative and would have been better relegated to footnotes. The style is easy, perhaps too much so, and short paragraphs of information and anecdote, sometimes lacking continuity, are delivered with a sense of familiarity. A bibliography is sadly lacking. The photographs of Saint Gaudens's sculptures, taken for the book by David Finn, highly acclaimed in the art of photographing sculptural work, are somewhat poorly reproduced in this paperback edition and sometimes in too small a format to do justice to the rather grand Beaux-Arts nature of the work.

Dr Paula Murphy is a Lecturer in the History of Art Department in University College Dublin

Irish Country Furniture, 1700-1950
By CLAUDIA KINMONTH
Yale University Press, New Haven and London, 1993. pp.242. £29.95 (h/b)

Timothy P O'Neill

FEW ATTEMPTS HAVE been made in the past to write about any aspect of Irish material folk culture and even fewer writers have looked at country furniture. A few isolated articles by Estyn Evans, A T Lucas, Kevin Danaher and Alan Gailey hinted that this might be an interesting topic. There was a mistaken belief that poverty prevented the Irish from acquiring any worthwhile pieces, that there was no great tradition of style, no outstanding furniture makers and that any attempt to write about country furniture would be an arid exercise. Ms Kinmonth's book should effectively lay most of that myth for ever. While no great craftsmen heroes emerge from this study, she shows that there is a significant body of surviving country furniture which, while plain and functional, is not lacking in design. This material is also important as the key to understanding

A 19TH CENTURY PINE SETTLE-BED. *(From Claudia Kinmonth, Irish Country Furniture 1700-1950).* The bed, which originates from east Co Waterford, is shown in its closed-up 'daytime' position.

the traditional lifestyle of country people. Country furniture has become very collectable in recent years.

This book covers the period from 1700, the earliest date from which many of the surviving pieces can be traced, to 1950, when vast amounts of furniture were removed from their traditional settings. After 1950 many pieces of old furniture were simply burned or dumped, but by the 1960s the passion for pine, especially stripped pine, created a new demand for it. Ms Kinmonth demonstrates that a significant amount of furniture survived both hazards. In this book she combines field work with a comprehensive combing of museum collections, large and small, to find her sources. Her work on West Cork is of particular interest and she demonstrates that the scope for field recording is far greater than most people would imagine. Her findings provide the fullest account to date of the different types of the main items of furniture. This will become the standard reference work for the dating and identification of Irish country furniture. Photographs and line drawings are essential in a book of this type where visual representations bring the material to life for the reader. Her illustrations and drawings from archival sources, old

publications and of furniture in situ are of an excellent quality and range.

There is an interesting historical introduction but the real strength of this book lies in the chapters on specific items such as stools and chairs, settles, beds, tables and hearth furniture. For each she provides the historical sources and examines the range, types, construction, decoration and function. This could make for dull reading but the discussion is lively and written in the style of constant discovery which carries the reader along. Anecdotes from writers are included with descriptions from older sources such as parliamentary papers and quotes from field recordings. She deals with the derivation of the names of objects and discusses regional peculiarities , including a brief account of associated beliefs and customs. Her explanations of the relationships between items, uses and form makes for fascinating reading.

This is a welcome addition to the small collection of works on Irish material folk culture. It is beautifully illustrated and will be of interest not just to folklorists but also to anyone who has an interest in history or antiques. Its publication unlocks the doors to many museum collections; some of the more striking objects mentioned are in the national collections in Daingean, Co Offaly. It is to be hoped that this publication will lead to the public display of some of this furniture which has never been seen by the general public. Ms Kinmonth has done an admirable job of rescuing this material and other artefacts from oblivion by presenting them to the wider public in a lively, stylish and professional manner.

Dr T P O'Neill lectures in the Department of Modern History in University College Dublin.

Art and the National Dream

EDITED BY NICOLA GORDON BOWE

Irish Academic Press, Dublin 1993. pp.214, 120 ills. £29.95

Paul Larmour

SUB-TITLED, 'The Search for Vernacular Expression in Turn of the Century Design', this sombre-covered book appears to be both an attempt to illustrate the general theme of national romanticism in turn-of-the-century design across much of Europe and the westernised world, and an attempt to provide a record of the papers given at one session of the Association of Art Historians Conference held in Dublin 1990. Not surprisingly, it falls between the two stools and fails to perform either function entirely satisfactorily.

The subject essentially comprises the use of indigenous vernacular features in the architectural or decorative arts of various countries as embodied in their arts and crafts movements, considered against an international background that embraces Symbolism, Art Nouveau and Modernism. The uneven representation of countries at the conference is reflected in the contributions to the book and means, therefore, that it cannot be taken as a comprehensive survey of the subject. There is much in the book that is good and interesting, but when we consider, for instance, that Ragnar Ostberg's Stockholm Town Hall, begun in 1909, perhaps the single greatest European exemplar of the 'national romantic' idiom, is nowhere mentioned because there is no essay on Sweden, it becomes obvious that the book has serious shortcomings as a general or comprehensive survey.

At the same time, when it is revealed that papers by some contributors to the conference have not been included, but essays by other people who did not contribute have been included here, it becomes clear that this book is far from being a reliable record of the proceedings of the conference.

As it stands, the book would be best described as a miscellaneous collection of essays which relate in varying degrees to the overall pattern of a (albeit limited) country-by-country exposition on the theme of emergent national revivalism in artistic design at the turn of the century. It starts with an introduction by Nicola Gordon Bowe in which the opportunity to make up for some of the deficiencies elsewhere (in terms of geographical range) in the book was not availed of; a really comprehensive overview was needed here.

Thereafter the book consists of a series of short essays of varying scope, but the majority are fairly wide-ranging and deal with entire countries or regions so that the first essay, in which Peter Cormack confines himself to a single artist, seems rather out of place and unduly specific by comparison. Whilst the editorial direction or selection may be at fault here, it must be said that there can be no complaint about the content of Cormack's contribution. It is a well-researched and well written account of the work of Christopher Whall, the great stained glass artist of the Arts and Crafts movement in England. It is all the more interesting to us here when we remember the crucial role Whall played in the development of twentieth-century stained glass in Ireland.

The subjects of the other essays include developments in America, Japan, Russia, Poland, Hungary, Norway and Finland, written by scholars mainly based in those countries. They vary in the degree to which their, at times limited, range of illustrations manages to convey the rich diversity of the period. More careful editing would also surely have eliminated some of the too numerous spelling mistakes or typographical errors which tend to spoil the book, and it is not just a case of translation difficulties brought about by the range of foreign contributors, as we can see from Dr Bowe's own repeated references to 'Thor Ballylee' instead of

'Thoor Ballylee' in her essay on Ireland with which the collection ends. This contribution on Ireland was not delivered at the 1990 conference. It is a revised and reworked version of an earlier article published in *Irish Arts Review Yearbook 1990-91*. It has been brought up to date for publication here in 1993, inasmuch as some new material has been added, but curiously any reference to a major new source of information published in the intervening period has been studiously avoided.

'It is not generally recognised that Ireland has her own Arts and Crafts movement,' writes Dr Bowe. That may have been a true enough assertion in 1990-91 but it is surely disingenuous of her to repeat it in 1993, a full year after the publication of the first full-scale study of the Irish movement.* That said, the Irish publishers may be congratulated on bravely venturing into this wider field of the decorative arts and architecture, but for a price of £29.95 one would have expected some colour illustrations.

*The Arts and Crafts Movement in Ireland, by Paul Larmour, published by Friar's Bush Press, Belfast, 1992.

Dr Paul Larmour is a Lecturer in the Department of Architecture in The Queen's University of Belfast

The Irish: A Treasury of Art and Literature

BY LESLIE CAROLA

Southport, Connecticut: Hugh Lauter Levin Association Inc., 1993 pp.368 (illus.) $75.00.

Michael Patrick Gillespie

IN BOTH FORM AND content *The Irish: A Treasury of Art and Literature* falls squarely within the category of 'coffee table book'. As such, the work immediately stands apart for other cultural studies. The term identifies a work whose size precludes reading it while standing on a subway and whose contents sample rather than exhaust a topic. Further conditions also obtain. One expects a coffee table book to confirm its presence through a physical attractiveness that establishes an aesthetic appeal operating independent of the response that one makes to its printed matter. In each of these areas *The Irish* meets the

BOOK REVIEWS

expectations of this genre.

The volume itself exudes a well-made aura. Its size, bindings, and pages all contribute to the sense of a physically attractive book. Its typography is sharp and clear, and its numerous illustrations, many on colour plates, provide a delightful complement to the printed page. In every respect, *The Irish* affirms the care that its editor and publisher have taken throughout its production.

The term 'coffee table book', however, carries negative connotations as well. One often finds it applied as a designation for works that fail to establish a topical, intellectual validity and remain solely a decorative feature.

Happily, *The Irish* complements its aesthetic appeal with scholarly credentials. As I will note below, in some aspects the book does not live up to expectations generated by its portentous title, for its design allows it no more than glancing views of the topics that it surveys. Overall, however, this edition gives a fine sampling of Irish writing and painting.

To offer a fair assessment of its value, of course, one must judge *The Irish* on its own terms. It does not in fact claim recognition as a scholarly work. Rather it stands as a reflective (and selective) response to a rich cultural heritage spanning two millennia. Thus the book emerges as evocative rather than instructive. One does not come away with a unified sense of Irish art and literature, but one does have a keener appreciation for its potential. Likewise, in the editor's choice to represent a conventional rather than a comprehensive view of the range of Irish art, the volume excites, but cannot, exhaust the reader's interest.

The Irish presents chronologically arranged selections of prose, poetry, and drama relating to and (generally) written by Irish authors. These pieces are punctuated by illustrations, predominantly of Irish paintings but also including examples of architecture, jewellery, and of course, illuminated manuscripts. The selection of writing represents some of the best Irish authors, and it generally covers a range of familiar writers and sub-genres. The same can be said of the examples from the visual arts. At the same time, and despite the chronological progression of the format, because of specific inclusions and exclusions made by the editor, the collection seems to

Phoebe Anna TRAQUAIR (1852-1936): Red Cross Knight and his Lady. *Completed 1914. Embroidered silks and gold thread on linen. (From Elizabeth Cumming, Phoebe Anna Traquair).* This catalogue traces Traquair's earliest work back to her Irish parents and Dublin art training.

lack a clearly defined goal and to operate without a unifying feature to bring these individual works together.

In some instances one can attribute such gaps, most notably in the sparse representation of work between the twelfth and eighteenth centuries, to the impact of colonial oppression on native Irish art. Nonetheless, with a more thorough examination of Irish artists the editor could have avoided the need to draw non-Irish writers into portions of the volume strictly devoted to Irish cultural achievements. (One need not be a Republican to question the wisdom of using the fiction of contemporary American writers like Tom Flanagan and Leon Uris to capture the ethos of political upheaval in nineteenth- and twentieth-century Ireland; or, even more to the point, including the arch imperialist Rudyard Kipling's offering of a patronizing lampoon of Irish oppression.) Likewise, the section on the Irish in America has some wonderful selections, but it also shows no awareness of the literary contributions of the comic writings of Finely Peter Dunne or of the letters and journals of numerous Irish participants in the American Civil War. These would be far more effective than the pieces by contemporary American writers and journalists, whose comments on the sense of Ireland are blurred by the detachment of several generations.

Admittedly, these are the cavils of a pedant asking why did you not write the book that I would have written. That aside, Ms Carola has produced a very fine collection that will introduce readers to the wealth of aesthetic pleasure to be found in Irish art.

Michael Patrick Gillespie is a Professor of English at Marquette University, Milwaukee, USA and has written books on Oscar Wilde and James Joyce.

Phoebe Anna Traquair (1852-1936)
BY ELIZABTH CUMMING

Catalogue of an Exhibition at the Scottish National Portrait Gallery, Edinburgh 1993

Nicola Gordon Bowe

'The nearer she approaches the Divine the more passionate become the lines' – W.B. Yeats.

WHILE THIS EXHIBITION admirably establishes, for the first time, the unique importance of Traquair as a prolific artist of exceptional versatility, skill and commitment in Scotland's Celtic Renaissance, it also traces her earliest work back to her Irish parents and Dublin art training. This is exemplified by the inclusion of evocative illustrated pages of her grandparents' homes in Co Wicklow, in her intricate, at times autobiographical illuminations to Rossetti's sonnets, *The House of Life* (1898-1902); also in two exquisitely observed studies of fossil fish, similar to those she executed as a Dublin Art School student for a Scots palaeontologist, Ramsay Traquair, visiting the Royal Dublin Society.

In 1873, aged twenty-one, she married him and they moved to Edinburgh on his appointment as Keeper of Natural

History at the Scottish Museum of Science and Art. This 'educational treasure-house' held international temporary exhibitions, some of decorative art, which stimulated her own deep love and observation of nature, and her early awareness of the current Art Needlework movement. Her earliest Edinburgh artwork was embroidered domestic linen, which she could do at home while raising three young children; it is a pity the V & A could not have lent more of their collection of Traquair's superb embroideries from different periods.

Gradually, her artistic and intellectual concerns drew her to those enlightened Ruskinian philanthropists, passionately versed in progressive aesthetic theory and practice, who had converged on Edinburgh; of initial and lasting influence were G Baldwin Brown, Professor of Fine Art at the University; John Miller Gray, newly appointed curator at the Scottish National Portrait Gallery; the architect Robert Rowand Anderson and, better known, Patrick Geddes, botanist, socialist and town planner. Through them, her love of the Pre-Raphaelites developed into a recognisably Edinburgh Arts and Crafts ideology, centred in the Edinburgh Social Union (founded 1884).

Phoebe Traquair's debut as a professional artist came a year later with her mural decoration of the mortuary chapel of the Royal Hospital for Sick Children. This seminal revelation of her lifelong thematic, iconographical, technical and spiritual preoccupations was painted, as W B Yeats observed, 'in stolen hours'. Her richly decorative symbolic programme synthesised past and present, the imaginative and the real, paying figurative and stylistic homage to Rossetti, Blake and the Florentine Quattrocento in a 'spirited mixture of Celtic and Byzantine, Gothic and Baroque.' Here is her first, profoundly moving, evocation of the redemption of mankind through love, what Yeats called 'the drama of the soul', which she would interpret thereafter in a variety of media. Sadly, none of Traquair's mural schemes (all three Edinburgh series, now misleadingly discoloured and in need of restoration, were accessible during the exhibition) could be represented except by related studies or rather poor photographs, but the subtle and sympathetic display of nearly every other aspect of her work more than compensated for this.

Elizabeth Cumming, in her exemplary catalogue, which is clear, informed, contextual and splendidly illustrated, emphasises the concern of Traquair and her colleagues with 'the relevance of historical prototypes to modern decorative art.' In true Arts and Crafts spirit, Traquair began to experiment with a variety of crafts, scales and media. Ruskin lent her medieval manuscripts to copy and she was soon designing and executing sumptuously detailed illuminated miniatures, virtuoso silk-embroidered panels, such as her large *Salvation of Mankind* triptych, exhibited to acclaim in 1895 in Dublin, book, jacket and magazine illustrations and painted panels for at least two oak cabinets and, later, a piano. One eminent Edinburgh printer was lucky enough to have his garden gates and railings designed by her. Her cover for *Women's Voices* (1887), an anthology of women's poetry, heralds her superbly graphic and expressive embossed, blind-tooled leather bindings. A distinguished Edinburgh silversmith, J M Talbot, forged details for these and, later, the settings for some of her subsequent wide range of enamelled art metalwork and jewellery.

Her decorative work, regardless of scale, is emphatically two dimensional, in true Pre-Raphaelite tradition, whether on paper, linen, canvas or leather. In all her work, her anachronistic preoccupation with salvation and redemption reveals an integral vision which was sustained in increasingly free linear and chromatic harmonies; seen in, for example, the tiny enamels, glowing in rich colours with childlike images, incorporated into caskets, pendants, necklaces, shell cups and miniature altarpieces. In several painted fragments and portraits (including her own searching but elusive self-portrait), occasional sketches and the few late works exhibited, a looser, more open, bolder treatment emerges. Her pantheistic empathy for all creatures, imbued with a passionate and poetic spirituality, was recognised at the time but has been less appreciated since. The purposefully modern idiom she sought is still deeply indebted to her own pantheon of the past, while her technical virtuosity allies her to an increasing number of contemporary craftspeople.

At the age of seventy, she embarked on her last mural scheme. By then, she had travelled widely, worked with the most distinguished architects, craftsmen and women and collectors of her day, made about one hundred and fifty enamelled pieces. She made some of her finest enamels and illuminations for her brother, William Moss, a successful cotton industrialist in Chester. Her niece, Beatrice Elvery, a major figure in the Dublin Arts and Crafts movement, was to embody many of her principles.

Dr Nicola Gordon Bowe, a lecturer in History of Art and Design at NCAD, Dublin, has published and lectured widely on early twentieth century decorative arts.

Decantations: A Tribute to Maurice Craig
EDITED BY AGNES BERNELLE
The Lilliput Press, Dublin, 1992 £35

Homan Potterton

MORE THAN TWO decades ago now a small publishing venture with an address in Ballycotton, county Cork commissioned me and a couple of others – all of us novices – to write a series of pamphlets on various topics of Irish art and architectural history. We were all thrilled when Dr Maurice Craig, then and now the doyen of Irish architectural historians, agreed to speak at a reception for the launch of the series although we were somewhat startled when after his speech – about which I recall nothing at all – he announced to us privately that he was going straight home to get a needle and thread to replace the binding of the pamphlets (a simple staple was all that Ballycotton could muster) with a hand-stitched one of his own devising. Authors and publisher alike were suitably chastened.

In light of this it would be a brave person who would set out to make a book for actual presentation to Maurice on such an auspicious occasion as his seventieth birthday and it is not surprising that his wife, Agnes Bernelle, found it impossible to get anyone to edit the *festschrift* she planned for the event. Stepping into the breach – and unknown to Maurice himself ('Why is Sir John Summerson writing to *you*?' he would occasionally sniff) – she set about the task in her own way and has brought out a volume that is as delightful and as diverse as the dedicatee himself. *Decantations* contains many gems, both literary and historical, with topics ranging over architectural history, archaeology, art, poetry, ship-modelling, fiction, and a myriad other subjects.

Some of the essays tell us about Maurice in his various guises: among the fine bindings of Trinity Library with William O'Sullivan about 1950; as a man of two cities (Belfast and Dublin) with Benedict Kiely; as the revered historian of Dublin with Frank McDonald; and meeting his match (not quite) with Colm Toibin on the waters of Lough Erne. Others, like the very clever essay, 'The Celestial Steam Packet' by C E B Brett, parody his style and in doing so make us grateful for the humour that is present in much of Maurice's most serious writings.

A number of contributions are particularly valuable for the reader of *Irish Arts Review* and as they might escape notice they are worth listing: Anne Crookshank on the conversation-piece in Irish painting; Jeanne Sheehy on Powerscourt; Jeremy Williams on the architect, William Atkins; the Knight of Glin on Dublin furniture makers; David Griffin on Leinster House; Frederick O'Dwyer on Dublin Castle; Edward McParland on Lovett Pearce; Jane Fenlon on the Ormonde inventories; Rolf Loeber on seventeenth century architectural sketches; and Peter Harbison on Raphoe.

The volume is elegantly assembled by the Lilliput Press and – to this reviewer's great relief – it is thread-sewn !

Images and Insights

Catalogue of an exhibition of works from the permanent collection at the Hugh Lane Municipal Gallery of Modern Art, Dublin, 1993. With essays by Barbara Dawson and Sean O'Reilly; catalogue entries by Christina Kennedy, Crista Maria Lerm, Catherine Marshall, Daire O'Connell and Wanda Ryan Smolin.
pp.287, fully illustrated in colour. £24.95 (h/b); £14.95 (p/b)

Rosemarie Mulcahy

THE HUGH LANE Municipal Gallery of Modern Art has the double attraction of an art collection of high quality and a distinguished classical building. In spite of these assets the Gallery is less well known than it deserves, largely due to

Antonio MANCINI (1852-1930): Portrait of Mrs Shine (detail). *Oil on canvas, 141 x 109 cm (from Images and Insights)*. The sitter was the sister of Hugh Lane who commissioned the portrait.

the fact that so little of the collection has been on view. It suffers from lack of space – the most common complaint of all galleries – and in addition from the lack of small exhibitions based on the Gallery's holdings, with accompanying catalogues; an illustrated Summary Catalogue is badly needed. The original catalogue, which was published in 1908, the year in which the Gallery was established at 17 Harcourt Street, contains three hundred works, many of them donated by Hugh Lane, its first Director. It also includes his gift of thirty-nine paintings of the Continental School, which was given on the condition that a suitable building be provided by the city – the controversy that ensued is complex and only in recent years seems to be reaching a resolution – as well as bequests and gifts from other sources. This very useful catalogue, which was complied by Sarah C Harrison, was re-printed by the Friends of the National Collections in 1984 in commemoration of their sixtieth anniversary. In 1958 a version of the original catalogue appeared, brought up to date by the insertion of subsequent acquisitions; this is long out of print. In a brief preface, Patrick O'Connor, then curator, issued a stern warning that 'Public Galleries must be vigilant to escape the invariably debased influences

of the Art Critics, Art Dealers and the coterie of shallow "progressives" and "intellectuals" who are forever buzzing around art and what passes for art.' We have come a long way since then.

With *Images and Insights* there is cause for celebration, for it is a landmark in the history and development of the Gallery. From more than two thousand works in the collection a hundred and seven have been selected – some having been in store for many years – and the ground floor rooms re-hung, giving new insights into the variety and quality of the Gallery's holdings. The accompanying catalogue, reviewed here, is a handsome publication in which all the works are illustrated with excellent colour plates and explained by informative and concise texts. This ambitious venture has been made possible by the enlightened sponsorship of ABN AMRO Bank.

In a well, documented introductory essay, 'Hugh Lane and the Origins of the Collection', Barbara Dawson, the Gallery's Director, outlines the persistent efforts of Hugh Lane to establish a Gallery of Modern Art for Dublin. After Lane's tragically early death on the *Lusitania* in 1915, the campaign was continued by his supporters, notably the painters Sarah Harrison and Sarah Purser. On Purser's initiative a permanent home was found for the Gallery in Charlemont House, which opened to the public in 1933. This distinguished building, designed by William Chambers for James Caulfeild, Earl of Charlemont, was an inspired choice. Charlemont, a discerning patron and collector, and his town house, are the subjects of Sean O'Reilly's succinct and entertaining essay. In recent years Charlemont House has been extensively renovated by Dublin Corporation.

Irish, British and Continental schools from the mid-nineteenth to the early twentieth century form the basis of the collection, with the addition of more recent acquisitions of contemporary works. Among the small gems from the Lane gift, Vuillard's *The Mantelpiece* is a masterpiece of *intimiste* painting, and it is very revealing to compare Degas's *Beach Scene*, so strikingly modern and yet painted only a decade later, with Boudin's charming *At the Seaside* of 1867. Some of the major masterpieces, such as Renoir's Les Parapluies, Degas's *Le Concert aux Tuileries*, will be returning to Dublin under a new agreement with the National Gallery, London, and the opportunity has been taken to illustrate these in the catalogue. However, an important aspect of the selection in *Images and Insights* is that it highlights the many excellent works acquired from other benefactors and shows the evolutionary nature of the collection: the ravishing *Blush Roses* by Fantin Latour was donated by Lady Ardilaun, Daubigny's *Un Coup de Vent*, presented by Alexander Young and an outstanding Lavery, *Sutton Court*, presented by Count John McCormack. The Friends of the National Collections have made major contributions to this selection and have shown themselves to be both discerning and brave in their purchases, which include fine examples of work by Segonzac, Rouault, Vlaminck, Albers, Lurçat and Hitchens, as well as excellent works by Irish artists. James White, an indefatigable member and officer of the society, and curator of the Municipal Gallery from 1960-64, was instrumental in organising an exhibition (Municipal Gallery and Ulster Museum, 1964) of the works acquired by the Friends since its foundation. Perhaps it is now time for another show of this kind, to complement the exhibition of the works by their founder, Sarah Purser, which is planned for this year.

There is strong emphasis on the contemporary part of the collection, to which Eithne Waldron (curator 1964-90) made some significant additions, notably, the Agnes Martin, a controversial purchase at the time; her recent retrospective at the Whitney established Martin as one of the major artistic talents of her generation. Waldron also purchased some good examples of Irish art of the 1970s and '80s by painters James Tyrrell, Patrick Graham, James Coleman, Brian Bourke, and sculptors Patrick Ireland, Kathy Prendergast, Michael Warren, and others. The works shown donated by The Contemporary Irish Art Society include Gerda Frömel, Gerard Dillon, William Scott, Camille Souter, and James Scanlon's stained glass, *Study no. 2 for Miró*, which is one of the delights – indeed the small selection of pieces in this medium, exhibited in a special room, is a welcome addition.

The present Director has, since 1990, strengthened the representation of contemporary Irish artists with outstanding works by Brian Maguire, Dorothy Cross, Michael Cullen and Tony O'Malley.

In some ways *Images and Insights* is tantalising, for it gives, and can only give, a partial view of this rich and varied collection. Dorothy Walker's article, published in *Irish Arts Review* (Vol. 4, no. 3, pp.28-36), is informative about other areas of the collection. A coherent programme of catalogued exhibitions designed around the Gallery's own holdings, perhaps supplemented by judicious loans, would offer exciting possibilities; as would small monographic exhibitions of Orpen, Yeats the elder, or Leech, along the lines of Julian Campbell's exemplary *Frank O'Meara and his contemporaries* (1989). It would be interesting to see the many superb portraits in the Gallery's collection exhibited together, including those by Mancini commissioned by Hugh Lane – and only one of which, that of his sister *Mrs Shine*, is shown here.

PS ... Of Course. Patrick Swift 1927-83

EDITED BY VERONICA JANE O'MARA

Gandon Books, Cork 1993
129 ills, 108 colour pl, pp.274, £27 (h/b)

Patrick Swift 1927-1983

CATALOGUE OF AN EXHIBITION AT THE IRISH MUSEUM OF MODERN ART

Dublin, December 1993
pp.80, 86 ills. 23 colour pl. £14.95

Wanda Ryan Smolin

PATRICK SWIFT, who has been virtually unknown to the public and whose painting has been overlooked by Irish art historians and critics in recent years, has only recently been recognised as an important artist entirely deserving of the acclaim which he steadfastly rejected during his lifetime.

Swift was born in Dolphin's Barn in Dublin and began to paint while still attending Synge Street Christian Brothers School. He held his first solo exhibition at the Victor Waddington Galleries in Dublin in 1952. By this time he was already known among artistic and literary circles in both Dublin and London. In Dublin he was part of the literary coterie which centred around McDaid's pub and close friends included

poets Patrick Kavanagh and Anthony Cronin. He gave up his job with the Gas Company to paint full time and he also contributed articles on art to John Ryan's journal Envoy. In London he associated with the poets and painters based in Soho, including Francis Bacon, Lucian Freud, George Barker, David Wright and others. He continued to paint and write in London and founded in 1959 with Wright the quarterly magazine "X". In "X" Swift promoted figurative artists such as Frank Auerbach, Craigie Atchison and David Bomberg and criticised abstract art as the art of the establishment. In 1962, having become thoroughly disenchanted with the art establishment and feeling increasingly marginalised by what he perceived as the dominance of abstract art over figurative art, he left London with his family and settled in a remote part of the Algarve. There he established a successful pottery and continued to paint in private but rarely exhibited.

Broadly speaking, his painting can be divided into two periods: – Dublin and London of the 1950s and Portugal of the 1960s and 70s. His early work was influenced to varying degrees by Freud (with whom he shared his Harcourt Street studio in the early 1950s) and Giacometti, while his Portuguese paintings acknowledge a debt to Cezanne and to Bomberg. However, above these and other stylistic influences, Swift's own individualism and strength of artistic vision asserted itself, not only in terms of his adherence to certain figurative themes, including portraits and trees, but more particularly through his ability to communicate certain truths on what one senses to be a deeply spiritual level. It is perhaps this quality in his work which links Swift with the world of poetry and poets. Apart from close family members, poets were the almost exclusive subjects of his portraits; the series of poet portraits shown at IMMA are quite exceptional by any standards and must place him among the very best Irish painters of the twentieth century. It is interesting that Edward McGuire, the only Irish artist to acknowledge the influence of Swift, was also to become similarly obsessed with poets as subjects.

In many ways the book *PS ... Of Course* and the Catalogue which accompanied the IMMA exhibition are

BOOK REVIEWS

complementary. The book, beautifully designed by John O'Regan, includes a diligently researched and laudatory biography of Patrick Swift by the editor Veronica Jane O'Mara, a collection of over twenty poems and essays dedicated to Swift by famous contemporaries and a compilation of Swift's own writing on art and poetry. Many of the essays and poems were written by close friends (including John Jordan, Anthony Cronin, Patrick Kavanagh, John McGahern and David Wright) and offer a fascinating insight into the extraordinary life and personality of Patrick Swift. The IMMA Catalogue, on the other hand, deals exclusively and in a more detached way with his painting (excluding his ceramic painting which did not figure in the exhibition but which is undoubtedly worthy of attention). Apart from Daire O'Connell's concise and clearly organised catalogue entries there are also essays by Anthony Cronin and Aidan Dunne. Cronin gives an interesting and perceptive personal view of Swift in his bohemian Dublin and London years; Dunne's essay charts the course of Swift's development as a painter against the complex backdrop of post-war British art and the artistic milieu to which the painter was drawn. He analyses the artist's own views on art which Swift expressed in a strong and thought-provoking,though not always clear or convincing, manner in his published writings.

Both catalogue and book are lavishly illustrated in colour and black and white, particularly the latter which includes some fine examples of Swift's drawings and illustrations as well as a superb portrait of the artist's mother and other works which were not included in the exhibition. The paintings illustrated in the book are accompanied by elaborate titles and an almost bewildering array of assorted quotations. Swift left most of his works undated and untitled and this explains the frequent discrepancies in titles and approximate dates between book and catalogue which would no doubt have amused the artist given his aversion to art history but may cause some angst to those who will now have to reassess Irish art in the twentieth century in the light of Swift's rediscovered talent.

Louis Le Brocquy: A Painter seeing his Way

By Anne Madden Le Brocquy

Gill and Macmillan, Dublin, 1994
pp.317, 123 (b/w) figs in the text

Alistair Smith

The last sentence of Anne Madden's book announces the forthcoming retrospective exhibition of her husband's work at the Irish Museum of Modern Art, thus making the publication of this biography particularly opportune, and essential reading for those looking forward to that event in 1996.

The seed of the book was planted by Ted Hickey (until recently Keeper of Art at the Ulster Museum), who suggested that Louis Le Brocquy write his autobiography. The idea was rejected with Le Brocquy understandably explaining that he wishes to devote all his time, which as he approaches 80 he construes as being limited, to painting. Hickey's idea has, however, been taken up by Le Brocquy's fellow artist and wife.

The book is, immediately, a rarity, in being a biography written by the subject's wife during his lifetime with his permission. It is also an oddity, falling, as explained by the author, into two distinct sections disparate in style, and relying on different sources.

The first deals with the period of Le Brocquy's life before he met Anne Madden, and is composed through the traditional means available to the biographer – the subject's own recollections of the first 40 years of his life, family legend and anecdote, and documentation through exhibition catalogues and reviews. These materials the author treats in a painterly fashion (as one might expect) and the narrative proceeds in a rather additive way, doubling back on itself on occasions as if sections were being overpainted, and perhaps reflecting the unchronological way that memory works. The 40 years are over in 109 pages which bring the subject to the early 50s when he had received considerable recognition, yet had not evolved the subject-matter and style for which he is now principally known, namely the extensive, obsessional series of *Heads* on white backgrounds. Thanks to the author's reticence, the principal voice heard throughout this first section is Le Brocquy's and a sense of his other-world-

ly qualities emerges from his earliest memories. It is interesting to speculate how emphatic this would have become, had Le Brocquy committed himself to an autobiography; and it brings to mind the early chapters of Oskar Kokoschka's autobiography. [I would have welcomed, in this section, some speculation on the relationship of Le Brocquy's Newgrange-related work (which surfaced in public form in the early 1950s) and Victor Pasmore's ostensibly similar spiral motifs of the same period. But perhaps this does not lie within the biographer's remit.]

The second part of the book deals with the following 40 years during which Le Brocquy and the author have spent their lives together, raised their children and painted side-by-side. It is partially based on Anne Madden's diary, and, unfortunately, the chronological structure buries any deep analysis. The reader might have been better served had the text been sectionalised into chapters dealing with family, friends, and, most important, with the *Heads*, both living and dead – W B Yeats, Joyce and especially Beckett and Francis Bacon. But God forbid that we should expect critical awareness or psychological objectivity of a long-term marital partner, and particularly so when those partners have led seamlessly entwined lives, sharing both a profession and, remarkably, a studio.

The diary-based section of the text has raised the hackles of those who prefer their artists to work in boiler-suits, and some of us might even find the index socially intimidating – 'de Chirico, de Gaulle, de las Torres, de Rothschild, de Valera, de Valois'. Nevertheless, in various eras, artists have been concerned to be seen as the social equals of their patrons, and the Le Brocquys have achieved this.

The book, however, conveys little sense of Le Brocquy being totally engaged within the process of the glamorous social life which is detailed here. This is, perhaps, the essential truth which the biographer conveys – of dedication to the muse rather than to the everyday. If the biographee seems somehow absent from his biography it is because, as artists do, he has invested himself in his work. We therefore await the revelations of the retrospective exhibition.

Alistair Smith is Director of the Whitworth Art Gallery, Manchester

1. William ORPEN: (1878-1931) The Roscommon Dragoon (detail). *Oil on canvas, 76 x 63.5cm. Sold at Sotheby's London, 30 June 1993 for £125,000.*

F or Irish art, as elsewhere in the art trade, where goods are fresh to the market, response is always healthy. Amidst much fanfare, Phillips Chester on 27 March 1993 offered a large (63 x 80 cm) 'rediscovered' Walter Frederick Osborne view of the picturesque village, Roundstone (*Life in Connemara: a market day*); estimated at £25-35,000, it was purchased by a private Irish buyer for £135,000 (hammer prices quoted). The atmospheric

Gertrude Prescott Nuding

introduces the price guide to Irish art with a note on international interest in Irish paintings.

painting had been purchased by Edward Lloyd Edwards after it had been seen in the 1898 Royal Academy Exhibition Show and since then it had remained in the possession of the family and in their home; Phillips made the strategic decision to keep the painting (and two original letters from the artist to Lloyd Edwards) in the sale of the contents of Bryn Oerog (near Llangollen, Clwyd). Another Irish painting that had remained in a private British collection (this time for thirty or forty years) and has returned to Ireland (a private collection) was Sean Keating's *The Feast of Bridget* which came up at Phillips London on 23 November 1993 (Fig. 3). The arresting image of the late fifth century saint fetched £13,500, within the estimate of £12-15,000. Repeating this pattern of repatriation, a Paul Henry view (*A Western Lough*, offered at Phillips 8 March 1994 sale after a sojourn in a British collection), went back to an Irish private collection (£14,000 against estimate of £7-8,000).

Also new to the market was a group of eight Jack Butler Yeats paintings collected by the American psychologist, Dr Eleanor de Bretteville Reid. Her collection was prompted by the chance discovery of a pen and ink and watercolour drawing of *Lafitte the Pirate* in an antique shop in San Francisco. Her enthusiasm kindled, she developed a friendship with Yeats through correspondence during the period 1953 to 1956, and became not only a collector but also firm advocate of his work. At Sotheby's on 24 November 1993, the consigned works from Dr Reid's collection offered a solid group into which trade and private collectors could sink their collective competitive teeth: *Lafitte the Pirate*, watercolour, pen and ink (1905), sold for £19,000 against estimate of £10-15,000; *The Brown-eyed Men*

2. Jack B YEATS: (1871-1957), The Great Tent has Collapsed. *Oil on canvas, 61 x 91.5cm. Sold at Sotheby's London, 24 November 1993 for £106,000 (inc. premium).*

3. Sean KEATING: (1899-1978), The Feast of St Bridget. *Oil on canvas, 96 x 117 cm. Sold at Phillip's London, 23 November, 1993 for £13,500.*

(1951), oil, sold for £31,000 against estimate of £25-35,000; *The Steep Way to Town*, oil, (1953) sold for £26,000 against estimate of £30-40,000; *Donkeyraces*, an early watercolour (1898), sold for £5,500 against stiff estimate of £10-15,000; *Caballero*, oil (1949) sold for £32,000 against estimate of £25-35,000; *A Speckled Memory* oil (1953), sold for £28,000 against estimate of £15-20,000; *Wait*, oil (1953), sold for £30,000 against estimate £25-35,000; *Sleep Sound*, oil, (1955), sold for £40,000 against estimate of £30-40,000. From another American source (descendant of Helen Hooker O'Malley Roelofs, Greenwich, Connecticut), *The Great Tent has Collapsed* at the Sotheby's November 1993 sale, fetched £95,000, well surpassing the £30-40,000 estimate (Fig. 2). That the market, during a recession, could absorb this many Yeats paintings in one go and at good prices should be read as an indication that the Irish art market has become firmly established. There is more to reading a market than merely taking its temperature based on 'world' records being set or failing to be achieved.

A more controversial consignment to the same Sotheby's sale was a group of thirty-one works (twenty-five of which were Irish) deaccessioned by the Arts Council of Northern Ireland. Presumably bowing to pressure, two of these were withdrawn from the sale and sold by private treaty to the Ulster Museum: Patrick Hennessy's *The Old Tree*, had carried a pre-sale estimate of £3-4,000 and Gerald Dillon's large oil *Self-Contained Flat* had carried a pre-sale estiamte of £10-15,000. Of the remaining works, a smaller Dillon oil, *The Fish-eaters* was sold for £10,000 (estimate £6-8,000); James Humbert Craig's *Races at Waterfoot* sold for £6,000 (estimate £4-6,000); and William Conor's *Hobby-Horses* sold for £11,000 (estimate £6-8,000). While the funds raised will help the Council continue in its stated aims, the dispersal of works which have acquired a historical contextual importance and served to spread artistic influences is certainly to be regretted.

Undoubtedly the most luscious painting of the year was Sir William Orpen's *The Roscommon Dragoon*, a 1913 portrayal of Vera Hone dressed in an Armagh Infantry militia tunic of about 1865 (Fig. 1). Full of nationalistic overtones, with allusions to similarly posed half-length self-portraits, the image transcends in importance other portraits of Orpen's favourite sitter. Against an estimate of £50-70,000, the 1913 portrayal sold at Sotheby's 30 June 1993 sale to a private British bidder (who at times buys for British corporate collections) for £125,000. A more atmospherically painted, aptly titled *Mrs. Hone in a Striped Dress* (1912) sold at Christie's 1 July 1993 sale for £62,000 (estimate £60-80,000) to the Pyms Gallery. Pyms Gallery also secured an early work by Orpen, the 1902 *Valuers* at the low estimate, £40,000, in the Sotheby's 24 November 1993 sale. Another work, standing between the early realist and the later society beauty portraits, also appeared in the November sale: the cockney working class mother, Lottie is shown feeding a toddler; estimated at £80-100,000, the painting amazingly sold for a low £50,000 – betraying its prior recent appearances both in the trade and at auction.

An encouraging note for the Irish market came in Christie's 11 March 1994 sale. Roderic O'Conor's *Village, Britanny* sold to the Pyms Gallery for £60,000 against an estimate of £25-35,000 and trade and commissioned underbidding.

DR GERTRUDE PRESCOTT NUDING writes regularly on art market issues for various publications.

PRICE GUIDE TO IRISH ART

An index of prices paid for Irish pictures at auctions in Dublin and London from May 1993 to May 1994

The following sale catalogues, referred to in the Guide by a single letter symbol, have been indexed:

A: James Adam – 16 June 1993; B: James Adam, Dublin – 5 October 1993; C: James Adam, Dublin – 1 December 1993; D: Taylor de Veres, Dublin – 25 May 1993; E: Taylor de Veres, Dublin – 15 June 1993; F: Taylor de Veres, Dublin – 12 October 1993; G: Taylor de Veres, Dublin – 14 December 1993; H: Taylor de Veres, Dublin – 8 March 1994; I: Adams, Blackrock – 4 October 1993; J: Adams, Blackrock – 21 March 1994; K: Christie's, Dublin – 26 May 1993; L: Christie's, Castle Upton, Co Antrim – 9 December 1993; M: Sotheby's, London – 24 March 1994; N: James Adam, Dublin – 30 March 1994; O: Sotheby's London – 24 November 1993; P: Sotheby's, London – 30 June 1993; Q: Denis Drum, Malahide, 24 March 1994.

The artist's name and date is followed by the painting's title. Next is the medium, referred to by a single letter symbol (as indicated below) followed by the measurements of the work. The letters 'S', 'D', or 'I' indicate whether the painting is signed, dated, or inscribed. The letter in parentheses refers to the sale and is followed by the lot number. Prices are quoted in local currencies.

A: Acrylic; C: Collage; D: Drawing; O: Oil; M: Mixed media; P: Pastel; Pr: Print; T: Tempera; W: Watercolour/Gouache/Wash.

ADAM, Patrick William (1854-1930)
  A Celtic Stone Cross / A Church, Glendalough
  W (2) 10 x 6.75", S, D, (K: 6)   £308
ADAMS, M. E. (19th/20th Century)
  Shipping in Rough Seas
  W 7 x 9.5", S, D, (J: 43)   –
ADAMS, Samuel (fl. 1884-1893)
  The Holz Market, Friburg - Baden
  O 16.25 x 20", S, (J: 31)   £2,000
ADDEY, Joseph Poole (fl. 1880-1914)
  Geese in a Landscape
  W 7 x 10", S, D, (G: 151)   £850
  Coastal Headland
  O 19 x 13.5", S, D, (J: 60)   –
ADDIS, Jonathan (20th Century)
  In Bewleys
  W 7.25 x 10", S, I, (E: 106)   £80
  The Canal at Huband Bridge
  O 12 x 16", S, (F: 193)   –
AITKEN, James Alfred (19th/20th Century)
  Coastal Landscape
  W 13 x 19.5", S, (H: 132)   –
  Landscape with Figure and Church Spire
  O 10 x 13.5", S, (I: 89)   –
ALEXANDER, Douglas (fl. 1930)
  Near Dhulough, Connemara
  W 14.5 x 21", S, (B: 129)   –
  On The Dargle
  W 8 x 9.5", S, (B: 141)   £220
  On Lough Anure
  W 10 x 14.5", S, (B: 149)   £320
  Coastal Landscape
  O 19 x 23", S (D: 2)   –
  Among the Mourne Mountains
  W 10.25 x 14.5", S, (D: 72)   £200
  Coastal Landscape
  O 8 x 14", S, (D: 152)   –
  Among the Twelve Pins, Connemara
  W 14.5 x 21", S, (E: 1)   –
  Among the Twelve Pins, Connemara
  W 15 x 20.5", S, (F: 124)   £340
  Coastal Landscape
  O 20 x 23", S, (F: 201)   –
  Bog Road, Near Maam, Connemara
  W 8.5 x 11", S, I, (G: 80)   £160
  Caragh Lake
  W 14.5 x 20.25", S, I, (G: 133)   £280
  Near Maam Cross
  W 14.5 x 21", S, (G: 175)   –
  Among the Connemara Mountains
  W 8.5 x 11", S, (I: 11)   –
  Near Maam– Connemara
  W 10 x 14", S, I, (J: 65)   –
  Dhu Lough, Connemara
  W 10 x 14", S, I, (J: 66)   –
  Bunbeg, Co. Donegal
  O 20 x 24", S, (N: 106)   £900
  Trout stream, near Leew, (Connemara)
  W 10 x 14.5", S, (N: 128)   £360

ALLEN, Harry Epworth (1894-1958)
  The Stalactites
  P 14 x 19.5", S, (D:151)   –
ANDERLE, Jiri (20th Century)
  Dam in Peltz
  Pr 26 x 20", S, (G: 179)   £90
ARMSTRONG, Arthur (b. 1924)
  Portrait of a hill
  O 18 x 36", S, (C: 3)   –
  Yellow headland (1968)
  O 110 x 14", S, (C: 15)   £500
  Connemara Landscape

Among the contents of Darver Castle, Co Louth (sold by Hamilton Osborne King, 23 June 1993) were several lots of fine silver including a claret jug and lid by the Dublin maker, Robert Sawyer. Hallmarked for 1843, the jug had an interesting inscription. It was presented in 1856 to Captain Hugh Daniell by the officers of the South Tipperary Militia Artillery.

O 27 x 33", S, (F: 214)   £950
  The Twin Beaches
  M 5.25 x 4.75", S, (G: 182)   £150
  The Twelfth of July
  C 18 x 14", S,(L: 378)   –
AYRE, Miss G. M. (fl 1859-1862)
  On the Avoca, Co. Wicklow
  O 12 x 17.5", S, (A: 51)   £1,100
BALLAGH, Robert (b.1943)
  Sketch of a Couple and Clifford Still, 1973
  D 19.25 x 19.5", S, (A: 105)   –
  Kaliber Girl
  A 35 x 23", S, (F: 44)   –
  View of the Examination Hall from the Chapel, TCD
  Pr 35 x 24", S, D, (G: 188)   £100
BALLARD, Brian (b.1943)
  Green Vase and Flowers
  O 24 x 30", S, D, (D: 23)   –
  Tulips in a Glass Bowl
  O 24 x 30", S, (F: 129)   £1,400
  Still Life
  O 15 x 11", S, D, (G: 37)   £620
  Glass Jar
  O 15 x 11.5", S, D, (H: 7)   £570
BARNARD, William Henry (b. 1767)
  Killarney
  W 10.5 x 17", (D: 141)   £240
BARRET, George (1728-1784) Attributed
  Cattle Watering in a River Landscape
  O 28.5 x 45", (A: 113)   £2,200
  Wooded river landscape with figure resting
  O 12 x 16.5", (A: 59)   £950
BARRY, Moyra (1886-1960)
  Apple blossom
  W 27 x 22", S, (A: 7)   –
  Still Life Flowers, 1936
  W 11 x 15", S, D, (E: 85)   £360
  Still Life
  O 29 x 24", S, (F: 22)   £800
  Still Life, Spring flowers
  W 11 x 15.5", S, D, (N: 120)   –
BARTLETT, William Henry (1809-1854)
  Preparing for the Catch
  O 17 x 13", S, D, (F: 130)   –
BARTON, Rose Maynard (1856-1929)
  Tom & Jack
  W (2) 3.75 x 6", S, D, (G: 17)   £1,800
  Daffodils and Wallflowers in a green Vase
  W 21 x 14", S, D, (K: 24)   £7,150
  Peonies in a blue Vase
  W 21.25 x 14.75", S, D, (K: 26)   £1,980
  Chilly
  W 13.75 x 10", S, D, (K: 37)   £1,650
BATE, Thomas (fl. c. 1690-c. 1710) Attributed
  A View of the Formal Gardens at Blessington, Co. Wicklow
  O 40 x 24", (K: 79)   £9,350
BATEMAN, Monica (20th Century)

Christie's sold (15 September 1993) the contents of Lyrath, Co Kilkenny, a house that had been the property of the Wheeler-Cuffe family since 1743. The sale included several exceptionally fine pieces of Irish furniture including a set of fifteen late-Victorian oak dining chairs. These were stamped by the Dublin furniture makers, William Fry & Company. The set of chairs sold for £6,000.

Still Life	
O 12.5 x 15", S, (E: 103)	£50
BEECHEY, Richard Brydges (1808-1895)	
Shipwreck off the Irish Coast	
O 36 x 53.5", S, D, (N: 28)	£480
BEWICK, Pauline (b. 1935)	
On the Circus Box	
M 30 x 22.5", S, D, (D: 34)	–
Mount Street	
W 20 x 25", S, (E: 66)	£280
Woman & Chickens	
M 44 x 29.5", S, D, (G: 21)	–
Reading Clare Boylan	
W 23 x 17.5", S, I, D, (G: 29)	–
September	
W 31.5 x 23.5", S, (J: 53)	£1,150
Hydrangeas in a Vase	
W 29.5 x 22.5", S, D, (K: 27)	–
Female figure and poppies	
W 21 x 15", S, D, (N: 85)	£750
BIANCHI, Patricia (20th Century)	
Bogs in Autumn	
P 12 x 8", S, (E: 38)	£60
BISHOP, John Henry (20th Century)	
Still Life	
W 9.5 x 14", S, (H: 23)	–
BLACKHAM, Dorothy Isobel (1896-1975)	
Stormy day, Keel, Achill	
O 6.5 x 10", S (B: 10)	–
Stormy day, Keel, Achill	
O 6.5 x 10", S, (C: 103)	£220
Stormy Day, Keel, Achill	
O 6.25 x 10", S, (E: 163)	–
St Stephen's Green in the Summer	
O 26.5 x 20.5", (K: 139)	£605
Amoreiro, Portugal	
O 20 x 30", S, K: 140)	£605

BLACKSHAW, Basil (b. 1932)	
Nude	
O 24 x 24", (D: 135)	£1000
Church	
O 19.5 x 15.5", S, (A: 103)	–
BLACKSTOCK, H. (20th Century)	
Looking out from Ballywilliam, Co. Down	
O 9.75 x 11", S, (G: 88)	£130
BLAKE, Lady Edith (1845-1926)	
Dogy Bay, Newfoundland	
W 10.5 x 7", (C:79)	£370
BLUCK, J. (after T.S. Roberts)	
A South view on The River Liffey, Dublin	
Pr 25.5 x 35.5", (N: 31)	£800
BLUNDELL, J.	
Ploughing a Field with 3 Cob Horses	
W 14 x 20", S, (I: 60)	£130
BOAK, Robert Cresswell (b. 1875)	
Sheep grazing by a Road	
W (12) 10.5 x 15.5" & various, S, (L: 301)	£88
White Park Bay, Co. Antrim	
W (11) 4 x 8" & various, S, I, (L: 302)	–
The Clonmany Hills, Co. Donegal	
W (11) 12 x 20" & various, I, (L: 303)	£77
White Park Bay, Co. Antrim	
W (12) 7 x 15.5" & various, I, (L: 304)	£77
Portmuck, Co. Antrim	
W (10) 8.25 x 11.5" & various, S, I,(L: 305)	–
The Marble Strand, Co. Donegal	
W (12)9.5 x 15.5" & various, I, (L: 306)	£77
Dundrum	
W (12) 9.5 x 17.5" & various, I, (L: 307)	£99
Lands End	
W (12) 7.75 x 11.25" & various, S, I, (L: 308)	£77
The Gobbins from Blackhead, Co. Antrim	
W (12) 7.75 x 22.5" & various, I, (L: 309)	£110
Rathlin Island from White Park Bay	

W (12) 15 x 22.25" & various, I, (L: 310)	£77
White Park Bay and Portbradden, Co. Antrim	
W (11) 11.25 x 15" & various, I, (L: 311)	–
A Cornish Bay	
W (12) 11.25 x 15.5" & various, S, I, (L: 312)	£77
The Bloody Bridge, Mourne Mountains	
Pr (18) 5 x 10", S, I, (L: 113)	£660
Fair Head from the Strand, Ballycastle	
Pr (20) 5 x 10", S, (L: 314)	£660
Belfast and Cavehill from Castlereagh	
Pr (20) 7 x 9.875", S, I, (L: 315)	£660
Derwent Water	
Pr (22) 6.5 x 9.875", S, I, (L: 316)	£352
Loch Maree, Ross-shire	
D & Pr (27) 7.25 x 10" & various, I, (L: 317)	£418
Rounding a Buoy	
Pr 4 x 8", (L: 318)	£2,640
BOLTON, Henry	
Lake & Mountain Scene	
O– x–", S, (I: 72)	£150
BOURKE, Brian (b. 1936)	
Landscape	
O 40 x 33", S, D, (D: 116)	–
Don Quixote de la Mancha	
M 23.5 x 18", S, I, D, (D: 133)	£400
Donegal	
W 29 x 19", S, (E 53)	£300
Switzerland, 1972	
M 19 x 14", S, D, (E: 64)	–
Winter	
M 25 x 22", S, I, D, (G: 115)	£700
Dublin Landscape (Diptych)	
P 18 x 25", S, (H: 58)	£370
Portrait of J. W.	
M 30 x 22", S, (H: 71)	–
Donegal	
W 30 x 20", S, I, (N: 142)	£350
BOWEN, Gretta (1880-1981)	
At the Seaside	
O 17 x 24", (F: 198)	£380
BOYD, Diarmuid (20th Century)	
Still Life	
O 13.5 x 13", S, (G: 4)	£220
BOYD, Ellie (20th Century)	
Venice	
O 12.5 x 14", (G: 62)	–
BOYD, Emma S. (20th Century)	
The Model	
W 20 x 13.5", S, (H: 108)	£800
BOYLE, Alicia (b.1908)	
The Frail Student	
O 26 x 28", S, D, (F: 74)	–
Market is Done	
O 17 x 25", S, D, (F: 86)	£550
Staircase	
O 30 x 19", S, I, (F: 24)	–
Sherkin Abbey, 1959	
W 19.5 x 30", S, (F: 203)	–
BRADY, Charles (b. 1926)	
An Italian Pear	
O 10 x 17.5", S, (F: 165)	–
Thursday's Match Books	
O 15 x 19", S, (H: 61)	–
Composition, c. 1970	
O 11 x 15", S, (A: 85)	–
Small Paint Brush	
O 8.5 x 11", S, (E: 11)	£300
Tennis Shoe	
O 12.25 x 16", S, (H: 143)	£360
Ball of Wool	
W 15.5 x 11.75", S, D, (I: 13)	£340
At Sandymount Strand	
O 11 x 16.5", S, (N: 13)	£400
BRANDT, Muriel (1882-1978)	
Memories	
O 17.5 x 13.5", S, (D: 55)	£750
Sandymount Green	
W 10.75 x 16", S, (H: 4)	£600
BRENNAN, James Butler (1825-1889)	
A Portrait of an Irish Peasant Farmer	

with Dog in an Interior
O 37 x 30", S, D, (J: 76)   –
His Only Pair
O 21 x 17", S, D, (C: 70)   £2,300
BRIDLE, Kathleen (b. 1897)
Coastal View
W 11.5 x 17.5", S, (F: 183)   £150
BRILLY, June
Rest in Summer
O 24 x 30", S, (I: 65)
BROCAS S.F. (1792-1847)
View in Co. Wicklow
W 13.5 x 18", S, D, (A 131)   –
BROCAS, William (1794-1868)
The Farrier's Shop
O 28 x 36", S, D, (C: 82)   £6,200
BROWN, Christy (20th Century)
Self portrait
O 23 x 21", S, D, I, (A: 71)   £2,400
BROWN, Hugh Boycott (20th Century)
Melmore Mountain, Co. Donegal
O 7 x 9.25", S, (K: 151)   –
Muckish Mountain, Carrigart, Co. Donegal
O 7 x 9", S,(K: 152)   –
Landscape Near Letterkenny, County Donegal
O 7 x 9", S, (K: 153)   £286
Sunset, Melmore Mountain, Near
Carrigart, Co. Donegal
O 7 x 9", S, (K: 155)   £264
BRUEN, Gerald (20th Century)
Italian Landscape
W 11 x 10", (H: 49)   –
Italian Landscape
W 11 x 10", S, (H: 49)   –
BURKE, Augustus Nicholas (1838-1891)
Sheep in a Landscape
O 14.5 x 20", (G: 3)   –
Evening Sketch on The Lagoon, Venice
O 8 x 16", S, (N: 33)   –
BURKE, James (20th Century)
Still life study of Spring flowers
O 36 x 27", (C: 55)   –
BURROWS, S.
Views of the Lakes, Killarney, 1883
W (2) 9.5 x 14.5", S, D, (F: 217)   £250
BURTON, A
Taking A Rest
O 17 x 21", S, (J: 33)   £460
BUTLER, Mildred Anne (1858-1941)
Herbaceous border at Kilmurry
W 14 x 20.5", S, I, (B: 106)   £5,200
Cottage By The River - Near Kilmurry
W 9.5 x 6.5", S, (J: 51)   £1,600
CAHILL, Richard Staunton (1827-1904)
Reading a Letter
W 9.5 x 13.5", S, D, (D: 101)   £170
Portrait sketch of an elderly lady / An elderly man
D (2) 20 x 14.5", S, D, (K: 8)   –
CAMPBELL, Christopher (20th Century)
Portrait of Laurence Campbell
P 20 x 14", S, (D: 87)
Reflection in a Mirror
M 18.5 x 13.5", S, (H: 32)
CAMPBELL, George (1917-1979)
Workers returning, Antequera
O 24 x 30", S, (A: 36)   –
Mountain Landscape with Ruined Cottages
O 20 x 30", S (A: 76)   –
Fruit Seller, Malaga Street
W 16 x 8.5", S, (B: 146)   £420
My Window
Pr 14.5 x 11", S, (B: 148)   £300
Three Men Resting
M 11 x 16", S, (B: 151)   –
Farm near Granada
W 8.75 x 11.5", S, (C: 14)   –
On Inishere
O 16 x 20", S, (C: 30)   –
First Communion, Gypsy Girls, Malaga
O 30 x 20", S, I, (D: 16)   £2,000

Mildred BUTLER (1858-1941), Herbaceous Border at Kilmurry. *Sold at James Adam, Dublin, 5 October 1993 for £5,200*

Clown and Horse
O 15.5 x 19", S, (D: 24)   £1,500
Three Arabs, Tetuan (c. 1960)
P 10 x 15.5, S, (E: 10)   £220
Street Scene, Malaga
M 15 x 10", S, (F: 7)   £600
Winter
O 14 x 17", (F: 21)   –
Spanish Village
P 4.75 x 6.25", (G: 183)   £180
Farms Near Granada
W 8.5 x 11.5", (H: 94)   £550
London after the Blitz
O 15 x 17.5, (I: 7)   –
Malaga Night
O 30 x 40", S, I, (I: 67)   –
Abstract
M 18.5 x 25", S, (I: 68)   –
Knight VI
O 36 x 24", S, I, (J: 24)   £600
Night in Malaga
O 30 x 40", S, I, (J: 57)   £1,300
Bog and Rock
O 20 x 30", S, I, (K: 135)   £1,100
Play of shapes, No. 15, Azteciana
O 50 x 18", S, I, (K: 136)   –
Winter Landscape, Spain
O 11.25 x 15.5", S, (M: 118)   £750
Fishing Village, Andalucia
M 8 x 10.5", S, (N: 6)   £200
Warriors
O 19.5 x 16", S, (N: 26a)   £3,000
Holyweek, Malaga
O 25 x 30", S, (O: 43)   £3,220
Turf-Cutters
14 x 18", S, (O: 47)   £1,610
No. 6 Patrol
O 20 x 24", (O: 49)   –
Dun Aengus Fort, Inishmore
O 35.5 x 50", S, (O: 52)   –
CAMPBELL, John Henry (1757-1828) Attributed
Wooded lake and mountain landscape
with figures
O 15 x 20", (A: 63)   £4,600
CAMPBELL, John Henry (1757-1828)
An Extensive View - Lough Glasbough,
Co. Monaghan
O 24 x 40", (J: 75)   –
CARACCIOLO, Niccolo d'Ardia (1941-1989)
The Red Car
O 17 x 22", S, (D: 63)   £2,500
The Courtyard of the Palazzo Pitti
W 12 x 9", S, (D: 71)   £850
Nude Study
D 16 x 12", S, (F: 18)   £600
Harvesting at Castletown, Co. Kildare
W 7.25 x 10.75", S, (F:162)   £750
Volterra, Italy (c. 1982)
W 7.5 x 11.5", S, (G: 153)   £600
CAREY, Joseph W. (1859-1937)

Glenetive
W 11 x 15.5", S, I, D, (B: 132)   –
Glengarriff
W 10 x 15", S, D, (B: 134)   –
Bantry Bay
W 8 x 14.75", S, D, (B: 135)   –
Continental Landscape
W 6 x 8.5", S, (F: 136)   £140
Howth
W 10 x 14.5", S, I, (J: 16)   –
Lough Gill, Sligo
W 9.75 x 14.25", S, I, (J: 17)   –
Bridge at Ballycastle
W 13 x 10", S, I, (J: 18)   –
The Mountains of Mourne, Co. Down
W 10 x 15", S, D, (K: 16)   £715
Lough Muick
W 10.375 x 14", S, D, I, (K: 17)   £770
Fair Head
W 8.75 x 21.75", S, I, D, (K: 18)   £1,430
The Giant's Causeway, Co. Antrim
W 11.25 x 15.5", S, D, (K: 19)   £1,210
Abernethy, Perthshire
W 13 x 10.125", S, D, I, (L: 337)   £220
The Annalong Valley, Mountains of Mourne
W 14.5 x 20.5", S, D, I, (L: 338)   £939
The Devil's Bite, Bryan's-Ford Mourne
W 8.5 x 10.75", I, (L: 340)   £308
Ireland's Eye from Howth
W 10 x 14.5", S, D, (N: 148)   £850
CARR, Tom (b. 1909)
Wooded landscape
O 16 x 18", S, (A: 13)   –
Lower Lough Erne
W 15 x 21", S, I, D, (H: 2)   £950
Children Paddling
W 4.5 x 4.25", S, (J: 6)   –
Give Way
W 10 x 14.5", S, (L: 388)   £330
Edenderry House
O 20 x 30", S, (L: 456)   £4,950
Girl reading
P 6 x 8", S, (N: 147)   £220
Two figures and a horse
W 9.5 x 13", S, (A: 58)   £450
CARRICK, Desmond (b. 1930)
On the Liffey River Bed, Ballysmutton,
Co. Wicklow 1981
O 16 x 20", S, (A: 18)   –
Winter Landscape
O 18 x 24", S, (E: 171)   £300
On the Liffey Riverbed, Ballysmutton,
Co. Wicklow (1981)
O 16 x 20", S, (F: 158)   £520
CARSON, Joy (20th Century)
A Gathering at a Country Fair
W 5.25 x 7", (F: 190)   £70
CARSON, Robert Taylor (b.1919)
September Evening, Cotswolds
O 28 x 42", S, (B: 65)   –
Maghera Cliffs, Co. Donegal
O 20 x 24", S, I, (D: 56)   £600
Beech at Downings
O 11 x 14.5", S, I, (I: 5)   £400
Glen Lough
O 12 x 15.5", S, (I: 9)   –
Spring Flowers
O 10 x 13.5", S, (I: 82)   £400
Children on the Pier, Roundstone
Harbour, Connemara
O 16 x 20", S, (K: 105)   £715
Achill Farmer
O 16 x 20", S, I, (K: 129)   –
Letterkenny Group
O 19.5 x 29.5", S, I, D, (N: 16)   £550
Pat's Kitchen
O 7 x 11", S, I, D, (N: 111)   £200
CARVER, Robert (1730-1791)
Figures by a Waterfall, possibly at Powerscourt
O 24 x 32", (K: 80)   £7,700

CLARKE, Carey (b.1936)
Galway Hooker
O 10 x 11", S, I, (I: 6) £300
The Wicklow Lands
O 22 x 33", S, I, (I: 53) £460
CLARKE, David (20th Century)
Ancient Oaks, Phoenix Park, Winter
P 19 x 25", S,(H: 73) £450
CLARKE, Harry (1889-1931) Attributed
Cartoon study for a stained glass panel
of St. Anne and a Child
W 73 x 29.5", (C: 49) –
CLARKE, Margaret (1888-1961)
The Mountain Goat
O 24 x 19", S, (F: 100) –
Flowers in a Vase
W 21 x 16", S, F: 113) £500
Aran Woman
D 20 x 14", S, (H: 68) £400
A Portrait of Sean Keating, seated quarter-length
D 13 x 9.5", (K: 11) £2,200
CLARKE, Terence (1917-1968)
Original design for Rose Window in
the Carmelite Church, Loughrea, Co. Galway
W 10" (diam.), I, (H: 117) –
Original design for Rose Window in
the East Transept, St. Michael's
Church, Renuera, Auckland, N.Z.
W 11" (Diam.), I, (H: 118) –
Original design for Rose Window
in St. Michael's Church, Renuera,
Auckland, N.Z.
W 16.5" (Diam.), I, (H: 119) –
Original design for Rose Window in
Parish Church, Wilton, Cork
W 15.5" (Diam.), S, I, (H: 120) –
COGHILL, Sir Egerton Bushe (19th/20th Century)
On the Moors, Glencolumbkille
O 14 x 20", S, (E: 159) £170
COLEMAN, Simon (b. 1916)
The Canal
O 17 x 21", S, D, (F: 20) £650
COLLINS, Patrick (1911-1994)
Study of Swallows
O 10 x 14", S, D, (A: 136) –
Unhappy Man, drinking beer
D 10 x 7.5", S, (A: 137) –
Mountains, Wicklow
O 11 x 14.5", S, (B: 88) £3,400
Carousel
O 16 x 23", S, D, (D: 45) £4,800
Studies of Miro
D (6) 5 x 6.25", S, I, D, (D: 136) –
Pere Lachaise
D 6 x 8", (D: 137) £100
In Pere Lachaise Cemetery, Paris
O 10 x 12.5", S, D, (G: 126) –
The Rook's Nests
O 17.5 x 11", S, (G: 159) £870
Still Life, Table & Chair
O 20 x 24", S, D, (I: 49) –
Kitchen sink
O 16 x 20", S, D, (N: 63) –
COLLIS, Peter (b. 1929)
Lough Tey
O 32 x 36", S, (E: 12) –
Thaw Murphystown
O 10 x 12", S, (N: 145) –
Wicklow Landscape
O 28 x 36", S, (E: 6) £820
Dun Laoghaire at night
O 7.5 x 9.5", S, (B: 77) £420
Wicklow mountains
O 8.5 x 9.25", S, (B: 85) £270
Wicklow
O 12 x 11", S, (B: 96) £ 270
Mountain side with trees
O 7 x 7.5", S, (C: 39) £160
Mayo Bog
O 5.25 x 7.5", S, (C: 101) £150

Margaret CLARKE (1881-1961), Portrait of Sean
Keating. Sold at Christie's, Dublin, 26 May 1993
(£2,200).

Landscape
O 7.5 x 9.5", S, (C: 105) £150
Still Life with Flowers
O 16 x 14", S, (D: 17) £400
Dalkey Island
O 20 x 28, S, (D: 47) £750
The Sugarloaf from Trooperstown
O 16 x 20", S, (D: 108) £500
A Small Reservoir, Glenasmole
O 22 x 24", S, (F: 23) £570
Still Life
O 28 x 20", S, (H: 122) –
Still life apples
O 18 x 22", S, (N: 134) –
Wicklow landscape
O 11.5 x 9", S, (N: 146) £400
Farm at Glenasmole with closed gate (1991)
O 30 x 34", S, (B: 6) £800
Mountain landscape
P 12 x 17", S, (A: 138) –
Ballycoyle, Forest Road
O 5.5 x 6.5", S, (D: 140) £160
Lough Dan
O 12 x 12", S, (H: 134) –
Sunset
O 22 x 24", S, (H: 137) £600
COLMAN, Eamon (20th Century)
Coming Storm
P 29 x 24", S, (E: 112) £100
COMERFORD, Oliver (20th Century)
Chicago Apartment
M 8 x 5.5", S, I, D, (E: 109) £90
CONNOLLY, Thurloe (20th Century)
Deer in the Forest
O10 x 19.5", S, I, D, (E: 102) £400
CONOR, William (1884-1968)
Churning
O 20 x 16", S, (C: 44) –
Study for the Launch
D 4.5 x 4.75", S, (F: 117) –
Figure Studies
D (2) 3.75 x 3", S, (F: 118) £400
Dublin Docks
W 6.75 x 10", S, (G: 5) £400
The Trial of Oscar Wilde -
Ned Carson for the Prosecution
W 8 x 4.5", S, (I: 41) £490

The Cottage -Stranmillis
W 8.75 x 12", S, I, (J: 3) –
A Politician
P 18.875 x 13.875", S, (K: 9) £2,090
Parading the Banner
P 11.75 x 9", S, (L: 362) £1,430
At the Races
W 10.5 x 8.125", S, (L: 363) £495
The Old Fiddler
P 10.25 x 8.625", S, (L: 365) £1,100
Women and Children in a Street
W 19 x 14.5", S, D, (L: 366) –
Near Bunbeg, Co. Donegal
P 14.75 x 19.25", S, (L: 368) –
Lough Erne
W 12 x 17", S, (L: 374) –
Study for The Launch
D 4.5 x 4.75", S, (N: 122) –
Fares Please
P 14 x 19.5", S, (O: 31) £5,620
Dough-Boys Enjoying a Ride on
a Jaunting-Car
P 14.75 x 17.25", S, (O: 33) £4,600
Chair-o-planes
P 19.75 x 14.25", S, (O: 34) £3,450
Ballad Singers
P 11.75 x 11.75", S, (O: 35) £4,887
The Road-Sweeper
P 17 x 12.5", S, (O: 36) £2,645
Sally
P 15.25 x 11.75", S, (O: 37) –
College Hill, Armagh
P 12.75 x 17.5", S, (O: 39) £2,300
Hobby-Horses
O 30 x 25", S, (O: 44) £12,650
Washing-Day
O 20 x 24", S, (O: 46) £9,775
COOK, Charles Henry (c. 1830-c.1906)
Young Man Drinking
O 12 x 9", S, (E: 33) £340
COOKE, Barrie (b. 1931)
Portrait of Lady Goulding
O 32 x 30", (B: 79) £750
Lough Derg from the Clare Shore IV
W 17 x 19", S, I, D, (D: 93) £400
Mountain Landscape
O 20.5 x 22.5", (F: 46) £870
Nude (c. 1985)
W 17 x19", S, (G: 95) £320
COOLT, B.
Trotting
O 17.75 x 26.25", S, (J: 72) –
COOPER, Margaret (1893-1992)
Winter Morning, Seine Woods, 1987
W & O (47) 8.125 x 11.625" &
various, S, I, (L: 319) £88
Misty Morning in Seine Woods
W & O (47) 8.875 x 12.875"
& various, S, I, (L: 320) –
Perranporth, Cornwall, 1934
W & O (48) 9.25 x 15.5"
& various, I, D, (L: 321) £132
COOPER, W. F. (20th Century)
Lake View
W 7.5 x 10.5", S, (G: 206) £80
COPE, Elizabeth (20th Century)
View of Carlow Town (1989)
O 24 x 30", S, (B: 9) £420
Still Life with Oysters
O 24 x 30", S, I, D, (D: 5) £570
Still Life
O 35 x 28", S, (F: 30) £820
Table & Sideboard
O 29 x 34", S, (G: 181) –
Sunflowers
O 13.5 x 11", S, (J: 63) £380
COSTELLOE, Eileen (1911-1976)
Rock Section, Sceiligmhicil
O 32 x 24", S, I, (F: 157) £400
CRADOCK, Marmaduke (After)

Peacocks in a Landscape/Rooster, Chicks,
Hen & Duck in a River Landscape
O (2) 11 x 17", (J: 64) —
CRAIG, Henry Robertson (1916-1984)
Spanish Child
O 30 x 18", S, (B: 90) —
Interior - a drawingroom with two gentlemen
O 20 x 25", S, (A: 22) £3,500
Cafe in Torremolinos
O 10 x 14", S, I, (H: 10) £650
Street Cafe
O 14 x 24", (H: 51) £500
Portimao Harbour
O 7 x 9", S, (L: 423) £308
Ulick
O 11.4 x 8", S, (N: 35) £500
CRAIG, James Humbert (1878-1944)
Bloody Foreland
O 14.5 x 19.5", S, (A: 79) —
River in Flood, Connemara
O 16 x 20", S, (A: 99) £2,600
Bloody Foreland
O 14.5 x 19.5", S, (B: 40) —
A Silver Day in The Rosses
O 11.5 x 16", S, (B: 55) —
The Bann Valley
O 18 x 24", S, (B: 72) £3,800
Tabulliagh Mountain
O 6 x 9", S, I, (C: 10) —
Evening on The Rosses, Co. Donegal
O 15 x 20", S, I, (C: 16) £3,800
Out Hunting
O 15 x 20", S, (D: 14) —
Weaving at the Cottage Door
O 18 x 14.5", S, (D: 77) £6,700
Near Salruck, Connemara
O 15 x 20", S, I, (F: 40) —
Showery Day, Donegal
O 15.5 x 19 S, (F: 89) —
South of Bloody Foreland
O 16 x 20", S, (F: 115) —
The End of Lough Mask
W 3.5 x 5", S, (F: 126g) £140
The Road to Burton Port
O 11.5 x 16", S, I, (G: 11) £2,500
Bringing Home the Catch
O 17 x 21", S,(H: 19) £4,600
Boats in an Inlet
W 6.5 x 9.5", S, I, D, (H: 33) —
Breaghey Head, Co. Donegal
O 21 x 29", S, (H: 149) £5,900
Gathering Turf, The Kenran Bog
O 16 x 20", S, (I: 47) £4,800
Galway Fisherfolk
O 18.5 x 24", S, I, (I: 59) £8,700
Children and Boats by an Esturary
O 10 x 14", S, (K: 160) £2,860
Bunbeg, County Donegal
O 16 x 20", S, I, D, (K: 174) £1,540
The Mayfly is up
W 3.5 x 5", S, (L: 360) £330
Lough Mask Castle
W 5.25 x 4", S, (L: 361) —
Unloading the Catch in a West of Ireland Bay
O 17 x 21", S, (L: 406) £2,640
Sheephaven, Co. Donegal
O 15 x 20", S, I, (L: 407) —
Alton Lough, Co. Donegal
O 15 x 20", S, (L: 408) —
Summer Morning, Cushendun Village,
Co. Antrim
O 15 x 19", S, I, (L: 409) £3,300
Horn Head, Dunfanaghy
O 12 x 17", S, I, (L: 410) —
Women Working by a Whaded Table,
Brittany /A Busy Market
O (2) 5.5 x 9.375", S, (L: 411) —
Cattle grazing in Glenwhirry, Co. Antrim
O 14.875 x 20", S, I, (L: 465) £1,760
Cattle grazing in a sunlit Mountainous

river Landscape
O 16 x 20", S, (L: 466) £1,540
Glendun, Co. Antrim
O 16 x 20", S, (L: 467) —
Potato Pickers in a coastal Landscape
O 15 x 20", S, (L: 468) —
Near Creeslough, Co. Donegal
O 15 x 20", S, I, (M: 115) £2,000
Sunday morning, Bloody Foreland
O 11.5 x 16.5", S, (N: 56) £4,800
Fisherman by a river
O 20 x 24", S, (N: 69) —
Donegal landscape with figure on a path
O 9 x 12", S, (N: 139) £1,200
Races at Waterfoot
P 15 x 20", S, (O: 32) £6,900
CRAIG, Michael (20th Century)
Russborough
D 4.5 x 7.5", S, (G: 180) —
CREGAN, Martin (1788-1870) Attributed
Portrait of a Gentleman
O 29 x 25", (C: 102) £1,100
CROZIER, William (b.1930)
Angel
O 24 x 22.5", S, I, (C: 97) —
Harbour scene, Granton
W 11 x 11", S, (C: 98) —
Landscape, Provence
O 13 x 19", S, D, (F: 14) £1,200
Field, Provence, 1983
O 13 x 19", S, (G: 23) —
North Star Venus
O 42 x 45", S, I, (M: 188) —
CUDWORTH, Jack (20th Century)
Still Life

O 14 x 16", S, (A: 31) —
Woman in Restaurant
O 11 x 13", S, D, (D: 113) £320
CUNNINGHAM, J. (fl. 1935)
View of Sandycove, Co. Dublin
O 14 x 24", S, D, (N: 83) —
Two race horses exercising
W 21 x 29", S, (B: 110) £2,800
Round the turn
Pr 19.5 x 28", S, I, (B: 111) —
A leisurely canter
W 14.5 x 22", S, (B: 112) —
Over The Chair Fence, Aintree
W 14 x 21", S, D, (G: 6) —
On the Rein
O 19.5 x 27", S, (G: 81) —
Approaching the Finish
W 14.5 x 26", S, D, (H: 12) —
Horse and jockey
O 25 x 33", S, (N: 112) —
The Home Straight
W 15.5 x 23", S, (N: 146a) £1,500
CURTIN, Isabel Mary (20th Century)
Nativity
O 27 x 22", S, (L: 425) —
CURTIN, Maureen (20th Century)
On the Canal
O 9.5 x 23, S, I, (E: 19) —
DANBY, James Francis (1816-1875)
View of the Killarney Lakes
W 6.25 x 9.5", (G: 130) —
DANBY, Thomas (1818-1886)
The Way to the Glen
W 9.5 x 21", S, D, (N: 150) £220
Landscape near Emmerdale

One of the highlights of the year's sales was the auction of the remaining stock of the late Ronnie McDonnell -considered by many to have been the doyen of Dublin antique dealers. This was conducted by Mealy's of Castlecomer in the august surroundings of the Royal Hospital, Kilmainham (20 October 1993)) and realised £1.2 million making it the most successful single-day sale ever held in Ireland.
The 18th-century bird pictures of Samuel Dixon were one of McDonnell's specialities and, among several examples in the sale, a particularly fine one went for £12,100.

W 13.75 x 19.5", S, (G: 174) –

DANIELL, William (1769-1837)
Dunluce Castle, Co. Antrim
W 6.125 x 9", S, I, D, (L: 329) –
Dundrum Castle, Slive (sic) Donard in the distance
W 6.125 x 9", S, I, D, (L: 330) –
Fair Head, Co. Antrim
W 6.125 x 9", S, I, D, (L: 331) –
Green Castle, Carlingford Lough, Greenwood Park, Rostrevor Mountain
W 6.125 x 9", I, D, (L: 332) –

DAVIDSON, Lilian (d. 1954)
Boats at Wicklow, Dusk
O 36 x 28", S, (B: 60) £10,000
The Road by Lough Fee, Connemara
W 11 x 18", S, (H: 154) –
Voyage Ended
W 23 x 19", S, I, (J: 25) –

DEEGAN, Philip (20th Century)
Near Howth (1942)
W 10 x 14", S, (B: 114) £90

DELANEY, Edward (b. 1930)
Untitled
Pr 15 x 13", S, D, (E: 135) £70

DICKINSON, Page L. (20th Century)
Evening - The Docks
W 9 x 13", S, (F: 184) –

DILLON, Gerard (1916- 1971)
Reclining nude
P 4 x 5", S, (A: 6) £200
Abstract
W 3.25 x 5", S, (A: 12) £130
Abstract
D 4 x 5.5" S, (A: 16) £220
Caged Bird
O 20 x 25.5", S, (A34) –
Dun Angus, Aran Boat
O 15.5 x 19", S, I, (D: 16) £11,000
Spanish Window Washing
O 17 x 22", S, I, (D:59) £5,500
Donkey, Innishlacken
O 14 x 19.5", S, (D: 73) £2,600
Mountain Farm
D/C 16 x 20", S, (E: 50) £970
Green Nude
O 20 x 24", S, (E: 61) £1,850
Coming Home
W 10 x 14", S, (E: 62) £820
Abstract, Spain
O 17 x 18", S, (E: 73) £800
Study of a Young Woman
W 11 x 8.5", S, (F: 8) £480
Aran Boys Lost in a Flooded River
O 12 x 17", S, I, (F: 73) £2,100
Girl at the Well
O 10 x 13.5", S, (F: 85) £4,200
Bathers on the Beach, Malaga
O 13.5 x 17.5", S, I, (G: 15) £3,000
The Holy Family
M 10 x 14", S, (G: 111) £700
Abstract Form
Sand 17.5 x 23.5", S, (G: 127) £600
Themes of the Sea
M 25 x 30", S, (G: 205) £1,600
The Wall
O 12.75 x 20.5", S, (H: 39) £4,500
Goodbye Old Paint
O/Sand 48 x 72", S, (H: 56) –
The Herring Man
W 15.5 x 19", S, (I: 66) –
Harvest Image
O 20 x 30", S, I, (I: 87) –
Inish Lacken
O 9.5 x 13.5", S, I, (J: 13) £3,000
A Figure in a Bedroom
O 11 x 15", S, (K: 106) £1,870
Herding Goats and Cattle over a stone Bridge
O 8.75 x 13.25", S, (K: 107) £990
Pierrot with Portrait
M 10.75 x 14.25", S, (L: 389) £990

Gerard DILLON (1916-71): Connelly's Bar, Inishlaken. *Sold at Sotheby's, 24 November 1993 (£6,900).*

Mellifont Abbey Ruins
W 15.875 x 20.625", S, (L: 390) £772
Still Life with Pears and Irish Stone
O 24.5 x 17.75", (M: 123) –
Decorated canoe
O 16 x 25", S, (N: 37) £1,200
The Fish-Eaters
O 17 x 20.75", S, (O: 29) £11,500
Self-Contained Flat
O 48 x 72", S, I, (O: 38) –
Connelly's Bar, Inishlaken
O 14 x 20", S, I, (O: 50) £6,900
Tea-Party
O 34.5 x 39.5", S, I, (O: 53) £12,650

DIXON, James (20th Century)
The 'Queen Mary' passing Tory Island
O 18.75 x 29.5", (L: 426) £1,650
Island Gull
O 10.625 x 23.625", S, I, D, (L: 427) £990
Tor Mor
O 19.25 x 29.5", (L: 428) £1,320
A sailing Ship passing Tory Island
O 19.75 x 29.5", (L: 429) £1,650
Ship aground off Tory Island
O 20.5 x 29.5", (L: 430) £1,320

DIXON, Sean (20th Century)
O'Connell Bridge

Lilian DAVIDSON (d.1954): Boats at Wicklow, Dusk. *Sold at James Adam, Dublin, 5 October 1993, (£10,000).*

W 16 x 12", S, (F: 138) £150

DOHERTY, John (20th Century)
Studio One, O'Connell Street
W 10.5 x 15.5", S, I, D, (H: 78) –

DONOVAN, Phoebe (20th Century)
Dinner Hour, Bray
O 20 x 28", S, (D: 50) £650
Figures on the River Bank
O 15.5 x 12", S, (E: 108) –
The Gate
O 9 x 13", S, (E: 115) £120
White Cherry
O 24 x 27.5", S, (F: 180) £200

DORAN, Christopher M. (20th Century)
Bridge over The Blackwater
W 11 x 15", S, (B: 143) £70

DUFFIELD, Michael (20th Century)
The Magician & Two Others
D (3) 18.5 x 12.5", S, (E: 118) £220

DUFFY, Patrick Vincent (1839-1909)
The Sugar Loaf Mountain from Bushy Park
O 14 x 22", (A: 60) £4,000
Skerries from The Balbriggan Coast
o 17 x 24", s, (A 64) £1,400
Killiney Bay and Bray from Killiney Hill
O 30 x 56", S, (C: 83) £3,800

DUNLOP, Ronald Ossory (1894-1973)
Swanbourne Park, Autumn
O 20 x 24", S, (N: 140) –

DUNNE, George (20th Century)
Couple in Interior
O 18 x 15.5", S, D, (E: 99) –
Landscape
O 18 x 20", S, (E: 104) £180

EGGINTON, Frank J. (1908 -1990)
Donegal Coast Scene
W 14.5 x 21", S, (B: 125) £800
The Rag River, Co. Donegal
W 21 x 29.5", s, (A 129) £1000
The Maam Valley, Connemara
O 24 x 36", s, (A 93) –
Connemara lake and mountain landscape with sheep on a road
W 21 x 29.5", s, (A 102) £1,500
An inlet near Recess
W 10.5 x 15", S, D, (A 110) –
Lough Tanny, Connemara
O 23.5 x 35.5", s, (A 20) –
Lackagh Bridge, Co. Donegal
W 15 x 22", S, D, (F: 33) £970
Hughie Strain's Cottage, Horn Head
W 10 x 14.25", S, D, (F: 34) £900
An Inlet Near Recess, Connemara
W 10.25 x 14.75", S, D, (F: 38) £620
View in Donegal
W 21 x 29", S, (F: 99) £1,700
The Vale of Avoca
W 10 x 14", S, D, (F: 120) –
Summers Day, Donegal
W 14 x 21", S, (F: 212) £1,000
Errigal from Gweedore, Co. Donegal
W 20 x 29", S, (G: 18) £1,600
Driving Home the Sheep
W 10 x 14", S, D, (G: 45) £750
Autumn, Sligo
O 19.5 x 25", S, D, (G: 112) £1,300
Autumn, Skibbereen
W 14.5 x 21", S, D, (G: 155) –
A Quiet Summer's Day
W 10.5 x 14.5", S, D, (G: 197) £500
Quiet Summer's Day
W 10.5 x 14.5", S, (I: 10) –
Lake & Mountain Scene - West of Ireland
W 14.5 x 20.5", S, (I: 91a) –
Peat Gatherers
W 10 x 13.5", S, (J: 52) –
Early Morning, Ballyconneely
W 20.75 x 29.5", S, D, (K: 28) –
The Ards Peninsula, Co. Donegal
W 21 x 30", S, D, (K: 29) £1,980

The Twelve Pins, Connemara
O 24 x 36", S, D, (K: 142) — £5,280
A Wet Day, Co. Down
W 14 x 21", S, (L: 352) — £990
A Cottage near Belmullet, Co. Mayo
W 10 x 14", S, (L: 353) — –
Near Cashel, Connemara
W 10.125 x 14.125", S, (L: 354) — £990
Glengariff, Co. Cork
W 9.5 x 13.75", S, (L: 355) — £495
A Donkey and Chickens by a
Thatched Cottage, Co. Mayo
W 14.5 x 20.5", S, (L: 356) — £1,540
A Wet Day, Connemara
W 14 x 20.75", S, (L: 357) — £1,045
At Rosbeg, Co. Donegal
W 14.5 x 20.75", S, (L: 358) — £1,100
Muckish from Bloody Foreland, Co. Donegal
W 14.75 x 21", S, (L: 359) — –
A Wet Day, Mournes, Co. Down
W 10.5 x 14.5", S, D, (N: 34) — –
EGGINTON, Wycliffe (1875-1951)
The Incoming Tide
W 11.25 x 15.75", S, (K: 2) — £330
Driving Sheep
W 6.75 x 9.25", S, (K: 15) — £715
Turf Gatherers and Ponies in a Bog Landscape
W 10.25 x 14", S, D, (L: 351) — £1,210
A walk on the Moors
W 11 x 14.5", S, (N: 129) — £300
EMMET, Roland (20th Century)
A Devonshire Lane
O 20 x 24", S, (G: 157) — –
ENGLISH, James (b. 1946)
The Broken Weir, The Boyne
O 16 x 11", S, (H: 52) — £200
FARRELL, Michael (b. 1940)
Yellow Press, 1972
Pr 26 x 29", S, D, (E: 86) — –
Anvers Sur Oise
W 22 x 36", S, I, D, (G: 100) — £560
La Ruche
Pr 26 x 32", S, D, (G: 177) — –
Alcool de Serpent
Pr 32 x 22", S, D, (H: 142) — £130
FAULKNER, John (1835-1894)
A Sheep Farm
W 17.5 x 29", S, I, (G: 49) — £1,700
Landscape
W 5.25 x 8.5", S, (G: 117) — £260
Cliffs, Blacksod Bay, Co. Mayo
26.25 x 46.25", S, I, (K: 23) — £3,520
A Mountain Top approach to Glen Cree,
Co. Wicklow
W 11.625 x 20.375", S, D, (K: 41) — £495
A Breezy Morning
W 22.5 x 29.5", S, I, (L: 327) — –
Sundown
W 17 x 30", S, I, (L: 328) — –
Faggot Gatherers and Sheep by a
Windmill in a Coastal Landscape
W 15.25 x 29.25", S, (L: 333) — £1,320
Cliff at Achill Island, Co. Mayo
W 40 x 25", S, I, (L: 339) — –
FISH, George Drummond (20th Century)
Bray Head and the Sugar Loaf from Killiney
W 12.5 x 18.5", s, (A 109) — £240
Lough Dan, Co. Wicklow
W 10 x 13.5", S, (F: 126) — £340
Lough Coomasaharn, Co. Kerry
W 10 x 14", S, I, (H: 53) — £270
FLANAGAN, Terence P. (b. 1929)
Grey Shore
O 25 x 30", S, (B: 82) — –
Benbulben from Grange
O 24 x 30", S, (C: 11) — £1,300
Bog 2
O 10 x 14", (E: 28) — £230
The Quarry
W 14.5 x 23", S, D, (F: 204) — £460

In the Woods
O 24 x 20", S, (G: 154) — £850
Grey Shore
O 25 x 30", S, (N: 136) — £750
FLYNN, Carmel (20th Century)
Still Life, Roses in a Vase
W 23 x 15", S, D, (G: 58) — £140
Sunflowers
W 22 x 15", S, D, (H: 112) — £200
FORBES, Alexander Stanhope (1857-1947)
Portrait of a boy
O 14.25 x 11", S, (C: 69) — –
Mousehole Harbour
O 17 x 13", S, D, (F: 164) — £5,600
FORBES, Ronald (b. 1947)
Creation with Fragments
A 54 x 45", S, D, I, (O: 42) — –
FOX, Kathleen (1880-1963)
A Moonlight Sonata
O 24.5 x 29.5", S, D, (G: 33) — £3,500
FRENCH, William Percy (1854-1920)
Evening light
W 7 x 10", S, (B: 108) — £1,700
Lakeland scene
W 6 x 9", S, D, (B: 131) — £1,200
Perfect peace - bogland landscape

A Path through a Bog, West of Ireland
W 6.5 x 9.5", S, D, (K: 35) — £660
A Cottage by a Road
W 6.5 x 9.375", S, (L: 345) — £825
A sunlit flooded Bog
W 6.5 x 9.375", (L: 346) — £715
Bog at Sunset
W 8 x 11", (L: 347) — –
A Cottage by a Lake in a mountainous
Landscape
W 6 x 11", S, D, (L: 348) — £528
A Fishing Boat in a Coastal Landscape
W 6.5 x 9.375", S, D, (L: 349) — £825
Trees by a Bog at Sunset
W 9.5 x 14", S, (L: 350) — £1,540
Ballinakill, Connemara
W 9.5 x 13.5", S, I, (N: 76) — £900
Breakers on the Rocks
W 6.5 x 10", S, (N: 125b) — –
FRIERS, Julian (20th Century)
Chaffinch / Goldcrests / Bluetits
W (3) 5" diam., S, (N: 131) — £400
FRIERS, Rowel (b. 1920)
Owl on a tree branch and kingfisher
W (2) 15 x 11.5", S, (N: 103) — –
Bluetits

There were a number of very good mahogany and brass-bound peat buckets in the Ronnie McDonnell sale (Mealy's, 20 October 1993). Several were sold as pairs. The two on the left fetched £9,400, those on the right, £12,100.

W 6 x 9.75", S, (B: 147) — £1,400
Dunfanaghy
W 7 x 10", I, (C: 43) — £900
Bogland river landscape
W 7 x 10", S, D, (C: 91) — £1,500
Mussenden, Portstewart
W 7 x 10", S, D, (D: 88) — –
Bog and River landscape
W 14.5 x 22", S, (A 56) — –
Evening Landscape
W 6 x 8", S, D, (F: 147) — £1,300
Evening Landscape
W 6 x 8", S, D, (F: 148) — –
Sunshine & Shadow on the Road to Leenane
W 8 x 11.5", S, (G: 136) — £420
The Bog Road
W 10 x 14", S, (H: 160) — £1,500
Cottage by the River
W 7 x 9.5", S, D, (H: 161) — £1,500
Sunset on the Shannon
O 9 x 27", (H: 162) — £1,500
The Canal, Dublin
W 8.375 x 9.625", S, D, I, (K: 32) — £1,760
An Irish Bog
W 9.25 x 14.25", S, (K: 33) — £2,420
A Bog Landscape with Hills beyond
W 7 x 10", S, D, (K: 34) — £880

W 18 x 15", S, (N: 104) — –
Coastal Landscape
O 16 x 20", S, (N: 127) — –
Bluetit feeding a cuckoo
W 17 x 14", S, (N: 133) — –
FROST, Stella (fl. 1940's)
Still Life
W 16.5 x 14.5", (E: 75) — £240
FRY, Windsor Arthur (20th Century)
Castle Market, Belfast, 1916
W 22 x 18", S, (L: 382) — £1,220
GALBALLY, Cecil (20th Century)
Guitar Player
O 20 x 18", s, (A 23) — £1000
GALLOWAY, Everett (20th Century)
A schooner-rigged Boat in a calm Sea
W 12.75 x 9", S, (L: 381) — £110
GANLY, R. Brigid (b. 1937)
Nasturtiums
O 12 x 12.5", S, (B: 57) — –
Anto's Jar with Apples
O 16 x 12", S, (B: 97) — –
Roses with salt cellar
O 14 x 18", S, (C: 32) — £420
Phlox - still life
O 15 x 18", I, (C: 42) — £500
Mead jar with pears

O 12 x 15", S, (C: 86) £360
Pink and White Roses in a Glass Vase
O 16 x 12", S, (D: 11) £700
A Lock on the Canal
O 9.5 x 13.5", I, (F: 5) £360
Convolvulus in a Glass (1964)
O 14 x 12", S, (F: 52) £360
A Still Life of Roses
O 12 x 16", S, (F: 178) –
Steep Cartrack, Tasmania
O 13 x 17.5", S, (I: 76) –
Upper Glenageary Road
O 20 x 16", S, (I: 79) –
Cretan Street
W 11 x 11.5", S, (N: 130) £200
GARNER, Philippa (20th Century)
Connolly's Folly, Celbridge
O 9 x 6.5", S, D, (G: 103) £220
The Circus Ring
O 22 x 23", S, D, (E: 3) –
GARSTIN, Norman (1855-1926)
A Country Cottage
P 22 x 16", S, (C: 77) –
GAULT, George (20th Century)
Flowerpiece
O 19.5 x 15", S, (K: 173) –
GENNARO, Gaetano De (20th Century)
Inishere
O 19 x 15.5", S, I, (H: 26) £470
Still Life – a jug of daffodils
P 16.5 x 24", S, I, D, (N: 8) £750
GIBNEY, Arthur (20th Century)
Front Square, Trinity
Pr 21.5 x 18.5", S, D, (G: 187) £140
GIBSON, Colin (20th Century)
O'Connell Street, Dublin
O 12 x 16", S, (N: 1) £220
GIFFORD, Grace (1888-1955)
On Board the H.M.S. Hi-You
W 10 x 10", S, D, (D: 128) £470
GILLESPIE, George K. (b.1924)
Farmstead Near Buncranna, Donegal
O 15 x 20", S, (D: 118) £600
Mulroy Bay, Co. Donegal
O 30 x 40", S, (E: 2) £770
Burtonpoint
O 20 x 30", S, (H: 64) £570
Reflections, Glanneagh, Co. Donegal
O 18 x 24", S, (J: 7) –
River Derg - Near Kellter, Co. Tyrone
O 20 x 30", S, (J: 34) –
Evening Light, Strangford, Co. Down
O 7.5 x 9.5", S, I, (H: 54) £420
Coastal landscape
O 20 x 24", s, (A 118) –
Antrim Coast and Garron Head
O 30 x 40", S, (L: 437) –
Summer in the Glens
O 20 x 24", S, (N: 2) £500
GLENAVY, Lady Beatrice (1883-1968)
The Family
O 16 x 15.5", S, (F: 144) £3,800
GOLDBERG, David (20th Century)
Autumn
O 19 x 23", I, D, (H: 124) –
GORDON, W.R. (20th Century)
Looking up the Glen
W 12.5 x 17.75", S, (O: 41) £460
GOSLETT
Farm House
O 12 x 16", S, (E: 165) –
GOWAN, Margaret (20th Century)
Cyclamens
W 8 x 13.5", S, D, (E: 167) –
The Eviction
O 17 x 22", S, D, (E: 170) –
Listening to Mozart
O 14 x 17.5", S, D, (E: 169) –
Listening to Mozart's Music
O 13.5 x 17", S, D, (G: 128) –

John FAULKNER (1835-1894): Cliffs, Blacksod Bay, Co Mayo. *Sold at Christie's, Dublin, 26 May 1993 (£3,520).*

Sheets in the Wind
W 10 x 11.5", S, D, (G: 149) –
GRACEY, Theo J. (d. 1959)
In the Mournes
W 11 x 15", S, (F: 107) £200
Landscape
W 10 x 14.5", S, (F: 108) £190
GREENLESS, William (19th Century)
Tynan Abbey, Co. Armagh
W 4.25 x 7", S, D, (B: 139) £100
GREY, Alfred (fl. 1873-1900)
On Guard
O 18 x 24", S, (A 128) £500
Extensive landscape with cattle drinking
O 28.5 x 42", S, D, (B: 21) £4,000
A Stag Amongst Heather
W 12 x 13.25", S, (K: 39) –
GUINNESS, May (1863-1955)
Tuscan Scene
P 12.5 x 9", (A 122) –
Mrs Hanlon taking tea
P 12 x 9", (C: 8) £600
Study of a Young Woman
P 10.5 x 8.25", S, (F: 17) £400
Autumn
P 12 x 9", (F: 57) £300
Lady in a Garden
P 9 x 15", (F: 84) –
Chateau de Josselin, France
W 12 x 11", (N: 4) £600
On the Seine
O 13.5 x 9.5", (N: 128a) £1,500
HALL, Kenneth (1913-1946)
Doorway Lr. Baggot Street
W 8 x 10", S, (H: 77) –
Train 1
O 19.5 x 24", S, (H: 106) –
HALL, Patrick (20th Century)
The Cockerel
O 24 x 19.5", S, (H: 126) –
HAMILTON E. H. (20th Century)
The Liffey, Strawberry Beds
O 14 x 18", (B: 63) £750
HAMILTON, Eva (1876-1960)
Celbridge Abbey
O 15 x 18", (F: 139) –
Coastal Landscape with Figure on the Rocks
O 12 x 16", S, (F: 80)-
A View of the Seine at Loire
O 4.75 x 6.5", (I: 15) £580
The Seine
O 4.75 x 6.5", (I: 16) £600
HAMILTON, Eve (Van Essen) (20th Century)
Cottage
P 12 x 16", S, D, (E: 121) –
HAMILTON, Letitia Marion (1878-1964)
Spring in Co.Wexford
O 20 x 24", s, (A 4) £1,500
Carrying turf
O 13 x 15.5", S, (B: 18) £850
Children on a beach
O 12 x 13.5", (B: 28) £450

View of a village below a castle ruin
O 17.5 x 11", S, (B: 41) £1600
Church ruins
O 12 x 16", (B: 50) £500
Oxen and cart, Italy
O 11.5 x 16", S, (B: 78) –
Path to the mountains
O 10 x 10.5", (C: 17) £550
Roundstone Harbour, Connemara
O 20 24", S, (C: 35) £4,600
Trammore, Connemara
O 11.5 x 16", S, I, (C: 40) –
In Dingle Bay
O 12 x 16.5", S, I (C: 73) £1,200
Canal scene, Venice
O 12 x 15.5", (C: 87) £1,000
Interior with Globe (c.1942-1944)
O 15 x 12", (D: 18) £720
Killougheboy Mountains, Sligo
O 12 x 14", (D: 111) £550
Apple Blossom
O 13.5 x 12.5", S, (G: 12) £1,400
Dooey Strand, Rosapenna, Co. Donegal
O 20 x 23.5", S,(G: 93) –
Venice
O 9.5 x 9.5", S, (H: 6) £1,300
The Polo Players
? x–", S, (H: 165) £820
The Fair
O 20 x 24", S, (J: 58) –
Sailing in Calm Sea
O 16 x 18.75", S, (J: 84) £3,200
A Queens County Bog
O 20 x 24", S, (K: 98) £4,950
Figures by a Thatched Cottage, The West of Ireland
O 20 x 24", S, (K: 102) –
Blanchardstown, Co. Dublin
O 7.5 x 9.5", S, (K: 103) £1,760
Ambledon, Dunboyne
O 5.125 x 7", (K: 104) £1,540
Dingle Bay
O 12 x 16.375", I, (L: 440) –
Thorn Tree, Lough Mask
O 12 x 16", S, (L: 461) £770
View through trees
O 20 x 24", (N: 9) –
Ireland's Eye from the 13th Tee, Portmarnock
O 20 x 24", S, (N: 14) –
Glengarriff
O 20 x 24", (N: 52) –
Stone Crushers, Dunmanus Bay
O 20 x 24", S, (N: 62) £2,800
Dunmanus Bay, Co. Cork
O 20 x 24", S, (O: 70) £7,130
HANLON, Fr. Jack P. (1913-1968)
Portrait (of a young woman)
O 23 x 20", S, I, (C: 52) –
Still Life with Flowers
W 23 x 16", (D: 4) £420
Celebration of Summer
W 9 x 12", S, (E: 67) £400
The Big House
W 9 x 12", S, (E: 68) £300
First Communion Procession
W 15 x 10", S, D, (F: 12) £620
The Flower Seller
O 14 x 21.5", (F: 47) £2,200
Still Life
W 9.5 x 7", (F: 109) £200
Bell Boy at the St. Isobel
W 19 x13.5", S, D, (G: 14) £370
View through the Trees
W 13 x 19", (G: 20) £520
Through the Trees
W 15 x 11", S, (G: 201) £420
View from Balcony
W 13 x 19", (G: 202) £620
Sweeney
W 15 x 21", S, (G: 203) –

Still Life
W 11 x 15", S, (H: 66) £500
Greystones
W 13 x 18", (H: 70) £300
Selskar Churchyard, Wexford
W 10.5 x 13.5", S, I, (I: 20) £480
Mother & Child
W 3.5 x 5.5", (I: 21) £400
Window Near Grasse
W 14 x 10.5", S, (I: 46) £510
Blue Corn
W 15 x 22", S, D, (N: 141) –
HANRAHAN, Mona
The Vico Road
W 8 x 10", S, (I: 71) £60
HARPER, Charles (b. 1943)
Nude
D 6.5 x 7, S, (E: 21) –
HARRISON, Sarah Cecilia (1861-1941)
Self-Portrait, as young woman
O 16 x 12", S, I, (C: 38) £800
Portrait Study of Emily McCord
O 19.5 x 15", S, (F: 116) £440
HARTLAND, Henry Albert (1840-1893)
Lake View with Figure & Boats
W 7 x 9.5", S, (G: 2) £300
Landscape
W 13 x 19.5", S, (G: 113) £720
Bog Pool
W 6.5 x 9.5", S, (H: 79) –
Shipping in a Lake & Mountain
W 6.5 x 12", S, D, (I: 85) –
A Mountain Road
W 11 x 17.375", S, D, (L: 325) £550
A Peat Bog, Connemara
W 13.5 x 27.5", S, (L: 326) £715
HASSARD, Tamison (20th Century)
Summer Cote d'Or, France
O 22 x 18", S, I, (F: 72) £1,200
HAUGHTON, Wilfred (20th Century)
Winter Road
W 4.75 x 6", S, (I: 2) £70
Misty Hedgerow
P 9.75 x 13.5", S, (A 134) £110
HAYDEN, Adrian Murray (20th Century)
Waterlilies
M 3.5 x 5.25", S, (A14) £50
Sunset over the coast
O 6.5 x 14.5", S, (A15) £100
Coastal scene
O 9.5 x 13.5", S, (A 24) –
HAYES, Claude (1852-1922)
A View Through the Trees Over a Lake
O 11.5 x 14", S, (F: 95) –
On the Stour
W 11.625 x 17.5", S, (L: 334) –
On the Stour
W 12 x 17.5", S, (N: 149) –
HAYES, Edwin (1820-1904)
Strangford Lough
O 7 x 11", S, (C: 80) –
Sands at Ostend
O 9 x 14", S, D, (B: 15) £2300
Southend
W 3.5 x 4.5", S, I, D, (D: 119) £450
Deal
W 4.25 x 6.75", S, I, (D: 120) £280
Sky and Sea Study
W 5 x 6.75", S, I, (D: 121) £300
Falmouth
W 6 x 3.75", S, I, (D: 122) £400
Padstow
W 4 x 6.75", S, I, (D: 123) £420
Beach, Hastings and Harbour View
W (2) 3.75 x 5.75", S, I, D, /
4 x 7.23, S, I, (D: 124) £600
Dutch Boats Running Free and 3 Others
W (4) 2.75 x 5", 3.75 x 6.25,
3 x 4.5, 3.25 x 5", S, I, (D: 125) £670
St. Ives

In a sale at Athassel House, Co Tipperary (12 July 1993), Hamilton Osborne King sold a Waterford mahogany long case clock of c.1820 for £1,600. The brass and steel dial was stamped by William Maddock of Waterford.

O 7 x 11", S, I, D, (G: 169) £750
Schooners Moored in Calm Sea
O 6 x 8.5", S, (J: 4) £1850
Scotch Fishing Boats off Gt. Yarmouth
W 5.25 x 8.75", S, I, (K: 22) £825
Fishing Boats in a choppy Sea

O 16 x 22.125", S, D, (L: 405) £1,525
Squall off the Needles
O 28.5 x 49", S, D, (N: 19) –
HAYES, Ernest (1914-1978)
Hardelot Plage, French Trawlers
O 14 x 18", S, (B: 69) –
Nettuno
O 13.5 x 17.5", S, I, D, (F: 10) £770
Venice
O 14 x 17.5", S, I, (F: 15) £800
Cupid's Flower
O 15 x 13", S, D, (F: 160) –
Landscape Portmarnock, Co. Dublin
O 20 x 24", S, (I: 77) –
HAYES, Michael Angelo (1820-1877)
Cavalry
W 10 x 16", S, D, (H: 125) –
HAYWARD, Phyllis (1903-1985)
Mediterranean town
O 14.5 x 10", S, (C: 104) £220
Man & Bird
M 23.5 x 18", S, (D: 115) £100
A Rose
M 18 x 14", S, (D: 114) –
Wooded Garden (plus 2 others)
W 17 x 11.5", S, (G: 196) –
HEALY, Henry (1909-1982)
Clare Island
O 20 x 23.5", S, (C: 1) –
Ringsend Basin
O 20 x 24", S, (E: 69) £460
West of Ireland Landscape
O 20 x 24", S, (E: 70) –
On the Canal at Sussex Terrace
O 19 x 24", S, (F: 39) £550
Near Ballyconneely
O 20 x 24", S, I, (H: 81) £650
On Achill Island
O 13 x 17", S, (I: 23) £410
Doonagh, Achill
O 11.25 x 15.25", S, (I: 24) £400
Harbour Innis Beg
O 20 x 24", S, (N: 61) £500
The Evening Walk
O 13.5 x 18", S, (A 54) –
The Evening Walk
O 13.5 x 18", S, (B: 12) –
HEALY, Michael (1873-1941)
Dubliners - Street Violinist
W 7 x 4.5", (C: 89) –
Dubliners - Men pushing a cart
W 4.5 x 7", (C: 22) £110
Dubliners - Woman in a blue shawl
W 7 x 4.5", S, (C: 23) £160
Man reading in Dublin Park
W 7 x 4.25", (C: 24) £140
*Dubliners - Two men with a cart
and boys talking*
W (2) 7 x 4.25", S, (C: 25) £220
*Dubliners - Man with a donkey
and tying his lace*
W (2) 7 x 4.25", (C: 26) £220
Dubliners
W 7 x 5", (E: 76) £140
Dubliners
W 7 x 5", (E: 77) £200
Dubliners
W 7 x 5", (E: 78) £140
Dubliners
W 7 x 5", (E: 79) £140
Dubliners
W 10 x 7.5", (E: 80) £160
Dubliners
W 8 x 5", (E: 169) £220
Cyclone Billy Warren
W 7.5 x 3.5", (F: 4) £200
Two Dubliners - Seated
W 5 x 4.5", (I: 31) £150
Left Profile of Mother & Child Walking
W 7 x 4.5", (I: 32) £150

Resting on The Park Bench
W 6.75 x 4.5", (I: 33) £170
Dublin Women Chatting
W 6 x 4", (I: 34) £190
The Flower Seller
W 7 x 4", S, (I: 35) –
Child Running & Mother & Child
W (2) 6 x 4.5" & 5.75 x 4", (I: 36)
The Actor
W 6 x 4.5" (I: 37) £190
The Coalman & A Seated Gentleman
W (2) 4 x 4.5", 5.5 x 3.5", (I: 38) £180
The Workers
W 6.75 x 4.5", (I: 39) £200
Dubliner
W 7.5 x 5", (D: 102) £160
Dubliner
W 6.5 x 5", (D: 103) £180
Dubliner
W 6.5 x 5", (D: 104) £200
Dubliner
W 6.5 x 5", (D: 105) £180
Dubliners
W 7.75 x 5", (H: 144) £120
Dubliners
W 7.75 x 5", (H: 145) £120
Dubliners
W 7.75 x 5", (H: 146) £120
HELMICK, Howard (1945-1907)
Discussing the Dowry
W 13.5 x 18.5", S, (D: 96) £1,450
HENDERSON, Nevill
Near Louisburgh with Croagh Patrick in Distance
O 20 x 30", S, (J: 83) £200
HENNESSY, Patrick (1915-1980)
Man and Horse at Pool
O 24 x 34.5", S, (A 32) £4,200
Fruit Stand
O 14 x 24", S, (A 107) £3,600
Figures in the Sand Dunes
O 10 x 18", S, (F: 65) £2,900
The Roman Fountain
O 24 x 34", S, (G: 82) £3,700
Conch Shells
O 13.5 x 19", (G: 92) £1,800
In the High Atlas
O 24 x 38", S, (I: 69) £2,300
Mare and Groom
O 16 x 25", S, D, (K: 162) £2,860
The New Walk
O 24 x 20", S, (K: 171) £4,180
Windy Brow, Lisburn
O 40 x 50", S, (M: 117) –
Serenade
O 25 x 35", S, (N: 54) –
Rose and Butterfly
O 14 x 12", S, (N: 117) £3,100
The Old Tree
O 25 x 35", S, (O: 30) –
HENRY, Grace (1868- 1953)
Lake and mountain landscape
O 15 x 18", S, (C: 95) £1,200
Houses by a River (Ennistymon)
O 5.5 x 7", S, (C: 114) £1,600
River Scene
O 10.5 x 13.5", (C: 115) –
Over the Shannon River
O 11 x 14", S, I, (D: 6) –
Cardinal
O 18 x 15", S, (E: 44) –
Female Study
O 17 x 14", S, (E: 146) –
Achill Landscape
O 7.5 x 10", S, (F: 27) £850
Landscape
O 20 x 24", S, (G: 131) £1,500
Conversation on Board the Corina
D 9.5 x 13", S, (F: 1) £360
Achill Landscape

Hamilton Osborne King's sale (1 February 1994) at Furness, Co Kildare included a mahogany sideboard of c.1840 stamped by Williams & Gibton of Dublin. It sold for £1,500.

O 7.5 x 10", S, (F: 27) –
HENRY, Marjorie (exh. 1942-1951)
Arabesque
O 21.5 x 24", S, (F: 127) –
The Gymnast
W 6.25 x 8.75, S, (J: 5) –
HENRY, Olive (1902-1989)
The Bridge
W 11.5 x 14.5", (F: 134) £100
Mending Nets
W 10.5 x 14.25", S, (D: 117) £400
A Roadside Cottage
W 10.5 x 14.5", S, (L: 377) –
HENRY, Paul (1876-1958)
Evening on the Bog
O 14 x 16", S, (C: 29) –
Near the Twelve Pins, Connemara
O 20 x 22", S, (C: 67) £33,000
Belfast Harbour
O 14.5 x 13.5", S, (C: 68) £4,500
West of Ireland Landscape with Cottage and Lake
O 19 x 24", S, (D: 69) £15,000
Farming Scenes
D (2) 7 x 4", S, (E: 57) £700
Driving Home the Sheep
D 8.5 x 11", S, I, (F: 25) £1,200
Mountain Landscape
O 11 x 13", S, (F: 77) –
Turf Stacks in Connemara Landscape
O 13 x 16.5", S, (I: 17) £8,000
Connemara, Lake & Mountain Scene
O 7.75 x 11", S, (J: 54) –
Fishermen in a Curragh by a Shore, Connemara
O 14 x 32", S, (K: 99) £7,150
A Western Landscape with Turf Stacks beside a Lake
O 9 x 11", S, (K: 100) £8,250
Turf Stacks and Cottages by a Coastal Inlet
O 14 x 16", S, (K: 101) £8,800
Achill, the Village by the Lake
O 14.5 x 16.5", S, I, (K: 148) £17,600
Turf Stacks
O 13 x 16.5", S, (L: 457) £12,100
Blasket Island
O 14 x 16", S, L: 458) £12,100
Achill Head
O 14 x 16", S, (L: 459) £8,280
An Achill Bog
O 12 x 14", S, (N: 24) –
The Blue Hills of Western Ireland
O 16 x 24", S, (N: 51) –
Cornwall, By the Cornish Riviera Express
W 24 x 22", S, (N: 59) –
Dusk, West of Ireland
O 16 x 24", S, (O: 8) –

HICKEY, Patrick (b. 1927)
The Marais after Two Months of Drought
P 9.5 x 12.5", S, (E: 55) £80
Brittas Bay
Pr 16 x 19", S, (E: 136) £40
XI Station of the Cross
Pr 18 x 12", S, (H: 60) –
The Summer Forests at Glendalough
O 40 x 50", S, I, (H: 148) –
HILL, Rowland (1918-1979)
Strangford, Co. Down
W 14 x 20", S, (G: 87) –
The White Chapel
O 24 x 30", S, (D: 58) £550
Donegal Landscape with Cottages
W 10.5 x 15.5", S, (J: 28) –
HOAD, Jeremiah (20th Century)
Distant Snow
O 19 x 23", S, I, (E: 18) –
HOLDEN, Liam (20th Century)
Naomhog, No. 2
O 14 x 18", S, D, (D: 153) £300
HOLLIS, George (1793-1842)
Notre Dame
D 7 x 10", S, (E: 95) £60
HONE, David (20th Century)
Pigeon House, Dublin
O 14 x 18", S, (C: 54) £850
Summer, Sandymount
O 10 x 14", S, (F: 51) £720
HONE, Evie (1894-1955)
St. Joseph and The Blessed Virgin
W (2) 38 x 14", (C: 106) –
Veronica Wiping the Face of Jesus
W 10.5 x 8.5", S, (C: 116) £200
Kitty & Danny at Marley
W 15.5 x 11.5", (D: 42) £750
Landscape with Rhododendrons
W 8.5 x 11.25", (E: 40) £400
Rainbow, 1945
W 9 x 12", S, D, (E: 42) £480
French Landscape
P 10.5 x 16", (E: 43) £360
Head of Christ
Pr 14.5 x 10.75", (E: 46) £80
Study Drawing
D 20 x 16", (E: 65) –
Abstract Composition
W 24 x 15", (F: 82) £1,500
Station of the Cross
W 12 x 9.5", (G: 31) £400
Abstract Composition - Musical Theme
W 15 x 12", (G: 124) £800
Composition
W 3.5 x 10", S, I, (G: 164) £360
Irish Landscape
W 10 x 13", (H: 17) £550
Study
W 9 x 4", (H: 72) –
Composition
W 8 x 8", S, (H: 116) £450
Abstract
W 6.5 x 5", S, (H: 130) £300
Our Lady of Mercy
W 6.5 x 17", (H: 163) –
Study -Stained Glass Window c. 1930
W 5.75 x 4.5", S, (I: 48) £350
HONE, Nathaniel (1718-1784) Attributed
Monochrome study of a marble bust of a cardinal
O 30 x 22.5", S, (A 115) £1,000
Monochrome study of an oval bas relief panel depicting the head of Christ
O 22 x 16", (A 116) –
HONE, Nathaniel (1831-1917)
Harvest Field and Trees
W 6 x 9.5", (G: 1) £720
Afternoon, looking towards Malahide
O 11.5 x 17.5", (A 21) –
Fishing Boats on the Strand, Normandy
O 25 x 36", S, (D: 32) £26,000

Stranded Ships in Tidal River
W 7.75 x 10.5", (E: 16) £850
Horse & Cart with Figures in the Vineyard
O 12.75 x 16", (G: 41) £4,800
Sea and Rocky Headland
W 4.5 x 6", (G: 56) £470
Three Pyramids
W 3.75 x 7", (G: 118) £400
Park, St. Doulough's
O 9.5 x 13.5", (G: 186) £1,400
On the Banks of the Seine
O 24 x 36", S, (K: 92) £31,900
A Hilly Landscape
O 9.5 x 14.5", S, (K: 141) £990
Ireland's Eye from Portmarnock
O 10 x 14", (N: 135) £1,000
HONTA, Rena (Mrs. Roderic O'Conor)
Apples
O 5.25 x 7.75", S, (K: 157) £1,320
HOPE, Elisabeth Lyn (fl. 1940-1958)
The Four Courts, Dublin
W 15 x 22", S, (N: 151) £500
HOUGHTON, Wilfred (20th Century)
Cattle grazing in a sunlit Landscape, Norfolk
O 16 x 20", S, D, (L: 462) £352
HUNTER, John (1893-1951)
Hallowe'en
O 21 x 18", S, (F: 9) –
ITEN, Hans (c. 1874-1975)
Summer - The Pond at Belvoir
O 10.5 x 13.5", S, (F: 81) –
In the Forest
O 18.5 x 12.5", (F: 145) £650
Souvenir de Normandy
W 12.25 x 9", S, (H: 9) £470
Bluebell Wood
O 5.5 x 7.75", (H: 31) £470
Winter Landscape
O 19 x 23.5", (H: 38) –
Rose Cottage, Dunfanaghy
O 7.25 x 10.625", S, (L: 414) £1,045
The Ploughed Field, Belvoir Park, Belfast
O 6 x 8.25", S, (L: 415) £1,100
JAMESON, Joan (1892-1953)
Garden at Derrynane c. 1936
O 16 x 20.5", S, C: 46) –
JELLETT, Mainie (1897-1944)
Wooded landscape
W 19 x 28", s, d, (A 91) –
Leafy river bank
W 14 x 9.5, s, (A 123) £670
Composition
W 12.5 x 6.5", S, D, (C: 66) £1,400
Coastal Storm
W 11.5 x 19.5", S, D, (D: 13) £1,100
Composition
W 11.25 x 16.5", S, D, (D: 37) –
Still Life with Palette
O 14 x 18", (D: 65) £3,400
The Four Seasons
W 8 x 11.5", (D: 85) £400
Two Nude Figures (c. 1940)
W 16 x 20", (D: 97) £500
Christ Carrying the Cross
W 26 x 14", (D: 98) £2,100
The Ninth Hour
W 15.5 x 11", (D: 138) £2,300
Seated Male Nude
D 18 x 14.5", (E: 152) –
Seated Female Nude
D 16 x 13" (E: 153) –
Head of a Boy
D 12 x 9", S, D, (E: 154) –
Standing Female Nude
D 12 x 9", (E: 155) –
Crucifixion
W 17.5 x 14", S, D, (F: 42) –
The Three Graces
O 32 x 21", (F: 45) £8,000
Abstract Composition (double sided)

Sean KEATING: *Waiting on the Pier, Aran. Bought in at James Adam, Dublin, 5 October 1993.*

W 6 x 5" / 10 x 7", (F: 76) £400
Abstract Composition
W 9.25 x4.5", (F: 168) £820
Abstract Composition
W 10 x 4", (F: 169) –
Abstract Composition
W 9 x 7", (F: 170) £960
Abstract Composition
W 9 x 6.5", (F: 171) –
Nude Study
O 24 x 18", (G: 94) –
Abstract
W 9.5 x 7", (G: 108) £1,400
Abstract
W 8 x 7.5, (G: 109) £1,400
Standing Female Nude
W 9.75 x 6.25",(H: 3) £720
Nymphs Dancing (1918)
W 9 x 6", S, (H: 22) £770
Seated Female Nude
D 12.5 x 9.5", S, (H: 76) £750
Seated Nude
W 9 x 7.5", S, (H: 98) –
Abstract Composition
W 15 x 11.5", S, (K: 40) –
Nude Model
O 12.75 x 10", (K: 128) £6,600
A Spanish Lady
D 11 x 8.375", S, D, (L: 364) £242
JENNENS & BETHRIDGE (fl. 1831-1864)
Blarney Castle, Cork
O 11.5 x 27", I, (H: 89) –
JOHNSON, Nevill (b. 1911)
Surreal Landscape
O 25 x 30", (E: 101) £260
Compotier & Finch
A 16 x 20", S, D, (H: 100) £1,100
Figures
P 9.125 x 7.25", (K: 42) –
Figures in a room
O 20 x 18", S, D, (B: 64) £700
Technological man
O 31 x 35", S, D, (B: 89) –
Body and Soul
A 16 x 20", S, D, (F: 112) –
Conversation Piece
A 20 x 16", S, D, (H: 128) £340
JONES, Nancy Wynne (b. 1922)
Harry's Barn
A 20 x 25", S, I, (E: 151) –
Harry's Barn
A 24 x 29", S, D, (G: 116) £650
JONES, Thomas Alfred (1823-1893)
Portrait of a boy and girl
W 18 x 15", S, (B: 105) £900
Portrait of a young gentleman in military uniform
W 14 x 10.5", S, D, (B: 127) –
JORDAN, A. (20th Century)
Western Landscapes
O (2) 9.5 x 13.5", S, (N: 152) –

JUDGE, Eugene (20th Century)
Playing the Piano
W 12.5 x 11", S, D, (D: 79) £370
Washing Her Hair
W 10.5 x 6", S, D, (D: 80) –
Study of a Young Girl
D 10.5 x 8", S, I, D, (E: 125) £160
Nude Study
D 11 x 8.25", S, D, (E: 126) £110
Female Study
D 10.5 x 8", S, D, (E: 127) £80
Female Study
D 10.5 x 8", S, D, (E: 128) –
Model Study
D 12.5 x 9", S, (E: 129) £110
JURY, Anne (b. 1907)
Secret Lough-Na-Ball, Co.Donegal
O 15.5 x 9.5", S, I, D, (H: 82) £450
KAVANAGH, Joseph Malachy (1856-1918)
An Old Flemish Draw-well, Merxem, 1883
O 26.75 x 17.75", S, (B: 54) £5
KEATING, Sean (1889-1977)
Dun Faoi na Greine
O 21 x 28", s, (A 74) £10,000
Man of Aran
P 16.5 x 12.5", s, (A 81) £950
Head of a man
P 18.5 x 14", s, (A 90) £1,300
Unloading the turf boat, Aran
P 31 x 40", s, (A 94) –
Aran Village
O 20 x 27", S, (C: 27) –
*Seashore with three fishermen and
a currach*
O 39 x 44", S, (C: 48) £11,700
West of Ireland fisherman
O 26 x 30", S, (C: 58) £13,000
The Bard
D 23 x 15.5", S, (E: 160) £600
Study from Life of James Larkin
D 32 x 16", S, (H: 139) £700
There you are Good Jumper/Grand Leper...
O 36 x 30", S, (I: 50) –
Thats a right toast, Sara Tansey...
O 36 x 30", S, (I: 51) –
*A Portrait of Desmond Stephenson,
seated three-quarter length*
D 19.75 x 14.5", S, (K: 5) £1,430
An Aran Couple by a Curragh
D 28 x 20", S, (K: 7) £2,420
*Fishing Boats returning to a Pier,
West of Ireland*
O 34.5 x 44.5", S, (K: 112) £26,400
Head of a Man - possibly a self portrait
P 26 x 19", S, (N: 107) –
Waiting on the Pier, Aran
O 35 x 47", S, (B: 71) –
Head of a Woman
P 9.75 x 11", S, (B: 130) –
Aran Playboys, c. 1916
M 32 x 33", S, (F: 26) –
Horse & Rider
O 30 x 21", (F: 140) –
*The Artist and his wife, dressed
as Aran Islanders, standing in a landscape*
O 36 x 36", S, D, (N: 72) £15,000
Aran Woman
P 20 x 15", S, (N: 102) £3,100
Profile portrait of a bearded man
P 12 x 17", S, (N: 113) –
KELLY, Frances (fl. 1929)
Still life with Ptarmigans
O 24 x 20", s, (A133) £850
Nude Study
P 7 x 10", S, (D: 112) £470
KELLY, Paul (20th Century)
A Still Life - Fish & Garlic
O 29.5 x 23.5", S, D, (J: 35) –
Landscape
19.5 x23.5", S, (J: 56) –

KELLY, Sir Gerald Festus (1879-1972)
Ma Seyn Sin (Dancing)
O 29 x 19", (B: 27) —
Coast of Tangier
O 14.5 x 17.5", S, D, (C: 45) £2,400
Portrait of Jane XXXII
S, I, D, (F: 126f) —
The Kuthodaw, Moonlight
O 6 x 7", I, D, (G: 40) —
A Spanish Lady
O 30 x 24", (K: 143) £495
Siamese Dancer, Ma Seyn Me Pose VIII
O 18 x 12.25", I, (K: 172) £528
A Burmah Boy
O 13.5 x 10.5", I, (N: 22) £1,500

KERNOFF, Harry (1900-1974)
Old Mill, Portmarnock, Co.Dublin
O 7.5 x 11.5", S, (B 3) —
Misery Hill
P 16 x 24", s, (A 19) £3,800
Western Madonna
P 8 x6", (A 82) £700
Miss Norma Barry
P 19.5 x 15", S, D, (A 97) £150
Nefertiti
O 8 x 6", S, (B: 26) £300
Kerry Bull after Sunset
W 10.25 x 14", S, (D: 38) £470
Bray Head, Evening
O 11 x 15", S, (D: 46) £720
Tralee Mountains from Killarney
O 25 x 37", S, I, (F: 35) £2,300
Messing about in boats
O 23 x 28", S, (F: 64) £3,800
New Year's Eve Party
O 19 x 22", S, D, (G: 30) £5,000
Floating Cubes
O 19 x 21", S, (G: 47) £1,500
Wind Blowing from the Left
O 8 x 6", S, (G: 173) £300
Killiney Village, Co. Dublin
O 11.5 x 15", S, D, (H: 46) £2,800
The Sailor
O 7 x 5.75", S, (I: 30) £420
Killiney Beach
O 26 x 37", S, D, (O: 114) —

KING, Cecil (1921-1985)
Circus Series c, 1965
P 11 x 7.5", s, (A 104) —
Willows
O 8.5 x 7", S, D, (E: 20) £140
Abstract
O 8 x 7", S, (E: 93) £150
Abstract
P 18 x 11", S, (E: 140) £150
Abstract
P 14 x 10", S, (G: 96) £280
Circus Pastel, 1965
P 11 x 7.5", S, (G: 193) £400
Abstract
M 22 x 10", S, (H: 95) £220
Celtic Motif
P 13 x 9.5", (I: 86) —
Still life - bottle and glass
O 14 x 10", S, D, (N: 100) £210

KINGERLEE, John (b. 1936)
Cornwall
M 9 x 14", S, D, I, (C: 36) £200
Mountain Valley
M 22 x 18", S, (C: 108) £450
Abstract
M15 x 10", S, D, (C: 110) £190
Several of Them
O 20.5 x 12.75, S, D, I, (D: 81) £370
Next Van
O 12 x 19", S, D, (D: 109) £400
Face
O 29 x 21", S, (E: 117) —
Figures at the Rock Face
O 11.5 x 22", S, D, (F: 135) £340

Harry KERNOFF (1900-74): Killiney Beach. *Bought in at Sotheby's, 24 November 1993 (est. £15-20,000).*

The Scholar & His Bird
O 8 x 6", S, (G: 120) £160
Abstract
O 22.5 x 18", S, D, (G: 145) £500
Untitled
M 9.5 x 9.5", S, D, (B: 92) £220

KINGSTON Richard (20th Century)
Snow, 1959
O 18 x 24", S, (A 5) —
The Old Mill
O 18 x 24", S, (A 35) £550
After the storm
W 14 x 18", S, (C: 13) £350
Marshland (1962)
W 12 x 20.5", S, (G: 72) £200
Spring - Marshland
O 11.5 x 22.5", S, (J: 81) —
Elements of Port Salou
O 30 x 38", S, (B: 45) —
Howth Harbour at night
O 23 x 35", S, (B: 66) £2,000
Co. Wicklow sketch
P 11.5 x 16.5", S, I, D, (B: 113) —
Corn poppies
P 12 x 16.5", S, D, (B: 136) £400

KINNARNEY, Bill E, (20th Century)
Still Life
P/C 22 x 26", S, (E: 141) £100

James LATHAM (1696-1747): Portrait of Ford Lambert, 5th Earl of Cavan. *Offered by Christie's at the Lyrath sale, Co Kilkenny, 15 September 1993, with an estimate of £6-8,000, it was bought in.*

Back Garden
O 11 x 12", S, (E: 83) —

KNEE, Howard (20th Century)
Throne Room, Dublin Castle
W 11.25 x 16", S, (I: 3) —
Dublin from the Mountains
W 9.5 x 14", S, (F: 185) £140

KNUTTEL, Graham (b.1954)
The Artist's Daughter
M 30 x 20", S, (A 2) £200

KYLE, Georgina Moutray (1865-1950)
A Steamer alongside
O 13.75 x 19.5", S, (L: 444) £825

LAMB, Charles Vincent (1893-1965)
Near Carraroe, Galway
O 10.5 x 14", S, (N: 12) £1,250
Cottage in coastal landscape
O 17 x 21", S, (N: 25) £2,200
Killowen, Rostrevor, Co. Down
O 20 x 24", S, (M: 116) £1,300
Tismane Beach
O 10.5 x 14", S, (A 111) £700
Cottages in a western landscape
O 12.5 x 16", S, (A 10) —
Struthan Harbour
O 10.5 x 14", S, (A 80) £1900
Cottages in a Western landscape
O 12.5 x 16", S, (C: 41) —
A Cottage in Co. Waterford
O 10.5 x 14", S, (C: 75) £1100
West of Ireland Landscape with Cottage
O 9.75 x 13.5", S, (F: 119) £1200
Killymore Lake, Co, Galway
O 12 x 15.5", S, (F: 141) —
Tishmane Beach
O 10.5 x 13.5", S, (G: 152) £970
Thatched Cottages - Near a Pool, Between Maam and Skreen, Connemara
O 10.25 x 13.75", S, (J: 69) £1,000
Rosses Tower from Rostrevor
O 20 x 24", S, (B: 53) £4,200
Cottages, Carraroe
O 11.25 x 15", S, (B: 86) £1,400
Hookers at Carraroe
O 10.5 x 14", S, (D: 10) £1,900
Slieve Ban, Mourne Mountains
O 8.5 x 11.5", S, I, (H: 37) —
Figures by a Village, Co. Galway
O 20 x 24", S, (K: 121) £4,950
The Coral Strand, Carraroe, Co. Galway
O 16 x 20", S, (K: 122) —
Bog Landscape, Connemara
O 20 x 24", S, (K: 123) —
In The Village of Carraroe
O 10.5 x 14", S, (K: 124) —
Killiney beach, Co. Dublin
O 20 x 24", S,(B: 95) —
Boats at Spiddal
O 24 x 18", S, (C: 96) £420
Hearing The News
O 24 x 20", S, (N: 60) £24,000
Cottages in a Western landscape
O 12.5 x 16", S, (N: 73) £1,400

LAVERY, Lady Hazel (d. 1935)
Female Portrait Study
O 23 x 20", S, (F: 194) —

LAVERY, Sir John (1856-1941)
Portrait of Lady Raeburn, seated half length, in a lace collared jacket, pearl necklace and black hat
O 36 x 28", S, I, D, (K: 96) £4,400
A Portrait of Miss Gentles, standing half length, in a brown jacket and floral bonnet
O 24 x 16.25", S, D, (L: 413) £1,980
A Woman and her Dog, Grez-sur-Loing
O 23.5 x 36.5", S, D, (O: 12) —
At Tangier
O 18 x 10", S, D, (O: 14) —

LAVERY, Sir John (after)

Portraits of Sir Arthur Griffiths and
Michael Collins
Pr (2) 21 x 17.5", S, (B: 142) — £370

LAWRENSON, Edward Louis (1868-1934)
Gathering Turf
O 25 x 30", S, (J: 23) — –
Cumulus Clouds
W 11 x 15", S, (D: 1) — –
Gypsies on the Downs
W 12 x 16.5", S, (G: 125) — –

LE BROCQUY, Louis (b. 1916)
Image forming on a red ground
Pr 26 x 19.5", S, (B: 145) — £370
Metamorphosis (The Tain Series)
Pr 21 x 14.5", S, D, (D: 129) — £190
The Tain Series
Pr 15 x 21", S, D, (D: 130) — £220
Man with Open Mouth
Pr 22 x 17.5", S, (D: 131) — £140
La Maine
Pr 22 x 17.5, S, (D: 132) — £140
The Tain
Pr (36) S, (F: 137) — –
Female Abstract
M 10 x 7.5", S, D, (F: 126a) — £1,500
Two Women, Connemara
W 8.75 x 4.5", S, D, (F: 126b) — £970
Still Life, Flowers in a Bowl
W 6 x 7", S, D, (F: 126c) — £850
Slain Figure (The Tain Series)
Pr 15 x 21", S, D, (G: 68) — –
Crouching Figure (The Tain Series)
Pr 21 x 15", S, D, (G: 69) — £180
Nude Study
O 14 x 10.5", S, I, D, (G: 98) — –
Boy & Fish
D 5.5 x 6.5", S, D, (G: 141) — –
Samuel Beckett
W 23 x 17", S, D, (G: 161) — £1,800
Figure against a Wall in Spain
W 7 x 8", S, D, I, (G: 162) — £650
Study of W. B. Yeats
D 8.5 x 7", S, D, (H: 28) — £1,100
Study of W. B. Yeats
D 8.5 x 7", S, D, (H: 29) — £1,200
Images of W.B. Yeats
W 24 x 18", S, (H: 90) — –
Carros Village 1988
W 7 x 10", S, (H: 164) — £1,100
W. B. Yeats
Pr 29 x 21.5", S, (J: 48) — £290
Procession
Pr 14 x 20", S, (J: 86) — £480
Standing Figure
O 48 x 36", S, D, (K: 132) — £10,450
Presence
O 30 x 25", S, D, (K: 133) — £5,500
Ancestral Head 1964
O 25.5 x 21", S, I, D, (K: 134) — £4,620
Canalside, Tullamore
W 3.5 x 6.5", S, D, (N: 70) — £700
Child Alone
O 34 x 39", S, D, (O: 110) — £20,700
Distant Image
O 58 x 45", S, D, (O: 129) — £6,900

LE JEUNE, James (1910-1983)
Across the canal from Herbert Place
O 16 x 20", S, (A:37) — £950
The Royal Exchange, London
W 12 x 15.5", S, (A; 95) — –
The Clock Gate, Main Street, Youghal,
Co. Cork
O 24 x 20", S, (A; 96) — £2,400
Northumberland Road
O 13.5 x 15.75", S, I, (H: 40) — £2,400
The Trout Stream
O 19.5 x 25", S, (I: 8) — –
Beauvais Cathedral
W 18.5 x 13.5", S, (K: 38) — £935
Blackmores Yard, Dun Laoghaire Harbour

William J LEECH (1881-1968): The River Wey.
Sold at Adams, Blackrock, 21 March 1994 (£5,000).

O 25 x 30", I, (K: 108) — £8,800
The Market at Annecy
O 20 x 22", S, (K: 109) — –
Capel Street, Dublin
O 14 x 18", S, (K: 110) — £3,300
The Rocks, Clogher Head
O 10 x 14", S, (K: 111) — £660
Cattle
O 9.5 x 13.5", S, (N: 81) — –
Children on the beach
O 14 x 17.5", S, (N: 132) — £1,600

LEECH, William John (1881-1968)
The Kitchen, 4 Steele's Studios, London
O 36 x 28", S, (G: 57) — £20,000
Interior with the bust of May
W 22 x 15", S, (G: 75) — –
Study for Studio Garden
O 17.5 x 19.5, (D: 51) — £9,000
Interior
O 26 x 18", (D: 68) — £5,000
Le Chateau, Nice
O 9 x 7", S, I, (D: 78) — £2,100
Self Portrait
W 22 x 15", S, (G: 76) — –
Quimper
O 24 x 20", S, I, (I: 45) — £17,500
The River Wey
O 14 x 17", S, (J: 37) — £5,000
Two Boats and a Barge, Billingsgate, Thames
O 15 x 18", S, I, (K: 126) — £18,700
Sunday morning in the Park
O 10.5 x 14", S, I, (K: 127) — £7,150

Still life, potted plant at a window
O 24 x 20", S, (N: 66) — –

LEONARD, Patrick (b.1918)
Tying up the Trawlers at Sunset
O 20 x 24", S, (A; 75) — –
Waiting for the bus
O 16 x 12", S, (A; 87) — £500
The Watchman's Hut
O 16 x 19.5", S, (B: 42) — –
Two donkeys in landscape
O 18 x 24", S, (B: 75) — –
The Circus Girls
O 23.5 x 19.5", S, (C: 9) — £600
The Old Lane, Skerries
O 16 x 20", S, (C: 111) — –
Belcalmed, Skerries
O 20 x 25", S, I, (I: 27) — £800
Skerries
O 15 x 23.5", S, (J: 10) — £720
Nearing the Pier Head
O 44 x 34", S, (L: 412) — –
Connolly Station, Dublin - 3.6.85,
4, 1.15pm
O 20 x 16", S, I, (L: 416) — £715
The Harbour, Kinsale
O 16 x 20", S, I, (L: 417) — –

LINDY, Philip (20th Century)
Holy Family
O 25 x 18", (E: 105) — £180

LUKE, John (1906-1975)
Landscape composition
O &T 16.75 x 23.25", S, D, (N: 39) — £70,000

LYNCH, Padraig (20th Century)
The Keep, Hospital Avenue,
Ardee
O 13 x 17", S, D, (E: 8) — £200

LYNDSAY, Roy (b. 1945)
Dingle
O 15 x 19", S, (I: 62) — –

LYSAGHT, Damaris (b. 1956)
Barn, Provence
O 24 x 17", S, D, (N: 15) — –

MacCABE, Gladys (b. 1918)
Before the Race
W 9.25 x 13.75", S, (F: 79) — £230
Mixed Flowers & Fruit
O 14.5 x 11.5", S, (G: 147) — –
Saturday Morning, Grafton Street
O 20 x 27", S, (G: 178) — £570
The Fruit Market
O 19 x 29", S, (E: 29) — –
Still Life
O 23 x 16", S, (H: 127) — –

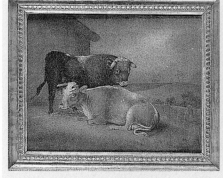
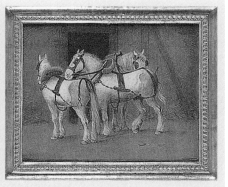

Christie's, London sale of Furniture on 18 November 1993 included a pair of intriguing and very unusual Irish sand pictures. These had the label of Joshua Kearney who worked at 49 Henry Street, Dublin between 1802-44. They sold for £3,100.

MacEGAN, D. J. (20th Century)
Wellington Monument, Phoenix Park
O 14.5 x 10.5" (B:11) —
MACEY, Pauline (20th Century)
Rhododendrons
O 15.5 x 17", S, D, (F: 92) £220
MacGONIGAL, Maurice (1900-1979)
Cill Maolceadair, near Dingle, Co. Kerry
O 20 x 24", S, (A; 121) £1,400
Finglas Wood (1964)
O 18 x 24", S, (A; 57) £1,700
Ciaran Asleep
O 17 x 25", S, (A; 100) £4,000
Sunbathing, Rush, Co. Dublin
O 12.25 x 12.75", S, (B: 46) —
The Dutch Barge
O 16 x 20", S, (B: 58) —
Michaelmas Daisies
O 14 x 14", S, (B: 68) —
A View of Clifden
D 13 x 19", S, (B: 150) —
Evening on the Connemara Coast
O 20 x 24", S, (C: 21) £1,500
Waiting for the boats - Fishermen's wives
O 25 x 19", S, (C: 53) —
The Deserted Farmhouse
O 20 x 24", S, (C: 62) —
Where the Liffey Begins
O 11 x 15", S, I, (D: 53) £3,000
Western Lake & Mountain Landscape
O 14 x 18", S, (E: 13) —
River Landscape with Two Swans
O 20 x 24", S, (F: 37) £2,800
Spring Waters on the Tolka
O 14 x 18", S, I, (F: 49) £1,400
Landscape with Cottage
O 10 x 14", S, (F: 98) £650
Boats, Dun Laoghaire
W 10 x 13.75", S, D, (F: 166) —
From Sandymount
W 11 x 16", S, D, (G: 7) —
Roundstone
O 20 x 23", S, (G: 64) £3,800
Reflections, Connemara
O 13.5 x 17.5", S, (G: 79) —
A View at Howth
O 13.5 x 18", S, (G: 102) £800
Boats on the Sticks, Dun Laoghaire
P 14 x 22", S, (G: 204) —
Two Men on a Connemara Street Corner
O 15 x 8", S, (H: 14) —
Evening Connemara
O 20 x 30", S, I, (H: 24) £4,700
Triangle, South Richmond Street
O 16 x 20", S, I, D, (H: 30) £4,800
Landscape, Connemara
O 24 x 28", S, I, (H: 48) —
Dingle Peninsula
D 11.5 x 17", S, I, (H: 74) —
Cattle Grazing
W 9.5 x 13", S, (I: 57) £500
Boatyard - Dun Laoghaire
O 16 x 30", S, (J: 27) —
Old Cross & Stone
O 20 x 30", S, I, (J: 36) —
Men and Women of Aran
O 42.875 x 51.25", S, I, (K: 113) —
Aran Folk with Animals
O 41 x 73.5", S, I, (K: 114) —
Aran Folk
O 43 x 64.25", S, I, (K: 115) —
Milking Cows, the Aran Islands
O 33.5 x 48.75", (K: 116) —
*Aran Folk with a Donkey and Cart
gathering Seaweed / Aran Folk and
Donkeys gathering Turf*
O (2) 43.25 x 60.75" / 41 x 64.5", (K: 117) £5,500
Fishermen by a Curragh
O 31.5 x 49", (K: 118) —
An Aran Woman Spinning

An Irish silver cup and cover by John
Hamilton of Dublin, hallmarked
1736 and engraved with the arms of
the 1st Earl of Ely sold at Christie's,
London (14 July 1993) for £7,130.

O 31.25 x 48.75", (K: 119) £2,640
Aran Women bathing Children
O 33.5 x 48.25", (K: 120) £3,080
Streamstown Bay, Connemara
O 24 x 28", S, (K: 125) £4,180
*Desmond Stevenson (sic) ARHA
coming home in Connemara*
O 14.25 x 10.75", S, I, (K: 161) —
Harbour Roundstone, Connemara
O 20 x 30", S, D, (N: 20) £9,000
Hero
O 16 x 12", S, (N: 67) £3,100
Black Cows, Connemara 1974
O 24 x 28", (N: 87) £3,900
Farmstead in Connemara
W 11.5 x 16", S, (N: 125a) £800
MacKINNON, Sine (b. 1901)
The Derelict Farm
W 9.5 x 14", S, I, (G: 134) £170
MacWEENEY, Leslie (b. 1936)
Head
M 19 x 13", S, (G: 70) £100
MADDEN, Anne (b.1932)
Lovers
M 25 x 20", S, D, (G: 101) —
Clare Bog
O 13 x 16", (G: 170) £550
MADDEN, Vincent (20th Century)
Still Life with Fish
O 20 x 16", S, (F: 56) £260
MAGUIRE, Brian (b. 1951)
Lovers
A 25 x 27", S, D, (G: 38) £300
MAGUIRE, Cecil (20th Century)
Boreen, Gortnagapull, Inishmor
O 16 x 24", S, D, (A; 26) £950
July Morning, Ervallagh, Roundstone
O 14 x 18", S, D, (A; 130) £800
Summer, Roundstone
O 14 x 18", S, D, (A; 86) £770
Slipway, Inishmaan
O 13.5 x 17", S, D, I, (D: 134) —
Summer, Roundstone
O 13 x 17", S, D, (F: 103) £570
High Water, Piazza San Mario
O 25 x 37", S, (F: 105) —
Currachs, Kilronan
O 13.5 x 17", S, D, I, (H: 41) —
MAHONY, James (1816-1879)
Figures sheltering by a ruined Bridge
W 8.125 x 12.75", S, I, D, (L: 324) £990

MANAHAN, Rosita (20th Century)
Mother & Child
W 11 x 9", S, (D: 106) £220
The Palm House, Botanic Gardens
W 20 x 13", S, (F: 192) £200
MANNING, Anthony (20th Century)
Dancer
O 16 x 12", S, (E: 81) —
MANNING, Jimmy (20th Century)
The Marchioness
O 18, 24", S, (A; 108) —
Western landscape
O 17 x 24", S, (C: 112) —
MARESCAUX, Kathleen (20th Century)
Orange Lillies
W 28 x 21", S, (F: 61) £300
Flowers of Gladness
W 22 x 30", S, (F 62) £240
A Bowl of Begonias
W 19 x 16", S, (F: 63) £220
Flowers of Gladness
W 21 x 30", S, (G: 138) —
MARJORAM, Gerard (20th Century)
*Western mountain &
river landscape*
O (2) 18 x 24", S, (C: 7) £750
MARQUIS, James Richard (fl.1853-1885)
Killarney lake by moonlight
O 12 x 16", (A; 127) —
MARSTON, M. G. (20th Century)
Still Life
O 25 x 18", S, (G: 59) —
MASON, William (20th Century)
The Picture Dealer
P 14 x 11.5, S, (D: 99) £450
Evening Regatta
P 5 x 7", S, D, (D: 100) £250
A Wet Morning
O 23 x 25", S, (G: 114) —
Beach Scene
O 20 x 27", S, (G: 171) £650
McALEER, Clement (b.1949)
Clare Landscape
O 35 x 37", S, I, D, (D: 92) £900
McAULEY, Charles (b.1910)
The Shire Horse & Groom
O 16 x 23", S, (I: 55) £820
The Flax Gatherers
O 16 x 21", S, (K: 163) £3,850
Fishing Boats
O 14.75 x 20", S, (L: 435) —
The Old Church
O 15.75 x 21", S, (L: 436) £2,200
River Dun, Glens of Antrim
O 16 x 30", S, (L: 445) —
Garron Point from Cushendun
O 16 x 24", S, (L: 446) £715
A Cottage by the Sea
O 10 x 15.5", S, (L: 447) £352
McCAIG, Norman J. (b. 1929)
Galway Hooker
O 18 x 22", S, (I: 63) —
Harbour Scene
O 14 x 9.5", S, (A 11) —
Roundstone Harbour
O 14 x 18", S, (A 119) £500
On Lough Inagh
O 14 x 18", S, (A 126) —
Ballinahinch River
O 24 x 36", S, (B: 51) —
Fishing boat, Lough Derg
O 18 x 20", S, (B: 87) —
Low Tide, Youghal Harbour
O 14 x 18", S, (B: 93) £500
Late Autumn
O 13.5 x 16.75", S, (J: 26) £360
In for the Night (1988)
O 12 x 16", S, (N: 23) £320
Burton Port, Co. Donegal
O 16 x 20", S, (N: 86) £700

Maurice MacGONIGAL (1900-79): Triangle, South Richmond Street. *Sold at Taylor de Veres, Dublin, 8 March 1994, (£4,800).*

McCREARY, James (20th Century)
She's a Lady
Pr 15 x 13", S, (E: 139) £20
McDONAGH, Bernard (20th Century)
Canal View, Dublin (c. 1943)
O 9.5 x 14", S, (E: 119) £120
The Canal (c. 1943)
O 10 x 14", S, (F: 101) –
McDONNELL, Hector (b. 1947)
Cafe Interior
O 36 x 46", S, (I: 64) £3,500
Lodge Gates, County Meath
O 5 x 9", S, (K: 149) £440
McEVOY, William (fl.1858-1880)
Glengariff from the Kenmare Road, Evening
O 28 x 52", S, D, (A 70) – /
£800 (A; 70a)
McGILL, Joseph Francis (20th Century)
After the Bull Fight, Valencia
O 36 x 40", S, (F: 69) –
McGORAN , Kieran (d. 1990)
In the Paddock
P 15.75 x 13.5", S, (L: 384) £1,065
Gossips
P 15 x 20", S, D, (L: 385) £330
A Game of Draughts
P 14 x 19", S, (L: 386) £440
The Shepherds
D 24 x 19.5", S, (L: 387) –
Horses & Jockeys
P 14.5 x 11", S, (I: 73) –
Kite Flying
P 11.5 x 16", S, (D: 91) £620
Card Players
P 13 x 17.5", S, (H: 109) £600
Old Men in The Park
P 14 x 18", S, (C: 4) £250
McGUINNESS, Norah (1903-1980)
Black Water Swans
O 20 x 28", S, (A; 53) –
Reading
W 21 x 16", S, (A 73) £1,200
A Wicklow Road
O 20 x 30", S, (B: 83) –
A Stroll in The Park
W 13.5 x 20", S, (B: 107) £1,200
Ballyvaughan
M 10 x 13.5", S, (B: 115) £320
Red House on The Liffey
W 7.5 x 10.75", S, (C: 2) £450
The Jagged Rocks, Ballycotton
W 13 x 19", S, (C: 5) –
Old Houses, Kinsale
W 7 x 10.5", S, D, (C: 90) £700
Le Petit Eglise
M 12 x 16", S, D, (C: 99) –
Harbour Sketch
P 7.5 x 11.5", S, (C: 100) £180
Picking Flowers
O 14 x 16", S, (D: 15) £2,600
Eileen Ganley & Gordon Glenavy at Rockbrook, Rathfarnham
W 11 x 14.75", S, (D: 29) £600

Borrishoole & Ballyhenan
M (2) 8.25 x 9.75", S, (D: 49) £500
Voyage of St. Brendan
M 9.5 x 7.5", S, (D: 57) £300
Smithfield Market
W 14.5 x 21", S, (D: 70) £3,200
Dublin Bay
Pr 13 x 20.5", S, (E: 51) –
Clondalkin Farm
W 6.5 x 9.75", S, (E:71) £700
The Mills, Wicklow
W 6.5 x 9.75", (E: 72) £460
Sea Shanties
D 6.25 x 8", (E: 110) £90
Sketch for Book Illustration
D 11 x 7", S, (E: 120) £130
Self Portrait
D 13 x 10", S, (E: 122) £270
Western Landscape (with Woman)
P 8 x 11.5", S, (E: 123) £220
Western Landscape (with Man)
P 8 x 11.5", S, (E: 124) £220
The Holy Family
P 11 x8", (E: 131) £130
Illustration for Kai Lung's Golden Hours
W 14 x 12", S, I, (F: 31) £620
The Elf
W 10.5 x 8", S, (F: 32) £350
Estuary Waters
O 17 x 21", S, I, (F: 41) –
Still Life, France
W 11.5 x 17", S, (F: 53) £700
The Farm Gate
O 17 x 23", S, (F: 75) £4,200
Landscape with Figure
P 14 x 17.5", (F: 111) £420
Bog Road
O 13 x 19", S, I, (G: 10) –
Vine Terrace
O 24 x 18", S, (G: 16) £8000
East River, New York
W 13 x 16", S, D, (G: 110) £2100
Donegal
W 12 x 19", S, G: 198) £870
Near the Slane
W 8 x 11", S, (G: 199) £620
Figure Bathing
P 9 x 12.5", S, (G: 200) £400
Dark Sands
O 20 x 36", S, I, (H: 8) £2,300
August Moths
O 23 x 11.5", S, (H: 47) £2,800
Donegal
W 12.5 x 19", S, I, (H: 50) –
Fishing Port
W 10 x 14", S, (H: 67) £570
The Italian Garden
M 12.5 x 9", S, (H: 80) £400
George Furlong, Director of the National Gallery
D 11 x 17", S, (H: 99) £200
In the Apple Tree
O 20 x 29", S, I, (H: 105) –
Sussex Landscape
W 12 x 19", S, (H: 111) –
Green Seaweed
O 16 x 22", S, I, (I: 26) £1,000
House through Leafy Landscape
O 15 x 19.25", S, D, (J: 22) £1,800
Still Life - fruit and flowers
W 14 x 18", S, D, (N: 10) £700
The Chestnut branch
W 7.25 x 10.5", S, (N: 68) £500
The Cherry Tree
P 8 x 10", S, (N: 77) £350
A Wicklow Road
O 20 x 30", S, (N: 137) £1,800
The Last of the Shellybanks
O 33 x 39", S, (O: 51) £2,645

Norah McGUINNESS (1903-80): Dark Sands. *Sold at Taylor de Veres, Dublin, 8 March 1994, (£2,300).*

McGUINNESS, William Bingham (fl. 1874-1929)
Street scene, Knightsbridge
W 12 x 6", S, (A; 65) £750
Mountain stream
W 12.25 x 8.25", S, D, (B: 140) £260
Winter Landscape
W 6.5 x 9.5", S, D, (E: 143) £140
Mountain landscape with River & Cattle
W 13.5 x 21", S, (D: 145) –
West of Ireland Landscape
W 19.5 x 29", S, (F: 206) –
Continental Street Scene
W 7 x 4.5", S, (G: 35) £400
Continental Lake Scene
W 12 x 6.5", S, (G: 46) £300
River Scene with Cattle
W 13 x 21", S, (G: 73) £400
On Kenmare Estuary, Co. Kerry
W 14 x 19.5", S, (K: 1) £990
A Bit of Old Venice
W 35 x 21", S, D, (K: 13) £2,200
A River Landscape
W 7 x 10", S, (K: 14) £440
Bringing Home the Turf
W 9.25 x 13.5", S, (L: 335) –
A Continental Waterway
W 18.5 x 13.5", S, D, (L: 336) £495
A Fisherman by a Boat in a Canal Landscape
W 20 x 13.25", S, (L: 343) £495
A bit of Venice
W 10 x 7", S, (L: 344) £132
Connemara lake and mountain landscape
W 9 x 13.5", S, D, (N: 29) £270
McKELVEY, Frank (1895-1974)
Portrait of a lady
W 13 x 10", S, (A; 135) –
Near Carrigart, Co. Donegal.
W, 9.75 x 13.5", S, (A; 8) –
The Footbridge
O 18 x 24", S, (A; 55) –
Tinkers Caravan by a river
O 17 x 23", S, (B: 62) £5,600
Silver day
O 15 x 20", S, (B: 84) –
Near Carrigart, Co. Donegal
W 9.75 x 13.5", S, (B: 137) £600
Harbour Port Na Blagh
O 10 x 13.5", S, (C: 61) £6,000
The Shower, theShores of Lough Erne
O 14 x 19", S, (C: 64) £4,000
The Wee Shop (1924-25)
O 15 x 19", S, (D: 75) £13,500
Young Girl Feeding Chickens
O 20 x 26", S, (F: 88) £17,000
Feeding the Swans, St. Stephen's Green
O 12 x 14.5", S, (G: 24) £12,500
Coastal Landscape
O 12 x 16.5", S, (G: 48) –
Female Portrait Study
W 12.5 x 9", S, (H: 150) –
Near Rathmullen, Co . Donegal
W 15 x 22", S, (I: 61) –

Landscape, Near Hillsborough, Co. Down
O 10 x 13.25", S, (I: 83) — —

Sheephaven Bay from Atlantic Drive, Co. Donegal
W 15 x 22", S, (K: 30) £1,540

A Farm among the Hills
W 10 x 14.5", S, (K: 31) —

On the River Bann, Co. Antrim
O 15 x 20", S, I, (K: 158) £8,800

River at Kells, Co. Antrim
O 16 x 20", (K: 159) —

A Thatched Cottage in a Coastal Landscape
W 10.5 x 14.5", S, (L: 379) £995

A Farm among the Hills
W 10 x 14.5", S, (L: 380) £495

ChildrenFishing by a Sunlit River
O 18 x 24", S, (L: 441) £4,950

Evening, Island Magee, Co. Antrim
O 10 x 14", S, (L: 442) £990

Near Rosbeg, Co. Donegal
O 12 x 17", S, (L: 443) —

Antrim Gypsies
O 20 x 27", S, (M: 64) £10,000

Looking towards Errigal from Dun Fanaghy
O 12 x17", S, (N: 26) —

Lough Gill, Co. Sligo
W 10.5 x 15", S, (N: 57) £550

Going off to War
W 15 x 10.5", S, (N: 128b) £550

Farm, Co. Antrim
O 27.5 x 35.5", S, (O: 9) —

Landscape, Co. Antrim
O 27.5 x 35.5", S, (O: 10) —

The Road to Derrybeg, Co. Donegal
W 14.75 x 22.5", S, (O: 111) —

Warrenpoint
W 17.75 x 23.75", S, (O: 112) £4,600

Atlantic Drive, Co. Donegal /
The Mournes form Rossglass, Co. Down
W (2) 10.5 x 14.5", 10 x 14.25", S, (O: 113) £1,840

McKENZIE, W. G. (1857 - 1924)
On the Donegal Coast
O 16.75 x 13.5", S, D, (H: 151) —

McSWEENEY, Sean (b.1935)
Island Road
O 9 x 6.25", S, D, (D: 9) £520

The Grey Road (c.1968)
O11.5 x 8.5", (D: 33) £720

Bogland Water
O 24 x 17.5", S, D, I, (E: 7) £400

Clothes Line in the Landscape
O 19 x 23", S, I, (E: 25) £400

Bogland Foliage
O 10 x 13.5", S, D, I, (E: 27) —

Evening Sky, Sligo
O 18 x 24", S, (E: 49) —

Scarecrow
O 40 x 44", S, (B: 91) —

Bowl of Flowers
O 23 x 28", S, D, I, (F: 55) £1400

Yellow Field, Wicklow
O 13.5 x 9.75", S, (G: 61) —

Landscape, Wicklow (Triptych)
O 23 x 45", S, D, I, (G: 97) —

The Lane, Lugglass
5.5 x 7.5", S, I, (G: 121) £260

Bogland Pools
O 17.5 x 23.5", S, I, D, (H: 11) —

Summer Shoreline
O 14 x 19", S, (H: 62) £360

Landscape
O20 x 14", (H: 69) £190

Island Shapes
O 20 x 25", S, (H: 121) £670

Willy's Bog
P 5.5 x 8", S, (I: 40) £260

The Pool
O 12 x 16", S, I, (J: 14) £600

MIDDLETON, Charles C. (1878-1935)
A Corner of St. Ives
W 10.5 x 14.5", S, D, (D: 94) —

Roderic O'Connor (b 1907): Portrait of a Lady.
Bought in at James Adam, Dublin, 5 October 1993.

MIDDLETON, Colin (1910-1983)
A View of Dick's Farm, Carnalridge, 1961
O 19 x 29", S, (D: 107) £3,600

Moonrise, Lough Erne, 1967
O 12 x 11.5", S, I, (E: 148) £500

Lady with Scarf
O 20 x 16", S, I, (F: 43) —

Woman Reading
O 18 x 24", S, I, D, (F: 155) —

March Landscape
O 19.5 x 23.5", S, (F: 208) —

The Temptation of St. Francis
O 20 x 23", (G: 25) £4,800

My Heart is in the Highlands (c. 1943)
O 20 x 24", S, (G: 42) —

Mother & Child
Pr 11.5 x 9", (G: 129) £110

Grace Darling/ Mother & Child/ Abstract
D (2) 5 x 22", (1) 8 x 11", S, D, (I: 78) £200

Continental Overtures
O 36 x 36", S, (J: 39) £1000

The Bride, Surrealist Composition
O 24 x 20", S, D, (K: 144) —

The Washing Line
O 24 x 18", S, D, (K: 145) £4,400

Nomads
O 30 x 24", S, I, D, (K: 146) £4,180

Canal: Damme
O 36 x 36", S, I, D, (K: 165) —

"Westerness Cycle" No 4: Samson Agonistes
O 24 x 24", S, I, D, (K: 166) —

Blue Landscape
O 24 x 24", (K: 167) £1,595

Horse and Chariot
O 6 x 6", (K: 168) —

Snow: Largymore
O 12 x 24", S, I, (K: 169) £550

The Rosses
O 3 x 3", S, D, I, (K: 170) £660

Naked Woman
D 12.25 x 8.75", S, D, (L: 371) £410

Naked Woman
D 12.375 x 8.875", S, D, (L: 372) £350

Young Woman
D 11.625 x 8.5", S, (L: 373) —

La Comedie
D 9 x 4", S, D, I, (L: 375) £550

Figure by a Window
D 12.25 x 9", S, D, (L: 376) £352

East Wind

O 20 x 24", S, I, D, (L: 424) —

The Refugee
O 24 x 20", S, (M: 122) £7,000

Marrakesh
O 24 x 24", S, I, (N: 110) £1,500

MILES, Miss R. H. (fl. 1891-1910)
Portrait of a young woman
O 20 x 15", S, (A; 117) £60

MILLIKEN, Robert W. (20th Century)
Wigeon flying over a coastal Cottage
W 10.75 x 14.5", S, (L: 383) £198

MITCHELL, Flora H. (1890-1973)
St. Stephen's Green East, Dublin
W 10 x 12.5", S, (A; 72) £700

Boyne Obelisk
D 12 x 9", S, I, (B: 116) —

The Old House
D 12 x 8", S, D, (B: 117) —

The Custom House, Dublin
D 9 x 10.5", S, D, (B: 118) £450

Fountains Hall, Yorkshire
D 7.25 x 9", S, D, (B: 119) —

Gateway to St. Sepulchre's, Kevin
Street, Dublin (1961)
D 9 x 10.5", (B: 120) £650

St. George's Church and Eccles Street, Dublin
D 11 x 10.5", S, I, (B: 121) £750

The Bank of Ireland, College Green
D 9 x 13.5", S, I, (B: 122) £800

Front Square, Trinity College, Dublin
D 14 x 9.5", S, I, (B: 123) £900

S. Aisle and Swifts Tablet, St. Patricks, Dublin
D 9.75 x 6.5", S, I, (B: 124) £400

The Ha'penny Bridge
O 15.5 x 11", (E: 142) —

Johnstons Court - Grafton Street, Dublin
W 12 x 9.25", S, I, (J: 11) £700

St Georges Church and Eccles Street, Dublin
W 8.5 x 10", S, I, (K: 25) £1,210

The Old House in Portsmouth Street, London
W 9.25 x 13", S, I, D, (N: 64) —

Shepherd Market, London
W 10 x 13.5", S, I, (N: 65) £700

MOLYNEUX, Major Edward (1869-1913)
Three figures around a fire
O, 25 x 33.5", (A; 39) £320

River landscapes in India
W 5.25 x 8.25", (A; 40) £50

A view of an Indian Dam
W 8.5 x 11", (A; 41) —

Views in the Sind Valley
W 5 x 6.5", (A; 42) £60

Mountain landscapes in the Sind Valley
W 4.75 x 6", (A; 43) £50

Pandritan and three other views
W 6.75" x 4.5, (A;44) £80

Balfal Glacier - Sind Valley and
Other mountain landscape
W 4.75 x 6.25", I, (A; 45) £90

Four Indian landscapes
W 5 x 6.5", (A; 46) £90

Simbal, Matungi and two other Indian views
W 5 x 6.5", (A;47) £60

MOONEY, Carmel (20th Century)
Field Patterns
O 10 x 12", S, (E: 52) —

MOONEY, Martin (20th Century)
Venice, Rear view of Rudentore
O 14.5 x 21", S, (N: 105) £650

Besalu Bridge, Gerona - Study (1991)
O 10.5 x 28.5", S, D, (N: 108) £600

Bathing Place at Bagnoles, Near Gerona
O 23.5 x 28.5", S, D, (N: 109) £950

Italian Study
O 25.5 x 18", S, (N: 115) £1,300

Killiney, Co. Dublin
O 28 x 36", S, (F: 15) £800

MOYNAN, Richard Thomas (1856-1906)
Portrait of a lady with a plumed hat
O 30 x 22", S, D, (N: 119) —

Dermod O'BRIEN (1865-1945): Sulphur Carnations. *Sold at Taylor de Veres, Dublin, 8 March 1994, (£1,200).*

MUIR, Moira (20th Century)
Hand Weavers
O 16.5 x 27", S, (F: 70)   £300
MULCAHY, Michael (20th Century)
Fellow Travellers
M 28 x 42", S, D, (E: 84)   –
MURPHY, Frank (20th Century)
A Busy Market Scene
10 x 14.5", S, (D: 110)   £220
Lough Gill, Co. Sligo
W 9.75 x 14", S, I, (J: 1)   –
In the Mournes
W 10 x 14.5", S, (J: 29)   –
MURPHY, Jay (20th Century)
Trees along a River, Galway
P 20 x 14", S, (E: 48)   –
MURRAY, Eileen (b.1885)
Horse & Rider, Donkeys Grazing
O (2) 12.5 x 9", S, D, (E: 132)   £100
Michael Corcoran & his Brother
O 24 x 19.5", S, (N: 74)   £1,900
NEILL, H. Echlin (b. 1888)
River & Mountain Landscape
W 10.5 x 14.5", S, (J: 50)   –
NICHOLL, Andrew (1804-1886)
Wooded Landscape with figures
W 12 x 17", S, (A; 140)   –
Water Carrier, Mournes
W 10.25 x 14.5", (G: 43)   £320
*Yachts in Dun Laoghaire Harbour
with Howth Head in the distance*
W 14.5 x 21", S, (K: 3)   £500
*Figures on a Road before The
Mountains of Mourne*
W 13 x 20", S, (K: 4)   £495
Sailing off the Giant's Causeway, Co. Antrim
W 17 x 24", S, (K: 20)   –
*Roundstone and the Twelve Pins
Of Connemara*
W 12.5 x 19.25", S, (K: 21)   £825
A derelict Churchyard
W 13.25 x 19.75", S, (L: 322)   –
NICHOLL, William (1794-1840)
Lough Dan, Co. Wicklow
W 9 x 13", S, (B: 133)   £380
NICOL, Erskine (1825-1904)
*A Dutch kitchen interior with an old
couple and a child*
O 19 x 24", S, D, (B:24)   –
The Love Letter
O 17 x 13", S, D, (G: 50)   £1,200
Waiting for an Answer
O 19.25 x 25", S, D, (K: 89)   £2,860
Notice to Quit
O 20.25 x 15.25", S, (K: 90)   £3,850
The Finishing Touch
O 40 x 32", S, D, (K: 91)   £18,700
A Peasant Girl

W 9.25 x 8.25", S, (L: 341)   –
Sixpence short
W 19 x 13.5", S, D, (L: 342)   £1,980
Figures on the rocks, near Glendalough
O 17.5 x 23.5", S, D, (N: 55)   –
NIETSCHE, Paul (1885-1950)
Malinmore, Co. Donegal
O 20 x 24", S, D, (L: 421)   £880
NISBET, Tom (b. 1909)
The Bridge at Donnybrook
W 10.5 x 14", S, (D: 155)   –
Fitzwilliam Lane, Dublin
W 11 x 15", S, (A; 1)   –
Trawlers at Howth
W 11 x 15", S, (A; 83)   £350
*Pepper Canister Church, Upper
Mount Street, Dublin*
W 12.5 x 15.5", S, (C: 31)   £300
The Bridge at Donnybrook
W 10 x 14", S, (H: 131)   £200
Autumn Near The Goat Pub & Mount Anville
W 10.5 x 14.75", S, (J: 79)   –
Grand Canal, Herbert Place
O 23 x 28", S, (N: 17)   £750
Entrance to the National Museum
W 11 x 15", S, (N: 82)   £240
NOLAN, Liam (20th Century)
The Burrow Strand, Howth
O 9.5 x 13", S, (E: 14)   £180
O'BRIEN, Dermod (1865-1945)
Summer Pasture
O 18 x 24", S, (B: 14)   –
Sulphur Carnations
O 9 x 13", S, (H: 21)   £1,200
The Windmill, Feltrim, North Co. Dublin
O 14 x 20", I, (I: 88)   £1,000
The Sand Pit
O 24 x 32", S, (K: 97)   –
Cattle watering in a river landscape
O 30 x 25", S, I, (N: 53)   £6,000
O'BRIEN, Gretta (20th Century)
The Trout Stream
O 26 x 20", S, (A; 30)   £300
Trees
O 15.5 x 23", S, (E: 162)   –
Autumn Fires
O 18 x 23", S I, (H: 113)   £440
Celtic Images
O 29 x 17", S, (I: 29)   £410

Erskine NICOL (1825-1904): The Finishing Touch. *Sold at Christie's, Dublin, 26 May 1993 (£18,700).*

James Arthur O'CONNOR: Extensive Wooded Mountain Landscape with Figures. *Sold at James Adam, Dublin, 5 October 1993 (£27,000)*

Coastal Scene
O 16 x 24", S, (J: 85)   –
O'BRIEN, Kitty Wilmer (1910-1982)
Sandymount Green
O 16 x 24", S, (B; 8)   £1,100
Beeches
O 13.25 x 16", S, (E: 74)   £500
*Winetavern Street & Wood Quay
from Christchurch Place*
O 11 x 28", S, (F: 146)   £800
The Twelve Pins, Connemara
O 10 x 13.5", S, (G: 28)   –
Howth from Sandymount
O 27 x10", S, (H: 91)   –
San Miniato, Florence
W 12 x 18", S, (N: 11)   –
O'CASEY, Breon (b.1928)
Blue Field
W 15 x 22", S, D, (O: 40)   £230
O'COLMAN, Seamus (d. 1990)
The Ally Ally O
O 8 x 10", S, (B 5)   £200
Street Scene
O 24 x 36", S, (E: 35)   £150
O'CONNOR, James Arthur (1792-1841)
*Extensive wooded mountain landscape
with figures*
O 24 x 29", S, D, (B: 22)   £27,000
Woman on a woodland path
O 8.5 x 11.5", S, (B: 81)   £3,300
Woman on a woodland path, by a river
O 13 x 17", S, (C: 71)   –
Figures by the Waterfall, Powerscourt
O 12.75 x 9.5", S, (K: 84)   –
*A Wooded Lake Landscape with Figures
Fishing*
O 9 x 11", S, (K: 85)   £3,520
*Figures on a Tree-Lined Road by
a Riverside Town*
O 20 x 23.5", S, D, (L: 401)   £2,750
Landscape
O 8 x 12" (Q: 237)   £3,500
O'CONNOR, Joseph (20th Century)
Footballers IV
O 17 x13", S, D, (G: 39)   –
O'CONNOR, Roderic (b.1907)
Portrait of a Lady
O 25 x 20", S, D, (B: 25)   –
O'CONNOR, Sean (d. 1992)
The Lower Lake, Killarney
O 13.5 x 17.5", S, (A 9)   £180
Kerry Landscape with Figure & Donkey
O 19 x 23", S, (E: 97)   £110
Killarney River & Mountain Landscape
O 15.5 x 20", S, (F: 186)   £200
18th Century Green, Mahony's Point, Killarney
W 10.25 x 12", S, (F: 187)   £130

Castle Lough, Killarney
W 10.25 x 12", S, (F: 188)   £130
Figures in a Sunlit Mountainous
Landscape, Connemara
O 16 x 19.75", S, (L: 420)   –
O'CONOR, Roderic (1860-1940)
Choufleur c. 1925
O 21.5 x 28.5", S, (C: 33)   £97,000
Femme A Contre Jour - Study'
O 24 x 19.5", S, D, I, (C: 51)   –
Jeune Femme sur le Divan
D 10 x 14.5", (F: 207)   £1,600
Neuil-sur-Layore, Maine et Loire
O 5.25 x 7.75", S, (K: 156)   –
Flowers
O 16 x 15.75", S, (O: 114a)   –
O'FLAHERTY, Michael
Mount Brandon
O 17 x 13", S, D, (F: 216)   –
O'HALLORAN, James (20th Century)
A day at the beach
O 20 x 26", S, D, (A: 33)   –
January in the Window
O 14 x 12", S, D, (H: 65)   £650
Summer Garden
O 10.5 x 12", S, (H: 123)   £280
Ballyalla Skies, Co. Clare, 1990
O 12 x 14", (H: 138)   £360
Happy Days - Summer
O 13.75 x 17.35", S, (J: 32)   –
Bantry Pier - Summer
O 13 x 15.75", S, (J: 38)   –
O'HARA, Helen (1881-1919)
Evening, After The Storm
W 14 x 20.75", S, (B: 109)   £1000
Shipping at dusk
W 10 x 13.5", S, (N: 30)   £500
O'KELLY, Aloysius (1853-1928)
Market in Brittany
O 10 x 13", (F: 67)   –
Tangiers Street Scene
W 10 x 7", S, (B: 126)   £1,200
The Lake, Van Cartland Park, New York
O 9 x 12.5", S, I, (F: 106)   £1,300
On the Sheepscott River, Maine
O 9 x 12", S, I, D, (G: 8)   £1,400
The Seaweed Gatherers
O 20 x 30", S, (G: 77)   £8,500
On the Sheepscott River, Maine
O 8.75 x 12.5", S, (H: 101)   £1,200
Breton Women by a Fireside
O 24.25 x 29.125", S, (K: 93)   £4,180
Figures on a sunlit Street, Cairo
O 20.25 x 13.75", S, I, (K: 94)   £10,450
Fishing Vessels, Concarneau, Brittany
O 10 x 12", S, (L: 403)   £3,850
O'MALLEY, Jane (b. 1944)
Lanzarote
W 14 x 21.5", S, I, D, (B: 138)   £220
November Fishing & Window Flowers
O 24 x 36", S, I, D, (G: 168)   £400
O'MALLEY, Michael A. Power (1878-1946)
Portrait of a girl
O 24 x 20", S, (B: 52)   –
O'MALLEY, Tony (b. 1913)
Big White Flower Pot
O 48 x 60" S, D, (D: 54)   –
St. Martin's
W 6 x 10.25", S, D, I, (D: 126)   –
St. Martin's
W 6 x 11", S, D, I, (D: 127)   –
Autumn (1967)
W 15 x 22", S, D (C: 12)   £450
Orzola, 1988
M 25 x 20", S, (E: 149)   –
Stormy Evening by the Sea with Bather
W 8 x 12.5", S, I, D, (F: 94)   £520
Warm Day, Kilkenny
O 6 x 16", S, D, (F: 167)   –
Big Poplar on the King's River

Walter OSBORNE (1859-1903): Billy. Sold at
Sotheby's, 24 November 1993 (£19,950).

O 14 x 18.5", S, I, D, (G: 22)
Patio Space
O 9 x 14", S, I, D, (G: 99)   £620
Red Gable Cottage, Curracloe, Co. Wexford
21.5 x 29.5", S, (J: 42)
Ardmore Sunrise
W 11 x 7.5", S, D, (K: 43)   –
O'NEILL, Daniel (1920-1974)
Shouting - Homage to Jack B. Yeats
O 24 x 35", S, I, (C: 65)   £5,000
Invented landscape (c. 1951)
O 16 x 18", S, (C: 88)   –
Study of a Young Girl
O 17.5 x 14", S, (D: 35)   £2,100
The Four Seasons
O (4) 11 x 17", S, (D: 86)   –
Two Girls in an Interior with a Cat
O 20 x 16", (F: 19)   £2,400
Interior with Yellow Hat
O 16 x 20", S, (F: 50)   –
Woman & Child
D 21 x 17", (F: 210)   £400
Man in a Bar
D 7.5 x 5.5", S, D, (F: 211)   £250
Mountain & Sky Study
O 4 x 8", S, I, (G: 163)   £550
Interior
O 30 x 24", S, (H: 15)   £3,800
St. Francis
O 11.5 x 16", S, I, (H: 27)   –
Bedroom Altar, Co. Donegal
O 20 x 24", S, I, (H: 166)   £1,300
Landscape with Figure
O 15 x 23", S, (I: 18)   £2,600
Low Tide
O 13 x 20", S, (I: 54)   –
The Musician
O 16 x 19", S, (J: 45)   –
Girl Fiesta
O 18 x 14", S, I, (K: 154)   £3,850
The Couple
W 13.375 x 8.5", S, (L: 369)   –
Profile
D 12.25 x 8.75", S, (L: 370)   –
Girl in Flowery Dress
O 26 x 20", S, (L: 431)   £3,860

Still life with Self Portrait
O 14 x 18", S, (L: 432)   –
Girl with Turban
O 24 x 18", S, I, (L: 433)   £4,620
Outside Theatre
O 12 x 16", S, (L: 434)   –
Landscape, Co. Donegal
O 16 x 20", S, (L: 460)   £3,300
Mother and Children
O 24 x 16", S, I, (L: 463)   £2,090
The Last Rose
O 16 x 20", S,(M: 124)   £1,800
Foreshore, Co. Antrim
O 20 x 27", S, (M: 137)   –
Girl in red
O 24 x 20", S, (N: 38)   £5,000
Glengad Head, Inishowen
O 10 x 6.5", S, (N: 125)   £600
Interior
O 18 x 24", S, (O: 48)   £7,475
O'NEILL, George Bernard (1828-1917)
Entertaining the Grandchildren
O 12.5 x 11", S, (G: 78)   £5,000
O'RYAN, Fergus (1911-1989)
Anglesea Market, Dublin
O 30 x 22", S, (B: 39)   –
Stephen's Court, Mount Street, Dublin
O 13 x 17", S, (B: 43)   £600
Canal Walk, Dublin
O 11 x 15", S, (B: 74)   –
Mill Race, Plassey
O 18.5 x 23.5", S, (C: 56)   –
Fishing on the River Bank
O 14.5 x 18", S, (E: 96)   £720
The G Boat at Baggot Street Bridge
O 18 x 22", S (F: 3)   £950
Mount Street Bridge
O 11.5 x 15.5", S, (G: 63)   £720
Island Bridge
O 9.5 x 13", S, (G: 71)   £320
Moore Street Market
O 27 x 35", S, (H: 36)   £1,400
The Pepper Canister Church
O 9.5 x 13.5", S, (H: 87)   £620
The Canal below Leeson Street
O 15.5 x 23", S, I, D, (H: 93)   £700
Findlaters Church, Parnell Square
O 16 x 20", S, (I: 56)   £500
Winter Landscape
O 12 x 20", S, (N: 101)   £600
Warners Lane, Leeson Park
O 12 x 15.5", S, (N: 123)   –
Canal, Wilton Place
O 10.5 x 15.5", S, (N: 124)   £600
O'SULLIVAN, Donal (d. 1992)
Two Nude Studies
P 14 x 14", S, (D: 154)   –
Contemplation
P 28 x 21", S, (F: 215)   £190
O'SULLIVAN, Sean (1906-1964)
Winter near Goatstown
O 6.5 x 9.5", S, (A: 17)   –
Mountain landscape
O 13 x 16", S, D, (A: 98)   –
Connemara landscape
O 20 x 24", S, (B: 29)   £450
Portrait of a gentleman in grey pin stripe suit
O 24 x 20", S, (B: 30)   –
Farmer at work in western landscape
O 20 x 24", S, (B: 31)   £850
Contemplation
O 24 x 20", S, D, (B: 32)   £350
Lady in Red
O 24 x 18", (B: 33)   £100
Portrait of a man in a white jacket
O 20 x 16", (B: 34)   £400
Portrait of a gentleman against a green background
O, 24 x 20", (B: 35)   –
Portrait of a woman wearing a green dress
O 24 x 20", (B: 36)   £100

Portrait of a woman wearing an orange scarf
O 24 x 20", (B: 37) £350
Portrait of a woman wearing a grey blouse
O 24 x 20", S, (B: 38) £180
Mountain landscape
O 13 x 16", S, D, (B: 94) £450
Outside Jammet's Restaurant
M 13 x 10.25", S, D, (D: 30) £500
Dublin from Ticknock
O 10.5 x 14", S, I, (F: 13) £720
Marble Hall, Co. Donegal
O 12 x 16", S, I, (G: 107) £550
Female Portrait
P 15.5 x 13", (H: 141) £220
Portrait of Paul Yandowski Sculptor
O 17 x 14.5", S, I, (I: 58) £2400

ORPEN, Bea (1913-1980)
Curraghs, Sheephaven
W 14.5 x 18.25", S, (D: 3) –
A Lake among the Hills
W 5.75 x 9.125", S, (L: 367) –

ORPEN, Richard Caulfield (1863-1938)
Dorset Landscape
W 9 x 14", S, D, (E: 147) £160
Irish Evening landscape with Figures
M 12 x 9", S, (F: 132) £440
An Evening in Newlyn
M 11 x 7", S, D, (F: 133) –

ORPEN, Sir William (1878-1931)
Portrait of Sister c. 1897
O 23.5 x 15.5" (A 78) £17,000
Female Nude Study
D 9.25 x 11.5", S, (D: 41) £1,500
The Breeze
Pr 9 x 5", S, I, (E: 37) £60
Standing Male Nude
D 8 x 6", (E: 156) –
Study for Statue
P 8 x 6", (E: 157) £300
Study for Swinford Family Portrait Group
D 11 x 8.5", (E: 158) –
Nude
W 12.75 x 8.75", S, D, (G: 119) £7,500
Self Portrait with Model (Emily Scobel)
D 11 x 8.5", (G: 142) –
Seated Woman
D 10.5 x 8.5", (G: 143) £600
Nude Studies
D 8.5 x 7", (G: 144) £500
Hugh Lane Asleep
K 9 x 12", (H: 34) £800
Sowing the Seed
Pr 12.5 x 8.5", (H: 96) £160
The Winner
Pr 12.5 x 8.5", (H: 97) £60
Open Air Theatre
W 7.5 x 9.25", (H: 107) –
Self-Portrait on a Cliff-top, Howth
W 20 x 14.5", S, (M: 119) £5,500
The Valuers
O 32.75 x 43", S, (O: 15) £45,500
Lottie Feeding a Baby
O 30 x 25", S, (O: 16) £56,500
The Entry into Jerusalem
O 29 x 30.5", S, (O: 26) £3,220
The Roscommon Dragoon
O 30 x 25" (P: 23) (see p.247) £125,000
The Refugees
O 25 x 30" (P: 25) £14,000

OSBORNE, Denis H. (20th Century)
Harbour, Portavogie
O 13.5 x 17.5", S, (A 92) £200

OSBORNE, W. F. & YEATS, John B.
*Patrick Street/ St. Patrick's/ Portrait
Of W. Osborne by John B. Yeats
(3 framed as 1)*
D (2) 4.5 x 3", (1) 6 x 4.5", S, I, (I: 43) £1,500

OSBORNE, Walter Frederick (1859-1903)
Coastal landscape near Rye, Sussex
O 10 x 8", S, (A: 69) –

Roderic O'Conor (1860-1940): Choufleur. c.1925.
Sold at James Adam, 1 December 1993 for £97,000.

Sunday School at St. Patrick's Cathedral, Dublin
D 16 x 12", S, (C: 47) –
St. Patrick's Close, Dublin - a sketch
O 9 x 5.5", S, (C: 74) £8,000
Cattle in a Landscape
O 12.5 x 15.5", (D: 40) –
String Quartet
D 5.75 x 11", S, I, D, (D: 44) £1,300
Near Didcot
O 5.5 x 8.5", (G: 32) –
Look Out
O 18 x 13", S, (I: 74) £1300
A Pensive Moment
O 7 x 10", S, D, (K: 95) –
Two studies of Yorkshire Terriers
D 3.75 x 5.75", (N: 75) £650
Billy
O 11.75 x 9", S, I, (O: 11) £19,550

OTTLEY, W.
Steel engravings (1808)
Pr (2) 14.5 x 9", (G: 189) –
Steel engravings (1808)
Pr (2) 14.5 x 9", (G: 190) –

PEACE, James (d. 1827)
River Landscape
W 15 x 19", (C: 78) –

PEARSON, Peter (20th Century)
Vico
O 10 x 10", S, I, D, (N: 79) £90

PERCY, L
The Little Sugar Loaf / Big Sugar Loaf
W (2) 19.5 x 14", S, (I: 80) £140

PETRIE, George (1790-1866) Circle of
Mallow Castle and the River Blackwater, Co.Cork
O 25 x 30", (K: 83) –

PIELOU, Florence (20th Century)
A Native of the Sugarloaf
O 10 x 14", S, (F: 156) £80

POTTER, George (20th Century)
Head of a Woman
O 10 x 10", S, (H: 59) –

POWER, Arthur (20th Century)
Underwater life
P 14 x 14", S, D, (A 88) –
The Abandoned Dog
M 22 x 15.5", (A: 124) £90
Weatherchart
W 13 x 20", (A: 125) –
Gardener with Pumpkin
W 14 x 10", S, (E: 90) –
The Swimmer
P 14 x 16", S, (E: 137) £190
Artist with Model
P 12 x 10", S, D, (H: 147) £190

POWER, James (fl.1940s)
Harbour View
O 15.5 x 19.5", S, (F: 71) £1,300

POWERS, Mary Farl (d. 1993)
Abstract

Pr 29 x 20.5", S, (N: 78) –

PRATT, C. V.
Birr 1853
D 6 x 9", S, D, (E: 94) –

PROUD, Paul (20th Century)
*View across the River with Cottage and
Mountains*
O 24 x 30", S, (E: 22) £100

PURCHAS, Thomas J. (fl. 1880-1894)
Rocky Valley, Kilmacanogue, Co. Wicklow
O 6.75 x 9.5", S, (B: 80) £400

PYE, Patrick (20th Century)
Early Morning in the City (after Seurat)
O 15 x 19", S, (D: 25) £1,900
Wynters Rest
Pr 14 x 12", S, (E: 138) –
Children in the Mill
O 14 x 12", S, I, (F: 36) –
The Ascension
T 7.5 x 17.5", S, I, (F: 60) £600
Agony in the Garden
P 24.5 x 19", S, D, (G: 26) –
The Children in the Mill
O 14 12", S, (N: 5) –

QUILLIGAN, Ita (20th Century)
Locks, Ringsend
O 9.5 x 12", S, I, D, (E: 26) –

RAKOCZI, Basil Ivan (1908-1979)
Fish Spirit
W 16 x 12.5", S, D, (D: 148) –
Le Compotier
O 15 x 18", S, D, (D: 149) –
Colloque
O 19.5 x 25", S, (H: 35) –
Still Life with Fish
O 28 x 21", S, D, (H: 44) –

REID, Eileen (1894 - 1981)
Nude Study
O 23.5 x 19.5", (G: 123) –

REID, Nano (1905-1981)
Donkey on the Shore
O 11.5 x 15.5", S, (D: 36) £2,600
Gate on the Lane
W 9.5 x 13.5", (E: 45) £500
Mountains and Sea
W 9.5 x 12.75", S, (E: 63) £400
Streetscape
W 10.5 x 14.5", S, (F: 125) £550
Fairy Thorn at Well
O 24 x 17.5", S, (F: 205) –
The Country Pub
O 29 x 23", S, (I: 22) –

RIDGEWAY, Helen (20th Century)
Purple Iris
W 22 x 30", S, D, (G: 132) –

RITCHIE, Anna (b. 1937)
Slow Elevation
M 16 x 10", S, (E: 100) £80

RIVERS, Elizabeth (1903-1964)
Woman in green hat
O 24 x 19.5", S, D, (N: 58) –

RIVIERE, Henry Parsons (1811-1888)
The Fortune Teller - An Irish Fair
W27 x 47", S, D, (D: 31) £5500

ROBERTS, Hilda (1901-1982)
Study of Sean Keating
D 21 x 16", S, (H: 140) –

ROBINSON, Henry Harewood (fl. 1877-1902)
Woman & Dog in Evening Landscape
O 12.5 x 11", S, (F: 174) –

ROBINSON, Maria D, (fl. 1873-1886)
Feeding the Calves, Evening
O 11.5 x 17.5", S, (F: 173) £500

ROBINSON, Markey (b. 1918)
Western village
W 12.5 x 20", S, (C: 109) £280
Cottage & Figure (20th Century)
O 12 x 19", S, (E: 23) £230
Islanders
O 4.5 x 7", S, (E: 41) £80

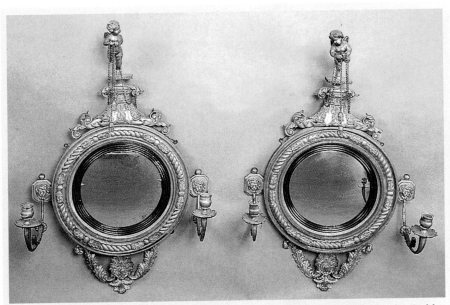

Two important Irish giltwood convex mirrors, one of which was labelled by the Dublin furniture maker, Cornelius Callaghan, were included in the Lyrath sale conducted by Christie's. They failed to sell. Callaghan, whose label describes him as 'Carver, Gilder, Looking-glass, Picture frame manufacturer' was listed at Clare Street, Dublin between 1823 and 1830.

Still Life	
O 6.5 x 10.75", S, (E: 54)	£160
By the River	
W 5 x 8.25", S, (E: 87)	–
North Africa	
O 5 x 8.25", S, (E: 88)	£80
Sailing Boats	
O 5.5 x 14.5", S, (E: 89)	£140
Two Nudes	
W 20 x 13", S, (E: 91)	–
Mother & Child	
O 29 x 21", S, (E: 116)	£340
Still Life	
O 14 x 19", S, (H: 63)	£450
Fishing Boats	
O 6.5 x 13.25", S, (I: 1)	–
The Clown	
O 10 x 10", S, (J: 2)	–
Bath time	
P 27 x 20", S, (L: 391)	£440
Figures and Cottages / Figures, Cottages	
and Trees	
P (2) 5.375 x 6.625", S, (L: 392)	–
Gossip	
O 16.5 x 28.5", S, (L: 418)	£1,760
Figures on a Village Street	
O 16.5 x 29", S, (L: 419)	£805
ROCHE, Samson Towgood (1759-1847)	
Lismore Castle	
W 12 x 19.5", S, Attrib. (A 132)	–
ROONEY, Lucas (early 20th Century)	
On The Sands, Rush, Co. Dublin	
O 9 x 13.5", S, D, (N: 21)	£1,100
ROTHENSTEIN, Michael (1908-1993)	
Bronze and Black, Spider Jazz, The Love	
Machine	
P (3) 00 x 00", S, (O: 45)	£345
RUSSELL, George 'AE' (1867-1935)	
Children on the Headland	
O 16 x 21", S, (B: 19)	£1,900
Spirit from the Sea	
O 19 x 24", (B: 59)	–

Gathering Leaves	
O 14 x 20", (C: 19)	£900
Pulling in the Nets	
O 19 x 23", S, (D: 60)	£6,000
Two Girls on the Donegal Coastline	
O 23 x 29", S, (F: 159)	£5,200
Figure in the Woods at Dusk	
O 18 x 24", S, (F: 195)	–
Woman & Child in Coastal Landscape	
O 15.75 x 20", S, (F: 209)	£3,200
Mythical Figure	
O 16 x 20", (G: 122)	–
Children Playing at the Beach	
O 14 x 22", S, (H: 55)	£2,000
Where Fades The Forty Lights of Day	
O 12 x 18", S, (I: 25)	£3,000
Hiding	
O 12.5 x 18.5", S, (J: 30)	£3,100
The Dim Blue Mantel of the Mountains	
Far Away	
O 16 x 21", S, (K: 137)	£1,540
Self-Portrait	
O 18 x 15", S, I, (K: 138)	£1,760
Coole Lake	
O 12 x 18.25", S, (L: 454)	–
Hiding	
O 12.5 x 18.375", S, (L: 455)	£2,200
RUSSELL, John (19th Century)	
A Good Days Catch	
O 16 x 23", S, (H: 156)	£350
RYAN, John (d.1992)	
Flower Study	
O 15 x 14", S, (A: 25)	–
RYAN, T. E. (19th/20th Century)	
Ponte Marina and St. Georgia in Venice	
W (2) 5.25 x 6.5", S, (H: 18)	–
RYAN, Thomas (b. 1929)	
Christchurch Arch and Assembly House,	
Dublin	
W 13 x 8", S, (A: 141)	£240
Cantolupo from Monte Fiolo	
O 15.5 x 19", S,I, D, (G: 19)	£600

Feeding Hens, Port-Na-Blagh	
O 11 x 9", S, I, D, (H: 1)	£650
St. Patricks Cathedral	
O 19 x 15", S, (I: 14)	–
May Altar	
O 19 x 15.5", S, I, (I: 19)	–
Kippers	
O 10 x 12", S, I, (I: 28)	£300
Christmas Carols & Studies	
D (1) 4.5 x 3.5", (2) 7.75 x 6.75", S, D, (I: 42)	–
Portraits of Michael Kelly and	
George F. Handel	
P (2) 22 x 18", S, (N: 143)	£800
Portraits of Mornington and Lady Morgan	
P (2) 24 x 19", S, (N: 144)	£800
SADLER, William II (1782-1839)	
Officers, Dragoons &Horses by an	
Inn in a Wooded Landscape	
O 15.5 x 23.5", (F: 58)	–
The Dublin Coach passing through the	
Glen O' The Downs	
O 8.5 x 12.5", (B: 20)	£1,600
Festive gathering, Glen of the Downs	
O 8 x 12.5", (A: 50)	£500
A View of The Liffey, Islandbridge and	
The Royal Hospital, from Chapelizod	
O 14 x 22", 4000 (A: 68)	
Donnybrook Fair, 1830 and 1835	
W (2) 9.5 x 14.5" & 10 x 14", S,	
D, I, (C: 84)	£900
Figures on Horseback Outside an Inn	
O 12 x 18", (F: 131)	–
Interior with Soldiers	
O 8 x 12", (H: 115)	£650
Sackville Street from Carlisle Bridge	
O 24.75 x 30.5", S, D, (K: 81)	£11,500
Merchant on Patrick Street, Dublin, with	
St Patrick's Cathedral and	
the Wicklow Mountains beyond	
O 10 x 11", (K: 82)	£7,150
A View of Dublin and the Liffey,	
from Phoenix Park	
O 11.5 x 17", (K: 87)	£6,050
Dockside scene with figures	
O 8 x 12", (N: 28a)	£650
SALKELD, Cecil Ffrench (1908-1968)	
Figures in a moonlit river landscape	
O 23.5 x 18", (C: 76)	–
SCANLAN, Robert Richard (fl.1826-1864)	
Blowing Stiff	
M 8.75 x 13.5, S, I, D, (D: 19)	£1,300
SCOTT, Patrick (b.1921)	
Footsteps	
O 48 x 33", (D: 66)	£1,000
Arcadian Fount Series	
Pr (2) 23.5 x 23.5, S, D, (D: 142)	£280
Head (1957)	
M 7.5 x 6", S, (D: 143)	£600
Aesops Fables (c. 1950)	
W (3) 8 x 7.5", S, (D: 144)	–
Fount Series 7	
T 32 x 31", S, D, (E: 161)	–
Gold painting No.32, 1965	
T 24 x 24", S, (A: 106)	–
Gold Painting No. 32, 1965	
T 24 x 24", S, (G: 192)	–
SCOTT, William (1913-1989)	
Untitled	
Pr 23 x 30 " S, (E: 56)	£450
Abstract Composition	
W 19 x 24", S, (G: 160)	–
SEMPLE, Joseph (19th Century)	
A Portrait of The Sloop Rig Cutter	
'Fanny' in full Sail	
O 20.5 x 24.5", S, (K: 88)	£1,540
SHACKLETON, Roger (1931-1987)	
Red Rocks of Aughadoon	
O 13.5 x 42", S, (E: 5)	–
Study - Male Figure	
D 16 x 14", (E: 92)	£80

Coastal view with House in Mayo
W 16 x 25", S, D, (G: 184) —
Magnolias
W 18 x 17.5", (G: 185) —
SHAWCROSS, Neil (b. 1940)
Cat on the Table
M 17.5 x 22", S, D, (D: 52) £300
SHELBOURNE, Anita (b. 1941)
Abstract
W 7.5 x 11", S, (E: 4) —
Cottages in a Landscape
O 22 x 30", S, (F: 191) £280
SHEPPARD, Oliver (1865 - 1941)
Dublin Bay from Howth
O 11 x 15.5", (G: 106) —
SHERIDAN, Noel (b. 1936)
Man and Chair
O 20 x 16", S, (E: 47) —
Untitled
O 30 x 27", S, (E: 150) —
Hanging Blackbird
O 19 x 26", S, (H: 57) £300
SHINNORS, John (b.1950)
Scarecrow and Magpie
O 16 x 16", S, (B: 7) —
The Embarkation
O 14 x 19", S, (G: 66) £750
SHORE, Henry (Lord Teignmount)
Views at Thomastown
W (3) 4 x 6", I, (D: 95) £420
SHORE, Robert S. (20th Century)
The River
O 24 x 36", S, (B: 16) £1,100
SIMMONDS-GOODING, Maria (b. 1939)
Rain from The West
Pr 12.5 x 11", S, I, (N: 80) £45
Sheep coming down the Hill
Pr 15 18", S, (E: 134) £30
SKELTON, John (20th Century)
A Break in the Clouds, Inishman,
Aran Islands
O 20 x 30", S, I, (F: 102) —
Lake View
W 17.5 x 23.5", (G: 191) —
Children in a Forest
W 19 x 25.5", S, (J: 62) —
SLEATOR, James Sinton (1889-1950)
Portrait of Sir William Orpen
O 19 x 15", S, I, (A: 77) £3,800
Still Life of Daisies in a Lustre Jug
O 26 x 26", (F: 175) —
Still Life of Sweetpeas
O 20 x 16", (F: 176) £2,600
Figure Leaning against a Tree with
House in Distance
O 22 x 16.5", (F: 177) £1,400
The Crutch-Frame Mirror
O 17 x 11", (G: 150) —
Still Life of Daisies in a Lustre Jug
O 26 x 26", (H: 16) —
Poppies
O 23 x 16.5", S, (J: 47) £1,250
SLUIS, Pieter (20th Century)
Young lady
O 24 x 20", S, (A: 52) £350
Circus artist
O, 18 x 24", S, (A: 29) £300
Still Life with Flowers (c.1970)
O 24 x 20", S, (D: 8) £570
Vase with Flowers
O 20 x 16", S, D, (H: 114) —
Still Life
O 20 x 26", S, (N: 7) £270
SMITH, Sidney (1912-1982)
November Hopfields
O 25 x 30", S, (N: 40) —
Whitstable Bay
O 20 x 24", S, I, (N: 41) —
Portrait of a young woman
O 12 x 9.5", (N: 42) £450

William SADLER II (d.1839): Sackville Street from Carlisle Bridge. *Sold at Christie's, Dublin, 26 May 1993 (£11,550).*

Extensive Continental River Landscape
O 20 x 30", S, (N: 43) £1,400
St. Mark's, Venice
O 9.5 x 13.5", S, I, (N: 44) —
Fort Antibes, Cote d'Azur
O 10 x 14.5", S, D, (N: 45) £450
Portrait of a young girl
O 14 x 10", (N: 46) —
A Tuscan farmstead
O 10 x 14", S, (N: 47) £750
The Winter Palace, Peking
O 20 x 24", (N: 48) —
Western Mountain Landscape
O 20 x 24", (N: 49) £700
SMITH, Stephen Catterson (1806-1872)
The Prince's Page
O 36 x 28", (C: 57) £3,800
SMYTHE, Anne (19th Century)
Forlorn girl seated by a tree
W 19.5 x 14.5", S, D, (N: 32) £300
SOLOMONS, Estella F. (1882-1968)
Carlisle Court
Pr 10.5 x 6.5", S, (B: 144) £100
At Howth
O 12.5 x 16.5", S, D, (C: 20) —
SOMERVILLE, Edith OEnone (1858-1949)
Upper Lake, Killarney
O 16 x 20", S, (L: 464) £715

Stephen SLAUGHTER (1697-1757): Portrait of Sir Edward O'Brien. *Sold at James Adam, Dublin, 25 August 1993, (£7,500).*

Study of a Young Woman
D 11 x 5.5", S, (G: 101b) £80
SOUTER, Camille (b. 1929)
The Rifle Range at the Summer Fair
Near Booterstown
O 22 x 15", S, (D: 74) £5,200
The Performers
O 16.5 x 14.5", S, D, (F: 54) £1,000
Abstract
M 14.5 x 10.5", S, D, (F: 83) £1,800
The Italian Easter Egg
O 13.5 x 15", S, (F: 163) £1,400
Town Creeping Out
O 18 x 14.5, S, D, (G: 9) —
Runway, Shannon
O 18.5 x 24", S, (G: 67) £1,400
Town Creeping Out
O– x–", S, I, (I: 12) £2,000
STAMPER, J. W. (19th/20th Century)
Still Life
O 20 x 26", S, D, (J: 44) —
STAPLES, Sir Robert Ponsonby (1853-1943)
Study from Life
O 8.5 x 4.75", (F: 90) £340
Bob
O 12 x 10", S, I, (G: 65) —
St. Patrick's Cathedral
P 13 x 9", S, I, D, (G: 104) £380
Giving the Degrees, Dublin University
M 9.5 x12.5, I, D, (G: 105) £260
STOKES, Margaret (1832 - 1900)
Landscape with Trees, Mountain Landscape
O (2) 12 x 12", S, (D: 20) —
At the Easel
W 19 x 15", S, (E: 24) £170
Close Roundstone (c. 1938)
O 14 x 18", (E: 111) £240
SUTTON, Ivan (20th Century)
Thrashing in Kilmore, Co. Wexford
O 16 x 19", S, (G: 148) £200
SWANZY, Mary (1882-1972)
The Victim
O 20 x 24", S, D, (B: 73) —
A Study of a Female Nude on a Sofa
O 25.5 x 21", S, (K: 130) —
Resistance Fighter
O 12 x 9", (D: 28) £2200
Slavic Landscape
O 12 x 19", S, (D: 48) —
Continental Lake View
P 9.75 x 7.5", (D: 82) £300
Child Studies
D (2) 10.25 x 8", (D: 83) £220
Market Day
P 7.25 x 10", (D: 84) £180
Donegal Coast
O 11.5 x 15", S, (D: 89) £1,500
Summer Shower
O 9 x 15", S, (E: 17) £1,200
Boat in Harbour
P 7.5 x 10", (E: 31) £210
Continental Cafe
P 7.25 x 10", (E: 107) £200
Continental Village
P 8 x 10.5", (E: 114) £260
Continental Village
P 10 x 7.5", (E: 130) £260
Reflections
O 16.5 x 12", (F: 59) £2,200
Still Life
O 20.5 x 17.75", S, (F: 93) £5,500
The White Horse
O 20.5 x 17.75", (F: 123) £1,800
Cubist Landscape
O 16 x 23", S, (G: 13) —
St. Tropez, with the Massif de
Maures Mountains beyond
O 16.25 x 25.5", (K: 150) £7,700
Above St. Tropez
O 17 x 18.375", (L: 422) —

Fete Champetre
O 18 x 21", S, (N: 84) £2,000
SWIFT, Patrick (1927-1983)
Landscape with Mountain Plateau,
Provence, 1982
W 17 x 24", (F: 48) 1500
The Carob Pickers (1972)
O 38.5 x 26", S, (G: 84) £4,700
Forget-Me-Knots on a Cane Table
O 30.5 x 25.25", S, (G: 156) £5,200
Chaves
D 17 x 13", I, (H: 92) –
TALLANTIRE, Anne (20th Century)
Still Life
O 20 x 30", S, (B: 2) –
TALLON, Desmond Charles (20th Century)
New Grass
O 7 x 10", S, (A: 3) –
TAYLOR, Maeve (20th Century)
On the Way to Lough Fada, Ardcroom
O 9.5 x 19", S, (F: 199) £240
TOOGOOD, Romeo (1902-1966)
Garden, Marlborough Park
O 23.5 x 19", (H: 45) –
TOPHAM, Francis William (1808-1877)
Praying at The Holy Well
W 16.5 x 20.5", S, (B: 128) £1,250
TREACY, Liam (20th Century)
Arklow Harbour
O 23 x 29", S, (D: 12) £950
Interior, The Auction Room
O 12 x 10", S, D, (F: 6) £320
TREVOR, George
Ray Valley, Co. Donegal
W 9.5 x 13.5", S, (H: 5) £130
TREVOR, Helen Mabel (1831-1900)
Study of a Monk
O 32 x 23", S, I, D, (L: 402) £770
TUOHY, Patrick Joseph (1894-1930)
Girl in a striped dress
O 36 x 25", S, (B: 56) £10,500
TURNER, Ken (20th Century)
Resting Doves
O 23.5 x 36", S, (H: 13) –
VERLING, Walter K. (b. 1930)
Connemara Faoi Caiso
O 13.5 x 17", S, D, (A 89) –
Massy, Paris
O 15 x 18", S, (A:27) –
Connemara landscape
O 13.5 x 17.5", S, (C: 6) –
WADE , Jonathan (20th Century)
Corridor
Pr 8.25 x 12", S, D, (A 112) £50
Relief Landscape
M 24 x 19", I, (E: 113) –
District 3 - The Liffey Bridge
O 23.5 x 22.5", S, (H: 135) –
Relief Landscape (Alexandra Basin)
M 24 x 24", S, D, (H: 136) £200
WALKER, J. Crampton (fl.c. 1895)
Martello Tower at Portmarnock
O 6 x 12.5", (B: 4) –
WALKER, Thomas Bond (20th Century)
Watching the Boat
O 11 x 15", S, (D: 90) –
WALSH, George (20th Century)
Clown
O 14 x 10", S, (A: 120) –
WALSH, Owen (20th Century)
Holy Week, Seville
O 18 x 15", S, D, (A: 38) –
WARD, Richard (20th Century)
Otters at Play
O 36 x 43", S, D, (F: 126d) –
WARREN, Barbara (b. 1925)
Eachros Mor
O 13.5 x 17.5", S, (E: 32) £230
Clifden, Connemara
O 5.75 x 9", S, I, (F: 11) –

Mary SWANZY (1882-1978): A Study of a Female
Nude on a Sofa. *Bought in at Christie's, Dublin, 26
May 1993 (est. £3-5,000).*

East Window, Aughrus Beg
O 5 x 21", S, (F: 91) £280
West of Ireland Coastal Landscape
O 21 x 36", (F: 202) –
On the Bog Road
O 20 x 16", S, I, (G: 44) £520
WATKINS, Bartholomew Colles (1833-1891)
*Summers Evening on The Liffey under
Leixlip Bridge, looking down The Vesey
Demesne.*
O 13 x 15", S, (A: 62) £1,500
*Ross Castle, Glena Mountain and
Toomie in the distance*
O 9.5 x 14", S, (A: 67) £450
*Glengariff, from the Windows of
Roches Hotel*
O 9 x 12", I, (K: 86) –
WATTERS, Una
Flower Piece
O 13 x 18", S,(J: 12) £300
WEBB, Kenneth (20th Century)
*Queen Elizabeth Gun and
Walker Monument, Derry*
O 20 x 24", S, (B: 45) –
Farmsteads in the West
O 12 x 36", S,(B: 49) £400 ·
Landscape with cottages
O 15 x 30", S, (B: 76) £600
Gorteen Bay
O 15 x 36", S, (C: 113) £450
Errelough, near Roundstone
O 14 x 29", S, I, (F: 29) £670
Sitting on the Beach
M 22 x 14.5", S, D, (G: 146) £260
Woodland Glade
O 12 x 9.5", S, (H: 88) £360
Summer Storm
O 16 x 40", S, (N: 18) £900
WHELAN, Leo (1892-1956)
*'Mine Host' - a Portrait of Jack Nugent
of The Dolphin Hotel, Dublin*
O 43 x 36", S, (C: 93) –
The Roadside
O 10 x 13", S, I, (G: 36) –
WILKS, Maurice C. (1911-1984)
Coastal Landscape, Co. Down
O 14 x 18", S, I, (B: 47) £1,000
*After the Storm, Atlantic Drive,
Co. Donegal*
O 16 x 30", I, (B: 13) £500

Girls Carrying Turf
O 20 x 26", S (B: 61) £5,200
River Landscape with Poplars
O 20 x 16.25", S, (B: 70) –
Silver Sea, Cushendun
O 20 x 26", S, (C: 18) £2,200
Co. Donegal Boglands, Gweedore
O 14 x 18", S, (C: 34) –
Lough Swilly from Malin Head, Co. Donegal
W 9 x 11.5", S, (C: 59) –
Dunmore Head, Co. Kerry
O 16 x 20", S, (C: 72) £2,700
*Cashel Mountain from Roundstone, Co.
Galway*
O 15.5 x 19.5", S, (d: 27) £3,000
Kelemore Lake
O 17.5 x 23", S, I, (D: 64) –
On the Quoile River
O 15 x 19", S, I, (D: 76) –
'Galway Girl' & 'Aran Man'
D (2) 21 x 15", S, (E: 98) £520
Lough Inagh, Connemara
O 13.5 x 17", S, I, (F: 97) £1000
Rough Seas Near Ballycastle
O 16 x 30", S, I, (F: 104) £800
Under Muckish (c. 1940)
O 24 x 30", S, (F: 114) –
Children at Ards, Nr. Cresslaugh
O 14 x 28", S, (F: 213) £1,300
Evening, Roundstone, Co. Galway
O 16 x 20", S, I, (G: 83) £1.200
Mount Errigal from Mount Rosses Country
O 11.5 x 15.5", S, (H: 20) £2,200
Low Tide, Cushendun, Co. Antrim
O 18 x 23", S, I, (H: 25) £1,800
Morning Light, Inagh Valley
O 11 x 15", S, I, (H: 110) £900
Above Kilkeel, Co. Down
O 16 x 21.5, S, I, (I: 81) £1,200
Misty Day, Ballynahinch
O 14 x 18", S, I, (J: 19) –
Near Clifden, Connemara
O 18 x 24", S, I, (K: 175) £1,980
On the Ross's Coast, Co. Donegal
O 16 x 20", S, I, (K: 177) –
White Park Bay, Co. Antrim
O 18 x 21", S, (K: 176) £2,420
Summer Evening, Cushendun, Co. Antrim
O 16 x 20", S, I, (L: 438) –
Maam Valley, Connemara
O 14 x 18", S, I, (L: 439) £990
North East Wind, Antrim Coast
O 20 x 24.5", S, I, (L: 450) £825
Thunder Clouds, Ballintoy, Co. Antrim
O 20 x 25", S, I, (L: 451) –
Sunny Day, Strangford Lough, Co. Down
O 14 x 18", S, I, (L: 452) –
The Japanese Fan
O 16 x 12", S, D, (L: 453) £495
Landscape, Connemara
O 16 x 30", S, (N: 3) £2,200
Co. Donegal Boglands, Gweedore
O 14 x 18", S, (N: 36) –
WILLIAMS, Alexander (1846-1930)
Glendarary River, Achill Sound, Mayo
W 13.5 x 23", s, (A: 114) £440
*Beached Brigantines on Sandymount Strand,
Dublin*
O 14 x 24", s, d, (A: 61) £5,500
*The Pigeon House Fort, Port of
Dublin - Sunset*
W 30 x 50", s, d, (A: 66) £8,500
Lake and mountain landscape
O 24 x 42", (A: 101) £500
Sailing Boat in an Estuary
O 7.5 x 14.5", s, (B: 23) £1000
Rosapenna Strand, Donegal
W 9.5 x 17.5", s, (C: 85) –
Carrying turf on a mountain road
W 18 x 30", S, (C: 92) –

Ringsend, 1892
D 4.25 x 6.75", (D: 21) —
Ringsend, 1892
D 4.25 x 6.75", (D: 21) —
Malahide
O 9.5 x 17.5", S, I, (D: 62) £650
Valley Sound, Achill, Co. Mayo
O 9.5 x 17", S, (D: 146) £620
A Cottage at Achill Sound, Co. Mayo
O 9.5 x 17", S, (D: 147) £650
Coastal View
O 7.5 x 14", S, (E: 164) £260
The Flag Pool, Glencar, Co. Kerry
O 12.5 x 23.5", S, (F: 2) —
Landscape
O 7 x 10", S, (F: 28) —
The Valley Strand, Achill
W 11 x 15.5", (F: 197) £520
The Rostrevor River
W 17.25 x 9.5", I, S, (F: 200) £420
River & Landscape
O 13.75 x 21", S, (G: 34) —
Rosapenna Rocks
O 7 x 14", S, I, (G: 139) —
In the Ladies Cove, Nr. Rosapenna
O 7 x 14", S, I, (G: 140) —
Wild Weather on the Achill Coast,
Blacksod Bay
W 17.25 x 29.25", S, (K: 36) £935
McCarthy Castle, Killarney
W 7.5 x 14.125", S, I, (L: 323) —
Fishermen's cottages
O 8 x 15", S, (N: 27) £370
Old houses at present in Cork Street, Dublin
W 10.5 x 15", S, D, I, (N: 114) £560
Mountain lake landscape
O 8 x 15", S,(N: 116) £420
The Gap of Dunloe /
Kenmare Bay / Atlantic Drive / Clew
Bay from Achill Sound / Coast of Achill
W (4) 10 x 17.5", S, I, (N: 138) £1,300
WILLIAMS, Lily (1874-1940)
Study of John Butler Yeats
D 9 x 8", S, (F: 154) £280
Study of a Child
P 18 x 14", (D: 67) —
WILLIAMS, Terence Attridge (20th Century)
Gap of Dunloe, Killarney
O 13.5 x 18", S, (A: 28) —
WILLINK, D. E. (20th Century)
Maghera, Co. Donegal
W 10.5 x 12.5", S, (E: 36) £50
WILSON, Ross (20th Century)
Horse and Rider, (1986)
P 8.75 x 7", S, D, (E: 39) —
WILSON, Thomas G. (20th Century)
A Village in Andalucia (1950)
O 20 x 24", s, (B: 1) £600
WOOD, Robert Sydney (b. 1895)
Coastal Village
W 6.75 x 10", S, (F: 189) —
WYNNE, Gladys (1878-1968)
Emell Castle, Clough Jordan, Co. Tipperary
W 9.5 x 7", (C: 37) £200
The Watergardens, Glendalough House
W 9 x 5.5", S, (F: 121) —
Pastoral Landscape
W 9.5 x 13.5", S, (F: 128) £130
Collecting Turf
W 11.25 x 18", S, (G: 172) £320

Jack B YEATS (1871-1957): Lafitte the Pirate. Sold at Sotheby's, 24 November 1993 (£21,850).

YEATES, Grace W. (19th Century)
Lough Dan, Co. Wicklow
O 14.5 x 17.5", S, D, (C: 107) —
YEATS, Jack Butler (1871-1957)
Rise Up Willie Reilly (1945)
O 14 x 21", S, (B: 67) £42,000
The Seanchai
D 8 x 10.5", S, D, (B: 104) £1,800
Western Man
W 12 x 9.5", S, (C: 28) —
The Player Dawn (1952)
O 14 x 21", S, (C: 50) £60,000
The Tall Lock House (1926)
O 9 x 14", S, (C: 60) £14,000
The Gay Moon (1949)
O 9 x 14", S, (C: 63) —
Crossing The Canal Bridge from the
Tram Top
O 9 x 14", S, (D: 61) £17,500
Errismore Races
W 3.5 x 4.75", (E: 58) £600
Errismore Races
W 3.5 x 4.75", (E: 59) £500
Connemara
W 3.5 x 4.75", (E: 60) £520
Original Drawing for Christmas Card
D 3.75 x 7", S, I, (E: 82) £870
The Old Picnic Ground
O 14 x 21", S, I, (F: 172) £51,000
Toney
W 5 x 3.5", I, (G: 51) £320
A Group of Farm Workers
W 3.5 x 5", (G: 52) £420
Donkey in a Field
W 3.5 x 5", (G: 53) £400
A man on his Horse
W 3.5 x 5", (G: 54) £450

Whitecaps
W 3.5 x 5", (G: 55) —
The Alibi (1947)
O 14 x 18", S, (G: 60) £23,000
The Derelict Ship (1946)
O 18 x 24", S, (G: 85) —
Broadsheet
Pr 20 x 14", (G: 137) £220
Kevin, The Shoe Maker
D 5 x 4", S, (G: 158) —
Masterman Ready
W 6 x 6", I, D, (G: 165) £800
Two Characters from Oliver Twist
W 4.75 x 4.75", I, D, (G: 166) —
Old John Barley Corn
W 3.5 x 5", (G: 167) £420
AE & W.B. Yeats Playing Cricket at Coole
W 5 x 3.5", I, S, D, (G: 176) —
The Feis
W 3.5 x 5", I, (H: 42) £550
The Feis
W 3.5 x 5", I, (H: 43) £620
Figure of Christ
D 4.5 x 3.75", S, (I: 44) £370
The Galloping Horse
D 6 x 8.5", S, (J: 73) —
The Chaney Stream
O 9 x 14", S, I, (K: 147) £25,300
Reveille (1946)
O 24 x 36", S, (N: 50) £155,000
A Quiet Death
O 24 x 36", S, I, (N: 71) £60,000
A Lane in Kerry
O 8.5 x 13.75", S, (O: 23) —
Roulette
W 10 x 6.75", S, (O: 80) —
Lafitte the Pirate
W 14.75 x 10.5", S, I, (O: 81) £21,850
The Brown-Eyed Men
O 14 x 21", S, I, (O: 82) £35,600
The Steep Way to Town
O 14 x 21", S, I, (O: 83) £29,900
Donkey Races
W 11 x 17.5", S, D, (O: 84) £6,325
Caballero
O 14 x 18", S, I, (O: 85) £36,700
A Speckled Memory
O 9 x 14", S, I, (O: 86) £32,200
Wait
O 14 x 18", S, I, (O: 87) £34,500
Sleep Sound
O 18 x 24", (O: 88) £45,500
The Great Tent has collapsed
O 24 x 36", S, (O: 109) £106,000
YEATS, John Butler (1839-1922)
Portrait Study of Elizabeth Yeats
D 9.75 x 7.25", S, I, (D: 43) £600
Portrait of George Russell, Called AE
D 7 x 5", S, I, (M: 55) £1,000
YOUNG, Mabel (1890-1974)
Winter Sunshine in Co. Wicklow
O 13.5 x 15.5", S, (A: 84) £800
The Lake
O 12 x 16", S, (N: 118) —
Wicklow Landscape
O 15.5 x 21.5", S, (N: 121) —
A Country Cottage in Summer
O 12 x 16", S, (N: 126) £20

PICTURE CREDITS FOR IRISH ARTS REVIEW YEARBOOK 1995

The numbers are those of the pages on which the photographs appear

2 Michael Blake; 60 Arc Survey Photographic Ltd; 82-87 Valerie Dowling, National Museum of Ireland; 88-95 Roy Hewson; 96, 97, 99 Fig.3, 100, 101 Paul Caponigro; 98 Pat O'Dea, Bord Failte; 108-111 Irish Architectural Archive; 112, 113 Fig.3, 115 George Munday, The Slide File Ltd; 114 John Kennedy. Repr. by permission of the Board of Trinity College Dublin; 118 Repr. by permission of Newman House, University College Dublin; 132, 135 Fig. 7 The Governing Body, Christ Church, Oxford; 134 Fig.5 Hugh Doran; 142 David Davison; 143 Manuscripts Dept, Library of Trinity College Dublin; 144 Fig.6 Jacqueline O'Brien; 145 Fig.8, 146, 147 Fig.13 David Davison; 155, 156 Sarah Cully; 169, 172 David Davison; 172 Fig.7 Derek Shortall; 173 Fig.9 Christie's,Glasgow; 182 Fig.3 Jacqueline O'Brien; 184 Fig.7 Roy Hewson; 196 Walter Pfeiffer; 204, 205 David Davison; 216-224 Michael Blake.

INDEX TO IRISH ARTS REVIEW YEARBOOK
VOL 11, 1995

INDEX OF ADVERTISERS IN IRISH ARTS REVIEW YEARBOOK 1995

Back Issues of the
IRISH ARTS REVIEW

Back issues of Irish Arts Review as listed below may be purchased from

> Irish Arts Review,
> P O Box 3500,
> Dublin 4,
> Ireland.

Prices (inclusive of post & packing)
Quarterlies : IR£5 each (Stg.£5;US$ 7.50)
Yearbooks - *Paperback:* IR£20 each (Stg.£22; US$35)
  -Hardback: IR£30 each (Stg.£33; US$55)

A discount of 10% is given on orders of IR£100 or more.

QUARTERLY Spring 1984 *(Vol.1 no.1)*
Contents include: Roderic O'Conor; Girona Jewels; Early Irish Chalices; The Shamrock Building, New York World's Fair 1939; Paintings of North-East Antrim; New Acquisitions at the National Gallery of Ireland; Textiles & Costumes in the Ulster Museum; Gheeraedts' Elizabethan portrait of Capt. Lee as an Irish kerne; Francis Wheatley's Lord and Lady Antrim

QUARTERLY Summer 1984 *(Vol.1 no.2)*
Contents include: Contemporary Irish Tapestry; Waterford Crystal; Charlemont House Medal Cabinet; Handel in Dublin;Hugh Douglas Hamilton's Letters to Canova;Wedgwood in Dublin 1772-77; a Belfast Patron of the Pre-Raphaelites; Frederick Buck's Cork miniatures (c.1768-1824); Irish Wooden Boxes; Cork Republican Silver

QUARTERLY Summer 1985 *(Vol.2 no.2)*
Contents include: Hughie O'Donoghue; Dun Emer; Daniel Maclise; Music in Paintings in the National Gallery of Ireland; a Dublin Dolls' House; Irish Silk Poplin; Old Master Drawings in the National Gallery of Ireland; Irish Provincial Chairs; Irish Artists at the Sao Paolo Bienal; Contemporary Ceramicists in Cork

QUARTERLY Autumn 1985 *(Vol.2 no.3)*
Contents include: Michael Warren; John James Barralet; History of the R H A; James Donovan's Irish China; Irish Glass Curiosities; Chinese Blue and White Porcelain; Letters of George Moore

QUARTERLY Winter 1985 *(Vol.2 no.4)*
Contents include: Hilda van Stockum; The Ulster Coat; Two Dublin Jewellers - West's and Weir's; Antiques Restoration; Roderic O'Conor; Art O'Murnaghan; Michael Mulcahy; James Arthur O'Connor; George Moore; University College Dublin Industry Centre

QUARTERLY Summer 1986 *(Vol.3 no.2)*
Contents include: Dundalk Courthouse; Goldsmithiana; Centenary of the Motor Car; Jack B Yeats; Patrick Scott; Dublin Society School of Landscape & Ornament ; Roderic O'Conor; Dublin Antique Shops; Barry Flanagan; Patrick Ireland; Women Stained Glass Artists

QUARTERLY Spring 1987 *(Vol.4 no.1)*
Contents include: French Textile Sculptures in Belfast; Francis Tansey; Belleek Pottery; Rathfarnham Castle; Mrs Delany's Drawings; Vodrey's Art Pottery; Patrick Hickey on Japanese arts; Sir Alfred Chester Beatty & the National Gallery of Ireland; the Parnell Monument & the American Beaux Arts movement; Armorial Blue & White Porcelain

QUARTERLY Summer 1987 *(Vol.4 no.2)*
Contents include: Matthew James Lawless; the Saatchi Collection; Richard Serra; portraitist Jean-Etienne Liotard; Rose Barton; John Shinnors; Mary Fitzgerald; Drimnagh Castle Restoration; Irish Bog Oak Carving

QUARTERLY Autumn 1987 *(Vol.4 no. 3)*
Contents include: Keely 'the Irish Pugin of America'; the Shrine of St Patrick's Hand; the Hugh Lane Municipal Gallery; Alfred Concanen, lithographer; Kilkenny miniaturist John Comerford; Patrick Collins; Wilhelmina Geddes; Centenary of James Adam & Sons

YEARBOOK 1988 *(Vol.5)*
Contents include: John Behan; Eyrecourt Castle, Co Galway; Mughal Paintings in the Chester Beatty Library; James Latham; Blessington Mansion; the Royal Hospital, Kilmainham; Clare Marsh; Hector McDonnell; Irish Rural Architecture; Limerick Lace; Irish Pianists; Irish Painters in 18th-century Rome;

Back Issues of the
IRISH ARTS REVIEW

Sackville (O'Connell) Street, Dublin; Allied Irish Bank's Art Collection; Irish Collectors of Indian Art; Contemporary Irish Ceramics; Frederick Burton; Alicia Boyle; Keating, MacGonigal & the National College of Art; the Lafranchini Brothers; Jack P Hanlon

YEARBOOK 1990-91 (Vol.7)
Contents include: Contemporary Cork Glass; the Ulster Museum's Portrait of the Elizabethan Earl of Essex; David Wilson; Oliver Sheppard; St Andrew's Church Dublin; Irish Georgian Garden Buildings; Jerpoint Abbey Sculpture; Pietro Longhi's Tipperary Giant; James Glen Wilson; Augustus Burke; Albert Power; the Arts Council of Ireland; the Book of Kells; Donegal Cottage Industries; Dublin Silk Weavers; Hughie O'Donoghue; William Kilburn and Samuel Dixon; Early Irish Sculpture; the Irish Arts and Crafts Movement; Celtic Metalwork; Irish Stamp Design; the National Heritage Council; Early Irish Crucifixion Plaques; Donegal Carpets; Paintings from the Ulster Museum; Irish Needlework; Irish Dolls and Dolls' Houses

YEARBOOK 1991-92 (Vol.8)
Contents include: Turner Watercolours in the National Gallery of Ireland; the Irish Museum of Modern Art; Terence Farrell; Nathaniel Hone the Younger; Louis Le Brocquy; Lutyens Gardens at Heywood, Co Laois; the Arts Council of Ireland; Kenmare Lace; the King's Inns Portrait Collection; Marie Foley; French Paintings in the National Gallery of Ireland; Tom Phillips' Portrait of Barry Douglas; Irish Sculptors and Church Patrons,

1922-45; Garret Morphy; Delamain Pottery; Edyth Starkie; Susan Mitchell; Thomas Bodkin; the Crawford Gallery, Cork; James Moore; the R H A Schools; Plasterwork Restoration at Birr Castle; Michael Mulcahy

YEARBOOK 1993 (Vol.9)
Contents include: Recent Dublin Architecture; Treasures of Trinity College; Jack B Yeats; Evelyn Montague; Belfast Harbour Office's Art Collection; Irish Restorers; T P Flanagan; Irish Gold of the Bronze Age; the Chester Beatty Library; Mainie Jellett; Grace Henry; James Dixon; William Crozier; Michael Healy; Irish Painted Porcelain; Thomas Farrell; Margaret Stokes; James Hore; W J Leech; Clement McAleer; Tony O'Malley; Albert Power; Graham Knuttel; Irish Silver

YEARBOOK 1994 (Vol.10)
Contents include: Sean Scully; the Book of Kells; de Blacam & Meagher's Chapel at Knock; Arthur Gibney's Irish Pavilion at Seville; the Celtic Revival; an Irish Monument by Grinling Gibbons; the Restoration of Newman House; Anne Yeats; Waterford Art Museum; Irish Art Needlework; George Barret; Borris Lace; Thomas Roberts; Early Irish Metalwork; the Watercolours of the Marchioness of Waterford; Irish Artists in Antwerp; Edward Martyn; An Túr Gloine; Wilhelmina Geddes; John Hughes' Sculptural Monuments; Irish Arts and Design Education; Henry Trench; Dürer's Irish Warriors; Leo Whelan; Sydney Smith; the Irish Pavilion at the St Louis World's Fair

OUT OF PRINT ISSUES
Irish Arts Review wishes to buy a limited number of the following back issues which are now out of print:
Quarterlies: Autumn 1984 (Vol.1 no.3); Winter 1984 (Vol.1 no.4); Spring 1985 (Vol.2 no.1); Spring 1986 (Vol.3 no.1); Autumn 1986 (Vol. 3 no.3); Winter 1986 (Vol. 3 no.4): Winter 1987 (Vol.4 no.4) **Yearbook:** 1989-90 (Vol.6)

ORDER FORM FOR BACK ISSUES
To: Irish Arts Review, P O Box 3500, Dublin 4, Ireland (Tel: 01-280 8461; Fax: 01-280 4190)

Please send me ....
PLEASE USE BLOCK CAPITALS

Name: ....

Address: ....

I enclose my cheque for .... or please debit my credit card (Visa, Access/Mastercard, American Express)

Card no: .... Expiry date: .... Signature ....